Zheng Chaolin, Selected Writings, 1942–1998

Historical Materialism Book Series

The Historical Materialism Book Series is a major publishing initiative of the radical left. The capitalist crisis of the twenty-first century has been met by a resurgence of interest in critical Marxist theory. At the same time, the publishing institutions committed to Marxism have contracted markedly since the high point of the 1970s. The Historical Materialism Book Series is dedicated to addressing this situation by making available important works of Marxist theory. The aim of the series is to publish important theoretical contributions as the basis for vigorous intellectual debate and exchange on the left.

The peer-reviewed series publishes original monographs, translated texts, and reprints of classics across the bounds of academic disciplinary agendas and across the divisions of the left. The series is particularly concerned to encourage the internationalization of Marxist debate and aims to translate significant studies from beyond the English-speaking world.

For a full list of titles in the Historical Materialism Book Series available in paperback from Haymarket Books, visit: www.haymarketbooks.org/ series_collections/1-historical-materialism.

Zheng Chaolin
Selected Writings, 1942–1998

Edited by
Gregor Benton and John Sexton

With an introduction by
Gregor Benton

With contributions by
Gregor Benton, Walter Daum, Donald Gasper, Sean A. James,
Gregor Kneussel, Tsim Shum Kow, Kevin Lin, Owen Miller,
John Sexton, Huang Ting, and Yang Yang

Haymarket Books
Chicago, IL

First published in 2022 by Brill Academic Publishers, The Netherlands
© 2022 Koninklijke Brill NV, Leiden, The Netherlands

Published in paperback in 2023 by
Haymarket Books
P.O. Box 180165
Chicago, IL 60618
773-583-7884
www.haymarketbooks.org

ISBN: 979-8-88890-006-2

Distributed to the trade in the US through Consortium Book Sales and
Distribution (www.cbsd.com) and internationally through Ingram
Publisher Services International (www.ingramcontent.com).

This book was published with the generous support of Lannan
Foundation, Wallace Action Fund, and the Marguerite Casey Foundation.

Special discounts are available for bulk purchases by organizations and
institutions. Please call 773-583-7884 or email info@haymarketbooks.org
for more information.

Cover design by David Mabb. Cover art is a detail from *Luibov
Popova Untitled Textile Design on William Morris Wallpaper for Historical
Materialism*, edition of 100, screen print on wallpaper, 2010.

Printed in the United States.

10 9 8 7 6 5 4 3 2 1

Library of Congress Cataloging-in-Publication data is available.

Contents

Introduction

Gregor Benton

Zheng Chaolin was a lifelong revolutionary socialist. After joining the movement in his late teens, his commitment to the cause never wavered despite the huge personal cost. He was born in 1901 and died in 1998, so his life was almost exactly coterminous with the twentieth century and can be viewed as a dramatic embodiment of the century's main passions and vicissitudes in China. Zheng spent all his adult life either making revolution or in jail. All in all, he was in jail for thirty-four years, first under the Nationalists as a revolutionary and then, under the Communists, as a so-called counter-revolutionary – because after the Chinese Communist Party's (CCP's) ill-fated alliance with the Guomindang led to catastrophic defeat in 1927 he joined the Trotskyist opposition. The Communist government could easily have coexisted with the few hundred Oppositionists, but in 1952, Mao Zedong decided to bury them alive in his prisons and Zheng, arrested along with his comrades, began his longest period behind bars.

Doubtless there are political prisoners in history, and perhaps even some today, who have spent longer in jail than Zheng, but they must be few in number. In revolutionary lore, Auguste Blanqui (1805–81) has always counted as the record-holder for political imprisonment, having spent thirty-three years behind bars for his beliefs, for which he was nicknamed '*l'enfermé*' ('the gaoled one'). Zheng had beaten Blanqui's record by a year when he finally stepped into qualified freedom in China in 1979, aged 78, nearly three years after Mao's death in 1976.

In the mid-1970s, together with Zheng's exiled fellow Trotskyist Wang Fanxi, by then in Leeds, I ran a campaign for Zheng's release, by publishing articles in the international socialist press and in *The Guardian*, *Le Monde*, and *The Washington Post* and getting Amnesty International to highlight his case, by naming him prisoner of the month in May 1979, shortly before his release. In the articles, I pointed out that Zheng had studied in France in the early twenties alongside China's newly rehabilitated paramount leader Deng Xiaoping (1904–7). When Wang and I started our campaign, we had no idea whether Zheng was alive or dead. I was astonished and delighted when Wang told me, in June 1979, that the Old Man was not only alive but had been set free.

After the death of Mao and the fall of his 'Gang of Four' in 1976, tens of thousands of political prisoners were liberated. The freeing of Zheng and his comrades happened in that context, and we were under no illusion that our campaign was the reason for Zheng's release. However, it might have speeded it, by jogging Deng Xiaoping's memory and pricking his conscience at a time when he was anyway freeing prisoners. (Deng's daughter later visited Zheng for an interview while she was researching her book on her father, whom Zheng had known in France.)

I met Zheng Chaolin twice in Shanghai in the mid-1980s, once on my own and once in the company of my friend the Danish Trotskyist Finn Jensen. Finn and I took him a bottle of French cognac (his favourite drink) and a long tape recording of a message from Wang, which he answered, also on tape. The meetings were semi-clandestine and a bit cloak-and-dagger, for Zheng was still closely monitored. My first impression of him at the door of his flat in Shanghai was not unlike that of the science-fiction writer and biographer Ye Yonglie, who visited him at around the same time: an old man, tiny and bent double, 'wearing a thick brown ski shirt, a blue woolen cap, and a pair of clamshell cotton-padded shoes'.

In 1990, several years before his death, Zheng Chaolin asked me to be his literary executor in the West, a request I took both as an honour and a challenge. Since then, I have done my best to repay his trust, by publishing translations of his books (his memoirs, his study on Chen Duxiu and Trotskyism, and his poems) and various other works. This collection of his writings, on which it has been my pleasure and privilege to work with several old and new friends, is probably the last in this series of publications, unless new texts suppressed by the Chinese Communists or lost in the chaos of Zheng's life and times come to light.

To present Zheng to a Western audience in various contexts, I have already written three general and largely overlapping accounts of his life, and this is the fourth. Regarding his biography, most of what I write here is adapted from those previous accounts, since I have nothing new to say. However, I have added a section discussing the writings collected in this anthology. My comments can be read together with Wang Fanxi's obituary of Zheng in the appendix, written after Zheng's death in 1998.

Like most Chinese Trotskyists, and for that matter most Chinese Communist leaders, especially in the CCP's early days, Zheng was by training and aptitude a thinker and a scholar rather than a man of action. Although never afraid to put himself in danger, his greatest contribution to the Chinese Revolution – both in the official Party before 1929 and, after that, in its Trotskyist offshoot – was in theory and propaganda rather than in practicalities. He despised the power struggles and organisational fights that punctuate political life and on which others thrive. Above all, he was an 'oppositionist for life' to all forms of established authority. This description, originally made by Hu Shi of Zheng's mentor Chen Duxiu,[1] fits Zheng to the letter, which is why he spent more than one third of his days as a prisoner of conscience under repressive régimes of different colours.

Comments I made in my introduction to Zheng's memoirs also apply, *mutatis mutandis*, to the work collected here:

> Zheng's writing is scrupulously truthful, accurate, and stringent. He tells us what he knows, how he came to know it, and what remained unknown to him, so his testimony is a perfect source for history-writers; and it is free from the self-exculpation and ideological axe-grinding that distorts most political memoirs of this sort. Chinese memoirs since 1949 have all the usual drawbacks of the genre, together with several more. They are winners' history written in a society where 'the loser is a thief'. They cleave closely to the dominant political line. They are ... meant to furnish 'concrete' illustrations of the general truths of Party history that dictate their framework and their setting. To quarry the few hard truths from [them], the historian must first hack through a dense layer of political shibboleths, editorial embellishment, and edifying anecdotes; even then, what remains is not necessarily the unvarnished truth. So Zheng's book is a lonely beacon that lights up a small patch on the great dark plain of China's recent past, and will be seen by fair-minded observers everywhere as something rare and precious.

Zheng was born into a declining old-style landlord family in Zhangping, a minor county capital in Fujian Province, in what was, at the time, a remote part of China. As a child, he read novels about heroic exploits and became dissatisfied with reality. Outwardly, however, he remained a quiet, obedient boy, ready to play the roles his grandfather and his father set him. He would probably have ended up like them – become a member of the lower gentry and stayed all his life in Zhangping, but for political developments on a national scale. He was saved from the likelihood of a boring, parochial existence by May Fourth, the movement for cultural renewal and political revolution that broke out in Beijing in May 1919, as a culmination of the New Cultural Movement that had begun in 1915. This movement led the Governor of Fujian, Commander Chen

---

1   In connection with *Chen Duxiu zuihou lunwen he shuxin* ('Chen Duxiu's last articles and letters'), first published posthumously by Chen's friends and later republished on Taiwan with Hu Shi's preface.

Jiongming, incongruously an anarchist, to order each county magistrate under his control to nominate two or three youngsters to go to Paris, where two of his anarchist comrades had set up a beancurd factory on the basis of which they ran a work-study scheme. The scheme was designed to provide young Chinese with a livelihood while at the same time training them in radical and scientific thinking, so that they could then go back to China and act as a revolutionary political yeast. Zheng was among more than thirty young Fujianese chosen.

In Paris, Zheng's revolutionary career began, after the Marxist Cai Hesen founded a Communist movement among the Chinese worker-students, which Zheng joined. While in France, he steeped himself in Marxist and other political and philosophical writings. Like other Chinese Communists who came to Communism through France, he had a broader mind and a freer, more Bohemian spirit than Communist leaders like Peng Shuzhi (who reached Russia in 1921 and later, in China, became a Trotskyist) and Wang Ming (the arch-Stalinist, who rose to power over the Chinese in Russia in 1927) – both Peng and Wang had gone straight to Moscow without first serving a revolutionary apprenticeship in China or elsewhere.

Among Zheng's comrades in France were Zhou Enlai, Li Weihan (later head of the United Front Department of the Chinese Communist Party [CCP]), and the sixteen-year old Deng Xiaoping. From Paris, Zheng travelled in 1923 to Moscow, where he was one of the first students at the new Communist University for the Toilers of the East.

Zheng stayed for more than a year in Moscow, where (by his own account) he learned no theory and spent most of his time carrying out 'individual criticism' by 'exposing' other comrades' petty-bourgeois or anarchist faults in meetings and having his failings picked out (he was apparently the main butt for it). This constant criticism and the system of 'commanding and submitting' was Zheng's most abiding memory of his time in the Soviet capital. However, the experience did not subdue him but made him even stubborner. The two criticisms that he was least willing to accept were that he 'read too much' (rather than take part in the 'training' he was meant to do) and that he was friends with a questionable person, the Esperantist Bao Pu, who hobnobbed with Esperantists of other nationalities in Moscow and was thought 'dangerous'. Zheng was also criticised for wanting to learn Russian – according to Peng Shuzhi, who already had some Russian and seems to have wished to monopolise it (and to use it like an old-style comprador used pidgin English), learning Russian was unnecessary, Chinese was enough. Thus friction arose between Zheng's broad, questing mind and Peng's narrow, carping one, a friction that survived the passage of both men into the Chinese Trotskyist Opposition in 1931 and lasted until their deaths.

In 1924, Zheng went back to China and was appointed Secretary of the Party's Propaganda Department. There he translated Nikolai Bukharin and Evgenii Preobrazhensky's *ABC of Communism*, written in 1919 during the Russian Civil War, as an elementary textbook of Communist knowledge. His translation became the standard work for generations of Chinese revolutionaries, and was for years the only book on Marxist theory that most of them had ever read. It was the inspiration for Zheng's own *ABC of Permanent Revolution*, a textbook of elementary Trotskyist knowledge, translated in this volume. As an aide in the Central Committee, he specialised in editing Party journals and writing for them.

The strategy imposed on the CCP by Moscow in the 1920s led to a devastating defeat in 1927, after which Zheng continued for a while to work underground for the Party. During this time, he came into contact with the views of Leon Trotsky, and he soon became Trotsky's follower.

The origins of the Chinese Trotskyist group were to be found in an earlier faction that had formed in China in the mid-1920s: the so-called Moscow faction, comprising Chinese students like Zheng Chaolin sent back from Moscow to China in 1924 to staff the infant CCP. These Russia-returned students – the first of several generations of such – became important leaders of the Party back in China; they were united as one and worked in close concert as a 'virtual clique', according to Zheng Chaolin.

The group's core was formed by Peng Shuzhi, Wang Ruofei, Yin Kuan, Zheng Chaolin, and Chen Qiaonian. Three of these people later became Trotskyists, while Chen Qiaonian died and Wang Ruofei became a secret sympathiser of the Trotskyists, though he remained within the official Party. All save Peng Shuzhi had spent some time working and studying in France before going to Moscow in the early 1920s. They had joined the revolution more or less simultaneously and gone through a long period of shared experiences at a most formative time in their lives. This naturally inclined them to group together. In France they had lived a hard and taxing life, as wage-slaves in capitalist industry; and Zheng Chaolin in particular had developed independent ways of thinking that were alien to Chinese students who had gone straight from China to Russia. Zheng knew that there could not be just one idea, one leader; his experience inclined him toward scepticism, intellectual curiosity, democracy, and internationalism. In Moscow, Zheng and some of his old comrades from France suffocated under the regime of stifling orthodoxy over which Peng Shuzhi and others presided. Zheng's habit of questioning accepted beliefs and values inclined him to an affinity with Chen Duxiu, Chinese Communism's founder, its most critical, free-thinking, and iconoclastic leader, and later its most prominent Trotskyist.

While this opposition was growing up in China, Trotskyists were also becoming active among the several hundred young Communist survivors who had gone to Moscow to study after the 1927 bloodbath. Though these students knew next to nothing about the Soviet Union or the world Communist movement when they first arrived in Moscow, within a matter of weeks they were 'more or less acquainted with the substance of the controversy' between Stalin and Trotsky.[2] What they lacked in theoretical grounding before going to Russia they made up for in direct experience of the events in China, which formed one of the main battlegrounds on which Stalin and Trotsky fought.

Even before the end of their first year in Moscow, the seeds of sympathy with Russia's Left Opposition had been sown in the minds of some of the new Chinese arrivals, who quickly progressed through sceptical neutrality to active support for the Opposition. Earlier, they had swallowed the official explanation that the policies followed in 1926 and 1927 were 'mistakes committed by Chen Duxiu in defiance of Comintern instructions'. Now, the truth dawned on them: the policies ascribed to Chen Duxiu were Stalin's. Nor was Stalin's policy for China the sole issue that exercised their indignation. They had arrived in Moscow fresh from battle. They were bursting with restless, frustrated energy, moral courage, and a strong antipathy toward the high-handed ways of Moscow's Chinese leaders. By the winter of 1928, Trotskyists were everywhere among the Chinese students there.

In late 1929, some two hundred of them were seized by the Soviet political police. Some were imprisoned for a while, expelled from the Party after recanting, and then deported (these numbered fewer than ten). Others were sent to labour camps in Siberia or the Arctic Circle, whence two escaped back to China sometime before 1949 to tell the tale. Some were shot. The number of those who made it back to China from Moscow just before this crackdown, with their beliefs intact, was fewer than twenty.[3]

In early 1929, the two currents of opposition, one formed in Moscow, tight and highly ideological, the other – looser and vaguer – in China, started out on the long and difficult journey that would eventually join them for a brief moment in Shanghai, under the leadership of Chen Duxiu, before catastrophe hit.

∵

---

2 Wang Fan-hsi, *Memoirs of a Chinese Revolutionary*, translated and with an introduction by Gregor Benton, Second Revised Edition, New York: Columbia University Press, 1991, p. 48.
3 Wang Fan-hsi 1991, p. 105.

The Trotskyist impact on the CCP in 1928 and 1929 was at first considerable. Those who became Trotskyists included Chen Duxiu, founder of the Party, and a score of other senior leaders. Trotskyists deported from Moscow formed several Oppositionist groups and began publishing journals. In January 1931, Trotsky wrote from Turkey urging them to unite, and in May they held a Unification Congress. However, within days the entire Central Committee except for Chen Duxiu was behind bars, and Chen Duxiu too was arrested the following year.

Zheng Chaolin had been expelled from the CCP as a Trotskyist in 1929, after which he became a leader of the Left Opposition and, later, of its offshoots. However, like most Chinese Trotskyists he spent more time in gaol under Chiang Kai-shek than out of it, not counting the eight years of the Japanese wartime occupation.

In August 1937, Zheng was released because of the war, and spent some time in Anhui recovering his health after his time in jail. In 1940, he and his wife Liu returned to Shanghai, where Liu taught in one of two workers' schools that the Trotskyists set up under the noses of the Japanese occupiers. During the war, Zheng's main activity was writing and translating. 'Most of the important articles [in *Internationalist* in the war years] were written by Zheng Chaolin', wrote Wang Fanxi.

> Zheng had long been famous as a contributor to the CCP press but it was only now that his talents as a creative theoretician began to bloom. During those darkest years he wrote his most brilliant and substantial pieces, including *Dialogue Between Three Travellers* (a theoretical treatise of revolution written in novel form), a book of memoirs (an inner history of the CCP from the early 1920s through to 1930), and the *ABC of the Theory of Permanent Revolution*. But the one work to which he devoted most care and attention was his *Critical Biography of Chen Duxiu*, which – to judge from a reading of the manuscript – was the most brilliant history of modern Chinese thought to have been written to date. The pity of it was that apart from the *ABC*, none of his manuscripts from this period ever saw the light of day. When the Chinese Trotskyist movement was destroyed during the nation-wide round-up in December 1952, they were locked up by Mao's political police together with their author.[4]

After the war, Zheng continued to work as a Trotskyist in Shanghai. In 1949, just a few months before Chiang Kai-shek's rule on the Chinese mainland ended, he

---

4   Wang Fan-hsi 1991, pp. 238–9.

helped found the Internationalist Workers' Party, which never had more than a few hundred members.

At first, Zheng's old friends in the new regime set up in 1949 tried to talk him into joining them. Li Weihan, acting through the intermediacy of Shi Fuliang, sought a reconciliation, but Zheng refused. Finally, on the night of 22 December 1952, three years into Mao's revolution, Zheng and two to three hundred other Trotskyists disappeared into prison, where some stayed for the next twenty-seven years under their onetime comrades.

Zheng's wife Liu Jingzhen was sentenced after a secret trial to ten years in jail but was released in 1957, due to illness. By then, her old lameness had worsened. Her rich family was afraid to keep up relations with her so she had become roofless. Fortunately, however, her earlier neighbours helped her find a room, and friends in Hong Kong secretly sent her money.

In the Cultural Revolution of the late 1960s, Liu, by then half-blind, was interrogated several times by Red Guards (though, thankfully, she was not maltreated). One of the charges against her was that in the 1930s, she had smuggled messages to and from the Trotskyist leader Chen Duxiu, at a time when Chen Duxiu had been in jail under Chiang Kai-shek as a revolutionary. In 1972, when Zheng was transferred from prison to the reform-through-labour glass-works in Shanghai's Pudong, Liu was allowed to join him. In Pudong Zheng's life eased slightly.

Did Zheng stay true to his Trotskyist beliefs after 1952? To anyone who knows even a little about the man, the question is ridiculous. That fact has not stopped Zheng's detractors from insinuating, wickedly and outrageously, that he traded his principles for his freedom in 1979 and 'is now happy to render dubious services to ... die-hard Stalinists',[5] Fortunately, there is ample evidence that Zheng's convictions, and his integrity, were one hundred percent intact when he walked free in 1979, having stayed in China thirty years earlier to hold the Trotskyist flag. Even in jail he secretly celebrated his admiration for Trotsky in a cryptic poem (translated in Chapter 10 of this book). Nor can the publication of Zheng's memoirs by the Chinese Communists be taken to imply that he compromised with the regime in Beijing. This is evident from the comment Zheng's official publishers attached to the book:

> Zheng Chaolin is currently a member, aged eighty two, of the People's Political Consultative Conference of the Municipality of Shanghai. He was an early member of the Chinese Communist Party. As he himself says,

---

5   Cheng Yingxiang and Claude Cadart 1986, 'Remarks on a Review of Peng Shuzhi's Memoirs', *China Quarterly*, no. 197 (1986), pp. 530–4, at p. 534. Cheng and Cadart are the daughter and son-in-law of Peng Shuzhi, Zheng's old adversary in the Chinese Trotskyist movement.

after the second half of 1927, he gradually departed from the line of the Communist International and the Chinese Communist Party and, after 1929, went over completely to Trotskyist positions; moreover, he became a main leader of the Chinese Trotskyist organisation ... To this day, the author fully upholds Trotskyist positions on various important issues in the Chinese Revolution and the Russian Revolution, and still supports various of Trotsky's and of Chen Duxiu's opinions. We are now publishing this book in a limited edition, restricted to internal circulation, as reference material for leading cadres in relevant departments and for scientific workers in the field of contemporary history.

The irony is that the purveyor of this attempt to defame Zheng was the daughter of Peng Shuzhi, leader of a Trotskyist faction hostile to Zheng, who fled China to spend the rest of his life in comfortable exile in France and America, whereas Zheng stayed and paid the price.

••

Most of the Chinese Trotskyist leaders were writers and several were poets – had they been made of rougher stuff or more soldierly, they might have followed a different path after the defeat of the revolution in 1927. When Mao and his comrades took to the hills, nearly all the Trotskyists stayed in the towns.

Zheng's Trotskyist comrade Wang Fanxi often said that Zheng, born in another age, would have shone as an academician or poet. Instead, he was born with the twentieth century, and into eventual martyrdom. In fact, Zheng's years in prison and his forced abstention from revolutionary activity gave him the chance and time he had previously lacked to write books and to compose poetry, which he loved to do.

Like Mao, Zheng Chaolin combined a belief in radical revolution with a love for poetry in the classical style. In a letter to the Communist poet Lou Shiyi, he explained his aversion to poetry in the modern idiom:

> For prose, the literary reform of May Fourth worked. Today no one writes in classical Chinese anymore. But for poetry, it failed. The first generation of literary reformers like Chen Duxiu and Lu Xun all wrote poetry in the old style. Poetry needs rules and forms. This is true of poetry (excluding free verse) in all the Western languages. I know of no new-style poetry in Chinese that is broadly read, like Lu Xun's old-style poems. So I take a very serious attitude to old-style poetry and would never stoop to writing doggerel.

In China far more so than in the West, poetry has always been a communal and collaborative activity, a main thread in the fabric of society and politics. Educated people celebrated events, friends, and heroes (past and present) and commemorated loss in 'exchange poems' that invoked someone either remote in time or space or with whom the writer was personally acquainted, whereas in the West poetry has long been a vehicle of mainly personal expression abstracted from society. Zheng, like Mao, was part of this poetic discourse.

But Zheng's poetry has none of Mao's brash self-regarding grandiosity and sense of personal uniqueness and superiority. This is because he was by nature a more modest and compassionate man than Mao, and his poetry reflects this difference as well as his defeat and calvary. Naturally he never wrote on martial themes, since he lacked Mao's experience of warfare. In any case, he doubted the advisability and long-term efficacy of a military road to power. Instead, he wrote in his poems – far more so than Mao – about personal loss and disappointment. Where he did tackle political topics, he cloaked critical or dissident opinions in cryptic language to fool the censor, using classical allusions to hint at the inevitability of great changes lying ahead. His poems are often bleak and tragic, but he sometimes makes fun of himself and the world.

∴

In his memoirs, Zheng frequently reviews the character, motives, and behaviour of his friends and enemies, but he rarely says much about himself. It is therefore helpful and appropriate to look at what other people have said about him over the years.

Wang Fanxi, Zheng's close collaborator in the Trotskyist cause, was struck above all by his formidable staunchness and his total disregard, like a Buddhist monk who has attained the Way, for his own personal fate. Wang wrote in 1957, in reference to the Trotskyists' decision not to flee China in 1949:

> Even if we leave aside Zheng Chaolin's other strengths, his Peter-like spirit of martyrdom alone will ensure him a lasting place in the history of the Revolution. Our dilemma was similar in many ways to that of the early Christians under Nero – should we stay in the capital or flee to a safe place? Some approached the question mainly from the point of view of their own fate, others from the point of view of the future of the organisation as a whole; but Zheng Chaolin did not wait for a voice from the heavens to ask 'Quo vadis?': his mind was made up from the very outset.[6]

---

6 Wang Fan-hsi 1991, p. 251.

Lou Shiyi, who knew Zheng Chaolin in the 1920s and visited him again in the 1980s, wrote a long appreciation of him in a preface to a volume of Zheng's poems, most of them written while Zheng was in jail under the Communists. Lou, a veteran and orthodox member of the CCP, was for many years a senior literary editor in Beijing. So his view of Zheng is not coloured by sympathy for Zheng's Trotskyist politics, and is therefore all the more remarkable and reliable:

> The old man Yu Yin, Comrade Zheng Chaolin, is my teacher. He is also my old friend – one of those with whom I shared many trials and who today number very few, as few as the disappearing stars in the early morning sky. It would be presumptuous of me to add mere tittle-tattle to my teacher's book. However, as his old friend, and in order to express my delight on this occasion, I shall venture to recall some events that happened during our long friendship and that younger readers may enjoy hearing about.
>
> I remember that several months after the end of the May Thirtieth movement of 1925 – winter had already set in – I and a few other young people attended night school several times a week in the home of a friend on Baotong Road in Shanghai's Zhabei. We were not many, but a group of people took turns at lecturing to us. We studied current affairs and the rudiments of Marxism. Our teachers included pioneers of the revolution like Qu Qiubai, Yun Daiying, Yin Kuan, and Zhao Shiyan; they also included Comrade Zheng Chaolin. In those days, he was still a young man, with a full head of black hair and an elegant bearing. He had probably not long been back in China. He had squeezed his plump body into a neat Western-style suit; a bright watch-chain protruded from his left-hand pocket and disappeared into his waistcoat button-hole. As far as I remember, his subject was 'The Meaning for the Chinese Revolution of the May Thirtieth Movement'. He was not a very fluent speaker and he had a slight Fujian accent, but he was very kind and approachable and left a deep impression on those of us who studied under him; in my mind's eye I can still see him to this day.
>
> The night school was abandoned before very long, and after that, I had no further occasion to meet Zheng. But fate is a strange thing, and ten or so years later, we renewed our acquaintance under remarkable circumstances – in the Guomindang's Central Military Prison in Nanjing. His solitary cell was on the same block as mine, just eight or nine doors away, but we rarely caught a glimpse of one another. One day, I was escorted to the Education Section, where a short thin man who was in charge talked cordially with me and allocated me to 'penal labour', after which I was

taken to a big room that had originally been part of the Education Section. It was bright and clean, with a row of ping-pong tables along the windows, each capable of accommodating six or seven people, who sat there doing literary work. I was allocated the German Military Code to translate. This threw me into confusion, for my German was quite elementary; I could remember little more than how to say the alphabet in it. How on earth was I to translate such a book? But when I lifted my head and looked around, I noticed several familiar faces. The first to greet me was Pan Zinian, who told me that I should accept the assignment, that everything would be all right. The person in charge of the Education Section was a man called Shen Bingquan. In order to make life easier for some cultural figures (I guess today you would call them 'higher intellectuals'), he had specially requested this cushy job from the Ministry of Military Administration. So we had a reason to leave our cells each day, we could get some exercise, and we got the chance to do some reading and writing. At my table were four other fellow inmates. All but one – even Pan Zinian – had only beginners' German. The exception, seated opposite Pan, was none other than Comrade Zheng Chaolin, whom I had not seen for a decade. He had aged somewhat in the meantime, and had lost his hair. He was the only true translator among us. All the rest of us learned German from him. In front of each of us was a German text, a dictionary, an exercise book, and a pile of loose writing paper. We spent our time reading and writing and called it translating, but in effect, all we did was learn from our teacher. A semi-literate warder on guard in the hall used to wander round the tables to see how conscientious and diligent we were; he thought that we were working hard and was very satisfied with us. We could get up and stretch our legs at will, or take time off for a quiet chat; no one ever interfered with us. Section Director Shen often used to visit us, and would sit down and talk with us about what was in the newspapers. We were not allowed to read the dailies, but we were allowed to receive large quantities of books and periodicals, so there was nothing that we did not know. Chaolin was of a different political persuasion from the rest of us, so we rarely discussed politics with him. Nevertheless, we viewed his big bald skull as a living encyclopaedia. He was never averse to answering our questions. At all times, he sincerely and tirelessly helped us. He not only taught us German; he also taught two youngsters French. At the same time, he helped us all with our translations. He was extraordinarily assiduous. He read and translated non-stop. I remember that he translated Thomas Mann's *Buddenbrooks* from German and D. Merezhkovsky's *Resurrection of the Gods* from Russian. We all vied to read this translation of Merezhkovsky's book, which was a fictional biography of Leonardo da Vinci. At one time, he translated from the French André Gide's *Retour de l'URSS*. Some of the people with us said that this book was anti-Soviet and told us to ignore it. But surreptitiously, I became the first reader of Zheng's Chinese translation, for which I was roundly criticised by my prison-mates. I was not convinced by their strictures.

The rest of us attended to our own research and translation. Section Director Shen helped us by posting our manuscripts to our friends in Shanghai, so they quickly appeared in print and we earned quite a lot of money. Some of us were even able to maintain our families. Chaolin, being the fastest and the most productive translator, naturally earned most. His wife Liu Jingzhen, who had stayed behind in Shanghai, came regularly and often to visit him in prison in Nanjing, and brought him large amounts of food, winter clothing, medicine, and nutriments. His own needs were few, and he often used to give away the larger part to prisoners whose distress was greater and who received no assistance from outside. He did this regardless of their political views, and did not even know some of the people he helped. There was one prisoner, a long-term inmate of the sickward stricken by tuberculosis of the lymphous gland, whom he met by accident only once in the clinic, while visiting the doctor. When Chaolin learned that this man was poor as well as sick, he got Jingzhen to bring a big bottle of cod-liver oil with her every time she came to the prison, and passed it on to this man through one of the prison guards.

We lived together in the same prison right through until 1937, when we were released after the outbreak in China of the full-scale War of Resistance against Japan. Actually, Chaolin had lost his freedom as early as 1931, and had been kept in various prisons before finally being moved to Nanjing's Military Prison, where he was an old lag. After our release, war beacons filled the sky all over China, and each went his own way. I heard nothing more of Chaolin after that. And so forty years passed. In the spring of 1979, I made a special trip to Shanghai to attend the service in memory of Fu Lei and his wife.[7] A friend in Shanghai told me that Chaolin had in the meantime spent another twenty years behind bars, and that he had just been freed; but he warned me not to visit him, for he was still under strict supervision. Not until a year or so later did I dis-

---

7   The parents of the famous pianist Fu Ts'ong. Fu Lei, who translated R. Rolland and H. Balzac into Chinese, committed suicide in the Cultural Revolution and was rehabilitated in 1979.

cover that Chaolin had already been restored to complete liberty, and that even though he still maintained his old political position, he had been invited to become a member of Shanghai's People's Political Consultative Conference. Just at that time, I was going to Shanghai on an official mission, so I visited my old teacher from half a century earlier, my prison mate from forty years earlier. Being the same age as the century, he was already an old man, but even so, he was warmly hospitable, tirelessly talkative, and overflowing with high spirits. It was as if he had sustained not the slightest damage from his trials and tribulations. But on the day[8] that he was restored to complete freedom, his wife Liu Jingzhen, who for twenty seven years had done everything possible from the other side of prison walls to alleviate his sufferings, who had defended him, and who had waited loyally for him, quietly left this world, after seemingly having completed her appointed task. And his only child, born during the War against Japan, has also left behind nothing but a precious wide-eyed photographic image pinned to the wall of Zheng's lonely study. Zheng lives a life of great calm and great intensity. He reads, he writes, and he receives and instructs an endless flow of comrades researching special issues in the history of the Chinese Communist Party.

Another brief pen-picture of Zheng can be found in the first volume of the memoirs of the Trotskyist Peng Shuzhi. There was no love lost between Zheng and Peng, but even so, Peng draws a rather affectionate picture of Zheng in the 1920s:

Zheng Chaolin was a strapping young fellow with a broad forehead, always smiling and extremely kind-hearted. There is no denying that he was something of a pedant. He had a stammer. And politically, he was rather uninventive. But in his way, he was a linguistic genius, in the very special sense that he could learn at high speed to decipher, read, and render into decent Chinese any language whatsoever, provided that it was at the level of political discourse and provided, above all, that he was never expected to articulate a single sentence or to understand it *orally*. For example, it only took him a few months in Moscow to disentangle Russian, just as it had taken him only a few months in France to familiarise himself – also

---

8   Actually, Liu Jingzhen died on 14 October 1979, four months and ten days after the release of her husband.

at the level of political discourse – with French. To the knowledge – political and bookish – of these two languages he soon added English, German, Italian, and Esperanto.[9]

∴

There have been many attempts to write an account of 'Chinese Marxism' as a *sui generis* philosophy with its own special characteristics drawn from traditional Chinese thought, shaped by the special experience of the Chinese Revolution and enriched by Mao's supposed personal genius. But none of these attempts to paint a picture of Mao as an independent philosopher and thinker of great stature has turned out to be convincing, for to make their case that Marxism *à la Mao* was an original and creative reworking of Marxist canon, they are forced to ignore its genesis, hardly hidden by Mao and his writing team, in Stalinist state ideology. Wang Fanxi, in his study on Mao thought, does full justice to Mao's contribution to the Chinese Revolution, and points to its sources in Confucianism and the *youxia* (knight-errant) tradition. However, he concludes that its Marxist component was derived chiefly from Stalinism and a product not of independent research and thinking on his part but of pro-Stalin plagiarism, exercised in the service of various inner-party struggles waged by Mao and his co-thinkers, chiefly against the Chinese Stalinist Wang Ming. Mao's knowledge of Marxism was thin, and even at the time of his longest immersion in it, in the late 1930s, as part of his striving to 'acquire the veneer of a philosopher and a theoretician and thus to outshine Wang Ming', he never achieved much depth. If anything, he and his supporters in the leadership 'disparaged revolutionary theory as "academic" chatter and preferred instead to knuckle down to hard work coupled with a mindless recitation of a handful of abstract programmatic goals'. So although a skilful tactician and military strategist and a man of action who made many practical innovations that played a central role in bringing the Communists to power in 1949, as a Marxist theoretician he achieved little of note – rather, he did great harm to the party's and to China's intellectual life.[10]

Marxism as a rich, complex, creative, and many-sided school of thought never figured in Mao's China, where for most of the time, except during brief

---

9   Claude Cadart and Cheng Yingxiang, *Mémoires de Peng Shuzhi: L'Envol du communisme en Chine*, Paris: Gallimard, 1983, p. 321. Actually, Zheng learned Esperanto in France.

10   Wang Fanxi, *Mao Zedong Thought*, edited and translated by Gregor Benton, Leiden: Brill, 2020.

interludes of relatively timid experimentation and debate, theory and philosophy were (and continue to be) reduced to a narrow, sterile, and highly selective orthodoxy, which its practitioners learned by heart and recited from memory and in chorus. For decades, the problem was not just the Stalinist poisoning of the party's intellectual wellsprings but a lack of access to the wide range of Marxist thought and even to the very writings of Marx, Engels, and Lenin, which only began to appear systematically in Chinese translation in 1953, a work that even now has still not been completed. The party was engaged almost from the start in a life-and-death struggle for survival on successive battlefields during which there was little opportunity for study, and some communists even saw 'too much study' as 'spouting hot air'. Under the warlord regime of the 1910s and 1920, Marxist writings were suppressed, and even after 1927 they were generally unavailable outside Shanghai. In 1937, after the party leaders had consolidated a new base in the northwest at the end of the Long March, they became acquainted with descriptions of Marxism sent back from Moscow, but it was no longer a living critical philosophy with competing schools but a closed ideology designed to justify Stalin's dictatorship and appropriated by Mao, with the help of the translator Ai Siqi, himself steeped in the Stalinist approach to theory, to establish Mao's credentials as a 'theorist'. Taking his cue from Stalin, Mao used the new ideology as a tool with which to shape and police his dictatorship.

To the extent that critical Marxist texts did appear in China, it was in large measure thanks to the Chinese Trotskyists, foremost among them Zheng Chaolin, who – as a virtuoso linguist – was the mainstay of their translating enterprise. Until their disappearance into prison for the first time in 1931, the Chinese Trotskyists published far more Marxist writings, including classics, than the official party. These writings included translations of Marxist classics and of histories of the European revolutionary movement. Besides their own writings, their publications included books by Marx, Engels, Plekhanov, Lenin, Trotsky, Preobrazhensky, Kant, Thomas Mann, Darwin, John Dewey, D. Merezhkovsky, André Gide, and Kropotkin. They even continued their translating in prison, to the extent that this was possible. 'In the early 1930s', according to Wang Hongmo, a CCP ideologue,

> the Trotskyists published a great many articles and books to spread their fallacious 'theories' about the nature of Chinese society and the Chinese revolution, which forced Chinese Marxists and Communist Party members into serious and vigorous polemics to counter their demagoguery and eliminate its negative influence.

So insofar as Marxism in its classical form reached China in the 1930s, it was mainly through the endeavour of the Trotskyists. To write independently, they needed money to feed themselves and their families, which they got by translating and by writing novels, short stories, biographies, political and social studies, and histories. 'Our "rice-bowl" literary activities during that period played no small part in popularising and deepening socialist thinking in China', wrote Wang Fanxi.

Their status as oppositionists, in China and in Russia after 1927, forced them to learn how to think against the stream and support unorthodox ideas. Within the Opposition, they enjoyed a freedom of thought alien to the official party, and had to argue their positions before an often sceptical audience of comrades.

One of their main outlets was the Oriental Book Company, a radical publishing house that had supported progressive movements in China ever since its founding in 1903 and was proudly described by its owner Wang Mengzou as 'a product of reform and revolution'. Starting in 1929, it published several dozen books written or translated by Chinese Trotskyists. Of some 140 books brought out by the company between 1929 and 1949, at least 61 were written or translated by Trotskyists; they included histories of various foreign revolutionary movements; economic studies; studies on dialectics, the philosophy of Kant, women's liberation, Japanese imperialism, the war in Europe, Darwinism, and science and social science; and several books by Chen Duxiu.

• •

Later the Chinese Trotskyists' foremost writer and translator, Zheng Chaolin made his first contribution to Marxist book-publishing in China in 1925, when he translated Bukharin and Preobrazhensky's famous ABC of Communism, which expounded the political programme of the Russian Bolshevik Party. The book immediately became a best-seller, and was the earliest and most influential Marxist textbook in Chinese and the standard work for generations of Chinese revolutionaries. Zheng edited Guide Weekly and Bolshevik for the Central Committee in the mid-1920s, and subsequently wrote and translated numerous books on Marxist subjects.

• •

This volume contains translations (presented in chronological order) of Zheng's articles, chapters, poems, and letters on a variety of themes to set alongside his full-length books (two of which have been translated into English – his memoirs, written in 1945, and his poems, most of which were composed in jail after 1952 and published in 1989). The writings' two main themes, which are treated separately in special articles but, in one way or another, inform most of the rest, are Trotsky's theory of permanent revolution and the non-Trotskyist (or Trotsky-related) theory of state capitalism, which Zheng called cadreism. Zheng and his comrades saw the idea of permanent revolution as an essential corrective to the Stalinist and reformist idea of a revolution enacted in discrete, impermeable stages. Cadreism referred to a social system that combined elements of capitalism with state ownership or control, and where the state acts as a single corporation extracting surplus value from the workers. (Zheng seems to have invented the term cadreism independently, while in prison under Mao, when he wrote a much longer study, of eighty five thousand Chinese characters, under the same title – it was apparently confiscated and destroyed by his Maoist captors.)[11]

Zheng's 'Introduction to the ABC of Permanent Revolution', modelled on Bukharin and Preobrazhensky's primer and drawing on his own translation of Trotsky's *Permanent Revolution*, was written in Japanese-occupied Shanghai in the dark days of 1942, in the middle of the Anti-Japanese War. Zheng wrote it as a contribution to the debate in China about the causes of the defeat of the revolution of 1925–7 and the best way to win the next one. His aim was to produce a clear and readable account of Trotsky's polemical work on permanent revolution, which Zheng saw as the key to victory in the coming struggle after the Japanese defeat. In it, he refutes the Stalinist misrepresentation of Trotsky's theory and shows how it was linked to Marx's writings on the German revolutions. He explains how the Russian Revolution of 1905 provided a negative and that of 1917 a positive confirmation of the theory, and demonstrates its applicability on a world scale, in the hope that revolutionaries in other countries will avoid China's disastrous error in 1927.

As John Sexton points out in his introduction to the ABC, Zheng has little to say about China in it, apart from giving a few Chinese examples. However, this was because Zheng, like Trotsky, wanted to put the Chinese Revolution 'on the same footing as revolutions in other countries' rather than discover 'special

---

11   See *Prophets Unarmed, passim*. Walter Daum has pointed out, in a personal communication, that Zheng thought that Stalinist state capitalism differed from other versions of it in that 'political and economic power have become one'. If so, 'cadreism' would simply be a way of specifying the nature of state capitalism as ruled by a party bureaucracy, and could be perhaps rendered as 'bureaucratism', in the same way that others have used the term 'bureaucratic collectivism' or 'bureaucratic state capitalism'. More recently, the term has been used in India and Africa to mean the appropriation by political cadres of what should be official government functions (John Plant, personal communication).

national characteristics' of the sort that the Maoists harped on about. Among these special characteristics was the military road that Mao took after 1927 – a strategy that Zheng doubted, and even saw as a road to disaster.

Zheng was wrong about the military road, for within seven years it had led Mao to power at the head of a peasant army. However, at the time of his victory Mao was promising decades of collaboration with China's national bourgeoisie. On this point, Zheng – though by then in prison – could at least take satisfaction from the fact that, within a decade of announcing his cross-class alliance, Mao had abandoned it and taken the capitalists' companies and factories into state ownership, in clear confirmation of the theory of permanent revolution that Trotsky had recommended 'for revolution in economically backward countries'.

Several years later, in an article published in 1946, Zheng used Trotsky's theory of permanent revolution to criticise Mao Zedong's plans for a New Democracy, a Chinese reincarnation of the Stalinist stages theory of revolution that had led to disaster in 1927, when the Chinese Communists had subordinated the interests of the Chinese working class to a 'bourgeois' revolution whose leaders first used and then slaughtered them. (In a linked article, Zheng accused his fellow-Trotskyist Peng Shuzhi, generally regarded in the Trotskyist movement as a dogmatist, of propagating a left-wing version of New Democracy.) By abandoning his planned alliance soon after winning power in 1949, Mao in effect implemented a distorted version of permanent revolution, even to the extent of proclaiming it as such by name (while insisting that it was not the same 'permanent revolution' as Trotsky's). However, Mao and his fellow-leaders continued to impose the doomed strategy of revolution in stages on Maoist parties in other countries, or to tolerate it in them.

∴

The second big theme of Zheng's writings in this volume is state capitalism, which features in several articles written at different times. Trotsky rejected the characterisation of the Soviet Union as state capitalist, but Zheng thought that the label accurately fitted the Soviet regime under Stalin and the regime in China under Mao. In that respect, he differed from his more orthodox Chinese comrades, who argued (like Trotsky) that the Soviet Union was a degenerated workers' state and that (by extrapolation from Trotsky's theory) the Eastern European 'People's Democracies' were, and had been from the start, deformed workers' states. It is possible that Zheng first became acquainted with the theory of state capitalism through the US Trotskyist Max Shachtman. Zheng's close friend and comrade Wang Fanxi was in correspondence at one point with

Shachtman (Shachtman published an article by Wang in his journal) and for a while shared Shachtman's view of the Soviet Union under Stalin as 'bureaucratic collectivist'. Although Wang himself soon gave up the theory of bureaucratic collectivism and reverted to a more orthodox Trotskyist position (i.e., the Soviet Union and its post-war satellites and China were workers' states of a sort), Zheng stuck to his theory of state capitalism for the rest of his life.

Zheng's view on state capitalism shows an evolution over time. In the article 'State Capitalism' written in 1950, before Zheng's arrest and soon after Mao had taken power (in 1949), Zheng argued that state capitalism was a late stage of capitalism that featured in the USSR after 1937 and in Eastern Europe and China after 1949. According to Zheng's theory, state planning and nationalisation was compatible with state capitalism thus conceived. As for the USSR, Stalin had overthrown the dictatorship of the proletariat and killed off the Bolsheviks. This theory is compatible, according to Walter Daum, who introduces the article, with the fact that in the 1980s the Maoists 'restored openly capitalist relations' without any need for a further revolution. (In Marxist theory, the transition from one form of class rule to another cannot happen without a revolution or counterrevolution.)

Daum questions Zheng's thinking on two grounds. First, he doubts Zheng's contention that Mao's China and Stalin's USSR were not workers' states 'because the broad masses cannot enjoy democracy', whereas they had done so in the early years of the Russian Revolution. Daum points out that democracy was short-lived in Russia before it collapsed as a result of Russia's international isolation, economic backwardness, and years of invasions and civil war, and according to Trotsky it remained a workers' state despite the early loss of democracy. Second, Daum questions Zheng's picturing of state capitalism as the most advanced form of capitalism. He argues instead that the rulers in both Russia and China thought that state capitalism (a) left them behind economically and (b) conceded too much to the workers, so the rulers eventually (in the late twentieth century) reverted to a more traditional form of capitalism dependent not on state ownership but on capitalist super-exploitation. On another question, Daum doubts Zheng's later contention, in a connected article written in 1992, that the coming revolution would happen not on the margins of capitalism, as in the past, and as Zheng had seemed to believe in 1950, but at its core in Europe and North America. Instead, Daum argues that rebel proletarians will strike first and hardest in countries like China, where the workers are most exploited and where the 'contradictions' that Zheng foresaw in 1950 will be hardest to mitigate.

In 1985, in the unpublished handwritten draft of a book titled *Waiting for a Return to Huilongwu* (the name of his family's 'ancestral mountain'), Zheng

develops an even more systematic critique of 'cadreism' in comparative perspective, with China and the Soviet Union as his comparands, noting their
commonalities and distinctions. In it, he traces the history of the term 'cadre' in
Stalinist and Maoist thinking, with its militaristic and authoritarian ethos. He
goes on to extend his critique of cadreism to China's incipient post-Mao market
reforms. Zheng's translator, Kevin Lin, points to the contemporary resonance
of Zheng's prescriptions for democracy in social movements.

In 1989, after the bloody crackdown on student and worker protests in May
and early June in Beijing's Tiananmen Square, in a brave criticism of the government, Zheng returned yet again (in an article translated by Tsim Shum Kow and
introduced by Owen Miller) to his analysis of the 'cadre class' as a bureaucratic
excrescence ruling over a society marked by commodities, classes, and a state –
thus ruling out workers' democracy and socialism. Now, unlike in 1950, he releg-
ates Stalinist-style state capitalism to a position behind 'traditional' capitalism,
which has shown itself to be the more flexible and efficient of the two forms.
State capitalism hastens to catch up, but the economic reforms it carries out
are no substitute for political reform of the sort demanded by critical citizens.
Zheng sees the inability of the cadre class to resolve this 'fundamental contradiction' as the biggest threat to its survival, but he was not able to foresee the
way in which it managed to overcome this contradiction in the following decades through high speed growth and continued authoritarian rule.

In 1991, after the fall of the Berlin Wall and the Soviet collapse, Zheng Chaolin
came back yet again, in an essay titled 'The October Revolution, Thermidor, and
the Stalinist Mode of Capitalism', to the question of state capitalism, copied
by Mao from the Soviet example. In his introduction to this article, Yang Yang
explains that for Zheng, the CCP's victory over the Guomindang had confirmed
the superiority of state capitalism over other forms of capitalism. After his
release from prison under the Communists in 1979, he continued to insist that
Russia and the countries in its supporting fringe had never been socialist, and
their demise was 'merely an expression of the bankruptcy of Stalinism, of the
doctrine of socialism in one country'.

As for the October Revolution, it too had failed, although Zheng continued
to believe into old age that October had been an experiment worth trying and
could, under different circumstances, have sparked world revolution. Why had
state capitalism subsequently succumbed to the traditional capitalism of the
West? Having abandoned his old belief that state capitalism was capitalism's
final and most efficient form, Zheng argues that it failed because it had been
left far behind by the postwar boom, despite having outstripped the West in the
Depression of the 1930s. Zheng acknowledged that he and the other Trotskyists
had failed to see traditional capitalism's capacity to renew itself and to incor-

porate older formations into the world market under its hegemony. This, he admitted, might mean that permanent revolution and world socialist revolution would be pushed further into the future and come only after many tides, both high and low.

Zheng's final essay on state capitalism, written in his very old age, titled 'On Cadreism', repeated Trotsky's view that socialism cannot happen in a single country, and built on his own view that Stalin's attempt to do so had led to the degeneration of the old revolutionary cadre into a new 'cadreist' class ruling over a form of late capitalism. In her introduction to the essay, Huang Ting explains that the persistence of scarcity was the material basis for the emergence of cadreism, and that cadreism is 'perfectly compatible with the existence of a ruling class that exploits the vast majority'.

• •
•

Other writings in this volume include a major study of the Trotskyism of Chen Duxiu, founder in 1921 of the Chinese Communist Party and in 1931 of the Chinese Left Opposition, written after Zheng's release from prison in 1979. Zheng's association with Chen Duxiu went back to the 1920s, when he was a mainstay of the Chen Duxiu faction. He continued to admire and respect Chen even after Chen began, in the late 1930s, to express doubts about Marxism in all its forms (though, as Zheng and Wang Fanxi always insisted, Chen's alienation never led him to make an explicit break with it). The essay on Marxism and alienation shows that Zheng remained alert to new developments in Marxist thought right up until the end of his life, although he stubbornly resisted jumping on the bandwagon of a fashionably 'humanistic' Marxism and called instead for a return to the fundamentals on which Deng Xiaoping (his old comrade from France in the early 1920s) had turned his back. The account of love and politics in China in the 1920s shows his fascination, as a man of great humanity and imagination, for interpersonal relations and their intersection with politics – a chapter in his memoir that the authorities in the 1980s saw as prurient and perhaps disrespectful and therefore banned, but one that actually brings into focus the richness of the human relations of the early Chinese Communists. Finally, Zheng's last correspondence shows that he retained his famously elephantine memory deep into old age, as well as his respect for accuracy and love of truth in all things, and the touching solicitude with which he treats his equally venerable correspondent across the Taiwan Strait.

ABC of Permanent Revolution (1942)

Translated by John Sexton

Translator's Introduction

In 1925, taking advantage of a brief lull in the mass movement that meant Communist Party printing presses were relatively idle, Zheng Chaolin translated Bukharin and *Preobrazhensky's ABC of Communism*. The revolutionary surge soon regained momentum and, to Zheng's surprise, the ABC became a best-seller around China, surpassed only by Sun Yat-sen's *Three Principles of the People* and beating a popular manual by the utopian sexologist Zhang Jingsheng into third place. For revolutionaries like Zheng, it was an optimistic period. He was a leading member of a rapidly growing party riding a revolutionary wave. His translation of the ABC became an indispensable educational text and a recruiting tool for the party. He could not know at that time that the upsurge would end in disaster, but when it did, he concluded that the debacle was caused by the fatal policies of the Stalinist bureaucracy that had obliged the CCP to cling to the coat tails of the Guomindang. The Nationalists, after squeezing all they could out of their alliance with Russia, turned troops trained by Red Army advisors and guns paid for by the Soviet Union against the Chinese workers and peasants. Tens, perhaps hundreds of thousands were wiped out and the CCP was reduced to a rump, some hiding in the mountains of Jiangxi and Hunan and the rest (including Zheng) in precarious underground urban networks, mainly in Shanghai.

As Zheng Chaolin notes in his introduction, the defeat of the revolution generated a wide-ranging controversy about the reasons for its failure. The debate began inside the Party but soon spread to broader intellectual circles and to Chinese society as a whole. Couched in sociological jargon so that they could be published in magazines and journals, articles by leading scholars discussed such questions as whether contemporary China was feudal or capitalist and indeed whether ancient China had ever been feudal or was an example of what Marx had called the Asiatic mode of production. But, as Zheng noted, the operational value of the debates boiled down to these two questions – why had the last revolution failed and how could the next one succeed?

Zheng noticed that the Left Opposition, after its emergence in the late 1920s, was at a disadvantage in these debates because it had no systematic and readily understandable account of its ideas. So in 1942, he decided to set out for a Chinese audience the theoretical basis for a correct revolutionary policy, which he did in this short book. His starting point was Trotsky's theory of Permanent Revolution. He had already translated Trotsky's eponymous work so why add his own exposition of the theory? Because, he said, Trotsky's book was a polemical work meant for an audience that already had a thorough grounding in revolutionary theory. Clearly Zheng was hoping that his *ABC of Permanent Revolution* would have the same educational and recruiting value as his translation of the *ABC of Communism*.

The circumstances in which he wrote the *ABC of Permanent Revolution* – in 1942 – could scarcely have been more different from the period in which he translated the *ABC of Communism*. The battle of Stalingrad was raging and the fate of the world depended on its outcome. Two great imperialist blocs – the 'democratic' empires and the Axis powers were locked in a struggle to the death for world mastery. The Soviet Union – the first and only workers' state – was on the brink of destruction. Zheng himself was no longer a member of a big party but of a small group persecuted by both left and right. Occasionally in his introduction he too appears to be near the brink of despair. The war in China has been going on for longer than the First World War and the war in Europe for three years, but there have been no revolutions. His lament is heartfelt:

> We cannot see the dawn ... all we hear about is war. People have forgotten everything but war. For the sake of war they have forgotten revolution.

There may also be personal reasons for Zheng's brush with despair. Around this time, his only son Frei died of tuberculosis.

Nevertheless Zheng continues to believe in the eventual victory of socialist revolution. By the time the book is published – five years after it was written – his optimism has returned.[1] The revolution is on the upswing, people who had forgotten about revolution in 1942 talk about nothing else in 1947. But mindful of how the last revolutionary wave ended in disaster, he expresses the hope that the publication of his little book will help shape events and push the movement to victory.

---

1 Both Zheng's translation of *Permanent Revolution* and his own *ABC of Permanent Revolution* were published in 1947 by Xin qi Press – the Trotskyist' imprint, along with Zheng's translation of Trotsky's autobiography *My Life*. See Wang 1991, 247–8.

> We are much closer to revolution than we were five years ago. So I dare
> to hope that the book, appearing so late, may prove more useful than if it
> had been published five years ago.

He divided his *ABC* into four chapters. Chapter 1 is devoted to refuting the Stalinist canard that Trotsky was the first to talk about "permanent revolution" and
that it was the fountainhead of all the blunderings of "Trotskyism."[2] In fact, as
Zheng demonstrates, the terminology and the fundamentals of the theory can
be traced to Marx's writings on the German revolutions of the nineteenth century.

In Chapter 2, Zheng examines how Trotsky rediscovered the permanent
revolution and described how the revolution of 1905 provided a negative confirmation of the theory. In Chapter 3, he demonstrates how the October Revolution in 1917 confirmed the theory and answered the objections of its opponents.
He also notes that for the revolution to succeed, Lenin had to re-arm the party
against the dogmatic schemas of the Old Bolsheviks, and how the latter revived
their schemas in their factional battle against Trotsky.

Finally, in Chapter 4, drawing on Marx, Lenin and Trotsky, he attempts a syn-
thesis and development of the theory to make it applicable on a world scale. In
this chapter Zheng also refutes another Stalinist charge – that Trotsky "underestimated the peasantry." Both Lenin and Trotsky believed the agrarian revolution
was the key task of Russia's bourgeois revolution and that peasant uprisings
were indispensable for overthrowing the ancient regime. They differed in that
Trotsky maintained that the peasantry was incapable of ruling a modern state
and must end up supporting one or another urban class – in Russia's case the
proletariat.

To better understand Zheng's text it will be helpful if the reader keeps in
mind the distinction between the *tasks* of a revolution and the *actors* (i.e. which
classes) will carry them out. Also, the related concepts of a *belated bourgeois
revolution* and a *backward country*. Zheng uses the term *backward country* not
to indicate the general level of development but in the special sense of a country where capitalism has created a conscious proletariat but the bourgeoisie, for
some reason or another, has not completed the bourgeois revolution. A backward country in this sense faces a *belated bourgeois revolution*. The *tasks* of such
a revolution are, or include, bourgeois tasks (such as the establishment of a
democratic republic, land reform and the sweeping away of feudal holdovers)
but these tasks will be carried out not by the bourgeoisie but by other *actors* for

---

2 Trotsky 1939, p. 1.

example the proletariat and/or the peasantry. This is because the bourgeoisie, faced with a class conscious proletariat, will be unwilling and unable to lead the kind of mass mobilisation necessary to complete its 'own' revolution.

For example both nineteenth-century Germany and early twentieth-century Russia, unlike seventeenth-century England and eighteenth-century France, already had a powerful organised working class when bourgeois revolution came on the agenda. Consequently, the bourgeoisie, far from leading the revolution, sided with the reactionary forces against it. This had crucial policy implications for socialists – for if the bourgeoisie was not going to lead its 'own' revolution, it would be of little use for the working class to offer support to it. As Lenin put it in March 1917 in his *Letters from Afar*:

> Ours is a bourgeois revolution, therefore, the workers must support the bourgeoisie, say the Potresovs, Gvozdyovs and Chkheidzes, as Plekhanov said yesterday.

> Ours is a bourgeois revolution, we Marxists say, therefore the workers must open the eyes of the people to the deception practised by the bourgeois politicians, teach them to put no faith in words, to depend entirely on their own strength, their own organisation, their own unity, and their own weapons.[3]

Trotsky explained the different positions within the RSDLP on the nature of the Russian revolution in *Three Conceptions of the Russian Revolution*, a text that Zheng does not refer to and probably had not seen when he wrote the ABC.

> The Menshevik attitude toward the revolution, stripped of episodic encrustations and individual deviations, is reducible to the following: The victory of the Russian bourgeois revolution is conceivable only under the leadership of the liberal bourgeoisie and must hand over power to the latter.

> Lenin's perspective may be briefly expressed as follows: The belated Russian bourgeoisie is incapable of leading its own revolution to the end. The complete victory of the revolution through the medium of the "democratic dictatorship of the proletariat and the peasantry" will purge the

---

3 Lenin 1960–78 [1917] p. 306.

country of medievalism, invest the development of Russian capitalism with American tempos, strengthen the proletariat in the city and country, and open up broad possibilities for the struggle for socialism.

> The perspective of the permanent revolution may be summed up in these words: The complete victory of the democratic revolution in Russia is inconceivable otherwise than in the form of the dictatorship of the proletariat basing itself on the peasantry. The dictatorship of the proletariat, which will inescapably place on the order of the day not only democratic but also socialist tasks, will at the same time provide a mighty impulse to the international socialist revolution.[4]

Transposed to China, both Lenin and Trotsky's position would seem to rule out the ill-fated alliance with the Guomindang. But Zheng contended that only Trotsky's position was internally consistent. In 1917, Lenin came around to Trotsky's point of view and quietly abandoned the formula of the "democratic dictatorship of the proletariat and the peasantry." That slogan remained in obscurity until revived by Trotsky's factional enemies in order to portray him as an opponent of 'Leninism'.

If there is a weakness in Zheng's short treatise it is that it makes use of so few Chinese examples to illustrate the theory. In the introduction he tells us little about the lively debate on the 1927 defeat beyond the fact that it took place. In the main text, almost all the examples he cites are from Europe and most are from the 1905 and 1917 Russian revolutions. But then as Zheng himself put it:

> For me, Trotsky's ideas meant putting the Chinese Revolution on the same footing as revolutions in other countries rather than ... discovering "special national characteristics" that restricted the application of Marxism to China.[5]

After the defeat of 1927, Mao and hundreds of others drew the obvious empirical conclusion that, at least in China at the time, political power grows out of the barrel of a gun. Zheng was sceptical. He maintained the Red Army was created not by a policy decision but by a series of accidents that were later rationalised. One reason for its growth was that while the remnants of the party in the cities felt the full force of repression, the mountains were for a while at

---

4   Trotsky 1939, pp. 71–2.
5   Zheng 1998, p. 239.

least, a safe haven. And it seems that, on principle, Zheng was hostile to the idea of a militarised party.

> We all thought the idea of a Red Army was dangerous ... that it would start representing the peasants or even bandits. At the time we never imagined that the Party would degenerate to the point it has now.[6]

Zheng wrote the ABC of Permanent Revolution seven years before Mao's mainly peasant army conquered power in 1949, in what was, so it seemed, a refutation of Trotsky's views on the peasantry and of his broader theory. However, within just a few years of seizing power, Mao had abandoned his plans to collaborate 'for several decades' with China's defeated capitalists, and for a staged progression rather than a revolutionary leap into state ownership, and had instead plunged into an all-out campaign to curb capitalism, in direct contradiction of his earlier promises and predictions. In effect, and by a grand irony, he had adopted the idea of permanent revolution, the Trotskyist strategy for revolution in economically backward countries. However, as Wang Fanxi observed at the time, he had done so blindly, under the pressure of events and crises, and seemed not to realise (or was unwilling to admit) that in doing so he had brought to naught all his previous attempts at theoretical analysis. (In 1958, Mao said 'I advocate the theory of the permanent revolution', but he immediately added: 'You mustn't think that this is Trotsky's theory of the permanent revolution'.)[7]

Translation source: *Buduan geming lun ABC* https://www.marxists.org/chinese/zhengchaolin/1947/marxist.org-chinese-zhengchaolin-1947.htm

The ABC of Permanent Revolution

1947 Preface
This little book has been printed at last. It was written nearly five years ago in the autumn of 1942 during the battle of Stalingrad, when the outcome of the Second World War was still in the balance.

Political books, especially revolutionary works, no matter how abstract or general or how much they try to avoid the concrete details of the contempor-

---

6 Zheng 1998, p. 238.
7 Schram 1971, p. 222.

ary struggle, cannot but be influenced by the setting in which they are written. Indeed when reading any kind of book one should bear in mind the circumstances in which the author wrote it.

For this reason, the introduction goes into some detail about the situation at the time of writing.

Five years on, of course, both China and the world have changed. If it was being written today, it would turn out a very different book. Apart from anything else, there is much more data available to supplement and strengthen its arguments.

But I have long since abandoned the idea of rewriting it, and I prefer instead to publish it in its original form. Its arguments and conclusions await your criticism. But when reading it, please bear in mind the context in which it came about.

We are much closer to revolution than we were five years ago. Today almost everyone is interested in politics and pays close attention to revolutionary developments. So I dare to hope that the book, though late in coming, may prove more useful than if it had been published five years ago.

21 May 1947.

1942 Introduction

Dear reader, you have in front of you a book about politics – more precisely, about revolutionary theory. I do not know when and under what circumstances you are reading this, but a little background about the conditions in which I am writing will help you understand the book.

I am writing in the middle of the Second World War. The great imperialist powers are divided into two hostile camps. On one side Britain, the USA, the Netherlands, Belgium and others, with their vast colonial possessions, form the so-called democratic camp. Facing them are the Axis powers, Germany, Italy, Japan and their allies, who, holding fewer colonies, are less able to develop their productive forces. The isolated Soviet workers' state, at the outset, tacitly supported the Axis powers as they conquered the democratic camp's European strongholds, continuing this policy even until France fell. But faced with invasion by the Axis powers, the Soviets allied with the democratic camp. The workers' state created by the first revolutionary wave of wave of the twentieth century has been officially at war for one year and three months. Right now, the greatest battle is raging in the Caucasus at Stalingrad (formerly Tsaritsyn). Egypt and the entire Near East are aflame. The only significant countries who are not at war are Spain, Turkey and Sweden. The Soviet Union and Japan are in a stand-off in the Far East, The Soviets have not involved themselves in the Pacific theatre and the Japanese have stayed out of the European war.

China was at war in the Far East before the main conflict broke out in Europe. The Sino-Japanese war has already lasted five years – longer than the First World War. It is three years since Germany invaded Poland – longer than Russia was in the First World War before revolution broke out. But so far there have been no revolutions. We cannot see the dawn. By closely inspecting news from the warring states we have learned of the great movement of the Indian people against British imperialism, of an independence struggle in the six counties of Northern Ireland, and of the resistance against German rule in occupied Europe.

But apart from these examples all we hear about is war. People have forgotten everything but war. For the sake of war they have forgotten revolution.

For the past hundred years all wars have given rise to revolutions. The First World War gave birth to several revolutions, led of course by Russia. The 1905 Revolution was provoked by the Russo-Japanese War. The Franco-Prussian War created the Paris Commune. Napoleon's wars sparked democratic revolutions in the backward countries of Eastern Europe. In China, the 1911 Revolution followed the Boxer Rebellion and after the Opium War came the great Taiping Rebellion. In the past hundred years can anyone cite a major war that did not end in revolution?

All the evidence suggests then that this war will also end in revolution and this century will see a second wave of world revolution. But the causal relationship is more complex. This war, or at least the form it has taken, was also the result of the failure of the last revolutionary wave. This is an important difference between this war and the last. In the run-up to the First World War there was no revolutionary wave in Europe. Half a century had elapsed since the Paris Commune. In fact the war came at the end of a long period of peaceful capitalist development. It was a golden age of bourgeois democracy. It was not just the capitalists who forgot their own revolutionary origins. Even so-called socialists thought the era of revolutions was over. Of course there was the failed Russian Revolution of 1905, just nine years before the war, which was echoed in Persia, Turkey and China. But Russia is a 'barbarian' country and the countries of the East even more so. In such countries, the reformists say, perhaps revolutions are necessary. But in civilised Europe, revolutions are not only not necessary – they are not possible. So on the eve of 1914, apart from a few extreme left wingers, Europe had entirely forgotten about revolution. It was not so on the eve of this war. The First World War was followed by a whole series of revolutionary waves; Russia, Germany, Austria, Hungary, Finland, Estonia, Bulgaria, Turkey, China, Spain all experienced one, sometimes two or even three revolutions. In Britain, France and the United States there were huge strike waves. In Ireland, Egypt, Monaco, Syria and other Arab countries, India and Iran there were great independence movements. But apart from Russia, all these movements failed. And history's first workers' state fell into a morass of bureaucracy and corruption. The First World War did not solve the world's problems. On the contrary it made another world war inevitable. So we can say that while the First World War was the inevitable result of the imperialist stage of capitalist development, the war this time was the result of the failure of the revolutionary wave that began in 1917. It was not simply the inevitable outcome of imperialist competition because if the revolution had succeeded in one or more major powers as well as Russia, the war could easily have been avoided. If for example the ferment in the most radical countries – Germany, China and Spain had succeeded, even if war could not be entirely avoided, it would not have reached its present scope and proportion.

But even if in the early period of this war the revolutionary movement has experienced a downturn, even a loss of hope, as Marxists we know that war cannot replace revolution as a solution to the tasks posed by history. War cannot abolish revolution – it can only delay it. After a period, revolution will inevitably break out again, with increased ferocity.

Imperialist war is different in another crucial respect from historical wars – the scope and power of its weapons, their unprecedented capacity for destruction. If revolution had not intervened, and the last war had been left to its own logic, the war might have wiped out humanity entirely, or at least set back civilisation by several hundred years.

But to ensure that war does not take over from revolution, we must not neglect revolutionary work even during the present downturn of the movement. On the contrary we must do everything possible, above all by preparing ourselves so as not to miss or fail to take advantage of the next revolutionary wave.

Revolutions proceed according to objective laws. They solve the tasks history sets them. Every stage of history has its own set of tasks to solve. The countries of the world are not all at the same stage of history and therefore the tasks facing them cannot be identical. Even if two countries are at the same stage of development, their histories are not identical, so the tasks that each needs to solve cannot be exactly the same. The equations of revolution allow for the substitution of different arithmetical values and therefore render differing solutions.

Before embarking on or planning a revolution in any country we must first determine what historical stage that country is passing through, as well as the specific features of its historical development and current conditions, its relations with other countries and so on. Only then can we understand the specifics of its revolution, what tasks it must solve and how they must be tackled.

This little book does not set out to analyse the Chinese revolution. China's historical development and its present situation are beyond the scope of this investigation. To adequately study such questions would require a much larger volume and more likely several volumes. Our offering here has a much more limited aim – to explain as far as possible in general terms the theory of Permanent Revolution – something that is a prerequisite for carrying out the kind of concrete analysis described above.

What is the significance of the theory of Permanent Revolution in examining the Chinese revolution? I am afraid there is little agreement or clarity on this but let us try as best we can to discuss the issue.

Let us for the time being set aside the question of how Chinese revolutionaries conceived of the revolution before Marxism arrived in China. Let us also ignore for the time being how Marxism was transmitted to China via Japanese or Western scholars, as well as the question of how to apply Marxist concepts to the study of ancient Chinese thought and society. The real entry of Marxism into China, in the sense of becoming a powerful and compelling school of thought, dates from the May Fourth movement. Debates about culture evolved into debates about politics and thence to socialism, trades unions were founded, strike waves followed and out of this ferment the party (CCP) was born. In this way Marxism took root and began to develop. Marxism is first and foremost a practical theory that emphasises the role of the proletariat in the revolution. Before the CCP was founded, how did Chinese revolutionaries conceive of the revolution? Did they have any definite ideas about the form it would take, its tasks, origins and direction? We can say that their ideas were confused and rather complicated. But one thing is clear – they did not include the dogma that the bourgeois democratic revolution must first be completed before the dictatorship of the proletariat can be attained. This idea only appeared in 1921 after the CCP joined the Guomindang. It continued to guide the conduct of the CCP through the 1925–7 revolution right up to the split between the Stalinist and Trotskyist factions that began in 1929. After the split, the Stalinists persisted with this theory and even today it guides their participation in the third revolution. This time it may well lead to the destruction of their party and of the revolution itself.

In some respects, the Russian and Chinese revolutionary parties developed in markedly different ways. In China, the debate on the nature of the revolution began ten years after the formation of the party. In Russia, the debate took place before the party was formed. If the RSDLP[8] had not had the debate at

---

8   Russian Social Democratic Labour Party.

that time it would be impossible to understand its subsequent conduct and policies. But how do we explain this difference between the parties? Only by applying the law of uneven development – a concept I will explore below. To put it simply, backward countries do not slavishly follow in the footsteps of the advanced countries. Sometimes they must skip stages that the advanced countries have already passed through. Just as Chinese factories employ the most modern equipment, although none of it was invented by Chinese scientists or engineers, the CCP did not develop its ideas through internal debate. It took them ready-made from the Third International – which created the party and defined the strategy and tactics of the proletariat in the revolution. But just as importing the most modern equipment does not mean an end to local scientific and engineering research, so the CCP cannot indefinitely postpone a debate on the fundamental problems of the revolution. If it is to become a real revolutionary party, it must debate these issues in the light of its own experience.

Nineteen-twenty-nine was a significant year in the history of the Chinese revolution for it was in that year that the CCP engaged in a fierce internal debate and began to split into two parties.

The debate revolved around the nature of the Chinese revolution. The Trotskyist faction maintained that only through the dictatorship of the proletariat could the bourgeois democratic tasks of the revolution be completed. But precisely because it would be a proletarian dictatorship, it would inevitably go beyond bourgeois-democratic limits and develop into a proletarian socialist revolution. The Stalinists, on the other hand, believed that the bourgeois democratic tasks of the revolution must be thoroughly achieved before the proletarian socialist revolution could begin. Until the democratic tasks were completed, there could be no dictatorship of the proletariat but only a democratic dictatorship of the proletariat and the peasantry and during that stage the revolution would remain a bourgeois-democratic revolution, in other words a nationalist revolution. The Trotskyists defended their claims on the grounds that China's economy was already overwhelmingly capitalist, whereas the Stalinists believed that feudal relations of production still predominated.

This dispute on these basic questions led directly to a debate on strategy. The Trotskyists maintained that the Second Revolution had ended in 1927 with the defeat of the Guangzhou Uprising and that it was impossible to predict when the Third Revolution would occur. At that time, 1929, we were in a period of reaction between two revolutions. Bourgeois rule had been stabilised and was being reinforced by economic recovery. The recovery would, in time, revive the proletariat, which would eventually return to the political arena at a higher stage of history. But at present, we should not call for the establishment of soviets and armed uprisings. Instead our slogans should aim to develop a broad democratic movement around the call for a National Assembly. But the Stalinists could not admit that the Second Revolution had been defeated. Although the first wave of revolution had receded, they believed a second wave was imminent and that therefore we should continue with the policies of the last few months of 1927 – that is to say, armed uprisings and the organisation of soviets, only this time not in the cities but in the countryside. The debate aroused public interest and spread into cultural movements, literary criticism and academic research.

At the outset the debate was a purely inner-party affair, taking place in secret meetings and by way of secret announcements and secret periodicals. But it soon emerged from the confines of the party, spread to its sympathisers and beyond, and became a subject of discussion in Chinese society at large. The internal debate in the CCP became the subject of articles in popular magazines, was discussed by famous academics and even became a homework assignment in some high schools and universities. Of course, precisely because the debate was taking place in the open, explicit reference to revolutionary politics had to be avoided. Nevertheless, this famous controversy on China's social history and the nature of its rural economy, was known by all to be a reflection of debates within the CCP. But the real point of the debates about ancient history, medieval and even more remote dynasties, the validity of archaeological evidence and so on, was not to decide whether Chinese feudalism began or ended with the Qin dynasty. The era of the emperors was over and done with, after all. The important issue was whether, at present, China's mode of production was predominantly capitalist or feudal. This was the main point of contention within the party, from its far right to its far left.

That the debate became a legal and open one had good and bad aspects. On the one hand, it demonstrated that these were burning issues in Chinese society. On the other hand, it made it easy for some participants, especially young intellectuals, to forget – and there were some who did not know at all – that in the final analysis the point at issue was the fundamental nature of the Chinese revolution, and thus the strategy of the revolutionary party. What is more, whether China's revolution was bourgeois or proletarian was not a question that could be decided with reference to China's stage of development alone. Whether China was predominantly feudal or capitalist still would not definitively decide the nature of its revolution. Furthermore, whose point of view should we accept when deciding which mode of production is dominant? It is clear that revolutionaries approach the issue very differently from historians and sociologists. These are all issues that need to be taken into account when discussing the theory of Permanent Revolution.

As the debate broadened and entered the legal, public sphere, the Trotskyist position increasingly came under attack. We were the only group in China that believed the third revolution would be proletarian and socialist in character. No other party held this view. The other parties united against us. We were isolated. If you are so right about this why don't people agree with you? Why are all the other parties against you? Many people rebuked us in this vein. But the criticisms had little substance. We should not forget that this debate took place in the context of a massive defeat of the revolution, when the masses were demoralised and not receptive to genuinely revolutionary ideas. But revolutionaries have to call things by their real names and state their views openly and honestly, whether or not the majority is ready to accept them. Revolutionaries need to know how to swim against the tide. They must not be afraid to stand alone against all other parties. But apart from these general considerations, there was, perhaps, a more specific reason why we were failing to win support: among the many who opposed our views on the Chinese revolution, very few knew about, and still fewer understood, the theory of Permanent Revolution. Perhaps not a single one of our critics really knew what Permanent Revolution meant. And if this was the case with the critics, how much more so with the retreating masses. Anyway, regardless of whether they agree with us or not, those who don't understand the theory of Permanent Revolution *ipso facto* don't understand the Trotskyist position on the Chinese revolution. In fact, very few people really understand the theory, not only because it is frankly rather difficult, but also because some authors have misinterpreted it or added unnecessary qualifications, and above all because up to now no popular presentation of the theory has been published in book form or in magazines. The theory of Permanent Revolution is the pinnacle of Trotsky's revolutionary activity and written work. To understand it thoroughly and correctly one should really read all his writings and study his career. He summed up the main points in a short eponymous book published in 1928. It is a very useful book. But it is not a systematic, popular and complete account of the theory. It is a polemical work written in the heat of controversy, and for people without a thorough grounding in revolutionary theory it is difficult to understand. As for gleaning the theory of Permanent Revolution from a study of Trotsky's other well-known works, that would be a still more difficult task for most people.

Since, as we have seen, the theory of Permanent Revolution is of such importance for the study of the Chinese revolution, a popular exposition of the theory is urgently required. It is this task that I have undertaken in this little book. In addition to explaining the basic concepts of the theory and the history of its development, it also pays particular attention to the application of the theory to the Chinese revolution.

I would also like to make clear, here and now, that I do not regard the theory of Permanent Revolution as a perfected, fixed and unchanging doctrine. Theories are not dogma, but guides to action, and this is especially true of revolutionary theories. The theory of Permanent Revolution was born from and grew into its present form through revolutionary practice and will continue to develop and improve in the same manner. If a theory is seen as fixed and complete, incapable of development, it is already dead. Such theories are mere dogmas, not living guides to action. Revolutionary practice especially has no use for theories of that type. Discussing Marxism, Lenin said:

> We do not regard Marx's theory as something completed and inviolable; on the contrary, we are convinced that it has only laid the foundation stone of the science which socialists *must* develop in all directions if they wish to keep pace with life.[9]

The theory of Permanent Revolution is itself a development of Marxism. If we wish to keep pace with life we must properly understand, explain, popularise, promote and develop it.

I should say a word or two about the approach taken in this book. It is not written in the form of textbooks that frequently use the deductive method whereby concrete propositions are derived from simple, abstract axioms. In practice, thought often proceeds from the concrete to the abstract, from the specific to the general, and this is the approach taken in this book. Trotsky himself took this approach when writing about the theory of Permanent Revolution.

> Even the truths of mathematics, the most abstract of the sciences, can best be learned in connection with the history of their discovery. This applies with even greater force to the more concrete, i.e. historically conditioned truths of Marxist politics.[10]

The theory of Permanent Revolution was first touched upon by Marx in an address to the Communist League in 1850.[11] Then it was forgotten. After the Russian Revolution of 1905, Trotsky revived the theory and went on to defend it against its opponents for more than a decade. The 1917 Revolution proved the validity of the theory and brought that phase of the debate to an end. In 1923 an

---

9   Lenin 1960–78 [1899], pp. 211–12.
10   Trotsky 2010 [1930], p. 173.
11   Marx and Engels 2010 [1850], pp. 277–87.

ideological reaction set in in the Soviet Union, attacking the ideas of the October Revolution under the guise of anti-Trotskyism, and revived the debate on the theory of Permanent Revolution. In 1928, Trotsky wrote his book *Permanent Revolution* in which he emphasised fourteen key points. His other relevant works, written both before and after *Permanent Revolution*, include *The Draft Program of the Communist International: A Criticism of Fundamentals*.[12] He wrote books about the future of Britain, the USA, France and Germany and articles on the problems of the Chinese revolution. Other works include *The History of the Russian Revolution* and *The Revolution Betrayed: What is the Soviet Union and Where is it Going?* In all these works, Trotsky applied the theory of Permanent Revolution to the prospects for revolution in the major countries of the world and to social and political developments in the Soviet state. In 1938, the Fourth International was founded and adopted the theory of Permanent Revolution as its basic theory of world revolution.

In what follows I will explicate the theory of Permanent Revolution as follows. I will first pay attention to its application to the problems of the Chinese Revolution. I will later touch on a number of directions in which the theory might be developed.

Chapter One – The Discovery of the Theory of Permanent Revolution
Most people associate the theory of Permanent Revolution with Leon Trotsky and assume that it was Trotsky alone who independently devised the theory. But in fact, it was Marx who originated it.

Ninety-two years ago in March 1850, the London-based central committee of the Communist League sent a circular to each of its branches setting out the lessons of the 1848–49 revolution in Germany and indicating the course that the German workers' revolutionary party should follow in future. The last line of the document read '[The German workers'] battle cry must be: The Revolution in Permanence'.[13] This notice, written by Marx, was the first exposition of the theory of Permanent Revolution.

This initial formulation of the theory can be summarised in this paragraph from the document:

> While the democratic petty bourgeois wish to bring the revolution to a conclusion as quickly as possible, and with the achievement, at most, of the above demands, it is our interest and our task to make the revolu-

---

12   Trotsky 1957 [1928], pp. 3–74.
13   Marx and Engels 2010 [1850], p. 287.

tion permanent, until all more or less possessing classes have been forced out of their position of dominance, the proletariat has conquered state power, and the association of proletarians, not only in one country but in all the dominant countries of the world, has advanced so far that competition among the proletarians in these countries has ceased and that at least the decisive productive forces are concentrated in the hands of the proletarians.[14]

This paragraph is very clear. The German Revolution, unlike the great vanguard revolutions of the past in England and France, should not stop at the democratic stage but should continue until the proletariat seizes political power and achieves its aims.

To understand why Marx held this view, we need to examine how the German Revolution of the mid-nineteenth century differed from the French Revolution of the late eighteenth century and the English Revolution of the mid-seventeenth century. The crucial difference was that by the time the bourgeois revolution reached Germany, a proletariat, in the modern sense of the word, was able to enter the political arena for the first time.

When the English bourgeois revolution took place there was no modern industry. There was only small-scale handicraft production. There was no modern proletariat, only petty-bourgeois artisans and the urban poor, who could at best be described as forerunners of the proletariat. By the time of the bourgeois revolution in France, however, the industrial revolution had taken place in Britain and steam-powered machines had even made their way to France giving rise to some industry and a modern working class.

The circular to the Communist League was later appended to Marx's book *Revelations Concerning the Communist League Trial in Cologne*.[15] But that is a little known work that has never been translated into Chinese, so the famous circular is hard to obtain. However, in this booklet I will need on many occasions to refer to it.

When there are only a few islands of modern industry in a sea of handicraft production, the minority of modern industrial workers will not be able to assert their independence but will be submerged in the petty-bourgeois mass. As for the petty bourgeoisie, due to its social position and outlook it cannot advance beyond the bounds of bourgeois society. It cannot create a more advanced social system or advance the revolution beyond its bourgeois stage. In these cir-

---

14   Marx and Engels 2010 [1850], p. 281.
15   Marx and Engels 2010 [1852], pp. 399–457.

cumstances, having achieved its democratic tasks, the revolution can proceed no further. Even if a section of the masses remains dissatisfied with the gains of the revolution and conspires to force it onward, the revolution will inevitably fall back within its bourgeois boundaries. Proof of this was seen in France in the failed revolts of the *enrages* and Babeuf.

The bourgeois revolution in Germany took place fifty years after the French Revolution. In this short half century, however, Western Europe had already embarked on a new economic era. Not only had Britain and France built entirely new social orders on the foundation of modern machine industry but even backward Germany had developed modern industrial areas, especially in the cities along the Rhine. Germany already had a modern proletariat which, although not large, was a real social force because of its role in production.

The German proletariat had not only begun to act spontaneously as a class but had begun to think of itself as a class. It had its own social ideals and demands. It is no accident that the founders of scientific socialism, Marx and Engels, were born in Germany. The German proletariat's brother, the French working class, had gone even further and raised the banner of socialism in the midst of capitalist society.

The belated German bourgeois revolution of 1848 raised unprecedented issues: What is the role of the proletariat in the bourgeois revolution? And, by implication, what is the relationship between the bourgeois and proletarian revolutions? History had so far given no examples on which to base a judgment because in the more advanced countries these questions had simply not arisen.

How did Marx approach the issue?

To answer this we should examine Marx's writings both before and after 1848. We can take the *Communist Manifesto* of 1847 as representative of his pre-1848 views, and the *Address of the Central Committee to the Communist League*, written in 1850, as representing his post-1848 views.

In Chapter IV of the *Communist Manifesto*, Marx wrote:

> The Communists turn their attention chiefly to Germany, because that country is on the eve of a bourgeois revolution that is bound to be carried out under more advanced conditions of European civilisation and with a much more developed proletariat than that of England was in the seventeenth, and France in the eighteenth century, and because the bourgeois revolution in Germany will be but the prelude to an immediately following proletarian revolution.[16]

---

16   Marx and Engels 2010 [1848], p. 519.

This indicates that Marx had already recognised that the German Revolution would be different from revolutions of the past. It is also clear, under these conditions, that he thought proletarian revolution would follow on directly from bourgeois revolution.

So what is the role of the proletariat in this bourgeois revolution? In the same chapter, Marx wrote:

> In Germany they fight with the bourgeoisie whenever it acts in a revolutionary way, against the absolute monarchy, the feudal squirearchy, and the petty bourgeoisie. But they never cease, for a single instant, to instil into the working class the clearest possible recognition of the hostile antagonism between bourgeoisie and proletariat, in order that the German workers may straightway use, as so many weapons against the bourgeoisie, the social and political conditions that the bourgeoisie must necessarily introduce along with its supremacy, and in order that, after the fall of the reactionary classes in Germany, the fight against the bourgeoisie itself may immediately begin.[17]

In other words, the proletariat should support the bourgeoisie until it completes the bourgeois revolution and replaces the feudal class as the ruling class. Then the working class should begin its own revolution and overthrow the bourgeoisie.

This view of the role of the proletariat in the bourgeois revolution was expressed more clearly by Engels than by Marx and the rest of the Communist League. In *The Movements of 1847*, written in the same year, Engels wrote:

> So just fight bravely on, most gracious masters of capital! We need you for the present; here and there we even need you as rulers. You have to clear the vestiges of the Middle Ages and of absolute monarchy out of our path; you have to annihilate patriarchalism; you have to carry out centralisation; you have to convert the more or less propertyless classes into genuine proletarians, into recruits for us; by your factories and your commercial relationships you must create for us the basis of the material means which the proletariat needs for the attainment of freedom. In recompense whereof you shall be allowed to rule for a short time. You shall be allowed to dictate your laws, to bask in the rays of the majesty

---

17   Marx and Engels 2010 [1848], p. 519.

you have created, to spread your banquets in the halls of kings, and to take the beautiful princess to wife – but do not forget that 'The hangman stands at the door!'.[18]

This was a natural view to take at that time, before the revolution had taken place. The German proletariat would, of course, take part in the bourgeois revolution. But its situation was very different from that of its forerunners in the British and French Revolutions. It would not be able to remain within the limits of the bourgeois revolution but would have to carry out its own revolution – and the gap between the two revolutions would not be wide. But how should the proletariat support the bourgeoisie in its revolution? How to make use of the conditions created by the bourgeoisie to defeat the bourgeoisie itself? How to start the proletarian revolution? How would the middle classes react to the two revolutions? There was no available evidence on which to base an answer to any of these questions.

The revolution of 1848–49 provided this evidence. The German bourgeoisie triumphed. In the wake of the 1848 March movement, it conquered state power. But it did not retain that power. It used its newly won authority not to clear out the feudal forces that had been defeated in March but to attack its comrades in arms, the German proletarians, and force them back into their previous, oppressed state.

> Though the bourgeoisie was not able to accomplish this without uniting with the feudal party, which had been ousted in March, without finally even relinquishing power once again to this feudal absolutist party, still it has secured conditions for itself which, in the long run, owing to the financial embarrassment of the government, would place power in its hands and would safeguard all its interests, if it were possible that the revolutionary movement would already now assume a so-called peaceful development.[19]

The strength of the German proletariat did not encourage the German bourgeoisie to take bolder steps on the road to revolution than the French bourgeoisie had in its revolution. On the contrary, it would become much more reticent than its French counterpart. In 1850, following the defeat of the revolution, Marx wrote:

---

18   Marx and Engels 2010 [1848a], p. 529.
19   Marx and Engels 2010 [1850], p. 278.

And the role which the German liberal bourgeois played in 1848 against the people, this so treacherous role will be taken over in the impending revolution by the democratic petty bourgeois, who at present take the same attitude in the opposition as the liberal bourgeois before 1848. This party, the democratic party ... is far more dangerous to the workers than the previous liberal party[20]

The petty bourgeoisie now began to call themselves 'republicans' or 'reds' but

It is evident, incidentally, that the altered name of this party does not make the slightest difference to its attitude to the workers, but merely proves that it is now obliged to turn against the bourgeoisie, which is united with absolutism, and to seek the support of the proletariat.

The petty-bourgeois democratic party in Germany is very powerful; it comprises not only the great majority of the burgher inhabitants of the towns, the small people in industry and trade and the master craftsmen; it numbers among its followers also the peasants and the rural proletariat, insofar as the latter has not yet found a support in the independent urban proletariat

The relation of the revolutionary workers' party to the petty bourgeois democrats is this: it marches together with them against the faction which it aims at overthrowing, it opposes them in everything by which they seek to consolidate their position in their own interests.[21]

By comparing these last few sentences with what the *Communist Manifesto* had to say about the liberal bourgeoisie, we can see clearly how Marx changed his views as a result of the revolution.

Before 1848, although Marx understood the fundamental antagonism between the bourgeoisie and the proletariat, and that the bourgeoise having seized power would use that power against the proletariat, nevertheless he believed the bourgeoisie would at least act in its own interests by destroying the feudal system and creating the conditions for capitalist development. In other words, it would carry out the tasks of the bourgeois revolution. The seizure of power by the bourgeoisie would mean the triumph of the bourgeois revolu-

---

20   Marx and Engels 2010 [1850], p. 279.
21   Marx and Engels 2010 [1850], pp. 279–80.

tion. But the lessons of two years of revolution taught him that, having taken power, the bourgeoisie would not necessarily destroy the feudal system and create the conditions for capitalism to develop. It would not necessarily create the social and political conditions that might permit the proletariat to take up arms against it. The seizure of political power by the bourgeoisie is not the same thing as the victory of the bourgeois revolution. They are two separate and sometimes contradictory things. We need to clearly distinguish them. It is true that the workers want the bourgeois revolution to succeed, but they do not want the bourgeoisie to rule them. They do not want the bourgeoisie to remain in power. The workers should from the outset oppose the new bourgeois regime; they should not allow it to stabilise but should continually harass it, even to the point of overthrowing it. And this goes for petty-bourgeois as well as bourgeois governments. The working class unites with the petty bourgeois to overthrow the bourgeoisie but 'opposes them in everything by which they seek to consolidate their position in their own interests'.[22]

The events of 1848 taught Marx an important lesson about the relationship between the bourgeois and proletarian revolutions. The key to understanding why the German bourgeois revolution had the capacity to turn into a proletarian revolution lies in the question of the transfer of political power. From the outset of the bourgeois revolution, the proletariat should strive by all means to wrest power from the hands of the feudal autocrats but should not allow it to remain in the hands of the parties of the liberal bourgeoisie, the democratic petty bourgeoisie or any propertied class. On the contrary, the proletariat should ensure that power swiftly falls into its own hands. Only in this way can the social transformation be guaranteed.

This is the theory of Permanent Revolution.

In the belated bourgeois revolution, 'it is our interest and our task to make the revolution permanent until all the more or less propertied classes have been driven from their ruling positions, until the proletariat has conquered state power'.

But how can we make the revolution permanent? How can we prevent political power remaining in the hands of the propertied classes? In the same address to the Communist League, Marx wrote:

> Alongside the new official governments they must immediately establish their own revolutionary workers' governments, whether in the form of municipal committees and municipal councils or in the form of workers'

---

22   Marx and Engels 2010 [1850], pp. 279–80.

clubs or workers' committees, so that the bourgeois-democratic governments not only immediately lose the support of the workers but from the
outset see themselves supervised and threatened by authorities backed
by the whole mass of the workers. In a word, from the first moment of
victory, mistrust must be directed no longer against the defeated reactionary party, but against the workers' previous allies, against the party
that wishes to exploit the common victory for itself alone.[23]

We now know, from this original document, what Marx meant by Permanent
Revolution when he first proposed it in 1850.

I will now try to analyse the theory of Permanent Revolution by examining
the German Revolution and subsequent belated bourgeois revolutions in other
countries.

Many people will say from the outset that Marx was wrong because history
did not bear out his predictions for the German Revolution. The 'imminent'
revolution – in which the petty-bourgeois democrats would overthrow the liberal bourgeoisie and seize state power – did not happen. This is quite true. Not
only in Germany but also in Britain, France and Germany, from 1849 onwards,
the revolutionary movement gradually declined in intensity. In this period,
capitalism developed rapidly across the whole of Europe. Countries like Britain and France, where the bourgeois revolution had already succeeded, made
rapid progress. At the same time, in countries where bourgeois revolutions
had failed, the reactionary aristocrats who still held state power, for reasons
of self-preservation, followed suit and encouraged capitalist development. But
what sort of development was it? The bourgeois representatives of capitalism languished in opposition, while the old aristocratic regime, which had
long resisted capitalism, remained in place. Capitalist development was doubly
hampered. The basic tasks of the bourgeois revolution – cleansing agriculture of feudal relations of production, unifying the nation state, establishing a
democratic republic and so on, which were accomplished so swiftly in France
by revolutionary means, were not fully resolved in Germany even after long and
troubled decades.

The 1848 German Revolution did not become permanent in the sense of pro-
gressing from bourgeois to petty-bourgeois and finally to proletarian power.
That is a historical fact. What is also a historical fact is that between its 1848
bourgeois revolution and its 1918 proletarian revolution, Germany passed
through an epoch of large-scale capitalist development.

---

23   Marx and Engels 2010 [1850], p. 283.

The explanation for these historical facts was not simply that the bourgeoisie preferred to submit to the aristocracy rather than see the proletariat take command of the revolution. The broader picture was that there was still scope for large-scale capitalist development in Europe. Marx only came to understand this later. In 1850, the Communist League still believed that another explosion of revolution was imminent. However, not long afterwards, a dispute broke out in the League over this issue. Marx's faction understood that the revolution had ended and only a new crisis would revive the movement. The opposing faction believed that the revolutionary situation was ongoing. The dispute resulted in a split. Engels later admitted that he and Marx's initial prognosis regarding the future of capitalism was wrong. But this was an error of fact rather than of methodology. In backward countries where capitalism has developed to an extent that there is a conscious proletariat, in order to accomplish its democratic tasks, the revolution must wrench state power from all the propertied classes and hand it to the proletariat. Marx's theory of Permanent Revolution can be applied to Germany in 1848, to Russia in 1917 and to China in 1927, and to all other backward countries that meet the above conditions.

We are talking about the original formulation of the theory of Permanent Revolution, not the theory in its developed form. But the relationship between the two is analogous to that between the sapling and the full-grown tree. The tree is more complex but its complexity can be traced back to the sapling's buds.

The developed form of the theory, inseparably linked to the name of Trotsky, is the subject of the next few chapters. We will see later that many points in Trotsky's theory can be traced back to their roots in Marx's original formulation, but for the time being I will continue to talk about two theories or at least two stages in the development of the same theory as I examine the question of how to assess the role of the peasantry in revolution.

Trotsky believed that although the Russian peasants would support the proletariat in the revolution, and indeed must do so if the revolution was to succeed, they nevertheless could play no independent role in the revolution. Marx, on the other hand, believed the German peasants would support the urban petty bourgeoisie and only agricultural labourers would ally with the proletariat.

Just as the democrats combine with the peasants so must the workers combine with the rural proletariat.[24]

---

24   Marx and Engels 2010 [1850], p. 285.

Marx saw the peasantry as the natural ally of the petty bourgeoisie and in 1850 he was still expecting the petty bourgeoisie to take power and implement its programme. But on this point Marx was wrong. The German petty bourgeoisie did not launch a revolution and did not seize power. In fact, it was impossible for it to do so, for once the proletariat entered the arena, not only the bourgeois liberals but even the petty-bourgeois democrats recoiled from revolution and ceased to play an independent role. The great revolt of the petty bourgeoisie in France could not be reproduced in Germany. Marx later came to understand this. Just as in 1848 the betrayal of the revolution by the bourgeoisie led him to formulate the theory of Permanent Revolution, so by 1850, having witnessed the impotence of the petty bourgeoisie, he concluded that the peasants could be allies of the proletariat. In 1856, he wrote to Engels:

> Everything in Germany will depend upon whether it will be possible to support the proletarian revolution by something like a second edition of the Peasant War. Only then will everything proceed well.[25]

Here we see the peasants as allies not of the petty bourgeoisie but of the proletariat. The support of the peasants is necessary for the success of the proletarian revolution, but since they are cast in a supporting role only, they do not play a leading or even independent role in the revolution.

After the defeats of 1848, the high tide of revolution receded and the reactionary forces consolidated their position. From then until 1905, apart from the short-lived counterexample of the Paris Commune, the world, and especially its backward countries, saw no revolutions. Revolution was forgotten and Permanent Revolution even more so. But Marxism – of sorts – flourished and crowded out all other theories of socialism. People who called themselves Marxists developed a theory according to which bourgeois society would, sooner or later, implement democracy and that, in the context of a democratic order, the proletariat would organise and introduce socialism. It is true that there were differing opinions on the transition to socialism. One side thought that the democratic order would, so to speak, be gradually filled with socialist content. Others thought that it would not be possible to avoid violence in the transition period. But both sides believed democracy and socialism to be two distinct phases of social development, separated by a long period of time. Both sides rejected the theory of Permanent Revolution.

---

25   Could not find this quote in Marx's 1856 letters to Engels in MECW, Vol. 40. But I have found it quoted by Riazanov at: https://www.marxists.org/archive/marx/works/1850/peasant-war-germany/chod.htm.

The theory of Permanent Revolution was forgotten and, to all intents and purposes, appeared to be dead. But half a century later it was revived and the setting for its revival was, like Germany, another backward country.

Chapter Two – The Rebirth of the Theory of Permanent Revolution

The experience of a bourgeois revolution in a backward country – Germany – gave rise to the theory of Permanent Revolution. A bourgeois revolution in another backward country – Russia – led to the theory's rebirth.

The German Revolution came half a century after the French Revolution; the Russian Revolution[26] half a century after the German. But the latter half-century cannot be mentioned in the same breath as the former. The half-century between the French and German Revolutions was an epoch of bourgeois revolutions in Western Europe; revolutionary waves rose and fell in succession. In the few periods of calm, lasting just a few years, the capitalists of each country did their best to develop the productive forces, repair the damage done by war and revolution, and consolidate their class rule. They were surprisingly successful. By the half-century between the German and Russian Revolutions, on the other hand, the West European bourgeoisie had already consolidated its ruling position (or at least consolidated the conditions for doing so) which freed it to launch an epoch of capitalist development. Industrial capitalism gave rise to finance capital and laid the foundations of imperialism. 'European civilisation' developed at a much faster pace than in the previous half-century – indeed, at a hitherto unheard-of pace. Russia, in 1848 seen as outside the boundaries of European civilisation, was now not only part of the European family of nations but could, in certain respects, be considered more advanced than the older, advanced European countries.

> England achieved her Puritan revolution when her whole population was not more than five and a half million, of whom half a million were to be found in London. France, in the epoch of her revolution, had in Paris also only half a million out of a population of 25 million. Russia at the beginning of the twentieth century had a population of about 150 million, of whom more than three million were in Petrograd and Moscow. Behind these comparative figures lurk enormous social differences. Not only England of the seventeenth century but also France of the eighteenth had no proletariat in the modern sense. In Russia, however, the working class in all branches of labor, both city and village, numbered in 1905 no less than

---

26   I.e. the Revolution of 1905.

10 million, which with their families amounts to more than 25 million –
that is to say, more than the whole population of France in the epoch of
the great revolution.[27]

Trotsky here compares early twentieth-century Russia with mid-seventeenth-
century England and late-eighteenth century France (all in eras of revolution).
He did not include a comparison with mid-nineteenth-century Germany, and
I have no figures to hand regarding the populations of Berlin and Vienna or the
size of the German working class at that time. But if my analysis of the development of European capitalism is correct, Russian capitalism in 1905 was more
developed than German capitalism in 1848, and its working class was correspondingly larger.

These, then were the conditions in this second great underdeveloped country – Russia – on the eve of its bourgeois revolution.

The German Revolution raised the issues of the role of the proletariat in the
bourgeois revolution and by implication the relationship between the bourgeois and proletarian revolutions. The Russian Revolution raised the same
questions even more acutely. Addressing these questions in the German Revolution led to the discovery of the theory of Permanent Revolution. To address
the same issues in the Russian Revolution it was necessary to revive the theory.

The term 'backward country' used here and throughout this book is not used
in its commonly accepted sense. Here by 'backward country' I do not mean a
country that lags behind others in terms of social development or economic
relations. Rather, I use the term to designate countries where capitalism has
developed to the extent that it has created a conscious proletariat, but where
the bourgeoisie has, for one reason or another, not undertaken, or not completed, the bourgeois revolution.

Section One – Characteristics of the 1905 Revolution

According to the above, we could classify the Russian Revolution of 1905 as a
bourgeois revolution in a backward country or a belated bourgeois revolution.

People may say the German Revolution of 1848 was also just such a revolution. But if they went on to say that there were no qualitative, only quantitative, differences between these two revolutions, that would be a grave mistake.
Many differing and even contradictory properties can hide under the terms
'backward' and 'historically belated'. First of all, the world-historical contexts
within which the two revolutions took place were completely different. In 1848,

---

27   Trotsky 2008 [1932], pp. 9–10.

capitalism was in its prime but by 1905 it was already approaching its late stages. Second, Russia's pattern of historical development was vastly different from Germany's. Russia's 'backwardness' and the 'delay' of its revolution were expressed concretely in the specifics of its historical development.

Russia spanned Europe and Asia not only geographically but also in terms of social development. In fragmented medieval Europe, the feudal system permitted the development of industrial and commercial cities that became independent of the rural economy, and over time came to dominate it. The merchants and master craftsmen congealed into a class, the precursors of the modern bourgeoisie. As their social weight increased, they played an ever more critical role in political struggles. First, they became the mainstay of the absolute monarchies and helped the autocrats weaken the power of the nobility. But when fully fledged and mature they overthrew the absolutists, transformed the feudal order and replaced it with their own social system.

The formation and development of medieval cities, and their burgher class, were key factors in Europe's modern history. Workshops gave birth to manufacturing and eventually to modern mechanised industry. Today's ruling bourgeoisie is descended from the merchants and master craftsmen of the past. But under Oriental Despotism there were no cities like those in medieval Europe. Asian cities did not play the same role in economic development and political struggles as their European counterparts. This is a crucial difference between historical development in the West and the East. Russia's development pattern was somewhere in between, sometimes leaning to the West, sometimes to the East. After Peter the Great's reforms, Russia decisively chose the Western path, but the Oriental elements in Russian history continued to influence its later development, and even now affect its post-revolutionary development.

The differences between the West and Russia can also be seen in the nature of its bourgeoisie and proletariat. Unlike in the West, where they evolved from the burgher and journeyman classes, the Russian bourgeoisie and proletariat were creations of imported capitalism. Russia never passed through an early manufacturing stage but jumped directly from household handicrafts to modern industry. The Russian bourgeoisie never participated in a struggle against the nobility alongside the autocracy because Russia's Oriental-style autocracy had no need of bourgeois support to establish itself. As a result, the Russian bourgeoisie was unencumbered by ideology and [its intellectuals] found it easier to accept the theory and practice of proletarian class struggle as found in the advanced nations.

The peculiarities of Russia's development explain why the Russian Revolution was so 'backward', that is to say how, with the world in the age of imperialism, the mode of capitalism gave birth to a numerous and deeply class-conscious proletariat even before its bourgeois revolution.

From this we can see that the difference between Russia's belated revolution and Germany's belated revolution was *qualitative*, not just a matter of degree. Without understanding Russia's specific type of 'backwardness' it is impossible to understand the 1905 Revolution or to assess the disputes between the various parties and factions.

But before examining the disputes between the parties in detail, I should first touch on some general issues.

In the debates, some took the view that, because of the peculiarities of Russia's development, its revolution would follow a completely different path from those in the West. In particular, they thought that Russia could skip directly to socialism without passing through a capitalist phase. Others thought that, because Russia was already integrated into the capitalist world, its revolution would necessarily follow the same path as Western revolutions and that it would have to pass through a distinct and separate democratic stage before a proletarian revolution entered the agenda.

Both points of view are mistaken and both fail to grasp the relationship between the general and the specific. That is to say, we cannot, on the basis of the generality of the capitalist world and the specificity of any given nation, regard the world as simply the sum of a group of nations all cast in the same mould, or any given nation as a mere concretisation of the general capitalist world system. The capitalist world is founded upon an international division of labour, within which each nation has its own specific features conditioned by its geography and history. The sum of these specific features constitutes the national peculiarity. A nation, with its peculiarities, integrates organically into the capitalist world. But no matter how exceptional a nation, it always remains linked to the world system and its so-called peculiarities are no more than variations on the fundamental patterns of world development.

We can deduce some general laws governing world history by studying the historical development of a few advanced countries. This was the method Marx used when writing *Capital*. But in practice, these laws of history do not strictly govern each nation's development. To put it another way, countries develop unevenly. In some countries, the forces of production develop rapidly, in others, more slowly. Here, a sector of the economy forges ahead, there the same sector lags behind, and elsewhere it may stagnate or fail to develop at all. The formation of institutions, culture and classes also proceeds unevenly. Furthermore historical epochs may be long or short. Sometimes two epochs may merge into one. Stages of history may be skipped altogether. This is known as the law of uneven development.

Without general historical laws we cannot understand the process of human history. Equally, without the law of uneven development, we cannot understand the specifics of each nation's development. In the final analysis, the particular features of a country are precisely the outcome of its experience of the law of uneven development.

The law of uneven development is expressed clearly, and in all its complexity, in the fate of late developing countries. Because they are relatively backward, these nations are forced to catch up with the advanced countries. To do this they must shorten each historical stage, reduce the gaps between stages, merge stages, mix ancient with modern. We see these phenomena in all backward countries as they develop. We call development under these conditions combined development.

These two laws – the law of uneven development and the law of combined development – are indispensable to an understanding of the specific nature of the Russian Revolution and the controversies surrounding it.

Section Two – Early Debates on the Russian Revolution

We begin with the debate between the Populists (Narodniks) and the Marxists.

Populism as an ideology arose in the mid-nineteenth century on the eve of the development of modern industry in Russia. Serfdom had not yet been abolished and there were many vestiges of communal ownership in the countryside. But Western capitalism was very advanced and its negative aspects were already evident. Progressive thought had already advanced beyond its utopian phase of dreaming about a future society to laying plans for the revolutionary overthrow of capitalism. At this juncture a petty-bourgeois school of thought arose – that Russia might bypass the capitalist stage of development and advance directly to socialism. This point of view was not a complete fantasy but was based on particular features of Russian society that preserved some aspects of primitive communism in the form of the village commune (*mir*).

When the populist movement was in its heyday its ideas dominated the debate. But by the 1870s, Marx's *Capital* had been published and was soon translated into Russian. It provoked a major controversy in Russia. Populists who accepted Marx's theories began to have doubts about their previous ideas. They asked themselves if Russia must first break up its rural communes and pass through a capitalist phase before arriving at socialism. The doubts deepened and the debates became fiercer. Because the debate originally arose from a reading of *Capital*, the protagonists often referred to Marx and argued over whether the laws governing the development of capitalism in Western Europe, as described in *Capital*, were universal and applied to all countries. As a result of these debates people learned more about Marx. What is even more interesting is that Marx, and later Engels, took part in the debate.

In 1877, Marx expressed his views in a letter to a Russian magazine. He wrote that the section in *Capital* on primitive accumulation was a description of the actual historical development of capitalism in Western Europe and should not be used as a general historical-philosophical law applicable to all countries. In order to decide whether Russia must pass through a capitalist stage of development, Marx said, one must examine the particular conditions prevailing in Russia, not simply impose a formula derived from his writings on the development of Western European capitalism. Marx taught himself Russian in order to research this issue and over many years studied many related published and unpublished works. The conclusion he reached was:

> If Russia continues along the path it has followed since 1861, it will miss the finest chance that history has ever offered to a nation, only to undergo all the fatal vicissitudes of the capitalist system.[28]

In 1882 Marx and Engels addressed this issue in a long preface to the second Russian edition of the *Communist Manifesto*.

> But in Russia we find, face-to-face with the rapidly flowering capitalist swindle and bourgeois property, just beginning to develop, more than half the land owned in common by the peasants. Now the question is: can the Russian *obshchina*, though greatly undermined, yet a form of primeval common ownership of land, pass directly to the higher form of Communist common ownership? Or, on the contrary, must it first pass through the same process of dissolution such as constitutes the historical evolution of the West? The only answer to that possible today is this: If the Russian Revolution becomes the signal for a proletarian revolution in the West, so that both complement each other, the present Russian common ownership of land may serve as the starting point for a communist development.[29]

The two founders of scientific socialism gave only conditional answers to the question of whether Russia would have to pass through a capitalist stage – 'If Russia continues to pursue the path she has followed since 1861', 'If the Russian Revolution becomes the signal for a proletarian revolution in the West',

---

28   Marx and Engels 2010 [1877] p. 199.
29   Marx and Engels 2010 [1882], p. 426.

etc. But the implied meaning was clear enough, even if the complete refutation of Populist ideas, and the recognition that Russia would have to pass through a capitalist stage, was achieved by the later efforts of Russia's young Marxist faction. Plekhanov's early works were crucial in this respect. Lenin's too. *The Development of Capitalism in Russia* gave the definitive answer to this question. This extremely important work, published in 1899, marshalled extensive field research and a host of statistics to demonstrate that the Russian countryside was already awash with commodity production and that therefore, whether run by landlords or peasants, Russian agriculture was already headed down the capitalist road. All Russia was forced along the path first blazed in 1861. The capitalist system developed at a hectic pace. Capitalist landownership outgrew its modest beginnings and eroded the communal ownership system to such an extent that the latter's fate was sealed and it could no longer be revived. By this time, even supposing revolutions in Russia and Western Europe, it was no longer possible to base future Communist development on Russia's rural communes.

Marx and Engels, while concluding that Russia would have to pass through a capitalist stage, hedged their judgment with conditions. The younger generation of Russian Marxists, especially Lenin, answered the question categorically. History showed that Lenin was right.

This first dispute following the arrival of Marxism in Russia was extremely important for the future of the revolution. Henceforth, all subsequent disputes about the Russian Revolution started from the premise that Russia could not avoid a period of capitalist development. But this debate has another important lesson, that is: although in the final analysis Russia would follow the same path of development as set out for Western European countries in *Capital*, Marxists should not see *Capital* as describing a kind of historical-philosophical law – and above all they should not use it to apply an arbitrary West European schema to Russia, regardless of the latter's specific characteristics. The development of capitalism in Russia did not follow any historical-philosophical or supra-historical law but proceeded in accordance with the law of uneven development and in particular with the law of combined development.

But unfortunately many Russian Marxists forgot this lesson, as we will see clearly when we examine later debates on the nature of the Russian Revolution.

Section Three – Russian Marxists Debate the Russian Revolution

Since Russia could not avoid a period of capitalist development and capitalism had already made great strides in the country, a bourgeois revolution was on the agenda. On this point, the Russian Marxists were united. But 'bourgeois revolution' is a general term. We have had the English bourgeois revolution, the French bourgeois revolution, the German bourgeois revolution – also the Dutch, the American and so on. And taking France alone as an example, we had the 1789 Revolution, the 1830 Revolution, the 1848 Revolution and so on. Is it possible to abstract a few general rules from these multifarious bourgeois revolutions and apply them to the Russian Revolution? Would the Russian bourgeois revolution have characteristics that differentiate it from the revolutions in the advanced countries? In what ways would It differ from the German Revolution? Finally, in what ways would the Russian Revolution differ from the revolutions in the advanced countries as a whole?

These questions triggered a debate among the Russian Marxists. The concrete issues they addressed were: what were the tasks of the Russian bourgeois revolution? What class would lead the revolution? What would be the relationships between the various classes in the revolution? And, finally, what sort of society would the revolution create? In short, these debates concerned the tasks, motive forces and outcome of the revolution.

I should first point out that the very fact that these debates took place demonstrates that the Russian Revolution was very different from previous revolutions in the advanced countries, for none of the revolutions in the advanced countries saw such debates – the issues did not even arise. The bourgeois revolution, seen as a historical phenomenon, solved bourgeois tasks, was led by the bourgeoisie, and gave birth to bourgeois society. In other words, the tasks, motive forces and outcome were all bourgeois. So much is indisputable. But the Russian Revolution was different from previous revolutions so these questions arose and were vigorously debated.

One might even say that the German Revolution was an exception to 'the revolutions in the advanced countries', because Marx's theory of Permanent Revolution raised these issues – if only in embryonic form.

The division of Russian Marxists into Bolshevik and Menshevik factions was, in the last analysis, the result of these debates.

The Menshevik position was that the Russian Revolution would solve the democratic tasks already accomplished in Western Europe and that the liberal bourgeoisie would naturally assume the leading role. The result of the revolution would be the creation of a democratic system. Although the Russian proletariat was far stronger than the English proletariat of the seventeenth century, the French proletariat of the eighteenth century, and even the German proletariat of the nineteenth century, the coming revolution would not be proletarian in character. The proletariat could not simply skip the democratic stage and proceed with its own revolution. It could not seize power for itself but could only play a supporting role in establishing bourgeois rule. And under the new regime it would constitute the opposition – defending the interests of the proletariat against the encroachments of the bourgeoisie.

The Mensheviks cited Marx in support of their position. Marx said:

> No social formation is ever destroyed before all the productive forces for which it is sufficient have been developed[30]

This showed – the Mensheviks maintained – that Russian capitalism had a long future ahead of it. It had only just embarked on its journey and the fact that it had not developed under the yoke of feudalism merely reinforced the conclusion that it had not exhausted its vitality. Marx also said:

> The country that is more developed industrially only shows, to the less developed, the image of its own future.[31]

Therefore – the Mensheviks concluded – the Russian proletariat should not seek political power. It should not try to go further than its counterparts in the advanced countries. On the contrary, it should follow their example in the bourgeois revolution, by helping the bourgeoisie overthrow the reactionary feudal authorities, and thereafter should be content with a subordinate role until the objective conditions for socialism have matured. The Mensheviks could also cite the *Communist Manifesto* to support their position on the strategy of the proletarian party in the bourgeois revolution. It said:

> In Germany [the Communists] fight with the bourgeoisie whenever it acts in a revolutionary way, against the absolute monarchy, the feudal squire-archy, and the petty bourgeoisie.[32]

If the German Communists could join hands and fight together with the German revolutionary bourgeoisie why should the Russian Social Democrats not join hands with and fight alongside the Russian revolutionary bourgeoisie? Do not the advanced countries show the backward countries the image of their own future? How faithful the Mensheviks were to Marx – or at least to his words!

---

30   Marx and Engels 2010 [1859], p. 263.
31   Marx and Engels 2010 [1867], p. 9.
32   Marx and Engels 2010 [1848], p. 519.

Lenin did not take Marx's words as his starting point. Instead he used Marx's method to analyse the problems of the Russian Revolution. By the turn of the century it was already clear that Russia's proletariat was greater in number, stronger and more class conscious than Germany's in the run-up to 1848. What is more, the Russian bourgeoisie was weaker than Germany's, had stronger ties to the feudal forces and was even more afraid to act decisively to complete its historical tasks. Under these conditions it was out of the question that the Russian bourgeoisie would lead the revolution. What I call the tasks of the bourgeois revolution – in the last analysis – boiled down to liberating the capitalist forces of production from the fetters of feudalism. On the face of it this was the most pressing task facing the bourgeoisie. But already in 1848, the greatest concern of the German bourgeoisie when it seized power was not how to complete its own tasks but how to suppress the proletariat. There was also another important difference between the Russian and German revolutions. The central task in Germany was to achieve national unity, while in Russia it was land reform. A thoroughgoing land reform that would suppress the landowning class and redistribute the land in a revolutionary manner was absolutely necessary if the productive forces of Russian capitalism were to be freed from their feudal restraints. But the Russian bourgeoisie with its innumerable ties to the landowning class could not resolve the land question in this way. So the success of Russia's land reform, and therefore of its bourgeois revolution as a whole, would depend on an alliance of the workers and peasants. The tasks of Russia's bourgeois revolution, since the bourgeoisie itself was incapable of accomplishing them, would pass into the hands of the proletariat and the peasantry. The revolutionary forces would be the proletariat and the peasantry – not the bourgeoisie.

The Mensheviks said: our revolution is a bourgeois revolution so the workers should support the bourgeoisie. Lenin said: our revolution is a bourgeois revolution so the workers should warn the people to open their eyes and be on guard against the tricks of the bourgeoisie. Both sides said the revolution was a bourgeois revolution, but they drew opposite conclusions. This was because, when considering the bourgeois revolution, the Mensheviks scoured history for examples and naturally concluded that the bourgeoisie would remain the driving force of the revolution. Lenin, on the other hand, drew attention to a new and very significant aspect of this bourgeois revolution. The bourgeoisie would no longer be its leading force.

It was the first time in history that anyone, when considering the bourgeois revolution, had so clearly separated the driving force of the revolution from the bourgeoisie. It was one of Lenin's major contributions. Three revolutions in Russia proved him right.

The result was a fundamental dispute between Lenin and the Mensheviks. Not only were they saying different things but even when they used the same words these words held different meanings. Both sides talked about 'the Russian bourgeois revolution', but for Lenin this meant a revolution whose central issue was agrarian revolution, whereas for the Mensheviks it meant the liberal bourgeoisie taking over from the monarchy. Both sides talked about the 'tasks of the bourgeois revolution' but Lenin meant the workers and peasants joining hands to create a democratic republic, expropriate the landlords and implement an eight-hour working day. For the Mensheviks it meant helping the bourgeoisie to take power and then allowing it to solve its own tasks in its own way.

For Lenin, the leading forces in the Russian Revolution would be the workers and the peasants. The strategic goal in overthrowing the monarchy would not be for the bourgeoisie take power but for the workers and peasants to unite and fight against the bourgeoisie to establish the 'democratic dictatorship of the proletariat and the peasantry'.

With his theory of the bourgeois revolution and the formula of the democratic dictatorship of the proletariat and the peasantry, Lenin gathered a group of supporters comprising the most revolutionary elements of the Russian Social Democratic Party (the RSDLP). This group later became known as the Old Bolsheviks.

Section Four – Trotsky vs Lenin on the Russian Revolution

The dispute between the Marxists and the Populists was essentially over by the end of the nineteenth century. The debate between the Mensheviks and the Bolsheviks about who would be the main actors in the Russian bourgeois revolution reached its peak in 1905 when Lenin wrote *Two Tactics of Social Democracy in the Democratic Revolution*.[33] After 1905 came the dispute between Lenin and Trotsky on their respective slogans – democratic dictatorship of the proletariat and the peasantry or dictatorship of the proletariat. This dispute continued until it appeared to be settled by the 1917 Revolution. Six years later, however, it resurfaced in a different form and remains a live issue to this day.

In the dispute between Lenin and the Mensheviks regarding the dynamics of the Russian Revolution, Trotsky was on Lenin's side and opposed the Mensheviks.

Like Lenin, Trotsky was convinced that the land question was the key issue in the Russian Revolution, and that the agrarian revolution, as well as the gen-

---

33   Lenin 1960–78 [1905], pp. 15–140.

eral democratic revolution, would only be achieved if the workers and peasants united in struggle against the liberal bourgeoisie. He said himself that on this issue he was Lenin's student. At the latest, in 1902, when he fled Russia into exile for the first time and met Lenin, he accepted Lenin's views on this issue. He continued to maintain this position when he took part in, and led, the 1905 Revolution. During the revolution he developed his own revolutionary theory. His theory was based on Lenin's, but he differed from Lenin on the question of political power. He opposed Lenin's formula of the democratic dictatorship of the proletariat and the peasantry and counterposed his own formulation – the dictatorship of the proletariat relying on the peasantry[34] – or, in short, the dictatorship of the proletariat.

Why did Trotsky oppose the slogan of the democratic dictatorship of the proletariat and the peasantry? Because he believed that it was flawed. It did not specify which of the partners in the dictatorship would hold the real power – the proletariat or the peasantry. Trotsky differed from the rest of the Russian Marxists in his estimate of the role of the peasantry in the revolution. Although he believed the peasants were very important in society and in the revolution, he did not believe they were capable of forming their own independent party, and still less would they be able to concentrate revolutionary power in their own hands. This was obvious from the experience of past revolutions. Starting in the Reformation in sixteenth-century Germany or even earlier, the peasants had risen in support of this or that faction of the urban bourgeoisie. Often the faction they supported had emerged victorious. But because it could only support one or another urban class, the peasantry could not lead the movement as a whole. In Russia's belated bourgeois revolution, since the urban proletariat would wage a fierce struggle while no faction of the bourgeoisie could help the peasants solve their pressing land question, a peasant insurrection would help the proletariat seize political power. The combined weight of the workers and peasants would carry out the bourgeois revolution – the workers and peasants would jointly take power. But the real dictatorship would be exercised by the workers. In order to call things by their real names and clearly define the role of the peasantry and the political relationship between the workers and the peasants in the dictatorship, Trotsky opposed the vague formula of a dictatorship of the proletariat and the peasantry and put forward the unequivocal slogan of the dictatorship of the proletariat.

Trotsky believed Lenin's formula – dictatorship of the proletariat and the peasantry – was ambiguous rather than wrong. He compared it to an algebraic

---

34   Trotsky, 2010 [1930], p. 211.

formula with an unknown variable x. The value of the formula depended on the value of x. The x in this case was the role of the peasants in the revolution.

In Europe there were people who called the peasantry the sphinx of Russian history – an enigma. It was quite a reasonable position to take. In the most backward major country in Europe, which had not yet experienced a bourgeois revolution, the role the peasants played in the revolution would be decided, in the end, by experience. Although it was his own slogan, Lenin never formed a consistent interpretation of the democratic dictatorship of the proletariat and the peasantry. Did it imply a coalition government formed by the proletarian and peasant parties, or just a government based on the support of the two classes? Nor did Lenin express a definitive view on the role of the peasantry in the revolution. Were the workers and peasants equal in status? Would the peasants accept the leading role of the working class? Would the peasants be in charge with the workers as their helpers? He shifted his position from one side to the other depending on the circumstances. He had been known to say that political power would lie in the hands of the peasantry. He had also said the proletariat would lead the peasantry in the dictatorship and, what is more, clarified that this was implied by the formula of the dictatorship of the proletariat and the peasantry. In between these two extremes, he expressed all sorts of intermediate positions. Looking at the formula itself, Trotsky's position could be accommodated within it as a variant, for the dispute was not really about the formula but whether, and to what extent, the Russian peasantry would play an independent role in the revolution.

Contrary to Lenin's more nuanced positions, Trotsky from start to finish insisted that the Russian peasants could not play an independent or leading role – their movement could only succeed under the leadership of an urban class. And in Russia, this meant that if the peasant revolution was to succeed it would be under the leadership of the proletariat. So he insisted on the slogan of the dictatorship of the proletariat and opposed the democratic dictatorship of the proletariat and the peasantry, which was open to many differing interpretations.

But since this would be a dictatorship of the proletariat, with the peasants consigned to a supporting role, although charged with carrying out the tasks of the belated bourgeois revolution, it would not be able to limit itself to those tasks. Having taken power, the proletariat would unavoidably take measures that would infringe on the rights of private property and would inevitably embark on the socialist road. The dictatorship would lose its 'democratic' character. The democratic dictatorship of the proletariat and the peasantry would lose its relevance as a slogan, not only because it failed to express clearly the relationship between the workers and peasants but also because it emphasised the democratic over the socialist. Because it stood for limiting the revolution to carrying out bourgeois-democratic tasks. With these issues as their starting point, Lenin and Trotsky debated the trajectory and tasks of the revolution.

What classes would be the driving forces of the Russian Revolution? Lenin's answer was the workers and peasants. Trotsky said the main protagonist would be the proletariat with the peasants taking part but in a supporting role.

What tasks would the Russian Revolution accomplish? Lenin's answer was the tasks of the bourgeois-democratic revolution. Trotsky said that, in addition to these tasks, it would also carry out some tasks of the socialist revolution, because the democratic tasks could only be accomplished by a proletarian dictatorship that would, by its very nature, carry out some socialist measures.

What would be the future of the Russian Revolution? Lenin said it would be capitalist. Trotsky said it would non-capitalist – that is to say, socialist.

So what exactly was the nature of the Russian Revolution? Was it a bourgeois revolution? Trotsky answered that it was and it wasn't. He said this question should not be approached in a formalistic way. One would have to look at how events developed. If the dictatorship of the proletariat was overthrown by other classes (including the peasantry recently liberated by the proletariat), then the revolution would remain within bourgeois bounds. On the other hand, if the proletariat was able to use its seizure of power as a springboard to spread the revolution to the democratic world, then the Russian Revolution could be the vanguard of a new era of world socialism. So what stage had the Russian Revolution actually reached? This question could only be answered conditionally.

Having come this far, you may be asking yourself – didn't I say earlier that all Russian Marxists agreed that the coming Russian Revolution would be a bourgeois one? Now I'm saying that Trotsky denied this, or at least did not definitely affirm that the revolution would be bourgeois. Isn't this a contradiction?

Trotsky addressed this issue himself. In *The Permanent Revolution* he wrote:

> I never denied the *bourgeois* character of the revolution in the sense of its immediate historical tasks, but only in the sense of its driving forces and its perspectives.[35]

Clearly the revolution was at one and the same time both bourgeois and non-bourgeois. There was no contradiction. It depends on from where you are looking at the revolution. From the point of its tasks? From the point of view of its driving forces? Or from the point of view of its perspectives?

---

35   Trotsky 2010 [1930], p. 200.

It was not only Trotsky who had such thoughts. Lenin did too. In 1906, in a preface to one of Kautsky's articles, he wrote:

> The revolution in Russia is not a bourgeois revolution, for the bourgeoisie is not one of the driving forces of the present revolutionary movement in Russia.[36]

We all know that Lenin, in other places, both before and later, talked many times about the bourgeois character of the Russian Revolution.

These apparent contradictions, which were really only on the surface, were the result of the specific characteristics or peculiarities of the Russian Revolution – its backwardness and its belated nature. These peculiarities prevented the Russian bourgeoisie from becoming the driving force in its own revolution and from accomplishing its assigned tasks, which would be left to other classes to carry out. The class that would replace it as the executor of these historical tasks turned out to be its gravedigger – the proletariat. What is more, at this stage of world history, the proletariat, having carried out the tasks of the bourgeois revolution, would not be able restrict itself to these tasks, but would necessarily start out on the tasks of its own revolution.

You may also ask – did not Lenin sometimes talk about a non-capitalist future for the Russian Revolution? Did he not say that the Russian democratic revolution would grow into a socialist revolution? So were not Lenin's views regarding the tasks and perspectives of the revolution exactly the same as Trotsky's?

But unlike Trotsky, Lenin did not argue that only a proletarian dictatorship could resolve the tasks of the Russian bourgeois revolution. He thought that a worker-peasant dictatorship could only go as far as completing the democratic revolution and that socialist revolution would not be on the agenda until the democratic revolution was complete, triggering socialist revolutions in Western Europe. His ideas of one revolution growing into another and of a non-capitalist future were qualified by these reservations. Only after the completion of the democratic revolution could the socialist revolution begin. He did not conclude that only a proletarian dictatorship could complete the democratic revolution and that some revolutionary socialist measures would be necessary in order to complete the democratic revolution. Lenin believed that the influence of revolutions in Western Europe was an important precondition for a socialist revolution in Russia. Until the influence of those revolutions was felt

---

36   Lenin 1960–78 [1906] p. 410.

in Russia, the Russian Revolution would not progress past the capitalist stage. He made these points very clearly in *Two Tactics of Social Democracy in the Democratic Revolution*, from which I reproduce a few extracts below:

> Marxists are absolutely convinced of the bourgeois character of the Russian Revolution. What does that mean? It means that the democratic reforms in the political system, and the social and economic reforms that have become a necessity for Russia, do not in themselves imply the undermining of capitalism, the undermining of bourgeois rule; on the contrary, they will, for the first time, really clear the ground for a wide and rapid, European, and not Asiatic, development of capitalism; they will, for the first time, make it possible for the bourgeoisie to rule as a class.[37]

> A bourgeois revolution is a revolution which does not depart from the framework of the bourgeois, i.e., capitalist, socio-economic system. A bourgeois revolution expresses the needs of capitalist development, and, far from destroying the foundations of capitalism, it effects the contrary – it broadens and deepens them.[38]

> All these principles of Marxism have been proved and explained in minute detail in general and with regard to Russia in particular. And from these principles it follows that the idea of seeking salvation for the working class in anything save the further development of capitalism is reactionary.[39]

Section Five – The Permanent Revolution Revived

Russia was facing a revolution that was the inevitable result of the contradiction between the productive forces of Russian capitalism and the prevailing feudal-serf relations of production. The revolution was bourgeois. Its task was to liberate the capitalist productive forces from the shackles of the feudal system and smooth the path for their further development. This is what Lenin said before April 1917.[40]

But it was a backward or historically belated bourgeois revolution. To begin with, it was not happening in the early period of world capitalism but in the era of late capitalism in a world where the conditions for proletarian revolu-

---

37   Lenin 1960–78 [1905], p. 48.
38   Lenin 1960–78 [1905], p. 49.
39   Lenin 1960–78 [1905], p. 49.
40   I.e. before he wrote the April Theses.

tion were already ripe. Second, Russian capitalism had already developed to the extent that it had created a numerically strong, powerfully concentrated and class-conscious proletariat. Naturally a bourgeois revolution that took place under these circumstances would be very different from previous bourgeois revolutions. It would be different not only from the pre-nineteenth-century revolutions in Holland, Britain, America and France but also from the mid-nineteenth-century revolution in Germany. The issues of national liberation and unification would figure less prominently in Russia's bourgeois revolution than in some others because Russia was already an independent and central-ised state. But the land question would be correspondingly more important because Russia was the last country to abolish serfdom and semi-feudal rela-tions still prevailed in rural areas. This bourgeois revolution would be based on an agrarian revolution. It would have to liquidate the landowning class and redistribute the land using revolutionary methods, as well as overthrowing the autocracy. But the Russian bourgeoisie, on the one hand feeling threatened by the proletariat and on the other intimately tied to the landowning economy, was in no position to lead such a revolution, and still less to rouse the peas-antry to carry out an agrarian revolution. The peasants were the overwhelming majority of the population and they would play a correspondingly huge role in the revolution. It was the joint action of the peasants in the villages and the workers in the cities that would carry the Russian bourgeois revolution through to completion. But the alliance of workers and peasants opposed not just the aristocracy but the bourgeoisie itself – the first time this had happened in a bourgeois revolution. Yet the peasants could not play an independent role, still less a leading role in the revolution. The peasant movements of the past could only succeed under the leadership of one or another faction of the bourgeoisie, and a faction might seize state power supported by a peasant uprising. The peasant movement in the Russian Revolution, no matter how important, was essentially no different. It could not play an independent or leading role. What was different was that the Russian bourgeoisie could not place itself at the head of the peasantry. The urban class that would lead the peasantry was the prolet-ariat and it would rely on peasant support to seize state power. The government formed by the victorious worker-peasant alliance was 'the dictatorship of the proletariat relying on the peasantry'. Only by establishing and maintaining this regime could it complete the tasks of the Russian bourgeois revolution. The Russian bourgeois revolution led to the dictatorship of the proletariat.

But the revolution would not come to a halt after the establishment of the dictatorship of the proletariat. The resistance of the defeated classes and divi-sions and conflicts between the allied classes would increasingly force the pro-letariat to carry out its own class policies, to encroach on private property rights and implement a number of socialist policies. To put it another way, in order to establish and maintain the proletarian dictatorship the revolution would have to put some tasks of the proletarian revolution on the agenda and carry them out.

How far would the Russian proletariat be able to go in implementing the tasks of proletarian revolution? How far would it be able to travel down the road of socialist revolution? There is no definitive answer to this question. The answer would depend not only on the domestic situation in Russia but also on the European and world situation. If the Russian Revolution provided the spark that set in motion proletarian revolutions in Europe, the European revolution could in turn support and ensure the survival of Russia's proletarian regime and Russia would be able to follow the advanced countries along the road to socialism. But on its own, Russia would not be able to progress to socialism.

Such is the theory of Permanent Revolution as revived in 1905.

The theory of Permanent Revolution had been buried under a heap of dusty papers for half a century when it was revived. But it was no surprise that it was resurrected at this time. Indeed, it was only natural that it should be, because the theory of Permanent Revolution was discovered and formulated when considering the role of the proletariat in the bourgeois revolution and the relationship between the proletarian and bourgeois revolutions. These were precisely the issues raised by the 1905 Revolution and the questions being discussed by Russian revolutionaries.

What is meant by the 'permanence' of the Russian Revolution? First, in Russia there would be no gap between the democratic and socialist revolutions. The socialist revolution would grow out of the democratic revolution. What is more, it would not be possible to complete the democratic revolution without embarking on the socialist revolution. There would be no prolonged democratic interlude between the two revolutions. Second, the socialist revolution would itself become permanent. From the seizure of power by the proletariat to the achievement of socialism, when the proletarian dictatorship will no longer be necessary, the political situation would inevitably see both cooperation and conflict between various social groups. It would be a turbulent time alternating between external wars and internal conflicts and periods of peaceful reform. The complex interplay of the economy, technology, science, households, ethics, and customs would not permit a state of equilibrium. Third, the revolution in Russia – in a single country – would permanently develop into a worldwide revolution. Socialist revolution could begin in a single country but could not be completed within a single country. The capitalist forces of production had already broken free of the confines of single countries and made the entire world their domain, and since this was the stage of development reached by capitalism, socialism – representing a yet higher stage of development of the productive forces – could still less be confined within the boundaries of a single country. So due to inevitable external and internal contradictions, the dictatorship of the proletariat could not be indefinitely sustained within a single country. The only long-term perspective would be the victory of the revolution in several advanced countries. Revolution in a single country is no more than a link in the chain of world revolution.

In section four of this chapter I already covered the disputes between Lenin and Trotsky regarding the Russian Revolution. You no doubt will be asking: did not Lenin reject the theory of Permanent Revolution in its entirety?

No, Lenin did not oppose the theory of Permanent Revolution as such; he only disputed one aspect of it, the role of the peasants in the revolution and whether the Russian Revolution would establish a dictatorship of the proletariat. As for the international and 'permanent' character of the socialist revolution, Lenin and Trotsky were in complete agreement. Trotsky's belief that the Russian bourgeois revolution could only be completed by a proletarian dictatorship was, in essence, derived from Lenin's own views. Later, during the 1917 Revolution, any remaining disagreements between Lenin and Trotsky fell away. Lenin abandoned his old slogan of the democratic dictatorship of the proletariat and the peasantry in favour of the dictatorship of the proletariat. So although this revived theory of Permanent Revolution is associated with the name of Trotsky, we might just as well say it was jointly proposed by Lenin and Trotsky.

I will explain in Chapter 3 how the 1917 revolution conformed to the theory of Permanent Revolution and how, in that revolution, Lenin and Trotsky united against those who opposed the theory of Permanent Revolution (the Old Bolsheviks). In Chapter Four I will examine how, during Lenin's last illness and after his death, these so-called Old Bolsheviks magnified Lenin and Trotsky's pre-revolutionary disagreements to claim that Lenin opposed the theory of Permanent Revolution to the very end (referring to various speeches by Stalin). For now, however I will stick to examining the relations between Lenin and Trotsky in the Revolution of 1905.

In 1903, at the second congress of the RSDLP, when the split between the Bolsheviks and Mensheviks took place, Trotsky stood with Martov and the Mensheviks against Lenin and the Bolsheviks. But the split took place on organisational issues – the famous debate on the first clause of the party constitution – not on political issues. The clear divisions on political orientation between the Bolsheviks and the Mensheviks appeared later and came about only gradually. Admittedly, from the outset, in the background of the split were the two political lines that emerged later but one thing is sure – Trotsky decided to stand with the Mensheviks against the Bolsheviks on organisational, not political grounds. On political issues, Trotsky stood with the Bolsheviks against the Mensheviks. He joined the Mensheviks only because of this one narrow and specific issue. He never agreed with the Mensheviks on political questions. Less than a year after the split he broke off organisational links with the Mensheviks. From then until June 1917 he remained aloof from the two main factions of the Russian Social Democratic Party. And it was as such that he took part in the 1905 Revolution. Nevertheless, he became one of the main leaders of the revolution (as secretary of the first-ever Soviet). During the revolution, on the main strategic issues, there was unanimity between him and Lenin. At the third congress of the Bolshevik faction, a motion proposed by Leonid Krasin on the provisional government was drafted by Trotsky. The overwhelming majority of resolutions adopted by the Petrograd Soviet of Workers' Deputies were drafted by Trotsky. These resolutions were all published by Lenin's newspaper *Novaya Zhizn* and approved by Lenin himself. After the defeat of the revolution, Trotsky, in prison, wrote a pamphlet on strategy that was in line with Lenin's positions. Lenin had it printed and published and sent a message to Trotsky to let him know he agreed with it.

You might think that Lenin agreed with Trotsky on tactical issues but continued to oppose him on the more important issue of revolutionary theory. But it was not so. In 1905, when Trotsky published his theory of Permanent Revolution, it attracted furious criticism from the bourgeois press. But *Novaya Zhizn*, a newspaper controlled by Lenin, defended Trotsky. The bourgeois paper *Nasha Zhizn* tried to draw a distinction between Lenin's 'more reasonable' position and Trotsky's theory of Permanent Revolution but the Bolshevik *Novaya Zhizn* replied as follows:

> This gratuitous assumption is of course sheer nonsense. Comrade Trotsky said that the proletarian revolution can, without halting at the first stage, continue on its road, elbowing the exploiters aside; Lenin, on the other hand, pointed out that the political revolution is only the first step. The publicist of Nasha Zhizn would like to see a contradiction here ... The whole misunderstanding comes, first, from the fear with which the name alone of the social revolution fills Nasha Zhizn; secondly, out of the desire of this paper to discover some sort of sharp and piquant difference of opinion among the Social Democrats; and thirdly, in the figure of speech used by Comrade Trotsky: 'at a single blow'. In No. 10 of Nachalo, Comrade Trotsky explains his idea quite unambiguously: 'The complete victory of the revolution signifies the victory of the proletariat:' writes Comrade Trotsky. 'But this victory in turn implies the uninterruptedness

of the revolution in the future. The proletariat realises in life the fundamental democratic tasks, and the very logic of its immediate struggle to consolidate its political rule poses before the proletariat, at a certain moment, purely socialist problems. Between the minimum and the maximum program [of the Social Democrats] a revolutionary continuity is established. It is not a question of a single blow; or of a single day or month, but of a whole historical epoch. It would be absurd to try to fix its duration in advance.'[41]

Given that Novaya Zhizn defended the theory of Permanent Revolution, we can conclude that on the fundamentals of the theory there was no dispute between Lenin and Trotsky. Their disagreements related to one subordinate issue only – the political relationship between the workers and the peasants.

The Revolution of 1905 failed. Not only did it not become permanent and develop into a socialist revolution but it failed even as a democratic revolution. Although, under the pressure of a general strike, the autocracy yielded for the first time and agreed to implement a constitution, it went on to use military force to crush the working class and the revolutionary people. The revolution languished in the doldrums for twelve years until it broke out again in 1917 and finally achieved victory. And this time it proceeded in accordance with the theory of Permanent Revolution.

Can we say that because, in 1905, the time was not ripe for Permanent Revolution, it was too early to put forward this theory? No. First, the theory of Permanent Revolution mapped out a path to the victory, not the defeat, of the revolution. Second, the defeat of the 1905 Revolution was a negative confirmation of the theory of Permanent Revolution in that, because a proletarian dictatorship was not achieved, the bourgeois tasks of the revolution could not be completed. Finally, the revolution demonstrated, through real experience, the crucial role of the working class. The autocracy conceded a Constitution not because of the political opposition of the liberal bourgeoisie, not because of the spontaneous, disorganised uprisings of the peasantry, and not because of terrorist acts carried out by intellectuals, but because it was faced with a general strike of the working class. This was an explicit confirmation of the theory of Permanent Revolution.

---

41   Quoted in Trotsky 2010 [1930], pp. 235–6.

Chapter Three – Permanent Revolution Put to the Test

After the final defeat of the German Revolution of 1848, the first adumbration of the theory of Permanent Revolution was forgotten and remained so for half a century. This was not only because, after 1850, the German Revolution failed to develop in the way Marx predicted. It was also because this 'belated' revolution took place when capitalism was flourishing, albeit along a winding path, and still had decades of peaceful development ahead of it. Under these circumstances, Germany was able to avoid the short cut of revolution and gradually to solve the tasks of the democratic revolution, albeit along a tortuous route. But this path was not available to twentieth-century Russia. It found itself in a period of capitalist decline. The imperialist world would not permit it to follow the leisurely path open to mid-nineteenth-century Germany. It could not avoid revolution. Following the defeat of 1905, its only way forward remained revolution, and exactly the same type of revolution that had been attempted in 1905 – a bourgeois revolution in a backward country. This explains why, following the defeat of 1905, the revived theory of Permanent Revolution did not disappear from the stage.

Quite the opposite. Although Trotsky was already struggling to revive the theory of Permanent Revolution in the summer of 1905, it was only after the defeat of the revolution that this actually happened. Trotsky of course fought unremittingly for the theory. But apart from him, there were others who stood up for Marx's revolutionary theory. One such was Rosa Luxemburg, whose name is well known in China. Another was Parvus, whose name is much less familiar, but who was at the time a well-known left-wing Marxist.

In 1917, twelve years after the failure of 1905, Russia was plunged once more into revolution, this time a successful one that not only completed its bourgeois-democratic tasks but, in line with the theory of Permanent Revolution, embarked on the path of proletarian revolution.

But before talking about the revolutionary test of 1917 I will first examine how the RSDLP debated the theory of Permanent Revolution.

Section One – The Question of Permanent Revolution, 1905–17

During this period the question at the heart of the debate was – could Russia implement the dictatorship of the proletariat before Western Europe.

Those who opposed the theory of Permanent Revolution unanimously held that it was out of the question to even mention the dictatorship of the proletariat in the context of Russia's bourgeois revolution. The purpose of the dictatorship of the proletariat was to implement socialism. But Russia was not ready for socialism. The tasks in Russia were to expunge feudal relations of production and clear the path for capitalist development. At this time what was needed was thoroughgoing democratic reforms. These reforms could provide a spark to ignite socialist revolutions by the working classes of Western Europe, which would establish their own dictatorships and set Russia an example to follow. Only at this point would it be possible to establish the dictatorship of the proletariat in Russia.

But Trotsky believed that the power and class consciousness of a country's proletariat was not mechanically determined by the degree of development of the productive forces in that country. Country A's productivity may be higher than country B's, but one cannot deduce from this fact that country A's proletariat has greater political weight. Not infrequently one finds that the proletariat of a backward country is politically stronger than its counterpart in an advanced country. The political strength of the working class is a function of the state of the class struggle in that country in conjunction with the conditions of the international situation. Whether we are talking about everyday politics or the dictatorship of the proletariat, the conclusion is the same. Political power does not sequentially fall into the hands of the proletariat in line with the degree of development of a given country. The proletariat of a backward country may seize power before that of an advanced country. It follows that the Russian proletariat may take power earlier than its British, French, German or American counterparts.

It was not simply that it was possible to take power earlier. Our analysis of the special circumstances of the Russian bourgeois revolution led to the conclusion that in order to carry the revolution to completion, it was necessary for the proletariat to take power. If not a proletarian regime, what kind of regime could complete the revolution? A bourgeois regime? But in the Revolution of 1905, the Russian bourgeoisie had shown itself to be not revolutionary but counter-revolutionary. Even before the revolution reached its climax, the bourgeoisie had begun to play a counter-revolutionary role. The urban petty bourgeoisie? But at each critical juncture of the revolution the Russian petty bourgeoisie displayed its impotence. A peasant regime? Across the country there were indeed peasant revolts of enormous scope and power. But this power was not independent. To contribute to the revolution, it had to attach itself to an urban class. But in Russia in 1905, the bourgeoisie was already in the camp of reaction. The petty bourgeoisie was weak and vacillating. The only class capable of playing a revolutionary role was the proletariat. The working class was the vanguard of the revolution. It had the strength and the courage to force the autocracy to yield for the first time in its history. And it showed itself capable of leading and giving direction to the peasantry. So the peasantry could only complete its own revolution by hitching its wagon to the proletariat. Since there was no other class capable of carrying the bourgeois revolution to its conclusion, it followed

that the revolution would either be completed by the dictatorship of the proletariat or, if the proletariat proved incapable of establishing its dictatorship, it
would not be completed at all. The latter, as we know, was the outcome of the
1905 Revolution.

The dictatorship of the proletariat in Russia was necessary precisely in order
to carry out the bourgeois revolution. If another class had been capable of carrying out the revolution, then the dictatorship of the proletariat would have
been impossible. In other words, the Russian proletariat would have had to wait
until socialist revolutions had taken place in several Western European countries before it could establish its own dictatorship.

It follows that the dictatorship of the proletariat in Russia was a means to
carry out the bourgeois revolution, not the socialist revolution. The Russian
proletariat would sweep away the autocracy and serfdom. In short, it would
carry out all the progressive tasks of the bourgeois revolution that in the past
would have been carried out by the bourgeoisie or the petty bourgeoisie, but
that now fell to the proletariat.

However, since it would be a proletarian dictatorship, it would not be able
to limit itself to carrying out democratic tasks but would be forced to address a
number of tasks associated with socialist revolution. The distinction between
the minimum and maximum programmes of the RSDLP would break down and
the revolution would grow over from a bourgeois-democratic one into a proletarian socialist one. How far would Russia be able to advance along the road to
socialism? That question could not be answered in advance as it would depend
on the national and international balance of class forces.

From 1905 to 1917, the debate on the theory of Permanent Revolution remained broadly as described above. Those who opposed the theory of Permanent Revolution were bourgeois commentators and Mensheviks, but also those
Bolsheviks who later became known as the 'Old Bolsheviks'.

But I do not count Lenin among the opponents of Permanent Revolution.
In section four of the previous chapter, I already set out the disagreements
between Lenin and Trotsky. They were not about the theory of Permanent
Revolution as such but about some minor aspects of it: the political relationship between the workers and the peasants, and the related questions of
whether the peasants could play an independent role in the revolution and
whether the revolution would limit itself to carrying out democratic tasks. Trotsky's views were very clear – the peasants would not be able to play a leading
or independent role – they would have to follow the lead of the working class.
Therefore the revolutionary dictatorship would not limit itself to carrying out
democratic tasks. Although Lenin held the opposite point of view, his opinions
were not set in stone but were rather a kind of working hypothesis that he was

prepared to modify or even abandon when faced with concrete evidence. It was precisely this flexibility that allowed Lenin to join hands with Trotsky in 1917 – and, on this issue, to part company with the 'Old Bolsheviks'.

Those who currently oppose the theory of Permanent Revolution[42] exaggerate the old disputes between Lenin and Trotsky, in order to make it seem as if Lenin opposed the theory in its entirety rather than just part of it. They selectively quote passages from Lenin's writings in which he opposes the theory of Permanent Revolution. To someone unfamiliar with the history of the controversy and the debating techniques used, it might appear that Lenin opposed the theory as a whole. The following points will clarify the issue.

First, Trotsky systematically expounded his theory in *Results and Prospects*, which he wrote while in prison and was published in 1906 as part of a collection of writings titled *Our Revolution*. His subsequent articles and speeches (up to 1918) touching on the theory of Permanent Revolution did not expand on this article – which was itself admittedly not a full treatment of the issue. But by examining Lenin's writings we can see that he had not read this article before 1919. In his debates with Trotsky the material he relied on was a few quotes from Trotsky cited by Parvus in the preface to another book and a proclamation written by Parvus mistakenly thought to have been written by Trotsky. He also used a few quotes from *Results and Prospects* but they were taken indirectly from an article by Martov, not from the original. In short, Lenin did not make a systematic study of Trotsky's theory as a whole. His opinions on the theory of Permanent Revolution were not consistent but could even be described as contradictory. It was probably only in 1919, when the State Publishing Bureau republished Trotsky's *Results and Prospects* as a pamphlet, that Lenin would have had the opportunity to read it. It was precisely around that time that Lenin had a conversation with Joffe about the theory of Permanent Revolution during which Lenin told Joffe that 'Trotsky's analysis was absolutely correct'.[43] In 1927, at the height of the campaign against the theory of Permanent Revolution, Joffe committed suicide. He related his conversation with Lenin in his suicide note.

Second, when Lenin opposed Trotsky, his real target was not always Trotsky himself. For the most part, while on the surface it seemed as though he was attacking Trotsky, he was really opposing Bukharin, Radek or Piatakov and other members of their tendency. They also supported the theory of Permanent Revolution but their views were immature and mechanical in comparison

---

42 The central points at issue in the debate are not the same as they were before the 1917 revolution – but we will talk more about this in Chapter Four. Footnote by Zheng Chaolin.

43 Joffe's suicide note actually said 'with my own ears I have heard Lenin admit that in 1905 it was not he, but you, who was right. In the face of death one does not lie'.

with Trotsky's. Lenin often used the technique of attacking people who were outside the party in order to correct what he saw as mistaken trends inside the party. Even if others did not understand his method, those who were being attacked knew full well they were the targets. Radek himself said that certain passages Lenin wrote were directed at their current/tendency, not at Trotsky. And when correcting mistaken trends in his party, Lenin did not restrict himself to correcting past and current errors but made great efforts to inoculate the party against possible future errors by criticising them in advance. Therefore, for preventative and educational reasons, he often exaggerated the mistaken tendencies of others.

With these points in mind, we can see that the belief that disputes between Lenin and Trotsky show that Lenin was fundamentally opposed to the theory of Permanent Revolution is simply inaccurate.

If we want to understand Lenin's attitude to the theory of Permanent Revolution, examining the real experience of the year 1917 is far more important than raking over old quotations.

Section Two – Rearming the Bolshevik Party

In 1917, revolution broke out once more in Russia, and this time it succeeded. What were previously merely theoretical questions were answered in real, revolutionary practice. That the revolution proved the theories of the Narodniks and the Mensheviks wrong can be taken as a given. Here I will talk only about two competing formulas – the democratic dictatorship of the proletariat and the peasantry versus the dictatorship of the proletariat.

This issue arose once more in 1917 and was debated very fiercely, precisely because this time the dispute was not a matter of conjecture but of concrete and pressing policy decisions that required immediate answers.

The strange thing is that this time it was not Lenin who defended the old formula of the democratic dictatorship of the proletariat and the peasantry and opposed the dictatorship of the proletariat but his former followers among the Old Bolsheviks. Lenin not only did not oppose the dictatorship of the proletariat but insisted on it in the face of opposition from Old Bolsheviks who clung on to the slogan of the democratic dictatorship. This struggle began *before* Trotsky returned to Russia. It was Lenin himself, on his own initiative, who proposed the slogan of the dictatorship of the proletariat at this time.

Lenin was not able to return to Russia until more than a month after the February Revolution. On April 3, when he returned to Petrograd, the activity of the Bolshevik Party was under the control of Kamenev, Stalin, Rykov and other Old Bolsheviks. On many issues their positions were more or less indistinguishable from those of the Mensheviks. On the government question, they were content to let the bourgeoisie form a government, while they themselves assumed the role of opposition party applying pressure on the government to implement its policies. On the question of the war, they abandoned revolutionary defeatism and adopted a position of 'revolutionary' defencism, arguing that since the first revolutionary regiment appeared on the streets of Petrograd the old slogan of revolutionary defeatism was no longer applicable. As soon as Lenin returned, he pointed out that this line was fundamentally wrong. Although Russia had gone through a revolution and replaced the autocracy with the provisional government, the reason for Russia's participation in the war had not changed. It was still a war undertaken for the sake of plunder. Therefore we must continue to advocate Russia's defeat and not switch to a policy of defencism. He also maintained that the revolution was passing from its first to its second stage. In the first stage, the bourgeoisie had taken power. In the second stage, the proletariat would take power. The new regime would be a dictatorship of the proletariat, not a democratic dictatorship of the workers and peasants. Lenin held fast to this idea from the moment he returned to Russia. As soon as he stepped off the train, he expounded it to the welcoming crowd. The same day, he set out his views even more clearly in a speech to comrades. The next day, he wrote down his ideas in the form of ten points that became known as the April Theses.

The effect of Lenin's theses on both Russia and the Bolshevik Party was akin to that of a bomb going off. Those who listened to him outline his theses were left in a state of shock. Among the leading Old Bolsheviks not a single person agreed with him. Even his old comrade Zinoviev, who had worked closely with him for so many years and had travelled back to Russia with him, opposed him, to say nothing of the attitude towards him of the other parties. But the lower ranks gradually began to listen and take note. By the end of April Lenin had won the party over.

Lenin threw himself into the struggle, but it was only after a fierce debate that he was able to win over the Old Bolsheviks. At the core of the debate was whether the bourgeois revolution had been completed. The Old Bolsheviks, headed by Kamenev, believed that although the autocracy had been overthrown, the bourgeois revolution, in particular the agrarian revolution, was not yet fully accomplished and that the party's task should be to complete this unfinished revolution. Only after this revolution was fully implemented would it be possible to start the proletarian revolution. In their view, there was currently a bourgeois government. After this government had exhausted its role, we would have a democratic dictatorship of the proletariat and the peasantry and after the latter had completed the bourgeois revolution, it would finally be possible to implement the dictatorship of the proletariat.

Lenin dismissed this view as

> reiterating formulas senselessly learned by rote instead of studying the
> specific features of the new and living reality.[44]

'In real life', at the outset of the revolution, power fell into the hands of the workers and soldiers. But because of the low level of consciousness of the masses,
they allowed themselves to be led by the petty-bourgeois Social Revolutionaries and Mensheviks, who handed political power to the possessing classes.
Only if the masses wake up will they be able to take the power back from the
bourgeoisie. But for this to happen they must cast off the influence of the petty
bourgeoisie. And to achieve this, the slogan of the democratic dictatorship of
the proletariat and the peasantry is useless because it does not prescribe, and
cannot bring about, a clear break between the masses and the petty bourgeois.
If the masses manage to break with the petty bourgeoisie and seize power, this
regime would be not a democratic dictatorship of the proletariat and the peasantry but a dictatorship of the proletariat.

On whether the bourgeois revolution was complete or not, Lenin's view was
that the bourgeoisie held political power and the transfer of political power is
the first step in a revolution. In this sense, the revolution was complete. But the
Old Bolsheviks said that the peasants were also bourgeois and it was also possible that they would take power and make a compromise with the bourgeoisie.
The reality, however, was that our starting point should be not possibilities but
actualities. If the peasantry were to cast off the influence of the bourgeoisie,
seize the land, take power and oppose the bourgeoisie, then the Russian bourgeois revolution would indeed have entered a new stage. But this just goes to
show that whether the bourgeois revolution is complete or not is the wrong
question to ask. We can see that Lenin's position was the same as that held by
Trotsky for many years.

In any case, the April Theses represented a change in the traditional views
of the Bolsheviks. The old viewpoint was that the Russian Revolution would be
restricted to carrying out bourgeois democratic tasks. The new doctrine said
that these bounds would be broken and raised the prospect of establishing the
dictatorship of the proletariat in the course of the bourgeois revolution.

But it was only Lenin who had changed. (To be exact, Lenin had clarified his
earlier ambiguous position in the light of events). The others clung to the old
theory and opposed him. Under pressure from the masses and from Lenin him-

---

44   Lenin 1960–78 [1917b], p. 43.

self, the Old Bolsheviks were forced to yield and follow the line set out in the April Theses, but in their heart of hearts, they were still wedded to the prejudice that the revolution must not *depasser* [go beyond] bourgeois democratic limits. It was only after the October Revolution and the dictatorship of the proletariat becoming an established fact that they cast aside and gave up this prejudice. This explains why the Old Bolsheviks often became an obstacle in the path of the revolution.

This is not difficult to explain. Humans are conservative in their thinking and revolutionaries are not immune to this. Often, even though history has entered a new epoch, revolutionaries still cling to old ideas that belong to the previous era and find it impossible to adjust their thinking to the new situation. So even in the most revolutionary of parties – like the Bolsheviks – every sharp turn in history will provoke a crisis. One the one hand, a leader of genius perceives a sudden turning point ahead and immediately abandons old slogans that are no longer suited to the new epoch, while on the other hand, his mediocre followers cling to the old ideas and oppose him. The famous chronicler of the 1917 Revolution Nikolai Sukhanov said this of the Bolsheviks:

> The few great generals were nothing without Lenin – they were like immense planets without a sun [to orbit] (of course here I exclude Trotsky who was not yet a member of the order – that is to say, he was still in the camp of the enemies of the proletariat, one of the lackeys of the bourgeoisie etc.).[45]

The so-called Old Bolsheviks stuck to their outdated formulas and slogans not only because of inertia. For months or even years before the revolution, they had been isolated from the masses. Hardly any had been involved in active revolutionary work in the lead-up to the revolution. Some were in prison; others were in exile and still others had lapsed into inactivity. When the revolution arrived, they immediately became its leaders because of their past prestige. But they had only just emerged from isolation and had not yet realised the extent to which the consciousness of the masses had changed since the revolution. Therefore they had not grasped the sharpness of the historical turn, to the extent that, as Lenin said at the time, the Old Bolshevik formula

> [that] the bourgeois-democratic revolution is not completed ... is obsolete. It is no good at all. It is dead. And it is no use trying to revive it.[46]

---

45   Sukhanov 1922.
46   Lenin 1960–78 [1917b], p. 50.

You may well say that Lenin, too, had been absent from the mass movement, and indeed was living an isolated existence in faraway Switzerland. How was he able to perceive this sharp historical turn? Simply because he was a genius? Or were there other reasons?

There were indeed other reasons. Even if the Old Bolsheviks had not been isolated, had taken part in the movement and experienced this historical turn side by side with the masses, even if they had all possessed the kind of genius required to recognise the historical shift, they would still not have been able to grasp its extent. Because this was an historical turn on an international scale. Its full significance could not be grasped in Siberia, in Moscow or even Petrograd. It could only be grasped in Europe, at the crossroads of world history. Lenin did not view the Russian Revolution from the point of view of Russia's development alone. He understood it in the context of the world revolutionary situation.

In April 1917, the Old Bolsheviks united against Lenin but were proved wrong by the actual course of events. They tried to confront the new Lenin with the old Lenin. They said Lenin had adopted Trotsky's position that he had always opposed in the past. They clung to the old formulas and slogans of the Bolsheviks. These old formulas may have been correct in the past but to cling to them in the present situation was a serious error.

What is more, these slogans had not been entirely correct even in the past. In a 1909 article by Trotsky there is a short passage that Stalin is fond of quoting to prove that Trotsky was opposed to Bolshevism.

> While the Mensheviks, proceeding from the abstraction that 'our revolution is bourgeois' arrive at the idea of adapting the whole tactic of the proletariat to the conduct of the liberal bourgeoisie, right up to the capture of state power, the Bolsheviks, proceeding from the same bare abstraction: 'democratic, not socialist dictatorship:' arrive at the idea of the bourgeois-democratic self-limitation of the proletariat with power in its hands. The difference between them on this question is certainly quite important: while the anti-revolutionary sides of Menshevism are already expressed in full force today, the anti-revolutionary features of Bolshevism threaten to become a great danger only in the event of the victory of the revolution.[47]

---

47   Trotsky 2010 [1930], pp. 265–6.

The political line of the Old Bolsheviks before Lenin returned to Russia and their opposition to him after he did return were omens of this great danger. That the great danger was avoided was entirely due to the fact that, happily, Lenin's April Theses won the support of the lower ranks and overcame the opposition. When this article was reprinted in 1922, Trotsky added the following note:

> As is known, this did not take place, for Bolshevism under the leadership of Lenin (though not without internal struggle) accomplished its ideological rearmament on this most important question in the spring of 1917, that is, before the seizure of power.[48]

The rearming of the party was crucial for the revolution. At the time, the Bolsheviks were the only truly proletarian party. If the Bolshevik party had not been rearmed, if it had undertaken the revolution using its old pre-revolutionary slogans, the pre-April line of Kamenev and Stalin, rather than Lenin's post-April line, the 1917 revolution would have been stillborn like the Chinese Revolution ten years later. This shows the enormous importance of Lenin as an individual.

If there had been no Lenin, would the Bolshevik party have been able to rearm itself ideologically in 1917? It is hard to say. Although we can reasonably conclude that even without Lenin an intense struggle would have broken out inside the Bolshevik party and that, from among the workers and younger Bolsheviks, something like Lenin's position would have emerged, the struggle would have been more intense and drawn out, and we cannot say which tendency would have won. Even supposing the new, radical tendency had prevailed, its victory might have come too late for it to lead the revolution to victory. In revolution, timing is everything.

Fortunately, Lenin was there to carry out the important task of rearming, and on this foundation the party developed in practice into a thoroughly proletarian party in time to lead the revolution to victory.

This is not to say that the rearming of the party could only be undertaken in April and not before – even before the revolution. In fact it should have begun long before. The democratic dictatorship of the proletariat and the peasantry was merely an algebraic formula in which the most important variable was the peasantry. Furthermore, just how far away the advanced countries were from the dictatorship of the proletariat was difficult to estimate before the revolution. This was also a factor in Lenin's reluctance to recog-

---

48   Trotsky 2010 [1930], p. 266.

nise that the dictatorship of the proletariat was the only possible outcome of the revolution. Both before and after the outbreak of the Great War in 1914, as the Western European proletarian revolution approached, the Russian peasantry had still shown no sign that it could play an independent role. Once the Great War started, Lenin should have put forward a different approach to replace the old formula of the democratic dictatorship of the proletariat and the peasantry, even if he had hedged it around with conditions and qualifications. But he only replaced the democratic dictatorship formula with the dictatorship of the proletariat *after* he returned to Petrograd, at the beginning of April 1917. A letter to the Swiss workers written on leaving Switzerland shows that at that time he had not yet resolved the issue:

> Russia is a peasant country, one of the most backward of European countries. Socialism cannot triumph there directly and immediately. But the peasant character of the country, the vast reserve of land in the hands of the nobility, may, to judge from the experience of 1905, give tremendous sweep to the bourgeois-democratic revolution in Russia and may make our revolution the prologue to the world socialist revolution, a step toward it.[49]

Here, although Lenin is still not proposing the establishment of a dictatorship of the proletariat in Russia, he is already hinting that the Russian proletariat might spark a socialist revolution. This short passage written in Switzerland shows Lenin adopting an intermediate position between his old and new viewpoints.

So why did Lenin not go straight to advocating the dictatorship of the proletariat? Why, after the war began, or even before the war, did he persist with the old formula of the democratic dictatorship of the proletariat and the peasantry?

Trotsky shed some light on this:

> It is self-evident that if Lenin had lived in Russia and had observed the development of the party, day by day, especially during the war, he would have given the necessary correctives and clarifications in time.[50]

---

49   Lenin 1960–78 [1917a], p. 371.
50   Trotsky 2010 [1930], p. 267.

To sum up, although the Old Bolsheviks continued (and continue) to insist on the old slogan of the democratic dictatorship of the proletariat and the peasantry, Lenin himself only ever viewed it as an algebraic formula whose arithmetic value would depend on changing circumstances and experience. But the Old Bolsheviks elevated this formula into a dogma, an empty abstraction to be applied regardless of changing historical circumstances.

Section Three – Was the Democratic Dictatorship of the Proletariat and the Peasantry Ever Realised?

Stalinism, representing the interests of the Soviet bureaucracy, 'rearmed' the Bolsheviks after 1924 or, more accurately, disarmed Bolshevism. The Stalinists refused to discuss whether the rearming of the party should have begun before April 1917. In fact, they basically denied that the party needed to be rearmed at all. As far as they were concerned the inner party crisis of April 1917 was a fleeting matter of no importance. Before and after April the Bolsheviks were equally well 'armed'. The Stalinists admitted that Lenin's April Theses had abandoned the old slogan of the democratic dictatorship of the proletariat and the peasantry and adopted the dictatorship of the proletariat. But that was not because the old formula was wrong but because the democratic dictatorship had been realised and it was now time move forward to the dictatorship of the proletariat. This was, they said, in line with the Bolsheviks' consistent view. When the bourgeois revolution is completed the proletarian revolution will begin. Kamenev's mistake was simply that, unlike Lenin, he had not realised that the bourgeois revolution was complete. So the dispute was simply about estimating the conjuncture and not about the correctness or otherwise of the traditional line. The above is a summary of the Stalinist view of the April crisis. To support their position, they cited various works by Lenin on the democratic dictatorship of the proletariat and the peasantry.

Was the democratic dictatorship of the proletariat and the peasantry realised during the 1917 Revolution? Has the democratic dictatorship of the proletariat and the peasantry ever been realised anywhere in human history? These are questions that demand definitive answers.

It is true that Lenin several times used forms of words that implied that the democratic dictatorship of the proletariat and the peasantry was realised after the February Revolution. But his words were hedged around with conditions, and he employed them in his battle against the Old Bolsheviks.

Here are a few examples:

'The revolutionary-democratic dictatorship of the proletariat and the peasantry' has already become a reality (in a certain form and to a certain extent) in the Russian Revolution ... 'The Soviet of Workers' and Soldiers' Deputies' – there you have the 'revolutionary-democratic dictatorship of the proletariat and the peasantry' already accomplished in reality.[51]

The revolutionary-democratic dictatorship of the proletariat and the peasantry has already been realised, but in a highly original manner, and with a number of extremely important modifications.[52]

A practical question. Who knows whether it is still possible at present for a special 'revolutionary-democratic dictatorship of the proletariat and the peasantry', detached from the bourgeois government, to emerge in Russia?[53]

All the above was written by Lenin in April 1917 in his *Letters on Tactics*. Around the same time, in other writings and speeches, he said things along the same lines.

Was the democratic dictatorship of the proletariat and the peasantry – the formula advocated for decades by the Bolshevik party – actually realised during the period of dual power following the February Revolution? Was it embodied in the Soviet that was dominated by the compromisers?

This cannot be true in the strict sense. During the period of dual power, the Soviet held only half the power. It did not have full control. An organ of power that holds only half the power must deliver the other half into the hands of the opposing organ. Or, as Lenin put it, the Soviet was

voluntarily ceding power to the bourgeoisie, voluntarily making itself an appendage of the bourgeoisie.[54]

So how could he call this a dictatorship? The democratic dictatorship of the proletariat and the peasantry, according to the sense in which it was defended for years by the Bolsheviks, was supposed to destroy the autocracy without trace and clear away the landholding system of the serf owners. Could the Soviet, dominated as it was by the compromisers, carry out these tasks? Clearly it would not and could not. Under the regime of dual power, the Soviet, so long as it left the petty bourgeois parties in control, would continue to pay dividends

---

51   Lenin 1960–78 [1917b], pp. 44–5.
52   Lenin 1960–78 [1917b], p. 45.
53   Lenin 1960–78 [1917b], pp. 50–1.
54   Lenin 1960–78 [1917b], p. 46.

to the other power – that of the bourgeoisie – until it was swallowed up and eliminated. To think that this sort of Soviet was the realisation of the Bolsheviks' long-standing formula, even 'in a certain form and to a certain extent', is simply not tenable.

So why did Lenin talk in this way? If we don't stick rigidly to Lenin's form of words but pay attention to the spirit of what he was saying, we can see that he was trying to wean the Old Bolsheviks away from their obsolete formulas and persuade them to embrace a new line. He was not trying to use the old formula to describe the historical particularity of dual power. His meaning was basically this: Look, that appendage of the bourgeois government – the Soviet – is the realisation of the old formula of the democratic dictatorship of the proletariat and the peasantry that you are so reluctant to part with. It has already been realised, albeit 'in a highly original manner'. Having been once realised in the form of an appendage to the bourgeois government, is it reasonable to hope that the democratic dictatorship of the proletariat and the peasantry will once again be realised in a manner in which it does not serve as an appendage to the bourgeois government? Lenin again:

> Who knows whether it is still possible at present for a special 'revolutionary-democratic dictatorship of the proletariat and the peasantry', detached from the bourgeois government, to emerge in Russia? [...] But if this is still possible, then there is one, and only one, way towards it, namely, an immediate, resolute, and irrevocable separation of the proletarian Communist elements from the petty-bourgeois elements.[55]

When Lenin said the democratic dictatorship of the proletariat and the peasantry had been realised under the dual power regime, he was defending his April Theses against the Old Bolsheviks. What is more, he said this only between April and October 1917. That is to say, before the revolution had succeeded.

After the October Revolution, Lenin had this to say. The dictatorship that the Bolsheviks had long advocated, the kind of dictatorship that would solve the tasks of Russia's bourgeois revolution (overthrowing Tsarism, expropriating the great landowners, implementing the eight-hour day) – had it been achieved? Yes it had. And when was it achieved? After the October Revolution, and not before.

---

55   Lenin 1960–78 [1917b], pp. 50–1.

In his 1918 book *The Proletarian Revolution and the Renegade Kautsky*, Lenin assessed the October Revolution as follows:

> Yes, our revolution is a bourgeois revolution *as long* as we march *with* the peasants *as a whole* ... Things have turned out just as we said they would. The course taken by the revolution has confirmed the correctness of our reasoning. *First*, with the 'whole' of the peasants against the monarchy, against the landowners, against medievalism (and to that extent the revolution remains bourgeois, bourgeois-democratic). *Then*, with the poor peasants, with the semi-proletarians, with all the exploited, *against capitalism*, including the rural rich, the kulaks, the profiteers, and to that extent the revolution becomes a *socialist* one.[56]

On the question of whether the Russian bourgeois revolution had been completed or not, I will try to compare what Lenin said when he had just returned to Russia, before the success of the revolution, with what he said *after* the success of the revolution. Before [October], he said the Russian bourgeois revolution had been completed by the February Revolution. Now he was saying that the bourgeois revolution had only been completed in October. For those who fetishise Lenin's every word, this sounds like a contradiction. But in fact it is not a contradiction at all. It was a long-standing view of the Bolsheviks that, in the sense of completing the bourgeois tasks of the revolution rather than the bourgeoisie simply taking political power, the bourgeois revolution would only be completed by an October-style revolution. The completion of the revolution and its tasks was in fact carried out in accordance with the Bolsheviks' forecast – not by a bourgeois-democratic republic but by a worker-peasant dictatorship, in opposition to the bourgeoisie. But it turned out that this dictatorship would be realised 'in a highly original manner', not as a democratic dictatorship but as a socialist dictatorship, a dictatorship of the proletariat supported by a peasant war. The algebraic formula acquired a particular arithmetic solution.

In fact the same solution can be found in Lenin's earlier work. In 1909, he said:

> The formula that the Bolsheviks have here chosen for themselves reads: the proletariat which leads the peasantry behind it. Isn't it obvious that the idea of all these formulations is one and the same? Isn't it obvious that

---

56   Lenin 1960–78 [1918], p. 231.

> this idea expresses precisely the dictatorship of the proletariat and peas-
> antry – that the 'formula' of the proletariat supported by the peasantry,
> remains entirely within the bounds of that very same dictatorship of the
> proletariat and peasantry?[57]

In short, the democratic dictatorship of the proletariat and the peasantry was
never implemented during the Russian Revolution. It was not implemented in
the period of Soviet power between February and October because it was a
period of dual power and the Soviet was dominated by the Social Revolutionaries and the Mensheviks, who turned it into an appendage to the bourgeois
regime. This was in no sense a dictatorship. Neither was it realised by the Soviet
regime after October, because although that was a dictatorship, it was socialist,
not democratic.

Was it accidental that the democratic dictatorship of the proletariat and the
peasantry was never realised during the Russian Revolution? No, it was not
realised because it contained elements that could not be implemented. When
Lenin first proposed this formula [of the democratic dictatorship], it was to
counterpose a worker peasant alliance *in conflict with* the bourgeoisie to the
Menshevik formula of allying with and supporting the bourgeoisie in its revolution, and to counterpose the idea of dictatorship to vulgar constitutionalism.
He was right, and indeed was proved right by the 1917 Revolution. But the problem lay elsewhere. The formula did not clearly define the relationship between
the workers and peasants in the worker-peasant alliance. It left open the possibility that the peasants might play an independent, even leading, role, and
therefore restrict the scope of the revolution to democratic tasks. He had not
foreseen that to resolve the democratic tasks completely, a proletarian dictatorship would be necessary, and it would be forced to go beyond democratic tasks
and implement a number of socialist measures. The 1917 Revolution exposed
the shortcomings of [Lenin's] formula.

After the revolution started, when Lenin returned to Russia and surveyed the
situation, he abandoned the old formula of the democratic dictatorship of the
proletariat and the peasantry and adopted the [formula of a] dictatorship of
the proletariat. This was a major change in the Bolshevik tradition and amounted to an ideological rearmament of the party. As the revolution unfolded, it did
so not in line with the longstanding predictions of the Bolsheviks but in ways
that contradicted their preconceptions.

---

57   Quoted in Trotsky 2010 [1930], pp. 221–2.

The difference between Lenin's genius and the mediocrity of the Old Bolsheviks was that Lenin spent his time 'studying the specific features of the new
and living reality',[58] not 'reiterating formulas senselessly learned by rote'.[59] The
Old Bolsheviks continued to

> cling to a theory of yesterday, which, like all theories, at best only outlines
> the main and the general, only comes near to embracing life in all its com-
> plexity.[60]

Hence the need for the April Theses which showed the way to victory in October.

Section 4 – Permanent Revolution Confirmed by the October Revolution

The 1917 revolution unfolded exactly as Trotsky had been predicting for years.
Russia's belated bourgeois revolution could not stop at the bourgeois-democratic stage but must inevitably, uninterruptedly develop into a proletarian
socialist revolution.

The Russian bourgeoisie, represented by Miliukov and Guchkov, was incapable of solving the tasks of Russia's bourgeois revolution. They originally did not
want to overthrow the monarchy, and when the workers and soldiers toppled
the Tsar, they did their best to find a replacement to put back on the throne.
All they wanted was a new Tsar who would allow them to enact a few reforms
in their own interests, but they were eventually forced to bow to the inevitable
and accept the abolition of the monarchy as an accomplished fact. They naturally had no intention of reforming the land system since they were heavily
invested in land. If the peasants were to seize the land from the landlords, they
themselves would suffer unimaginable losses.

The parties of the urban petty bourgeoisie – the Social Revolutionaries and
the Mensheviks – performed pitifully in the revolution. After the February
Revolution, the masses – whose level of consciousness was still fairly low –
handed the power that had fallen into their hands over to these two parties
because they trusted them and were willing to follow their lead. The two parties
could not have wished for a better opportunity to carry out the tasks of the
bourgeois revolution, following in the footsteps of their predecessors, the British and French petty bourgeoisies. But what did they do with this power that

---

58   Lenin 1960–78 [1917b], p. 43.
59   Lenin 1960–78 [1917b], p. 43.
60   Lenin 1960–78 [1917b], p. 45.

had fallen into their hands from the sky? At first, they refused to accept it, and when they could no longer refuse it, they handed it over to the bourgeois liberals and restricted themselves to putting pressure on the bourgeois government. From February to October, they rebuffed the demand of the masses that they take back the power that they had given away. They also opposed the efforts of the Bolsheviks to seize power from the bourgeoisie on behalf of the proletariat and spared no effort to help the bourgeoisie retain power and resist the onslaughts of the masses. Why so pathetic? First, because in the mature stage of capitalism the conflict between the bourgeoisie and the proletariat eclipsed all other conflicts and the petty bourgeoisie, buffeted by both sides, had no chance to assert itself. Second, the Russian petty bourgeoisie was especially weak because Russian capitalism had developed in a great leap straight from domestic handicrafts to large-scale industry, skipping over the stages of urban handicrafts and small-scale manufacturing. Because of this, Russia never experienced anything like Western Europe's history of citizens' movements against the aristocracy and, as a result, Russia's urban petty bourgeoisie lacked a long revolutionary tradition. Finally, from simply observing its performance we can see that the Russian petty bourgeoisie was incapable of leading a revolution to carry out the tasks set by history.

The role of the Russian peasantry was finally determined by the revolution. The self-proclaimed peasant party – the Social Revolutionaries – proved to be no peasant party at all. It did nothing to help the peasants get land. On the contrary, several of the party leaders actively tried to stop them. The peasants, when all was said and done, no longer had a party of their own. No matter how boldly the peasants acted in the revolution, no matter how violent and radical the land seizures, without the support and leadership of the urban proletariat, the scattered and diffuse rural struggles would be suppressed by the landowners and the bourgeois government. On the one hand, the revolution proved that the peasantry could not play an independent or leading role. On the other hand, it showed that a peasant war could help the proletariat to seize power as Marx foresaw in his 1856 letter to Engels. In April, Lenin could not say for sure that the peasants would help the proletariat seize power. He believed they would continue to listen to the petty-bourgeois Social Revolutionary party – they would not begin land seizures but would wait for the convocation of the Constituent Assembly. In this way, the peasants would compromise with and even cooperate with the bourgeoisie. The course of the revolution proved this conjecture of Lenin's to be over-pessimistic. The peasantry as a whole, not just a part of it, supported the proletarian revolution. But its role was nonetheless limited to a supporting one. It could not lead the revolution and could not play an independent political role.

So the leadership of the revolution had to fall to the Russian proletariat. As expected, the Russian bourgeois revolution could not but push the proletariat to seize power. Moreover, the Russian proletariat seized power before the working classes of the advanced Western European countries. The Russian proletarian dictatorship carried out the tasks of the bourgeois revolution. But the proletarian dictatorship could not restrict itself to carrying out the tasks of the bourgeois revolution. In order to maintain and consolidate the dictatorship, the proletariat was daily forced to violate the rights of private property. It could not help but implement its own proletarian policies and, in doing so, it split the peasantry and supported its poorest, semi-proletarian elements in their struggle against the village bourgeoisie, the so-called rich peasants or kulaks. Just as the alliance between the proletariat and the peasantry as a whole opposed the autocracy and the aristocracy to carry out bourgeois revolution, so the alliance of the proletariat and the poor peasants opposed the bourgeoisie in town and country to carry out socialist revolution. In this way, democratic revolution grew into socialist revolution. This was how the two revolutions developed *permanently*.

The October Revolution verified Trotsky's formula of the dictatorship of the proletariat, proposed twelve years earlier.

You may well ask – did the October Revolution refute Lenin's formula of the democratic dictatorship of the proletariat and the peasantry? I would answer:

First, the dictatorship of the proletariat was a particular solution to the algebraic formula of the democratic dictatorship of the proletariat and the peasantry. Showing the first to be correct does not show that the latter is mistaken.

Second, just because Lenin proposed, and persisted with, this algebraic formula does not show that he was wrong. We should bear in mind that Lenin worked by successively approximating to the truth. This method is perfectly valid and indeed unavoidable in some contexts, e.g., in solving simple problems of arithmetical division. When dividing a multidigit number we often have to make several approximations before arriving at the right answer. Artillerymen must fire several spotting rounds before hitting the target. This method is also unavoidable in political affairs. The key is to understand promptly which shots miss the target and realign the gun muzzle accordingly.

Lenin's formula of the democratic dictatorship of the proletariat and the peasantry was of great historical significance. He had solved one of the most pressing contemporary theoretical and political questions – the extent to which the peasantry and other petty-bourgeois layers are politically independent. But on the basis of the rich experience and practice of the Bolsheviks between 1905 and 1917, Lenin closed the door on the formula of the democratic dictatorship. He wrote on that door in his own hand: *No Entry*. He also wrote that if the peasantry does not follow the bourgeoisie it must follow the proletariat. This was where the old slogan of the Bolsheviks ended up.

In 1917, the Russian Revolution triumphed and eliminated the old dispute between Lenin and Trotsky. The theory of Permanent Revolution conceived by Marx's genius finally became a reality. The theory had evolved and will continue to evolve because the creation of the first workers' state by this successful revolution threw up new tasks, quite unlike and beyond those posed by a simple bourgeois revolution in a backward country: how to develop a revolution in one country into a world revolution and how to cleanse the new workers' state of the vestiges of its pre-revolutionary past so as to fully realise a socialist society.

But history does not travel in straight lines. It follows a tortuous route and often retreats after advancing a few steps. The Russian Revolution confirmed the theory of Permanent Revolution. Paradoxically, however, a large scale campaign to refute the theory of Permanent Revolution erupted just a few years later in the new workers state created by the revolution. The old, long-solved and long-forgotten controversies between Lenin and Trotsky were dug up and distorted for factional purposes.

But this also gives us an opportunity to examine the theory of Permanent revolution from yet another angle.

Chapter Four – The Theory of Permanent Revolution as a Formula for World Revolution

Section One – Bureaucracy, Thermidor and 'Socialism in One Country'

The term Permanent Revolution does not imply that revolutions develop ever ascendingly. Revolutions, like history in general, do not proceed in a straight line. They have rising curves and descending curves. This applies to all revolutions, and the Russian Revolution was no exception.

The declining curve of the great French Revolution began with the coup of the 9th Thermidor (27 July) 1794 in the third year of the Republic, when the revolutionary leader Robespierre was overthrown by moderates. Starting from that date, the reactionary forces became bolder day by day until Napoleon proclaimed himself Emperor. This was a crucial turning point in the French Revolution and happened when the revolution was not yet five years old. Historians now routinely use the term Thermidor to refer to the point at which a revolution, having reached its peak, begins to retreat. The Russian Thermidor began in 1923 when Lenin was forced to retire from government due to illness, again only a little over five years after the revolution. From then on, the masses were gradually excluded from taking part in politics, and political affairs became the preserve of a bureaucratic layer that had risen above the people. Today the Soviet Union – the state born of the October Revolution – is ruled not by the masses who made the revolution but by a privileged bureaucratic elite that reaps its benefits.

How to explain this? It is not enough to rely on the abstract law that all revolutions produce a corresponding reaction. We need to examine the specific conditions that caused this particular reaction.

First, the revolution did not happen in an advanced country of Western Europe but in backward Russia. The dictatorship of the proletariat in Russia was the result of a particular combination of the world situation and internal conditions in Russia. It was not the result of internal conditions alone. The Russian Revolution, far more so than the French Revolution, was the product of the international situation. But unfortunately the wave of revolution that flooded west from Russia, despite severely shaking several of the great powers, failed in the end, and when a corresponding wave spread east, it also failed. Capitalism was somehow able to heal the scars of war and revolution and gradually stabilise itself. The Soviet Union was left isolated and surrounded in a conjuncture in which the immediate prospects for revolution were bleak.

Second, Russia's backwardness exacerbated bureaucratic tendencies in the new country. Since, it was not possible to immediately abolish the state in the aftermath of the proletarian revolution, it was necessary to assign a portion of the population to exercise state functions, the bureaucratic element. If Russia had been an advanced country, or if the world situation had been more favourable, this bureaucratic element might have become a loyal servant of society, serving the masses. But Russia was backward and the world situation was anything but favourable. These 'servants of society' were themselves dissatisfied with their lot. When the New Economic Policy was implemented, they consolidated their petty-bourgeois status and began to assert themselves. When the civil war ended and five million soldiers were demobilised, officers accustomed to giving orders were reassigned to administrative organs at all levels and gradually stifled soviet democracy. These factors all favoured the growth of the bureaucracy.

Finally, very many lower-level revolutionary cadres sacrificed their lives in the revolution and civil war. Some survivors were integrated into the state machine, rose several levels in the bureaucracy and became estranged from the masses. The masses themselves, having had their hopes raised and then dashed, became dispirited and demoralised. When they saw that the bureaucrats had usurped their power, they were unwilling (or, more precisely, unable) to rise up again. So their 'social servants' became their 'social masters'.

The change in status of the bureaucrats from servants of society to masters of society did not happen overnight. It was a drawn-out process. At the start of 1923, the social base of this transformation was beginning to take shape. The emerging bureaucratic forces assembled around a section of the Old Bolsheviks whose thinking and spirit was epitomised by the figure of Stalin. But they encountered obstacles. One obstacle was the system of thought created by the October Revolution. Without smashing this system of thought they could not brazenly assert themselves as masters of society. But if they openly confronted it, they would provoke resistance from the masses and rekindle the spirit of October. It was necessary to adopt an oblique approach.

This was not too difficult. The two leaders of the October Revolution were Lenin and Trotsky. Lenin was ill and would soon die. During the revolution and afterwards, Trotsky had been at one with Lenin. But he had clashed with Lenin in the past, not only on organisational issues but also on matters of theory. This provided the bureaucrats with the excuse to attack the ideas of October. It appeared as though they were not attacking those ideas but 'Trotskyism', not attacking Lenin but Trotsky. And what was this thing called 'Trotskyism'? It was the theory of Permanent Revolution.

At the outset, the ideas of this anti-October, so-called anti-Trotskyist movement were inchoate and self-contradictory. Although it represented a new and different ideological trend it had as yet developed no consistent theory. That had to wait until the autumn of 1924, six months after Lenin's death, with the emergence of the theory of Socialism in One Country, whose author was Stalin.

The fundamental point of this new 'theory' was that in the special circumstances of Russia, the Russian proletariat had conquered political power. The revolution had therefore ended and there would follow a period of social reform that would continue until a socialist society had been successfully constructed in this one country – Russia. Even if there was no world revolution and no other proletarian countries came to Russia's aid, this would not hinder the building of socialism in one country.

This 'theory' fundamentally contradicted the ideas of Bolshevism. But Stalin and his supporters maintained that it was consistent with Bolshevism, and that it was what Lenin and the Bolsheviks had always stood for. They claimed that one of the main points of contention between Lenin and Trotsky was that Lenin thought Russia could build socialism on its own while Trotsky said it could not.

But this was Stalin's 'theory', not Lenin's. And there is a further complication. Stalin first put forward this theory in the autumn of 1924. He had never before asserted that Russia could build socialism in one country. On the contrary, he had explicitly stated that without aid from advanced proletarian countries Russia would not be able to build socialism. In the spring of 1924, just six months before the appearance of his new theory, he wrote the pamphlet *Problems of Leninism*, in which he had this to say:

> But the overthrow of the power of the bourgeoisie and establishment of the power of the proletariat in one country does not yet mean that the complete victory of socialism has been ensured. The principle task of socialism – the organisation of socialist production – has still to be fulfilled. Can this task be fulfilled, can the final victory of socialism be achieved in one country, without the joint efforts of the proletarians in several advanced countries? No, it cannot. To overthrow the bourgeoisie the efforts of one country are sufficient; this is proved by the history of our revolution. For the final victory of socialism, for the organisation of Socialist production, the efforts of one country, particularly of a peasant country like Russia, are insufficient; for that, the efforts of the proletarians of several advanced countries are required.[61]

This extract demonstrates that in the spring of 1924 Stalin himself did not believe that Russia could build socialism in one country. But now it is impossible to find this passage in the book *Problems of Leninism*. It does not appear in the Chinese, the Russian or any other edition of the book. Instead, in its place, we find this:

'After consolidating its power and leading the peasantry in its wake the proletariat of the victorious country can and must build a socialist society.'[62]

Stalin had changed his mind by the autumn of 1924 and recalled the original edition of the book containing the first passage and replaced it with the second. The original edition with the uncorrected text was banned.

Are the ideas expressed in the long paragraph quoted above correct? Yes, because they do not express Stalin's own theory but traditional Bolshevik thinking. Stalin himself concluded by saying:

> These, in general, are the characteristic features of Lenin's theory of proletarian revolution.[63]

The theory of Socialism in One Country was first proposed in the autumn of 1924 and definitely contradicted traditional Bolshevik thinking. We don't need to look to others for evidence of this. Stalin himself provided the evidence.

---

61   Stalin 1924, p. 157. Cited in Deutscher 1949, 282.
62   Stalin 1924a, pp. 110–11.
63   Stalin 1924, p. 111 (This however is from the revised text).

Stalin said the theory of 'Socialism in One Country' is inconsistent with 'Trot-skyism'. He was right about this as well. 'Trotskyism', the theory of Permanent Revolution, indeed maintains that

> [f]or the final victory of socialism, for the organisation of Socialist pro-duction, the efforts of one country, particularly of a peasant country like Russia, are insufficient; for that, the efforts of the proletarians of several advanced countries are required.[64]

The 'anti-Trotskyist' movement had hit upon its central idea.

Here I should note that before the February Revolution in 1917 what was referred to as 'Trotskyism'[65] was the idea that if the Russian bourgeois revolu-tion did not propel the proletariat into power it would not be able to accom-plish its own tasks. After the reactionary movement of 1924, so-called 'Trotsky-ism' meant the stance that after seizing state power the Russian proletariat, relying solely on its own resources, would be unable to construct a socialist system in a single country.

Before the revolution, it never occurred to those who opposed 'Trotskyism' after 1924 that Russia could build socialism on its own. In fact, they went fur-ther, maintaining that it would be impossible for the Russian proletariat to even seize political power until after the dictatorship of the proletariat had been established in several Western countries.

But as far as 'Trotskyism' itself was concerned,[66] the above two ideas were really one and the same. They amounted to the two main components of the theory of Permanent Revolution.

There was never a dispute between Lenin and Trotsky about the second com-ponent of the theory of Permanent Revolution, because it was, as Stalin himself said, one of 'the characteristic features of Lenin's theory of proletarian revolu-tion' and a tenet of Bolshevism's theoretical tradition. In Lenin's writings, from the earliest right up to the last, whenever he mentioned socialist construction, he always adopted this internationalist stance: that without proletarian revolu-tions in the advanced countries, it would be impossible to build socialism. You will never find a quote that contradicts this. Lenin never says that one country on its own can construct socialism.

But Stalin nevertheless quoted Lenin in support of his 'theory'. He insisted that Lenin had said it was possible to build socialism in one country.

---

64   Stalin 1924, p. 157. Cited in Deutscher 1949, p. 282.
65   That is to say, by its opponents.
66   That is to say according to Trotsky and his followers.

Stalin only cited two passages from Lenin (by contrast Trotsky quoted thirty or forty – see *The History of the Russian Revolution*, vol. 3, Appendix II: *Socialism in a Separate Country*[67]). The first passage Stalin cited was from *On the Slogan for a United States of Europe*, written in 1915. The second was from *On Cooperation* written in early 1923.[68]

In *On the Slogan For a United States of Europe*, Lenin said:

> Hence, the victory of socialism is possible first in several or even in one capitalist country alone. After expropriating the capitalists and organising their own socialist production, the victorious proletariat of that country will arise against the rest of the world – the capitalist world[69]

Stalin was delighted to discover this passage. He believed that Lenin had put forward, for the first time in Marxist literature, the idea of Socialism in One Country. If Lenin really had intended this literal interpretation, I would find it hard to explain how he later forgot this idea and always contradicted it. Happily, an examination of his article *Several Theses* shows that in the same year Lenin gave voice to his real meaning:

> The task confronting the proletariat of Russia is the consummation of the bourgeois-democratic revolution in Russia *in order* to kindle the socialist revolution in Europe. The latter task now stands very close to the former, yet it remains a special and second task, for it is a question of the *different classes* which are collaborating with the proletariat of Russia. In the former task, it is the petty-bourgeois peasantry of Russia who are collaborating; in the latter, it is the proletariat of other countries.[70]

So Lenin believed that for the Russian socialist revolution to succeed it must receive cooperation and support from the working classes of other countries.

In his unfinished article 'On Cooperation', Lenin wrote that the Soviet Republic had 'all that is necessary and sufficient' for the transition to socialism, without the need for a new revolution. Stalin believed that this passage too supported the idea of Socialism in One Country. But in the context of the article it is clear that 'all that is necessary and sufficient' referred to political and legal preconditions. Lenin never forgot to remind people that Russia's productive

---

67   Trotsky 2008 [1932], p. 890.
68   Lenin 1960–78 [1923] p. 467.
69   Lenin 1960–78 [1915], p. 342.
70   Lenin 1960–78 [1915a], pp. 402–3.

capacity and level of cultural development were insufficient for the introduction of socialism. In another article written around the same time he wrote:

> We, too, lack enough civilisation to enable us to pass straight on to socialism, although we do have the political prerequisite for it.[71]

In March 1923, in one of his last articles, Lenin wrote:

> Thus, at the present time we are confronted with the question – shall we be able to hold on with our small and very small peasant production, and in our present state of ruin, until the West-European capitalist countries consummate their development towards socialism?[72]

From this we can see that right up until his death Lenin believed that the solution to the Soviet Union's problems lay in the support that would be provided by proletarian revolutions in other countries, not in the building of socialism within the borders of one country.

Why is the theory of Socialism in One Country a reactionary fantasy?

Because socialism is a higher level mode of production than capitalism. Although in its early stages capitalism was able to develop with the confines of the nation state, with the emergence of finance capital, the boundaries of nation states became too restrictive to contain its advance. Imperialist war is the most obvious sign that capitalism has breached national borders. If capitalism cannot be contained within national borders, still less so can socialism. If it is confined within the boundaries of a single state it is not socialism; if it is socialism, it must transcend those boundaries. Socialism in One Country is a contradiction in terms, equivalent to a square circle or a circular square. If this fantasy is put into practice anywhere, if one managed to establish 'socialism' in a single, isolated country, then that country's forces of production would be at a lower level than those of capitalism. It would not be socialism at all. To recklessly pursue the creation of such a society is a quest to build a reactionary utopia.

Proletarian parties, whether before or after the conquest of power, must never forget the contradiction between national boundaries and the forces of production, that under the capitalist system the forces of production are international in scope, that they impose an international, not national, division

---

71   Lenin 1960–78 [1923a], p. 501.
72   Lenin 1960–78 [1923a], p. 499.

of labour, and that they require not national markets but the world market. The so-called world market is not simply the sum of more or less equivalent national components, as some people believe, but an independent and over-arching entity based on the differences rather than the commonalities between countries. Each country's place in the world division of labour is determined by these differences. Countries complement each other, depend on each other. They are all indispensable and what happens in any country affects the whole world. Since the world market predominates over national markets, the class struggle also takes place on an international scale. So the victory of a proletarian revolution in one country is not a definitive victory but merely the beginning of a revolutionary wave. The task of a proletariat that has seized political power in one country is not to build socialism but to help the working classes of other countries make revolutions, to support them by all means, and to wait for successful revolutions in the great powers to come to their assistance in building socialism. If the world revolutionary tide raised by victory in one country fails in other countries then the proletarian dictatorship, although it may be maintained and developed for a period, will eventually be brought down by internal and external contradictions.

The history of the Soviet Union, the first country to establish the dictatorship of the proletariat, bears this out, no matter how much the new Thermidorians in the party protest that it has already built socialism.

But these problems are not restricted to backward Russia. Even if a proletarian revolution succeeded in advanced Britain, it would not be able to build socialism on its own. A British proletarian dictatorship left to itself would also encounter difficulties and contradictions no less severe than those the Soviet Union faces now and India may face in the future. Although the nature and scale of these difficulties and contradictions would be different in each of these three countries, the way of overcoming them would be the same in each case – advancing the international revolution.

> Section Two – On 'Underestimating the Peasantry' and 'Skipping
> the Bourgeois Stage of the Revolution'

The new Thermidorians, the official Bolshevik Party after the death of Lenin, having jettisoned the ideas of the October Revolution and the living tradition of Bolshevism, could do and say as they pleased. They say the Soviet Union is a country that has successfully built socialism. But in reality, it is a transitional country where the principal means of production are owned by the state but whose productivity lags far behind that of the great powers of Western Europe and which is striving by all means to catch up with those great powers. What is more, political power is in the hands of a Bonapartist bureaucratic caste. If a second wave of revolution does not rise in time, then sooner or later the revolution will be lost. The character of the Soviet Union has not yet been decided by history.

The mere fact that the new Thermidorians, the Soviet bureaucratic caste, declared in their propaganda that the Soviet Union possessed all the preconditions for building Socialism in One Country could not change the future of the country. On the contrary, it set the Soviet Union on the course to collapse. They carry out their reactionary line supposedly in the name of the October Revolution and Bolshevism, just as they employed the ideas of the October Revolution and the Bolshevik traditions to justify abandoning those same ideas and traditions. And they gave their actions the fine-sounding name of 'anti-Trotskyism'.

This approach was very convenient. They abandoned the old traditions, but not openly. On the contrary, they used the authority of the old traditions to justify their reactionary line.

But what did they mean by Trotskyism? In the last analysis, what were the ideas that they opposed?

They naturally opposed the idea that socialism could not be built in a single country and the idea implicit in the theory of Permanent Revolution that socialism must by its very nature be international in character. But they did not stop there. Following the logic of their position they went a step further and revived old and long-forgotten controversies between Lenin and Trotsky dating from before the February Revolution. As we have already seen, these arguments had nothing to do with whether socialism could be built in one country. On that point, Lenin and Trotsky agreed with each other. At the time, the point in dispute was whether the Russian bourgeois revolution could be completed only by the proletariat. By 1923, when this latter debate revived, it was not in order to study the history of the matter, for by then the October Revolution had taken place and decided the issue. The October Revolution had confirmed that a proletarian dictatorship was necessary to complete the Russian bourgeois revolution. So how could this verdict of history be overthrown six years after the revolution?

They naturally used all sorts of sophistry but it all boiled down to saying that the October Revolution did not take place in accordance with the theory of Permanent Revolution but in conformity with the old theory of the Bolsheviks. Let us remind ourselves that this said: we will first carry out the bourgeois revolution and establish the Democratic Dictatorship of the Proletariat and the Peasantry. The February Revolution of 1917 marked the completion of the bourgeois revolution and the establishment of that Democratic Dictatorship, so starting in April we began the second stage of the revolution, the proletarian revolution, and prepared to install a second type of dictatorship – the dictatorship of the proletariat. At the time, although certain old comrades mistakenly believed that the bourgeois revolution had not yet succeeded and the Democratic Dictatorship of the Proletariat and the Peasantry had not yet been established, when Lenin returned and corrected these mistakes, these views faded away. As for Trotsky's theory of Permanent Revolution, it did not conform with the revolutionary process. Trotsky underestimated the role of the peasantry in the revolution. He raised the slogan 'Down with the Tsar, For a Workers' Government'. But during the revolution, the peasants in uniform (i.e., the soldiers) joined hands with the workers while peasant uprisings in the villages helped the urban workers seize political power. Trotsky failed to distinguish the bourgeois and proletarian stages of the revolution. He did not understand that the proletarian revolution must grow out of the bourgeois revolution. He maintained it was possible to jump straight from feudalism to socialism. But during the revolution we had to pass from autocracy through two regimes to arrive at the dictatorship of the proletariat.

The above arguments are a mixture of ignorance and guile. Between April and October 1917, although Lenin said that the Russian bourgeois revolution (the Democratic Dictatorship of the Proletariat and the Peasantry) had succeeded, he meant it in a particular sense, different from the old formulation in the Bolshevik programme. By the success of the bourgeois revolution Lenin merely meant that the bourgeoisie had taken political power, whereas in the old programme it meant the completion of the tasks of the bourgeois revolution. The so-called Democratic Dictatorship of the Proletariat and the Peasantry (April to October) was nothing more than an appendage to the bourgeois government, not an independent government in its own right as set out in the old programme. To grasp Lenin's position there is no need to cite what he said before the October Revolution – we can simply repeat what he said after the revolution. We have already seen how in *The Proletarian Revolution and the Renegade Kautsky*, Lenin said that the Russian bourgeois revolution was completed in the first period *after* the October Revolution. The completion of the bourgeois tasks referred to in the old programme was carried out in this period and the regime that solved these tasks was not the Democratic Dictatorship of the Proletariat and the Peasantry but the Dictatorship of the Proletariat. We can see that for the Russian bourgeois revolution to succeed, it had to propel the proletariat into power regardless of whether the proletariats of the advanced countries had already taken power.

The two charges they adduce to attack the theory of Permanent revolution – underestimating the peasantry and skipping the bourgeois stage – simply do not stack up.

In the second chapter, I showed that although Trotsky said that the peasantry could not create a political party independent of both the proletariat and the bourgeoisie and could not play an independent role in the Russian bourgeois revolution, he never underestimated the power and force of the peasantry in the revolution, and never underestimated the importance of land revolts in the revolution. On the contrary, his starting point was that the land question was the key issue of the Russian bourgeois revolution and that its main driving force would be the alliance of workers and peasants. It was on this basis that he formulated his theory of Permanent Revolution. Since neither the bourgeoisie nor the urban petty bourgeoisie could lead the peasants to victory in the land revolution, and since the peasants themselves, using their own forces and under their own leadership, could not solve their own historic tasks, the Russian bourgeois revolution must of necessity become 'permanent' until the establishment of a proletarian dictatorship that would resolve these tasks.

The idea that the peasants could not form an independent party did not begin with Trotsky. In *The Eighteenth Brumaire of Louis Bonaparte* Marx wrote:

> Insofar as there is merely a local interconnection among these small-holding peasants, and the identity of their interests begets no community, no national bond and no political organisation among them, they do not form a class. They are consequently incapable of enforcing their class interests in their own name, whether through a parliament or through a convention. They cannot represent themselves, they must be represented.[73]

If this amounts to underestimating the peasantry then Marx himself is guilty of the charge.

Admittedly Marx was talking about the French peasantry (a peasantry *after* the victory of the bourgeois revolution) and one cannot simply apply this model to the Russian peasantry. One has to analyse the concrete conditions of the Russian peasantry. Trotsky's conclusions flowed from just such a concrete analysis and did not simply reproduce Marx's views on the matter. Lenin's own analysis of the same conditions arrived at a conclusion not all that different from Trotsky's.

---

73   Marx and Engels 2010 [1851–52], p. 187.

It is also possible that the objective difficulties of achieving political unity among the petty bourgeoisie will prevent such a party from being formed and, for a long time to come, will keep the peasant democracy in its present state as a loose, amorphous, jellylike Trudovik mass.[74]

However, in 1909, Lenin returned to the same theme and wrote:

> there cannot be the slightest doubt that a revolution carried to such a 'conclusion', or rather, to such a high stage of development as a revolutionary dictatorship, will produce a more definitely constituted and stronger revolutionary peasant party. To think otherwise would be like supposing that some vital organs of an adult can retain the size, shape and development of infancy.[75]

This conclusion is at odds with Trotsky's.

The Russian peasantry was an unknown quantity. It is perfectly understandable that, before real evidence was available, there should be speculation about the role of the peasants in the revolution. But after the 1917 revolution [s] Lenin arrived at a definite conclusion:

> The whole of political economy, if anybody has learned anything from it, the whole history of revolution, the whole history of political development throughout the 19th century, teaches us that the peasant follows the worker or the bourgeois ... If you do not know why, I would say to such citizens ... consider the development of any of the great revolutions of the 18th and 19th centuries, the political history of any country in the 19th century. It will tell you why. The economic structure of capitalist society is such that the ruling forces in it can only be capital or the proletariat that overthrows it. There are no other forces in the economic structure of that society.[76]

If this is underestimating the peasantry then Lenin, or at least the post-1917 Lenin, also underestimated the peasantry.

In any case, it is illogical to conclude from Trotsky's belief that the peasantry would not play an independent role that he underestimated it.

---

74   Lenin 1960–78 [1907], p. 121.
75   Lenin 1960–78 [1909], p. 374.
76   Lenin 1960–78 [1919] pp. 367–8. Here presented as quoted in Trotsky 2010 [1930], p. 284.

But having come this far, the new Thermidoreans retort: During the 1905 Revolution Trotsky raised the slogan 'No Czar, but a workers' government.'[77] Does this not show that he underestimated the peasantry? I will try to answer this question.

Nowadays, in the worldwide 'anti-Trotskyist' movement, when it comes to discussing Trotsky's mistakes, 'underestimating the peasantry' is always brought up and this famous slogan is cited as evidence. But this slogan had nothing to do with Trotsky! In fact, the slogan 'No Czar, but a workers' government' was the title of a pamphlet distributed outside Russia in 1905. The proclamation was actually printed by Parvus. At the time, Trotsky was living clandestinely in St Petersburg and knew nothing about it. Much later, he heard about the proclamation from articles written by others to attack him but he never set eyes on the proclamation itself.

Is this enough to demonstrate that the accusation that Trotsky underestimated the peasantry is unfounded? Here's another fact: at the same time as Parvus was distributing his proclamation outside Russia, Trotsky wrote another proclamation to be distributed clandestinely in St Petersburg the title of which was *Neither Czar nor Zemtsi, but the People!*[78] The People here was clearly meant to include both workers and peasants. This proclamation was later reprinted by the Soviet State Publishing House in Trotsky's *Collected Works* (vol. II, pt. 1, p. 256). It seems that Trotsky, presumably gifted with foresight, wrote the proclamation specifically so as to be able to refute later misrepresentations. In the same volume of his writings there are several proclamations to the peasantry that were printed and distributed in the name of the Central Committee of the Bolshevik Party, but actually penned by Trotsky. From all this we can see the absurdity of the charge that Trotsky 'underestimated the peasantry'.

The slogan 'No Czar, but a workers' government' was often cited to prove that Trotsky not only underestimated the peasants but also believed the bourgeois stage of Russia's revolution could be skipped. This argument does not on its own stand up to scrutiny, but can the substantive charge be made to stick? Let's put this particular argument aside and see if there is any tendency in Trotsky's theory to assert that the bourgeois stage of the revolution could be skipped over.

The theory of Permanent Revolution does not deny that the Russian Revolution must pass through a bourgeois stage. What it does say, however, is that

---

77   Trotsky 2010, [1930] p. 206.
78   Trotsky 2010 [1930], page 251. The Zemtsi were liberal nobles who made up the Zemsta – local assemblies with limited powers.

the bourgeois stage could only be completed under the dictatorship of the proletariat. The seizure of power by the proletariat is not the same as socialist revolution. In a backward country, it is the only way to carry the bourgeois revolution through to completion. This was how Lenin described the October Revolution and the regime it gave birth to. The course of the Russian Revolution was that before the land question (the basic issue of the Russian bourgeois revolution) was solved even in the slightest, the proletariat took power, and only afterwards solved it. If you want to call this 'skipping a historical stage' then it was the revolution that skipped the stage, not Trotsky or Lenin.

Trotsky himself particularly emphasised the bourgeois character of the Russian Revolution. He said it was precisely because Russia's bourgeois revolution had not taken place that its proletariat would take power before those in the advanced countries. Otherwise a dictatorship of the proletariat in Russia would be out of the question.

Since the new Thermidorians believed that the bourgeois revolution had been completed and the democratic dictatorship of the proletariat and the peasantry had been realised during the period of dual power, they concluded that the Russian Revolution had not skipped any stages and set out to popularise their conclusion that history never skips stages. The 'impermissibility of skipping historical stages' became a main pillar of Thermidorian theory.

But they concluded wrongly. Although Trotsky never confused the Russian bourgeois revolution with the proletarian revolution and never advocated a direct jump from feudalism to socialism, he opposed this 'theory of non-skipping of stages'. He believed it was nonsense because the real, living process of history often skipped the stages set out in the work of theorists and researchers. Revolutionary policy, if it is to avoid falling behind the objective process of history at critical junctures, must therefore also skip those stages. The key difference between revolutionaries and vulgar evolutionists is that revolutionaries recognise that history skips stages, whereas vulgar evolutionists do not. It is because of this that revolutionaries are able to recognise critical junctures and take advantage of them.

Let us take Russia as an example. Marx distinguished three stages in modern social and economic development – handicrafts, manufacturing and modern mechanised industry. This was a classic theoretical exposition of stages, but did Russia pass through them? Not at all. Russia passed directly from household handicrafts to modern mechanised industry, 'skipping over' the stages of rural and urban manufacturing. Russia's political history also skipped over many stages. It missed out the Reformation as well the democratic parliamentary system and went straight to the soviet system. (This is not to say that the theoretical analysis of stages is of no value in the study of Russian history. On the contrary, without an understanding of these stages we would be unable to understand Russian history – and the Bolshevik party would not have been able to arrive at the correct policies to lead the revolution to victory.)

It follows that some stages seen as inevitable from a theoretical point of view can, in the real course of development, above all in revolutionary periods, be shortened to the point that in practical terms they do not exist. Conversely, some stages that are not at all foreseen as inevitable at the level of theory, under certain sets of circumstances, may appear and even become prolonged. Some people may object that Russia actually went through the manufacturing stage and it is just that it was very short. Russia also went through the parliamentary stage with the convening of the Constituent Assembly after the revolution and its dismissal shortly afterwards. This is not wrong as such and one could look at things from this point of view. You could even go as far as to say that Russia went through all the same stages as Western Europe, the difference being merely that some of the stages were extremely short and took a peculiar form. But such stages are so short that they can be regarded as embryonic forms that had no effect on history. To all intents and purposes, it is as if they never took place at all.

In short, it is wrong to say that no historical stage can be skipped.

Section Three – Generalising from Russia to All Backward
Countries

In 1923, when the debate over the theory of Permanent Revolution revived, the main question at issue was whether Russia could build socialism in one country, so the question of the transition from bourgeois revolution to proletarian revolution became secondary and simply a matter of settling old scores. This was because this transition, as far as Russia was concerned, belonged to the past.

When the new Thermidorians attacked Trotsky for his pre-revolutionary position on this question they used it as a debating point to attack Trotsky's on the theory of Socialism in One Country. They considered the question *in its own right* to be of no practical significance.

This is more or less correct, but things are not so simple. The new Thermidorians took a firm stand on the primary question,[79] but they were forced to defend their position on the old, secondary issue.[80] So they were forced to twist the facts to prove that the course of the Russian Revolution had confirmed

---

79   Socialism in One Country.
80   The transition from bourgeois to socialist revolution.

their old point of view. Worse still, they began to apply their old views to new, current revolutions – and this time it was not the Russian Revolution that was at stake but the revolution in another enormous, backward country – China.

The new Thermidorians steered the Chinese Revolution of 1925–7 in line with their old standpoint of opposition to the theory of Permanent Revolution, with the result that they destroyed a revolution that had every hope of success. After the failure of the revolution they did not correct their mistakes but instead prepared to repeat them in the case of future revolutions in China and in backward eastern countries in general. So this old controversy suddenly took on an enormous contemporary significance.

The new Thermidorians brandish Lenin's name and that of the Bolsheviks to oppose the theory of Permanent Revolution. But we should remember: the pre-revolutionary controversies between Lenin and Trotsky were settled in the 1917 Revolution. After the revolution, the ideas that Lenin developed on all kinds of questions concerning the Russian Revolution were at one with Trotsky's positions and, what is more, were in line with Trotsky's pre-revolutionary positions. There were no further disputes between the two regarding these issues. The new Thermidorians claimed the mantle of the Old Bolsheviks, but how did they perform in 1917? After the February Revolution, they all, without exception, adopted left-wing democratic positions. At the time, they all regarded the dictatorship of the proletariat as a vague and distant prospect and dismissed the idea of setting out to establish it as ridiculous (as 'Trotskyism', in fact). When Lenin returned to Russia, he corrected the mistakes of the Old Bolsheviks. But Kamenev continued to oppose him, stuck to the old positions and organised a democratic wing in the Bolshevik Party. He was soon joined by Zinoviev, who had travelled back to Russia together with Lenin. Stalin was cleverer. He knew that the standpoint he had taken in March was not in line with Lenin's views but hoped that people would forget his woeful articles and speeches and that he could then gradually shift towards Lenin's new position. These three were representative of the rest. In short, the so-called Old Bolsheviks failed the test of revolution. The 'Bolshevism' they now uphold is precisely the inconsistent part of Bolshevism – the part that Lenin himself abandoned. Strictly speaking, the 'Bolshevism' they espouse is, in essence, Menshevism, but even more dangerous since it is dressed in Bolshevik clothing.

The theory of Permanent Revolution must inevitably clash with the doctrines of the new Thermidorians, not only on the issue of Socialism in One Country but also on the artificially revived pre-revolutionary disputes. The latter issue is not simply about defending historical accuracy. Far more important is its significance for the fate of the Chinese Revolution and revolutions in the East in general.

For this reason, the theory of Permanent Revolution must pass beyond Russia's borders to become a theory applicable to all revolutions in backward countries, and indeed to the world revolution as a whole.

I would remind you that Marx based his theory of Permanent Revolution on the particular conditions in one country – Germany. His *Address to the Communist League* makes this clear. Trotsky originally based his theory of Permanent Revolution on the particular conditions prevailing in Russia. We know this because his arguments in support of the theory were based on Russia's particular qualities. For example, in his 1906 work *Results and Prospects* he wrote:

> The Russian Revolution has a quite peculiar character, which is the result of the peculiar trend of our whole social and historical development, and which in its turn opens before us quite new historical prospects.[81]

In short, before 1928, neither Marx, Trotsky, nor anyone else regarded the theory of Permanent Revolution as applicable to backward countries in general and still less to the world revolution as a whole.

It was only in his book *The Permanent Revolution*, written in exile in 1928, that Trotsky, for the first time, elevated the theory of Permanent Revolution into a general formula applicable to all backward countries and the world revolution as a whole.

In this book, Trotsky wrote that the theory of Permanent Revolution combines three lines of thought. The first is that belated democratic revolutions turn into socialist revolutions. The second is that socialist revolution itself becomes permanent revolution. The third is that the socialist revolution is an international revolution. The second and third points are of particular importance for combating the doctrine of Socialism in One Country. These two points are not only applicable to the Soviet Union but to all future revolutions around the world. This implies that the theory of Permanent Revolution is a formula applicable to the world revolution as a whole. The first point applies particularly to backward countries. Whether bourgeois revolutions in backward countries can or must turn into proletarian revolutions is an issue that concerns not only Germany and Russia but backward countries in general. Whether what is at stake in the revolution is land, independence or national unification, the bourgeoisies of backward countries are not up to the task because they are inextricably linked to the landowners or foreign oppressors and already face strong and conscious working classes that they simultaneously fear and oppose. They

---

81   Trotsky 2010 [1906], p. 41.

therefore prefer to take the reformist rather than the revolutionary road. At the same time, the petty bourgeoisie in backward countries, including among the peasants, cannot play the same independent, leading role as in previous revolutions, for the proletariat has already stepped into the political arena. It follows that the bourgeois revolution can only succeed under the leadership of the proletariat. But a proletarian dictatorship will not be able to avoid implementing at least some socialist measures. This applies to all backward countries that have reached the conditions necessary for a bourgeois revolution. It follows that Trotsky's theory of Permanent Revolution, conceived in response to Russia's peculiarities, can be applied to backward countries in general.

In 1929 the new Thermidorians expelled Trotsky from the Soviet Union. In exile in Turkey he summarised the theory of Permanent Revolution in fourteen points. Here is the full text:

> 1. The theory of the permanent revolution now demands the greatest attention from every Marxist, for the course of the class and ideological struggle has fully and finally raised this question from the realm of reminiscences over old differences of opinion among Russian Marxists, and converted it into a question of the character, the inner connections and methods of the international revolution in general.

> 2. With regard to countries with a belated bourgeois development, especially the colonial and semi-colonial countries, the theory of the permanent revolution signifies that the complete and genuine solution of their tasks of achieving democracy and national emancipation is conceivable only through the dictatorship of the proletariat as the leader of the subjugated nation, above all of its peasant masses.

> 3. Not only the agrarian, but also the national question assigns to the peasantry – the overwhelming majority of the population in backward countries – an exceptional place in the democratic revolution. Without an alliance of the proletariat with the peasantry the tasks of the democratic revolution cannot be solved, nor even seriously posed. But the alliance of these two classes can be realised in no other way than through an irreconcilable struggle against the influence of the national liberal bourgeoisie.

> 4. No matter what the first episodic stages of the revolution may be in the individual countries, the realisation of the revolutionary alliance between the proletariat and the peasantry is conceivable only under the political leadership of the proletarian vanguard, organised in the CCP. This in turn

means that the victory of the democratic revolution is conceivable only through the dictatorship of the proletariat which bases itself upon the alliance with the peasantry and solves first of all the tasks of the democratic revolution.

5. Assessed historically, the old slogan of Bolshevism – 'the democratic dictatorship of the proletariat and peasantry' expressed precisely the above-characterised relationship of the proletariat, the peasantry and the liberal bourgeoisie. This has been confirmed by the experience of October. But Lenin's old formula did not settle in advance the problem of what the reciprocal relations would be between the proletariat and the peasantry within the revolutionary bloc. In other words, the formula deliberately retained a certain algebraic quality, which had to make way for more precise arithmetical quantities in the process of historical experience. However, the latter showed, and under circumstances that exclude any kind of misinterpretation, that no matter how great the revolutionary role of the peasantry may be, it nevertheless cannot be an independent role and even less a leading one. The peasant follows either the worker or the bourgeois. This means that the 'democratic dictatorship of the proletariat and peasantry' is only conceivable as a dictatorship of the proletariat that leads the peasant masses behind it.

6. A democratic dictatorship of the proletariat and peasantry, as a regime that is distinguished from the dictatorship of the proletariat by its class content, might be realised only in a case where an independent revolutionary party could be constituted, expressing the interests of the peasants and in general of petty-bourgeois democracy – a party capable of conquering power with this or that degree of aid from the proletariat, and of determining its revolutionary program. As all modern history attests – especially the Russian experience of the last 25 years – an insurmountable obstacle on the road to the creation of a peasants' party is the petty bourgeoisie's lack of economic and political independence and its deep internal differentiation. By reason of this the upper sections of the petty bourgeoisie (of the peasantry) go along with the big bourgeoisie in all decisive cases, especially in war and in revolution; the lower sections go along with the proletariat; the intermediate section being thus compelled to choose between the two extreme poles. Between Kerenskyism and the Bolshevik power, between the Guomindang and the dictatorship of the proletariat, there is not and cannot be any intermediate stage, that is, no democratic dictatorship of the workers and peasants.

7. The Comintern's endeavour to foist upon the Eastern countries the slogan of the democratic dictatorship of the proletariat and peasantry, finally and long ago exhausted by history, can have only a reactionary effect. Insofar as this slogan is counterposed to the slogan of the dictatorship of the proletariat, it contributes politically to the dissolution of the proletariat in the petty-bourgeois masses and thus creates the most favourable conditions for the hegemony of the national bourgeoisie and consequently for the collapse of the democratic revolution. The introduction of the slogan into the program of the Comintern is a direct betrayal of Marxism and of the October tradition of Bolshevism.

8. The dictatorship of the proletariat which has risen to power as the leader of the democratic revolution is inevitably and very quickly confronted with tasks, the fulfilment of which is bound up with deep inroads into the rights of bourgeois property. The democratic revolution grows over directly into the socialist revolution and thereby becomes a permanent revolution.

9. The conquest of power by the proletariat does not complete the revolution, but only opens it. Socialist construction is conceivable only on the foundation of the class struggle, on a national and international scale. This struggle, under the conditions of an overwhelming predominance of capitalist relationships on the world arena, must inevitably lead to explosions, that is, internally to civil wars and externally to revolutionary wars. Therein lies the permanent character of the socialist revolution as such, regardless of whether it is a backward country that is involved, which only yesterday accomplished its democratic revolution, or an old capitalist country that already has behind it a long epoch of democracy and parliamentarism.

10. The completion of the socialist revolution within national limits is unthinkable. One of the basic reasons for the crisis in bourgeois society is the fact that the productive forces created by it can no longer be reconciled with the framework of the national state. From this follows on the one hand, imperialist wars, on the other, the utopia of a bourgeois United States of Europe. The socialist revolution begins on the national arena, it unfolds on the international arena, and is completed on the world arena. Thus, the socialist revolution becomes a permanent revolution in a newer and broader sense of the word; it attains completion only in the final victory of the new society on our entire planet.

11. The above-outlined sketch of the development of the world revolution eliminates the question of countries that are 'mature' or 'immature' for socialism in the spirit of that pedantic, lifeless classification given by the present program of the Comintern. Insofar as capitalism has created a world market, a world division of labor and world productive forces, it has also prepared world economy as a whole for socialist transformation. Different countries will go through this process at different tempos. Backward countries may, under certain conditions, arrive at the dictatorship of the proletariat sooner than advanced countries, but they will come later than the latter to socialism. A backward colonial or semi-colonial country, the proletariat of which is insufficiently prepared to unite the peasantry and take power, is thereby incapable of bringing the democratic revolution to its conclusion. Contrariwise, in a country where the proletariat has power in its hands as the result of the democratic revolution, the subsequent fate of the dictatorship and socialism depends in the last analysis not only and not so much upon the national productive forces as upon the development of the international socialist revolution.

12. The theory of socialism in one country, which rose on the yeast of the reaction against October, is the only theory that consistently and to the very end opposes the theory of the permanent revolution. The attempt of the epigones, under the lash of our criticism, to confine the application of the theory of socialism in one country exclusively to Russia, because of its specific characteristics (its vastness and its natural resources), does not improve matters but only makes them worse. The break with the internationalist position always and invariably leads to national messianism, that is, to attributing special superiorities and qualities to one's own country, which allegedly permit it to play a role to which other countries cannot attain. The world division of labor, the dependence of Soviet industry upon foreign technology, the dependence of the productive forces of the advanced countries of Europe upon Asiatic raw materials, etc., etc., make the construction of an independent socialist society in any single country in the world impossible.

13. The theory of Stalin and Bukharin, running counter to the entire experience of the Russian Revolution, not only sets up the democratic revolution mechanically in contrast to the socialist revolution, but also makes a breach between the national revolution and the international revolution. This theory imposes upon revolutions in backward countries the task of establishing an unrealisable regime of democratic dictatorship, which it

counterposes to the dictatorship of the proletariat. Thereby this theory introduces illusions and fictions into politics, paralyses the struggle for power of the proletariat in the East, and hampers the victory of the colonial revolution. The very seizure of power by the proletariat signifies, from the standpoint of the epigones' theory, the completion of the revolution ('to the extent of nine-tenths:' according to Stalin's formula) and the opening of the epoch of national reforms. The theory of the kulak growing into socialism and the theory of the 'neutralisation' of the world bourgeoisie are consequently inseparable from the theory of socialism in one country. They stand or fall together. By the theory of national socialism, the Communist International is downgraded to an auxiliary weapon useful only for the struggle against military intervention. The present policy of the Comintern, its regime and the selection of its leading personnel correspond entirely to the demotion of the Communist International to the role of an auxiliary unit that is not destined to solve independent tasks.

14. The program of the Comintern created by Bukharin is eclectic through and through. It makes the hopeless attempt to reconcile the theory of socialism in one country with Marxist internationalism, which is, however, inseparable from the permanent character of the world revolution. The struggle of the Communist Left Opposition for a correct policy and a healthy regime in the Communist International is inseparably bound up with the struggle for the Marxist program. The question of the program is in turn inseparable from the question of the two mutually exclusive theories: the theory of permanent revolution and the theory of socialism in one country. The problem of the permanent revolution has long ago outgrown the episodic differences of opinion between Lenin and Trotsky, which were completely exhausted by history. The struggle is between the basic ideas of Marx and Lenin on the one side and the eclecticism of the centrists on the other.[82]

---

82   Trotsky, 2010, [1930], 310–15.

Commemorating Comrade Chen Duxiu (1942)

Translated by Donald Gasper

Translator's Introduction

When Zheng Chaolin delivered his article commemorating Chen Duxiu follow-ing the latter's death on 27 May 1942, he was undoubtedly the most suitable person for the job. Chen was the former Dean of Peking University, a key figure in the New Culture movement, one of the two co-founders of the CCP and its General Secretary for its first five congresses. Zheng Chaolin was many years his junior. He became Chen's most loyal disciple and stuck with him till the end of his life, although the views of the two eventually sharply diverged on a number of important issues.

Zheng recalls in his memoirs how while sailing to France in November 1919 to take part in the work-study movement, he had come across a copy of the magazine *Xin qingnian/La Jeunesse* (New Youth), of which Chen was the editor, and how it had revolutionised his thinking. As he wrote in his diary at the time, however, he was initially repelled by Chen's attacks on Confucius.[1] In France he was a co-student of Chen Yannian and Chen Qiaonian, two of Chen's four sons, murdered by the Guomindang in 1927 and 1928. He went on to study in the Soviet Union with them, having joined the communist movement, which in China was then headed by Chen Duxiu, in 1922.

In his memoirs Zheng wrote of the high regard in which Chen was held by progressive youth: 'We worshipped Lenin as the supreme leader of the Soviet Republic – and in China we worshipped Chen Duxiu'. He described the situ-ation within the CPC in 1925 when Peng Shuzhi and others were sent back to China to become key cadres in the party: 'As long as they got on well with Chen Duxiu, they would control the feudal lords [i.e. other party officials] by using the emperor's name and so take over the Party's commanding heights. And this is more or less what happened'. Similarly, rivals of Zheng later noted that he 'always held high the great banner of Chen Duxiu'. Zheng for his part claimed that Peng 'tightly latched on to Chen Duxiu in order to make himself more important'.[2]

---

1 Zheng Chaolin, in Benton 2015, p. 177.
2 *Prophets Unarmed.*

Peng emerged after 1929 as a leader of the Chinese Trotskyists and at one time was seen as being very close to Chen. After the defeat of the revolution in 1927 and Chen's own removal from the post of General Secretary (at a Politburo meeting attended by Zheng Chaolin), Chen too became attracted to Trotsky's theories. Zheng became a Trotskyist at almost the same time.

Following his imprisonment by the Guomindang in 1932, Chen's thinking underwent a change and he moved away from his former views. Zheng refers to this in his valedictory article, saying that by the early 1940s Chen had major differences with his erstwhile comrades: 'There were differences of opinion between us and him and these differences became greater over the last five years of the war [of resistance against Japan]'. Whether Chen actually broke with the Trotskyist movement has been the subject of debate. Gregor Benton has pointed out that Chen continued his personal links with the Communist League of China, one of the two rival Trotskyist organisations in the 1940s, right up to the unification convention of May 1941.

However, there was in my view a clear ideological rupture. This is indicated by Chen's opposition to any attempt to rebuild a Trotskyist organisation. In a letter to Trotsky of 3 November 1938, Chen said that 'a closed-door ultra-left sect [...] cannot hope to develop and if it could, it would be an obstacle to the Chinese revolutionary movement'.[3] Between 1931 and 1932, Chen had issued a call for joint action against Japan with bourgeois, petty-bourgeois and other 'democratic' parties, such as the Salvation Society, the Democratic League and the Workers' and Peasants' Party.[4] He had moved away from the slogan of a purely proletarian dictatorship (the Trotskyist position) back towards the notion of a revolutionary democracy of workers and peasants supported by other classes. However, his appeals to the 'democratic' parties fell on deaf ears. The CPC's own united front offered such parties 'a far more viable alternative'.[5]

Starting in January 1931, his attitude to the CPC-led Red Army (which he had previously claimed would collapse or become a 'White Army') also changed. He called also for working with the CPC, taking the initiative in January 1932 to publish his 'Letter to All Comrades'. Peng Shuzhi attacked Zheng Chaolin and Wang Fanxi for their articles mourning Chen, criticising them for the non-political attitude they had taken in singing the praises of a former comrade who ideologically had gone over to the enemy camp.[6] Wang conceded that 'Chen Duxiu's thinking in the final years of his life was already far from Trotskyism'. However,

---

3   Benton 2015, p. 716.
4   Miller 2016, p. 18.
5   Benton 2015, p. 30.
6   Benton 2015, pp. 562–3.

he argued that 'in mourning Chen Duxiu we had to do everything within our powers to restore him to his rightful position as the most outstanding figure in the history of modern Chinese thought and the embodiment of the entire period of Western political thought from Rousseau to Marx'.[7]

One of Zheng's motives in writing the article honouring Chen in 1942 was to defend the memory of his former mentor from the criticisms of other Trotskyists like Peng Shuzhi. Earlier, Zheng had continued to look up to Chen at a time when some Trotskyists condemned the former General Secretary as an 'opportunist'. (According to Pu Qingyuan, Chen brushed off these attacks, speaking contemptuously of his critics as 'young pups still smelling of their mother's milk'.)

Zheng's article was written at the time of the Yan'an Rectification Movement, which some say was a drive by Mao Zedong to further reduce the influence of his main rival in the Party, Wang Ming. Zheng repeatedly attacks Wang Ming, stressing that Chen Duxiu was a quite different kind of leader. Yet not once does it name Mao, who had become the party's leader seven years before at the Zunyi Conference of January 1935.

Source: Zheng Chaolin, *Huiyi lu*, (Neibu xianliang faxing [Issued in a limited edition for internal party use]), edited by Fan Yong, Beijing: Dongfang chuban she, 2004, 3 vols, vol. 2, pp. 413–417

Commemorating Comrade Chen Duxiu

Comrade Chen Duxiu has passed away.

On May 27, 1942, Comrade Chen Duxiu died of illness in Jiangjin county, Sichuan. The world revolution thereby lost a veteran commander and the Chinese proletariat a great leader.

His 64-year life is full of symbolic significance. He took an active part in the Xinhai Revolution of 1911 as a leader of the Guangfu (Restoration) movement in Anhui; he was a main leader of the May Fourth Movement and the Chinese Enlightenment. He shifted the direction of the New Culture Movement, leading its left wing to socialism. He initiated and led the Chinese labour movement during its initial phase and founded the Chinese Communist Party (CCP). He led the 1925–7 Revolution and, discarding Stalinism which buried the revolu-

---

7   Benton 2015, p. 563.

tion, accepted Trotsky's theory of permanent revolution. He became the leader of the united Chinese Left Opposition and, as a representative of the Chinese Trotskyists, was imprisoned for five years by the counterrevolutionary Guomindang government. In this capacity he also became the target of attacks by the Stalin party [i.e., the CCP] and it was in this same capacity that he died.

In the modern history of China we can find no other revolutionary of his like. From the Sino-Japanese War of 1895 to the end of the Xinhai Revolution of 1911, we have had many bourgeois leaders, including some calling themselves 'socialist' or even 'Marxist,' but when socialist ideology merged with the workers' movement they recoiled, not only abandoning socialism but sinking into the most reactionary camp. From the events of 1927 to today we have also had many leaders who have emerged from the workers' movement, but they have all been tainted by the poison of Stalinism or the line represented by Wang Ming [Stalin's most prominent agent in the CCP] and have been unable to rid themselves of these poisons. Only Comrade Chen Duxiu was able to advance from the teachings of Rousseau to Jacobinism, from there to Marxism and then to Leninism and Trotskyism. This complex and dramatic process was completed during the lifetime of one individual and it was evidently no ordinary thing that at each stage he was always in an active position of leadership. This person needed to be of an extraordinary revolutionary character, with outstanding intelligence, strong willpower and a sharp instinct, who did not make obeisance to any idol or old conventions. Comrade Chen Duxiu's character was exactly such.

In his life, Chen's transformation from the leader of the Stalin party to the leader of the Trotsky party was in our view even more difficult than his transformation from a bourgeois revolutionary to a proletarian revolutionary. After the First World War, the movement of the proletariat was already shaking the whole world. At this time it was not difficult for genuine revolutionaries to cast off the influence of the bourgeoisie and throw themselves into the proletarian movement. However, the evils of Stalinism were still fresh and one needed to have personal experience before becoming aware of them. What determined Chen Duxiu's abandonment of Stalinism was not so much Trotsky's theoretical explanation as the Revolution of 1925 to 1927, which was overseen by Stalin. Comrade Chen Duxiu was himself the one who during this revolutionary process implemented this bankrupt line.

Here we come to the issue of the responsibility for the failure of the revolution. Stalin and all the Stalinists blame it completely on Chen Duxiu's 'opportunist line.' This is at variance with the facts. The failure of the Chinese Revolution was due to the official theory of the Third International, namely, regarding the Chinese Revolution as a bourgeois democratic revolution and not as a proletarian, socialist revolution. In the course of implementing it, Chen Duxiu had already partially become aware of the error of this official theory, based on his own experiences. In 1926, he secretly proposed to the leading organ of the Third International that the CCP should withdraw from the Guomindang but this was rejected by the Third International. Naturally, he could not completely understand the tendency whereby Bolshevism was turning into Stalinism. Although he had a glimpse of the degeneration of the Soviet Union and the Communist movement in various countries, he could not explain this theoretically. This was the reason for his inability in the midst of the revolution to resist the leadership of the Third International in a resolute fashion and get the revolution onto the right track with the same resolution that he had displayed many times in his life when there had been a shift in the situation. This was the reason why he took responsibility in Stalin's stead for the failure of the revolution.

But there is one point to which we must pay attention: The spineless leaders of the CCP cannot be mentioned in the same breath as this veteran. Comrade Chen Duxiu could not renounce his views from the presidium of the Third International and adopt those of his opponents just for self-protection. Nor could he issue a *mea culpa* and beat his breast for being a despicable individual. In short, he was not one of the adherents of the Wang Ming line, not a 'leader' of this type. They are products who appeared after Lenin withdrew from work and do not have their own views, or, if they do, they do not dare reveal them. Their will is that of their superiors. They place excessive trust in the will of their superiors and their thinking is the thinking of those in the rank-and-file who have been granted the favour of the superior organs. What is valuable to them is not their own strong character but, on the contrary, their spineless-ness. What they value is not the analytical methodology of the authorities [of Marxism] but their set phrases, even the set phrases in notifications and res-olutions. Whenever new opinions are put forward, they pay attention not to whether these new opinions are in keeping with an analysis of the facts but to whether they are in accordance with the 'line' or the set phrases of the author-ities. In a nutshell, 'leaders' of this type are those who are most suitable for carrying out Stalin's line. They are not, or rarely, mass leaders who have natur-ally emerged in the course of work but people whom the superior organs take a shine to and promote. Currently the leaders of the various national sections of the Comintern are, with very few exceptions, all of this type. When Comrade Chen Duxiu was the leader of the Comintern's Chinese section [the CCP], this type of leader had already begun to emerge and there were clear signs of this. But Chen was definitely not this type of leader. He was definitely not a 'follower of Wang Ming'. His leading position in the party and his position in general in the eyes of all classes throughout the whole country was entirely the result of his own efforts. One could say that this was precisely the result of his not being in accord with Wang Ming.

However, in other respects, Chen Duxiu was, in the last analysis, a product of the special development of the Chinese Revolution. We know that there was a distance of half a century from Rousseau to Robespierre and Babeuf and another half century from Rousseau and Babeuf by way of Fourier to Marx. From Marx and Engels to Lenin and Trotsky there was another half century. However, China was able to telescope this long transition that Europe had made into just half a century. Russia's development from Chernishevsky to Trotsky was not something that a single generation of men could duplicate but China shortened this development to the lifetime of a single person and the distance was only a few years. From this it can be seen that Chen Duxiu symbolises the way China's bourgeois revolutionary movement drew closer to the country's proletarian revolutionary movement, so that one generation was able to take part in both. Chen Duxiu symbolises China's 'permanent revolution'. The drawing closer and fusing together of the two revolutions like this made it impossible to determine where one ended and the other began – this was something unprecedented in all advanced nations, including Russia. Therefore, the question of 'permanent revolution' presents itself before all revolutionaries with a special force in China, even more so than in the advanced nations.

What then is the relationship between the bourgeois revolution and the proletarian revolution in China? On this question there are differences of opinion among revolutionaries, so it is not only possible but also inevitable that there should be all sorts of differences of opinion as to the question of the strategy and tactics of the revolutionary party. Revolutionaries can definitely not suppress the existence of these divergent opinions; on the contrary, it is only if there is a thorough discussion of them that correct conclusions regarding strategy and tactics can be arrived at.

After 1929, Comrade Chen Duxiu expressed relatively many opinions on this question and these have been quite profound. Although he has passed away, his views have been left for the discussion that continues. We [Trotskyists] regard him as a leader but the fact that we regard him as the most experienced leader and the one who is most loyal to the revolution and possessed of the strongest character does not mean that we regard him as an infallible Pope. In sum, we regard him as a comrade and debate with him, even till we are red in the face. He was not a follower of Wang Ming and we definitely do not adopt the position of followers of Wang Ming in our attitude towards him. There were differences of opinion between us and him and these differences have become greater over the last five years of the war [of resistance against Japan, starting in 1937]. His article 'My Basic Views', written at the beginning of this year, may be taken as representing his last systematic views.[8] This is the last thing written by him that we have seen. Before we received news of his death, we had already decided to publish this article while at the same time expressing our different opinions, in the hope that comrades and readers would discuss his views. This is the best way for us to commemorate him.

In 1912, the year of the establishment of the Republic, Lenin wrote the article 'Democracy and Narodism in China'. It draws a comparison between the Western bourgeoisie and the Eastern bourgeoisie: 'The Western bourgeoisie has already become corrupted. It is confronted by its own gravediggers – the proletariat. But in Asia there is still a bourgeoisie which can represent the true militant democrats. It is a worthy comrade of the great thinkers and great personalities of France at the end of the 18th century'.[9] This passage was correct when it was written in 1912. However, not long afterwards the 'gravediggers' of the Chinese bourgeoisie were already standing before it. Hence China too only has a corrupted bourgeoisie, not one 'able to represent the true militant and thorough-going democrats'. For individual elements within it, bourgeois revolutionaries, to be 'true militant and thorough-going democrats', they must oppose the bourgeoisie itself and become proletarian revolutionaries. This was the path taken by Comrade Chen Duxiu. Therefore he, and not Sun Yat-sen, was China's worthy comrade of the great thinkers and great personalities of France at the end of the eighteenth century. Chen Duxiu was also a worthy comrade of Lenin and Trotsky, a Chinese Bolshevik and leader of the party of Lenin and Trotsky. His life reflected the special characteristics of the Chinese Revolution. The Chinese section of the Fourth International can be proud that it once had such a great thinker and great personality as its leader.

31st May 1942

---

8   Chen 1940. Zheng was mistaken about the date. Perhaps (because of the war) he had only recently received Chen's article.

9   Lenin 1912, p. 165.

CHAPTER 3

Love and Politics (1945)

Translated by Gregor Benton

Translator's Introduction

In 1944, Zheng Chaolin started work on a memoir, which he finished in February 1945. At the time, he never got round to publishing it. However, in 1986, after sitting on the manuscript (newly unearthed from a government vault) for several years, Chinese Communist officials authorised its publication minus the chapter 'Love and Politics', and later ordered a second printing. Access to these editions was, at the time, restricted to privileged categories of officials and researchers. Sometime in the 1980s, i.e., before the memoir was officially printed, a few copies of the manuscript were mimeographed for Party history workers, but I do not know in what form. This translation of the chapter was, at the time I first published it in 1997, the only published version of the chapter to date, for Party officials cut it, for reasons of prudery, from the 1986 Chinese edition. Even Zheng wondered in 1945 if the chapter should be published. He wrote:

> I originally intended to scrap the chapter 'Love and Politics' because it might be deemed too close in content to the gossip columns of the Shanghai yellow press and might attract adverse comment. My aim in writing it was to describe different sorts of love among revolutionaries of that period and to throw light on the character of certain revolutionaries; it was in no way to pass moral judgments. Love of any sort is permissible in a revolutionary party so long as it does not cause political damage. Most of the men and women I write about in that chapter lost their lives in the White terror and some survivors have abandoned the revolution for a genteel life. They will probably think my descriptions of their youthful love affairs slanderous. All I can do is apologise. Unfortunately, the events described in 'Love and Politics' have broader implications; otherwise I would have left them out. Readers should not forget that I, too, was implicated in them. Now as then, I am completely without feudal or bourgeois prejudice concerning relations between the sexes.

Although deleted by Zheng's official Chinese editors from the 1980 Chinese edition and consigned to the Party archive, a copy of it was discovered by chance in Hong Kong in 1990, as part of a manuscript sent there by the author in 1950. I published it in 1997 without Zheng's authorisation. In this chapter, Zheng talks not of 'husbands and wives' but of 'lovers', or *airen* in Chinese. The use of this term by revolutionaries is a reflection of the revolt by Chinese young people, in particular students, in the early twentieth century against old-fashioned views of marriage, and of their advocacy of 'free love' as opposed to marriages arranged by parents and through match-makers, 'commercial unions', sexual inequality, and wedding ceremonies in general. When young men and women fell in love, they simply began to live together. They might or might not have marked the occasion by inviting some of their relatives and friends for a meal, but they dispensed with all ceremonies, either civil or religious. Though they lived as man and wife, they avoided using these terms. Before 1949, this practice was mainly confined to Communists and progressive intellectuals, but after the Chinese Communists assumed power it became – with modifications – a national way of marriage. Now, however, China has undergone a revival of the old-fashioned style of marriage.

Love and Politics

Two or three months after I returned to Shanghai, an unexpected event disturbed my life: I fell in love and got married.

In this political memoir, I have been unable to abide by the principles that I originally set myself and have written a great deal about personal affairs and about issues that bear no relation to politics. I shall cut them. In this chapter, I do not intend to write about my own affairs of the heart, which I shall keep for a memoir of a different sort (should I ever write one). However, I will say a few things about other people's love affairs – love affairs that do bear directly on politics.

From its very inception right up to when I left France, the Communist Youth Party lacked poetic quality, and could boast not a single romance. The reason was quite simple: there were no women comrades. Cai Chang, the younger sister of Cai Hesen, was still in France. I do not know if she took part in our organisation, but I never saw her at either of the two Congresses or on any of my frequent trips to Paris. Her lover Ouyang Ze, one of my philosopher friends, was deported from France after the Lyon University campaign. Cai Chang's mother did not like Ouyang Ze. Instead, she had set her eyes on Li Fuchun, whom she urged Cai Chang to marry while she was in France. While I was in Moscow,

Ouyang Ze heard a false report that Cai Chang was also in the Soviet capital, so he sent a long diary for her to read, and it came into our hands; it was truly a tear a word. Ouyang Ze fell ill and started spitting blood, but he could never forget his lover back in France, and many worrying rumours reached his ears. In his diary, he recorded everything, from recollections of his life with Cai Chang to his outlook on death. I suspect that there was blood between the lines – blood from his tubercular lungs. In the spring of 1926, in Shanghai, I met Cai Chang for the first time, after she had just returned from Moscow. When I mentioned the diary to her, she gave an indifferent laugh.

In Moscow, too, there were no women comrades. That is to say, while I was in Moscow, there were none. It's quite obvious from the nicknames we gave each other that we were longing for the Party back in China to send some women to join us in the Soviet Union. We used to call Ren Bishi 'Girl Student' and Wang Renda 'Women's Delegate': a brilliant contrast to Li Weinong, whom we called 'Peasants' Delegate'. Whenever Wang Yifei introduced Chen Qiaonian to foreign comrades, he called him Kitayanka ('Chinese woman' in Russian). At KUTV, there were Korean women, Persian women, Indian women, Caucasian women, and women of many other nationalities. The only ones missing were Chinese women. We all felt very ashamed by this lack. When Bu Shiqi went back to China and arrived in Beijing, he immediately made a pass at He Mengxiong's wife Miao Boying, which caused quite a commotion. Even we in Moscow heard about it. Those returning home from Moscow seemed like sex maniacs to the comrades back in China. Luckily, the following groups to return – our groups, in 1924 – turned out to be rather more civilised. That proved that we were no crazier about sex than the comrades back in China.

When we got back, it was a long time before any of us had a love affair. It was as if we were reacting against the sacred view of love promoted by the May Fourth Movement. Jiang Guangchi was a typical example of the May Fourth attitude, for which we ridiculed him. He corresponded for many years with a girl student in Henan. Their relationship was like in a romantic novel. He used to boast about it to other people, but no one appreciated him. We all thought that 'love is petty-bourgeois'. Unlike young people in the early period of the May Fourth Movement, the great majority of those of us who had been in Russia were not against arranged marriages. Xue Shilun got leave to go home and get married, after which he stayed in Hunan to work for the Party. When He Jinliang returned to China from Vladivostok to take part in the Fourth Congress, he took advantage of the occasion to go home and get married, and he even held a traditional wedding feast. Ren Zuomin went home and brought back a wife, who turned out to be a most virtuous woman. In 1926, in Shanghai, she fell ill and died. Through carelessness, I neglected to give Ren Zuomin my condolences when I met him, which upset him a lot. Ren Bishi, our 'girl student', went back to Hunan to get married and brought his 'little wife' back to Shanghai with him – 'little wife'[1] not in the usual but in the literal sense, for she was a tiny slip of a girl. She used to deliver documents between different offices of the Central Committee, and seemed to be very capable and efficient.

The first big love storm in the Party after my return to China involved Zhang Tailei. None of the parties to it had been in Moscow. After the end of the Jiangsu-Zhejiang war, Zhang sent his mother, wife, and children back to Changzhou, and stayed on by himself in Shanghai, in a house on Moulmein Road. At night, he worked in the editorial office of Republic Daily. At that time, the Central Committee's Propaganda Department and the editorial office of Guide Weekly had both moved from the Moulmein Road premises, while Qu Qiubai and Yang Zhihua, having started an affair, had gone off to live together elsewhere in a rented room. There were many empty rooms in the Moulmein Road house, so Shi Cuntong and his family moved in. His was a university professor's family, with a mistress of the household, children, guests who were received with polite ceremony, and mahjong parties during the New Year festivities (for Shi Cuntong was a mahjong fanatic). The house on Moulmein Road took on a new air; it was no longer a nest of Bolsheviks. Gradually, Zhang Tailei and Shi's wife Wang Yizhi (when Shi published articles in Awakening he used to sign them 'Yizhi' or 'Banjie'[2]) started becoming friendly and often went out together to the Great World Amusement Centre or the Tianyunlou Variety Centre on the roof of the Wing On Department Store. One night in the editorial office at Republic Daily, Shi leant his head on his desk and started to cry his eyes out. It was a long time before he stopped. Ye Chuchang and Shao Lizi were at a loss to know what was going on, and Shi was not minded to tell them. Shortly after that, Wang Yizhi officially moved in with Zhang Tailei. At the time, Zhang was the new General Secretary of Communist Youth. Lots of people attacked him, so he failed to settle into his new job. Perhaps it was the Shanghai University students who denounced him. I heard that at one time, the Central Committee wanted to send him to Outer Mongolia to represent the Chinese Communist Party. Qu Qiubai said: they want to exile him. Because Qu spoke up for him, this General Secretary of Communist Youth was sent, instead, to Guangzhou to interpret for Borodin. He took Wang Yizhi with him, together with Shi Cuntong's child, which seemed to drive Shi mad, for he was, anyway, a very nervous sort of person. So he was admitted to hospital. Zhong Fuguang,

---

1 *Xiaolaopo*, literally 'little wife', actually means 'concubine'.
2 *Yizhi* means 'to know one thing'. It is used in a phrase together with the word *banjie*, meaning 'to understand half of it'. Together *yizhibanjie* means 'to have scant knowledge'.

a woman student at Shanghai University, wrote to him expressing sympathy and indignation. Gradually, Shi Cuntong became his old self again.[3] As I said earlier, this was the first time after arriving back in China that I had witnessed a stormy love affair. Later, in Wuhan, where I worked together with Zhang Tailei, we resolved another love problem in the Organisation Bureau of the Hubei Provincial Committee concerning an aide called Wei. Zhang suggested that we apply the following principle: 'As long as love does not harm politics, it should be considered a personal affair and the organisation should not meddle in it'. I raised my head to look at him. No one else present noticed the expression on my face, nor were they aware of all the implications of Zhang's comment, for they were ignorant of his romantic past.

I have already mentioned Qu Qiubai and Yang Zhihua, and here I would like to say something about their love history. It started before the Zhang Tailei problem, but was not among the affairs that 'harmed politics'. Yang Zhihua was pretty, gentle, soft-hearted, clever, and able, but she was also the daughter-in-law of Shen Xuanlu. Wu Ming, my fellow-member of the 'library' in France, who was arrested and deported back to China during the Lyon University campaign, ran the Central Committee of Socialist Youth in Shanghai. On one occasion, when they were about to hold some meeting or other, Shen Xuanlu wanted them to go to Xiaoshan,[4] because Shanghai was inconvenient for him. Wu Ming was infatuated by Yang Zhihua's beauty and almost went out of his mind. He wrote her a great number of despairing letters, but she ignored him. These letters infuriated Shen Xuanlu, who said, 'there are swindlers in the Communist Party'. The first time Shen Xuanlu left the Party was not unrelated to this problem. But his son and his daughter-in-law did not love each other. Shen Jianlong[5] loved a Korean girl and grew cold toward Yang Zhihua, who named her daughter Duyi[6] to demonstrate her sadness and left home to study at Shanghai University. Qu Qiubai had lost his wife, who died of TB, shortly before this happened. Her name was Wang, and she was a friend of Ding Ling[7] (then called Jiang Bingzhi). No one knows how Yang Zhihua and Qu Qiubai fell in love. One morning, at around the time of the Huang Ren case, not long after Qu Qiubai and He Shizhen had both quit Shanghai University, we got up one morning to find three strange advertisements in Republic Daily: one said that 'on such-and-such a day of such-and-such a month in such-and-such a year,

---

3   Here, there is a play on Shi Cuntong's other name Fuliang, which means to 'restore the shine'.
4   Shen Xuanlu's native place, near Hangzhou.
5   Shen Xuanlu's son.
6   Literally, 'only she'. Yang meant by this that in the world, only this girl was truly hers.
7   Ding Ling is the Chinese Communist movement's best-known woman writer.

Shen Jianlong and Yang Zhihua formally stopped being a couple'; another said that 'on such-and-such a day of such-and-such a month in such-and-such a year, Qu Qiubai formally started living with Yang Zhihua'; the last one said that 'on such-and-such a day of such-and-such a month in such-and-such a year, Shen Jianlong and Qu Qiubai formally became friends'.[8] Zhang Danfu (alias Zhang Danweng), editor of Jingbao ('Crystal'), the best-known of the Shanghai tabloids, wrote an article about the affair but gave new names to the people in it. He disguised Shen Jianlong as Shen Daohu,[9] Qu Qiubai as Qu Chunhong,[10] Yang Zhihua as Liu Shiye,[11] Shen Xuanlu as Shen Heidian,[12] Shanghai University as Lower Chang Jiang University, and the Commercial Press as the Industrial Press. For a long time after that, we called Qu Qiubai 'Spring Red'. Once, when I went to Qu Qiubai and Yang Zhihua's new house, a man came in while we were talking together. They introduced him: 'This is Shen Jianlong'. He and Qu Qiubai were like old friends. Yang Zhihua fussed over him like a girl who has left home after getting married might fuss over her older brother if he arrived on a visit. Later, Yang Zhihua once told me: 'Jianlong is noble and refined, I am too vulgar for him, I am no match for him'. But Shen Xuanlu was less magnanimous than his son. He maligned Qu Qiubai behind his back: 'He has a narrow face, he obviously has a crafty and treacherous mind'.[13] Shortly after that, Shen Xuanlu left the Communist Party for the second time. That act and his son's divorce were not unrelated. But even without this affair, he would still have left.

During this same period, student circles in Beijing were shaken by another love affair. The main female role in it was played by a friend of Ms Lu Yin, who wrote a novel about it called Xiangya jiezhi ('Ivory ring'). In Beijing's Taoran-

---

8   I have traced the advertisements. They were placed on November 17, 1924. [Note by Zheng Chaolin.]

9   Jianlong means 'sword dragon', Daohu means 'knife tiger'.

10   Qiubai means 'autumn white', Chunhong means 'spring red'.

11   Yang Zhihua means 'poplar flower', Liu Shiye means 'willow leaf'.

12   Both Xuanlu and Heidian mean 'black shop'.

13   Yang Zilie paints a completely different picture. She recalls Yang Zhihua telling her: 'My former husband led a life of debauchery. He had the habits and characteristics of the pampered son of an influential family. After my parents had decided to marry me to him at the age of nineteen, I gave birth to a daughter I called Duyi. Naturally, I tried to persuade him to put some effort into his study. My father-in-law Shen Xuanlu, a modern-minded person, asked me to stick closely to his son. I even used to traipse round the brothels after him. There was no way I could reform him. Father-in-law wanted me to go to Shanghai University to study and to divorce his son. He approved my marriage to Qu Qiubai' (Yang Zilie, Zhang Guotao furen huiyilu ('Memoirs of the wife of Zhang Guotao'), Hongkong: Zilian Chubanshe, 1970, p. 196.).

ting district, there is still a bizarre tombstone where emotional people go to pay their respects after reading Ivory Ring. The story will last forever with the novel and the tombstone. The male role in the drama was played by our comrade Gao Shangde, alias Gao Junyu, an early member of the Communist Party and of Guide Weekly's editorial board. When I first arrived in Shanghai, he happened to be there, and I met him on several occasions in the editorial department. Not long afterwards, he returned to Beijing, and not long after that, he died.

We certainly did not envy these members of the May Fourth school of love, whom we called 'petty-bourgeois'. Those playing the female role in them were not comrades; the love affairs were not grounded in the revolutionary cause. But we did envy the marriage between Cai Hesen and Xiang Jingyu, whom we called a 'model couple'. Xiang Jingyu, who was short and slight, always dressed like a woman student, and had not been at all polluted by Shanghai-style frivolity. She formed a sharp contrast with Yang Zhihua. She was a very active person who participated in the workers' movement, the students' movement, the women's movement, and the Guomindang movement, and frequently wrote short articles for Guide Weekly. She detested romantics in the Party. During or after meetings, Chen Duxiu used to like to make jokes about relationships between men and women, but if Xiang Jingyu was present, she was quite likely to protest or to say a few serious words that would embarrass him. The other comrades were even less inclined to let themselves go in her presence. All our women comrades, especially Yang Zhihua, feared her. Because she was fond of giving people advice and lectures, she acquired the nickname 'Granny' or 'Granny of the revolution'. Qu Qiubai once said, 'In our Party we have Han-Confucian Marxists, like Li Ji; and Song-Confucian Marxists, like Xiang Jingyu'.[14]

Immediately after my return to China, I lived in the same house as this 'model couple', first on Moulmein Road, then in Minhouli, and finally on Fusheng Road. After we had been living in Minhouli for some time, Cai Hesen went to Beijing to recuperate from an illness. Xiang Jingyu stayed behind in Shanghai, and threw herself into the May Thirtieth Movement. Shortly before the Mid-Autumn Festival,[15] we moved to Fusheng Road, without waiting for Cai to return. At around the same time, Peng Shuzhi returned from having fallen ill in February and gone into Baolong Hospital. He had missed the strike movement that preceded May Thirtieth and the spectacular movement of May

---

14   Confucian scholars of the Han dynasty (206 BC to AD 220) were famous for the diligent scrutiny of texts; those of the Song (960–1279) paid more attention to the essence of Confucian ethics, and in particular emphasised the importance of suppressing human desire.

15   The fifteenth day of the eighth lunar month.

Thirtieth itself; by the time that he recovered, the movement was already on the retreat. On the evening of the Mid-Autumn Festival, we threw a sumptuous dinner to celebrate the festival, the move, and Peng's discharge from hospital, and after the meal we held a soirée, which was a practice we had learned in Russia. Everyone had to give a short performance to entertain the rest. Apart from the three hosts, present were Zhang Bojian, Shen Zemin, and Shen's wife Zhang Qinqiu. Peng Shuzhi danced a Caucasian dance, Zhang Qinqiu sang 'Wretched Qiuxiang',[16] and the rest of us gave performances, too. Xiang Jingyu did not want to sing, nor did she did want to put on any other act. But we refused to let her get away with it. Finally, she recited a poem by Li Houzhu:[17] 'Silently and alone I climb the western tower …'. After the guests had left, I returned to my pavilion room to sleep, but Xiang Jingyu stayed in Peng Shuzhi's room. It was a hot night, and the doors of both my room and the front room on the same upstairs floor had been left ajar. I awakened to hear Xiang Jingyu still talking. I could not believe my ears: she was telling Peng Shuzhi that she loved him. Presently, she went up to the second floor. Peng came to my room and said:

'Something really strange has happened!' He repeated to me what I had just heard Xiang saying.

'I would never have dreamed it', he told me.

'Don't carry it any further', I told him. 'It could harm the functioning of the organisation'.

'Don't worry, I'm not interested. She knows as well that it's not right. She says she only wanted to bare her heart to me'. What he said was true.

From that day on, Xiang frequently came down from the second floor to talk with Peng Shuzhi, often for hours on end. The first few times, Peng reported to me what she had said and discussed with me 'what to do about it'. I could see that he was gradually beginning to waver, so I warned him even more urgently. After that, he did not come to discuss with me anymore. He had accepted Xiang Jingyu's love.

Cai Hesen was about to return to Shanghai from Beijing. First, he wrote to Xiang Jingyu telling her on what day and at what hour he would arrive at Shanghai's Northern Railway Station.

That day, I asked Peng Shuzhi, 'Will you tell Cai Hesen?'

'Comrade Jingyu thinks it's not necessary'.

When the time came, there was a knock at the door. I went down from my pavilion room to open it. It was Cai Hesen, his luggage loaded, together with

---

16   A popular song of the 1920s.
17   Last king of the Southern Tang dynasty, and a well-known poet.

a basket-full of Tianjin pears, on a rickshaw. He asked me where Xiang Jingyu was. 'Upstairs', I replied. He was a bit surprised that Xiang Jingyu had not come to fetch him from the station, and he thought something must have happened. The next day or the day after, the affair came out into the open. Xiang Jingyu, our 'Song academician', was unable to keep up the deceit. Cai Hesen asked her what was up. At first, she said, 'I'm trying to think out an article;' afterwards, she told him the whole story. That day or the next, the Presidium of the Central Committee met in the downstairs guest-room. Chen Duxiu, Cai Hesen, Zhang Guotao, Qu Qiubai, and Peng Shuzhi were all there, together with some non-voting attenders (whose names I forget) from Communist Youth and the Shanghai District Committee; I also forget what the meeting was about. I was present in an unofficial capacity, as was Xiang Jingyu. At the end of the discussion, Chen Duxiu was about to proclaim the meeting closed when Cai Hesen suddenly stood up and said that there was another matter he wanted to raise for discussion.

'Comrade Jingyu and Shuzhi have fallen in love ...', he said.

Chen, Qu, Zhang, and the rest of them looked like the characters in the last scene of Gogol's Government Inspector. For a long time, no one said anything, so surprised were they.

Finally, Chen Duxiu said, 'Comrade Jingyu must decide for herself'.

Xiang Jingyu put her head in her hands and wailed. Not a word passed her lips.

Chen Duxiu: 'Who do you love, Shuzhi or Hesen?'

Still Xiang Jingyu did not answer. In the circumstances, the Presidium had no choice but to decide on her behalf. The Central Committee, i.e., Chen Duxiu, Qu Qiubai, and Zhang Guotao, decided to send her to Moscow with Cai Hesen. Cai had gone south from Beijing precisely to go to Moscow to be the Party's permanent representative there. Xiang Jingyu raised no protest, so in this way, the matter was resolved. Chen Duxiu swore those present to strict secrecy about the affair, and he especially forbade Qu Qiubai to tell Yang Zhihua. Everyone promised to keep quiet about it, but pretty soon, it had become common knowledge. I think it highly unlikely that Yang Zhihua was the last to get to hear of it.

I doubt very much whether the Central Committee's decision was a right one. Of course, Xiang Jingyu did not want to decide one way or the other, but it's easy to imagine that she preferred Peng Shuzhi to Cai Hesen. Even if her mind was still not made up, in the course of time her old love was definitely likely to fade and her new love to grow. If the Central Committee had decided the other way round, or if it had let the matter take its own course and had not interfered, many later wrangles could have been avoided, for the affair had a big aftermath.

At the end of the meeting, Xiang Jingyu accused Cai Hesen of 'selfishness'.

'You knew beforehand that the Central Committee would back you up', she told him. 'Otherwise you wouldn't have raised the matter'.

What could Cai say? After supper, instead of going up to the second floor, he stayed downstairs and paced about the room. I, too, stayed downstairs.

'Chaolin', he told me, 'it's as if my heart had been cut by a knife'.

I suggested that we go and see a film. He agreed. This was something new, for in the past he had never gone to watch films or Beijing operas. We went to the Odeon Cinema, newly opened, which was showing Love Parade, starring Janet Macdonald and Maurice Chevalier. It had some beautiful scenes, bustling with noise and excitement, but Cai's heart was not in it. During the interval I invited him for a cup of coffee. The film started up again, but he was not interested, so I had no choice but to sacrifice my evening's entertainment and escort him back to Fusheng Road.

Several days passed by. On the second floor, a person lay sighing on a bed; on the first floor lay another, similarly sighing, with Xiang Jingyu constantly climbing up and down between them. It was obvious to me that things could not go on like that, so I went to see Chen Duxiu and asked him to propose a solution. After thinking for a while, he raised his pen and wrote a short note telling Cai Hesen and Xiang Jingyu to move at once to a hotel and await the steamer for Vladivostok. I took the note home and handed it to Cai Hesen, who accepted it, but Xiang and Peng hated me bitterly. Peng even had a row with me.

I said just a moment ago that the affair had a big aftermath. What I meant was that it had numerous implications, and that it influenced the later course of the inner-Party struggle. As a result of it, Cai Hesen and Peng Shuzhi became sworn enemies. At the Fifth Congress, Cai launched a ferocious attack on Peng. In the autumn of 1927, when Cai was in charge of the Party's Northern Bureau and outranked Peng, who was then Secretary of the Shunzhi[18] Provincial Committee, he reported to the Party centre that Peng had informed the police, as a result of which Wang Hebo and other comrades were arrested. The charge was so absurd that even Peng's political opponent Qu Qiubai, then in charge of the Central Committee, did not believe it.

The 'model couple' finally broke up after reaching Moscow. Li Lisan and his wife Li Yichun accompanied them on the journey. To lessen Cai's grief, Lisan told Yichun to console him en route to Moscow, but during the consolation, Hesen and Yichun fell in love. Some say that Lisan did this deliberately to get rid of Yichun so that he could fall in love with Yichun's younger sister, but whatever

---

18   Shuntian and Zhili, now Beijing and Hebei.

the case, Lisan and Hesen became deadly enemies. Not long after the Central Committee elected at the Sixth Congress in Moscow in 1928 had returned to China and started work there, an internal struggle broke out in the course of which Cai Hesen, then an important leader of the Party, was ousted from power by Li Lisan, who took his job. The incident had a bearing on my own work – I will come back to it in a later chapter. In Moscow, Xiang Jingyu fell in love with a Mongol. In 1927, she returned to China alone to work for the Party. In Wuhan, she had a tussle with Cai Hesen and accused Li Yichun of wronging her and called her names. In Wuhan, she poured herself into her work and stayed on even after the government there had turned reactionary. She never fell in love again to the day she died, as a martyr for the revolution.

Greater still were the implications for those left behind in China. Before Cai Hesen's return from Beijing to Shanghai, a vivacious woman student arrived one day at the Propaganda Department on Fusheng Road and asked me, 'Is this where Peng Shuzhi lives?' It was Chen Bilan. She had a letter of introduction from Luo Yinong to Peng asking him to look after Bilan, because she was young and green. We already knew Chen Bilan's name; in fact, she was quite famous, though she had gone to Moscow only after we had returned to China. She was Huang Rikui's wife. Chen Bilan, Shi Jingyi (Liu Renjing's wife), Cai Chang, Guo Longzhen (who had both been in France), and others formed the first group of Chinese women students at KUTV. So now, the Chinese men in Moscow could hold their own with students of the other nationalities. Li Heling (i.e., Li Helin), Huang Guozuo (i.e., Huang Ping), and Luo Jiao (i.e., Luo Yinong) immediately made advances to Chen Bilan, who was the prettiest of the batch. Luo Jiao was the leader, being Secretary of the Chinese Communist Party's Moscow branch, so he had a head start. Huang Guozuo beat a quick retreat, Li Heling cried his eyes out. Luo Jiao returned home before Chen Bilan. Though Chen Bilan had broken with Huang Rikui, she kept Luo Jiao at arm's length, for she was not really in love with him. After her return to China, she shunned him. He was in Beijing, she in Henan; when he hastened to Henan, she rushed off some-where else. Luo Yinong bit his finger until it bled and wrote Chen Bilan a letter in blood; her defences weakened and she promised to get back together with him. Later, in gaol, He Zishen told me, 'The blood was fake. Luo Yinong dis-cussed his plans with me in Beijing. I told him that if you mix milk with red ink the effect is the same'. He Zishen also told me that afterwards, he had met Chen Bilan in Shanghai and told her, but she had only laughed and tried to hit him.

Later, Chen Bilan often used to turn up at the Propaganda Department. Xiang Jingyu knew Chen Bilan from before, having advised and lectured her in Shanghai in the old days about romance. But now, Xiang had another reason to dislike her. Every time Chen Bilan turned up, Xiang Jingyu urged her to leave early, saying that Fusheng Road was too far from Chen's home in Caojiadu, that she would miss the last tram, that she would get stranded and have to stay the night. After Xiang Jingyu and Cai Hesen left for Russia, Peng Shuzhi became melancholic and depressed. He started drinking and used to get hung-over. Qu Qiubai advised him to stop drinking Chinese spirits and switch, instead, to foreign brandy to stop the hang-overs, so Peng got himself a bottle of brandy and carried it round with him in his overcoat pocket. Zhang Guotao invited him out for a walk and tried to console him by telling him about his own romantic disappointments. It turned out that Zhang had fallen unrequitedly in love with Liu Qingyang. But Chen Bilan's consolation proved more effective than Zhang Guotao's. This time, Peng initiated the courtship, to fill the hole left in his heart by Xiang Jingyu. And this time, the affair lasted.[19]

In 1925 or early 1926, Luo Yinong came to Shanghai. He had been transferred from Beijing on the recommendation of Zhang Guotao to become Secretary of the Jiangsu-Zhejiang Regional Committee. Peng Shuzhi did not oppose the appointment, but we were all worried that there would be a row, for Luo Yinong was unaware of what had happened. Wang Yifei, who was Acting Secretary, told me: 'When Yinong gets here bring him to my place first, I'll have a word with him about it'. The day that Luo arrived, Peng was not at home, and I, too, was out somewhere on business. Suddenly, Luo dashed in and went straight up to the first floor looking for Peng. The only person at home was Chen Bilan. Luo noticed that there were two beds in the room, together with some women's things. 'Has Shuzhi found a wife?' he asked Chen Bilan. Chen did not know what to say. Just at that moment, Wang Yifei turned up and took Luo off. I only found out about this incident from Chen Bilan, after I got back.

Qu Qiubai proposed trying to reconcile the two old friends. One evening, we all met together in Peng Shuzhi's room: Qu Qiubai, myself, Luo Yinong, and Peng and Chen, who hosted the gathering. First, Qu Qiubai mouthed a few pious words, intermingled with criticism of the three concerned. All I remember is a Russian word he used while criticising Chen Bilan. It was legkomyslennaya, which you can translate as 'light-minded' or 'fickle'. After Qu Qiubai, it was Luo Yinong's turn. Luo said the whole thing was unimportant, as if there were no problem. Peng Shuzhi disagreed. 'He is being pompous', he protested. 'Pompous' is the only other word I can remember from our attempt at conciliation.

---

19   Peng Shuzhi and Chen Bilan stayed married to one another for the rest of their lives; Peng died in 1983, Chen in 1987.

So after that, 'there was no problem'. Luo Yinong frequently came to the Propaganda Department to pass the time of day, and Peng and Chen frequently visited him in his home, where they laughed and joked together. During Chen Duxiu's 'disappearance', on several occasions, Luo turned up early in the morning at the Propaganda Department to ask for instructions concerning his work on the Shanghai Regional Committee from Peng Shuzhi, representing the Central Committee, and Luo sat there and talked to Peng while Peng lay in bed with Chen Bilan. At the Fifth Congress, both men were subjected to attack. After the Wuhan debacle, Luo gradually rose again in status. At first, he became Secretary of the Hubei Provincial Committee, then, he joined the Standing Committee of the Politburo, then, he became Secretary of the Chang Jiang Bureau and directed the Autumn Harvest Uprising in Xiang'egan,[20] and, finally, he became Director of the Central Committee's Organisation Bureau, like Stalin in the Soviet Union. When Peng came back from Beijing, he had to report to Luo and ask for instructions. Luo added his own big stone to Cai Hesen's secret denunciation of Peng.

One day, while I was talking and joking with Wang Ruofei and Zhao Shiyan at Luo Yinong's place, the conversation naturally turned to Luo's love life. Later, Luo said to me: 'Today at an activists' meeting there was a woman student who kept on staring at me. Do you know who she is?' He began to describe her, and I quickly realised who he meant. 'That's Zhu Youlun', I told him. 'She is He Chang's wife. Don't do anything silly'. He replied that he had no intention of trying to steal a comrade's wife. Indirectly, he was criticising Peng Shuzhi. At the time, He Chang was in Moscow. After a while, Zhu Youlun and Luo Yinong started living together. Just at that time, Zhu's mother brought her youngest son with her to Shanghai from Sichuan and moved into Luo's residence as his mother-in-law. Several of us used to spend a lot of time there playing mahjong with her.

It was not He Chang himself but two professor comrades, Shi Cuntong and Li Ji from Shanghai University, who protested at this love affair. Shi Cuntong's protest was entirely reasonable. He proposed a principle: if a female comrade wants to live with another male comrade, she should first formally break with her original lover. Li Ji's protest was harder to explain. He argued from the point of view of Party interest. He said: 'Luo Yinong told us in one of his speeches: we should hate as deeply as if he had dug up the grave of one of our ancestors anyone who harms the Party. Luo Yinong's behaviour today has harmed the Party'. There was an imminent danger of revolt by the students and teachers of Shang-

---

20   Xiang'egan means Hunan, Hubei, and Jiangxi.

hai University that was averted only by the intervention of Peng Shuzhi, who went to speak with these people on behalf of the Propaganda Department.

He Chang himself suppressed his feelings right up to the time of the defeat of the revolution, when Luo Yinong took over as Director of the Organisation Bureau. Only then did He Chang join together with Lin Yunan, Liu Changqun, and a few other Hubei comrades to denounce Luo to the Central Committee for various crimes committed in the course of his work in Hubei. So Luo was toppled from his special position on the Central Committee, and was even removed from the Organisation Bureau. Other members of the Central Committee, for example, Li Weihan, also had a hand in his toppling.

Zhu Youlun lived for more than a year in Luo's residence before going to Moscow to study. In Moscow, she fell in love with Shao Lizi's son Shao Zhigang. In 1928, she drowned while out rowing on the Moscow River.

When Zhu Youlun went to Moscow to study, we all sweated for Luo Yinong. When people coming back from Moscow began to gossip about her, no one dared tell Luo – not until after he had become Secretary of the Hubei Provincial Committee and joined the Politburo did he finally hear the news. At the time, Wuhan was already under the pall of reaction. Of the beautiful women comrades who had previously sought the limelight in Wuhan, some had gone to other places and others – especially the local ones – had withdrawn from the Party. But there was one exception. Li Zheshi, who had been in charge of the Hubei Women's Association during the high tide of the revolution, continued to work actively for the Party. Li Zheshi was an advised spinster and an intellectual, no longer young. A few months before, during Wuhan's great storm of romance, she had stayed a spectator, but this time, she was unable to withstand the determined advances of Luo Yinong and ended up abandoning her celibacy. I knew about this liaison even before I left Wuhan. Not long after I had gone back to Shanghai, Luo Yinong, too, arrived there with his new lover. More than half a year later, Li Zheshi went to Longhua to collect Luo's corpse. After that, she went to Moscow to study.

Only now did the sequence of events set in train by Xiang Jingyu on the night of the Mid-Autumn Festival in 1925 draw to a close. How much distress and hatred it had provoked, how many struggles it had unleashed within the Party! Cai Hesen against Peng Shuzhi, Li Lisan against Cai Hesen, He Chang against Luo Yinong, Luo Yinong against Peng Shuzhi! In the New Huizhong Hotel in Shanghai, I saw with my own eyes how He Chang asked Zhou Enlai for an interview, and how venomously he denounced Luo to Zhou. I realised even then how intimately love and politics are intertwined. It struck me that various other struggles had also been caused by love. Generally speaking, if love is not involved in an internal struggle, then both sides are cooler, more objective, more rational, and more restrained; whereas in every struggle that is excessively violent and heated, a love entanglement can generally be detected. Once, I half-jokingly, half-seriously, developed this argument in the presence of some friends, but none of them could be persuaded. They said it was 'un-Marxist'. I certainly did not base my case solely on facts, which may be incidental. What I meant was that if a comrade or a friend steals your lover, then even if you can reason it away and regard it as something separate from politics and revolution, subconsciously you will find it hard not to develop an antipathie[21] toward the thief, and if a quarrel develops, and you might otherwise have stayed neutral, you will come out against him; and if you would have come out against him anyway, you will do so all the more bitterly; and if you might otherwise have joined him, you will hesitate to do so. He Chang did not necessarily oppose Luo Yinong out of a sheer feeling of revenge, but since he anyway felt an antipathy to Luo, he used the opportunity to vent it. And it was less because of the revolution in Hubei than because of Zhu Youlun.

But there were exceptions. I still remember to this day my friend Yan Changyi, who was so noble-minded that even when his lover was stolen away from him he harboured not the slightest rancour. He and Xia Zhixu had been together for many years, but at a certain point one had to go to Shanghai for the Party while the other stayed in Beijing. One day, when Zhao Shiyan was passing through Shanghai, someone – I forget who – invited us out for a meal at the Xinya Cantonese Restaurant on North Sichuan Road, and Yan Changyi was among the guests. At the time, I had never met Xia Zhixu; all I knew was that she was Yan's lover. During the meal, I asked Yan whether she had written recently. 'She is Zhao Shiyan's lover now', he told me. He said it quite innocently, but Zhao Shiyan blushed violently. It was only then that I realised that I had said the wrong thing. Yan was not being insincere – I knew his character quite well; he was not that sort of person.

Chen Qiaonian lacked Zhao Shiyan's good fortune. His love affair with Shi Jingyi happened at more or less the same time as Zhao Shiyan's with Xia Zhixu, but it caused an almighty storm. Shi Jingyi had originally been Liu Renjing's wife, but after Liu brought her to the city, he fell out of love with her, so he sent her to Moscow to be a student. After she had become more cultured, she, in turn, fell out of love with Liu Renjing, who then gradually fell back in love with her. When she returned to China, she stayed in Beijing to work for the Party, having no wish to go to Shanghai to live with Liu Renjing. Liu Renjing was then editor of China Youth, and since I often used to go to Communist Youth

---

21   This word is in French in the original.

headquarters to pass the time of day, I became his friend and wrote something for China Youth almost every week. One Sunday in the autumn of 1926, some young people at Communist Youth decided to organise an outing to Wusong. Liu Renjing and I went along with them. Liu seemed downcast throughout the entire trip. On the way back, while we were waiting for the train at the railway station, I suddenly noticed that Liu Renjing had a bandaged finger. I asked him what had happened. He did not answer, and someone else steered the conversation round to another subject. I thought it was all very strange. Later on, someone else – perhaps it was Liu Changqun – quietly told me, 'Liu Renjing cut his finger on purpose to write a letter to Shi Jingyi. We organised the excursion to drive away his cares'. And it was true! His was real blood, not milk and ink.

Shortly afterwards, Liu Renjing went to Moscow to become a student. It was not Liu Renjing himself but Liu's fellow-provincials from Hubei who criticised Chen Qiaonian. They all along harboured an antipathy toward Chen. Later, when the Hubei comrades were accusing Luo Yinong, one item on the charge sheet was that when Chen Qiaonian had fallen ill with typhoid fever (at the time he was in charge of the Hubei Committee's Organisation Department), he had been given several thousand dollars for his medical expenses by Luo, who was Secretary of the Committee. Before the Fifth Congress, Chen Yannian went to Beijing for a meeting and found out about the attacks on Chen Qiaonian. Passing through Shanghai on his way back to Guangdong, he revealed to me his dissatisfaction with his younger brother. It was the first time I had heard him speak like that.

Chen Yannian never had a single love affair, from the day that he was born to the day he died.

Like Chen Qiaonian, Yin Kuan and Wang Ruofei also got into trouble over women. Yin Kuan was sent to Shandong to be Secretary of the Provincial Committee. In that land of Confucian rites,[22] the boundary between men and women was extremely sharp. When Yin Kuan first arrived, the women comrades in the organisation always used to sit with bowed heads whenever there was a meeting, so Yin Kuan worked hard to raise their self-esteem. In their eyes, his theories, his methods of work, and his ways of dealing with problems were quite new. Everyone believed in him, worshipped him. We in Shanghai heard nothing but good about him. It would have been wonderful if only he had not become involved in a love affair. His lover Wang Bian was a girl of talent, a pearl in the palm of her ageing father. Her father was a veteran Shandong Communist; the daughter, too, was a Party member. She and Yin Kuan had fallen

---

22   Qufu in Shandong is the birthplace of Confucius.

secretly in love. Shortly after that, the Central Committee transferred Yin Kuan to Shanghai to be Secretary of the Jiangsu-Zhejiang Regional Committee. I am talking about 1925, in the wake of the May Thirtieth Movement, when Party activity was on the rise. Zhuang Wengong was not up to his job, so the Central Committee, impressed by Yin Kuan's record in Shandong, decided to give him Zhuang's post. I went to say hello. In his room was a short fat girl. 'This is Comrade Wang Bian', he said, though I had already guessed who she was even before he told me. She bowed her head and smiled.

Soon after that, I heard that some of the comrades in Shandong had written to the Central Committee denouncing Yin Kuan for 'abducting' Wang Bian to Shanghai. They were highly indignant and demanded that Yin Kuan should be punished. Most indignant of all was Wang Bian's father, who was prepared to go to Shanghai with a dagger to fight Yin Kuan to the death. To my knowledge, this was the sole occasion that a comrade was ever denounced to the Central Committee for a love affair, and in such sharp terms. (It could only happen in the land of Confucius.) But the Central Committee did not handle the question. Later, the Shandong comrades wrote a second letter announcing that Wang Bian's father had set a condition, and that if it was met, he would consider the matter a fait accompli. He said that Chen Duxiu representing the Central Committee and Yun Daiying representing Communist Youth should be chief witnesses at the couple's wedding. Again, the Central Committee ignored him. It so happened that at around this time, Yin Kuan, stricken yet again with TB, started spitting blood and was unable to work, so the Central Committee let him go on leave and sent Wang Yifei to replace him. The Comintern wanted the Chinese Party to send a batch of students to Moscow, so the Central Committee sent Wang Bian. As a result the people in Shandong calmed down. But Wang and Yin stayed in love and kept in regular touch by letter.

Moscow at the time was a hive of '"flag-switching"',[23] by which I mean that women with lovers back in China were dropping them for men in Moscow. The men whose lovers were away in Moscow – Yin Kuan included – considered themselves under threat. Comrades who came back to China after attending meetings in Moscow often used to tell stories about the Moscow love scene. Once, when Li Lisan came back from Moscow, I asked him on behalf of Yin Kuan whether any stories were circulating about Wang Bian. 'How could anyone suspect Wang Bian?' he asked me. 'She is completely loyal to Yin Kuan'. That put Yin Kuan's mind at rest.

---

23   'Flag-switching' was the term used at that time to denote General Feng Yuxiang's rebellion against his superiors Cao Kun and Wu Peifu during their war against the Fengtian warlord Zhang Zuolin. Communists applied it, by extension, to relations between men and women.

Wang Bian arrived back in China from Moscow shortly before the Guang-zhou Insurrection. The Central Committee sent her and another woman com-rade to Guangzhou to work for the Party. She knew that Yin Kuan was head of the Guangdong Committee's Propaganda Department. Her arrival in Guang-zhou coincided with the Guangzhou Insurrection, so she and the other woman comrade sought out the insurrectionary troops on the Guangzhou streets. Clutching her identity papers, she told the troops that she was looking for the Provincial Committee, but they paid her no attention. Actually, by then Yin Kuan had already returned to Shanghai, where he contacted the Central Com-mittee on behalf of the Guangdong Provincial Committee. He was staying in a hostel. When he heard that Wang Bian had already returned to Shanghai and was unable to track down the Central Committee, he placed an advertisement in the missing persons column of a newspaper. After that, the Central Com-mittee sent Yin Kuan to be Secretary of the Anhui Provincial Committee. Wang Bian, too, returned to Shanghai from Guangzhou and went to Wuhu, where she and Yin Kuan were finally reunited.

But shortly after that, Wang Bian was arrested and sent to gaol, and Yin Kuan escaped back to Shanghai to await another assignment. It was then that he joined the Left Opposition and was expelled from the official Party. Wang Bian served her sentence in Anhui and was released, and then she, too, came to Shanghai. The Central Committee told her that Yin Kuan had already been expelled, but she demanded to see him, so the Central Committee allowed her to pay him a visit. She stayed with him for two or three days; on one occasion, I met her there. She was already a fat woman and no longer a shy young girl.

In Moscow, Wang Bian had been an anti-Trotskyist, and during her brief reunion with Yin Kuan in Wuhu, he had not yet seen any Trotskyist documents, so there were no differences in their thinking. But now, in Shanghai, they no longer had a common language, so eventually, she went back to the Central Committee

Wang Ruofei's love affair caused just as great a storm as Yin Kuan's, but unlike his, it did not end in tragedy. Li Peize was a woman student from Baoding who went to Henan to work for the Party. I never met her, but people told me that she had the classical feminine graces. She Liya and Wang Ruofei both pursued her, and Wang won, so She Liya kicked up a big fuss, and some other comrades joined him. The question was raised at the Central Committee. The reason Wang Ruofei was transferred from his job as Secretary of the Henan-Shaanxi Regional Committee to Shanghai, where he led the Central Committee's Sec-retariat, was obviously because he was needed there, but it was also a way of resolving this love entanglement. At the same time, Li Peize was sent to Moscow to be a student, like Wang Bian. You can split couples up and make them live in different places, but they may still keep loving one another. Whether they manage to do so in the long run depends on who they are. In 1928, when the Chinese Communist Party convened its Sixth National Congress in Moscow, Wang Ruofei was sent as head of the Jiangsu delegation. After the Congress, he stayed on in Moscow as Party representative to the Comintern, and started living with Li Peize again.

Love affairs in Moscow must have been much livelier than back in China. I heard any number of stories, but now, I have forgotten them. In a word, Wang Bian and Li Peize in Moscow were considered 'backward' because they stuck to their old lovers. Sometimes, women left their men, sometimes vice versa. But it's up to someone else to tell these stories.

In China in those years, I only knew of one case where a male comrade left behind in China gave up his lover in Moscow. That case was Wang Yifei. When Wang Yifei first got back to China, he felt so deprived of female company that any woman would do for him, and he quickly ended up married to one called Zhang Liang. But they soon discovered that they were mismatched in character, and found it hard to keep their relationship going. So Wang sent Zhang to Moscow to be a student, while he quickly found another lover whose character was more compatible with his own. Zhang Liang in Moscow bitterly denounced Wang Yifei. When she returned to China she proved to be capable and efficient. She stayed behind in southern China after the start of the Long March in October 1934. Later, she and a group of people under Qu Qiubai tried to slip through the blockade thrown around the old Central Soviet and to reach Shanghai, but they were caught in Fujian and someone revealed who Qu Qiubai was.[24] I was in prison at the time, but in a newspaper, I read a report about this episode. Some people say that by then, Zhang was the wife of Liang Botai, others, of Xiang Ying. I do not know which if any of them is right.

At the start of this chapter, I said that I only intended to write about other people's love affairs and not about my own. However, having got this far, it seems wrong not to say a few words about myself. But I will keep my remarks short.

Not long after I had got back to Shanghai from Wuhan, I arranged to meet Jiang Guangchi in a room above the Creation Society publishing department on North Sichuan Road. After talking for a while about what each of us had been up to since we had last seen each other, Jiang took out from under his coat the latest edition of a Shanghai tabloid. It contained a news item the gist of which

---

24   The first person to identify Qu was a cook-soldier, but according to a Guomindang newspaper, Zhang Liang, too, confessed. Zhang later joined the New Fourth Army and was reprimanded by Xiang Ying, its leader.

was as follows. 'Zheng Chaolin and Jiang Guangchi have fallen out within the Chinese Communist Party over a woman. Zheng has stolen Jiang's wife. The two men took their quarrel to the Central Committee; the outcome was that Chen Duxiu decided that the woman was Zheng Chaolin's wife. So Jiang buried his head in his hands and wept bitterly'. I laughed, and so did Jiang. I forget which tabloid it was. Naturally, I knew that Jiang had been married, for he was always boasting about his Henan student wife. But I had not even seen her face, for she had died of TB at Lushan. So the report was completely without foundation. Even so, weakness lends wings to rumours, and the report can be seen as a distorted reflection of the numerous love affairs in which senior Party members became entangled in those years.

After getting back to China from the Soviet Union, for some inexplicable reason it seemed to me that I had already outgrown the age of love, so I had no interest in it and made no preparations for it. The disintegration of the 'model couple' made me even warier of romance. But at more or less the same time as Cai Hesen was languishing in agony, downstairs I was laughing and joking with Yang Fulan. Yang Fulan was a girl student at Shanghai University who used to come to the Propaganda Department every day to do two or three hours' administrative work: clipping newspaper articles, sticking up posters, sorting out materials, that sort of thing. I was in charge of this work. One day, when I had just got back from a workers' branch meeting in east Shanghai and was still wearing my workers' clothes, Cai Hesen – who happened to be in the guest-room at the time – said to me:

'Chaolin, I've got some good news for you'.

I asked him what good news.

'We'll speak about it later', he said. While this conversation was going on, Yang Fulan was sitting there with her head bowed. After a while she went out. Then Cai told me,

'You should hurry up and propose, she has fallen in love with you'.

He explained: 'I've just spoken to Fulan, I knew she wasn't married, so I said jokingly that I had to introduce you to her. To judge from her expression, she agreed'.

He seemed to me to be talking nonsense. But after that, I began to pay attention to this nineteen year-old girl, and it gradually dawned on me that maybe Cai was right. So I became friends with Yang, and we often used to go out together. In those two months, I had numerous chances to 'say what was necessary', but I did not, and later, she left Shanghai and went to Guangzhou. She was Lin Boqu's adopted daughter. When Chen Yannian met her in the Propaganda Department on one of his visits to Shanghai, he recruited her to work for the South China Regional Committee. There she got to know my friend Huang

Guozuo (Huang Ping), and after a while, they became partners. After she had left Shanghai, instead of waning my feelings for her intensified, and I regretted never having 'said what was necessary'. I tasted the bitterness of love lost. Only after Zhao Shiyan got back from a meeting in Guangzhou and told me about Fulan and Huang Ping's marriage did I gradually forget her.

But the interlude was not without its uses, for now I realised that the age of love had not yet passed me by after all, and that I could still find a girl to love me, even though I had still not vanquished my antipathy toward the love wrangles of which I had been witness in the Party.

In mid-November 1927, more than a month after reading in the tabloid about my alleged theft of Jiang Guangchi's wife, Wang Ruofei came to my home to take me out for a meal at the Jufengyuan Restaurant after two comrades had got married. The bridegroom worked in the Organisation Department of the Jiangsu Provincial Committee. It was the first time I had ever met him. But I had known the bride for a long time; her original lover had worked in the Central Secretariat, and had been seized and shot by Yang Hu half a year earlier. Another person I had never met before was a women companion of the bride who also worked in the Jiangsu Organisation Department. She was wearing a padded jacket and a black skirt. She had a plump face, white skin, and rosy cheeks, and she was wearing a pair of thick spectacles. Wang Ruofei introduced her: Comrade Liu Jingzhen[25] from Yunnan. During the course of the meal, somehow or another my attention was focused less on the bride than on Liu Jingzhen. After the meal, I sought out Wang Ruofei to make some enquiries about her. Wang told me that he had deliberately engineered the meeting because he knew that her views on love were more or less the same as those of his friend Chaolin.

Whereupon, battle commenced between me and her. She was not averse to seeing or talking with me, but she acted as if she were ignorant of my intentions toward her, and whenever I visited her, she pretended to treat me just like any other comrade. Just as we started becoming amicable, she told me she was preparing to go back to Yunnan. On several occasions, I actually lost hope, but then she would reawaken it with a few words or gestures. For several weeks, I was swayed violently this way and that, wanting to win her and at the same time fearing to do so. Every time we met, it was at her home, never at mine.

On December 24, 1927, the Central Committee wanted to discuss something with Chen Duxiu, so they sent a car to fetch him to my home, which was in the editorial offices of Bolshevik on Yuyuan Road. He was going to stay for three

---

25   Later, Liu Jingzhen adopted the alias of Wu Jingru.

days. I prepared a dinner to entertain them. 'Do you want to meet the Old Man?' Wang Ruofei asked Liu Jingzhen. 'We're eating together tonight, I'll take you if you like'. Naturally, she agreed. Only when she got there did she realise that the dinner was at my home, by which time, she had no choice but to stay. After the meal, I escorted her home. We walked together as far as the Bubbling Well Road Tramcar Station, and from there, we each took a rickshaw to her house at the intersection of Avenue Foch and Route Père Robert. On the way we arranged to meet the next day and go together to Castle Bay for an outing.

I was not involved in the discussions between the Central Committee and Chen Duxiu, so the next morning, I apologised to Chen and went to fetch Liu Jingzhen. We went together to the Northern Railway Station and took the train to Castle Bay, and after that, we went for a walk on the sandy beach fringing the Yangtze estuary. From then on my mind was made up.

We began to live together in early April, at around the time as the Festival of Pure Brightness.

Our love definitely 'did not harm politics', for there were no complications.

CHAPTER 4

Discussion on Problems of Revolution (1946–79)

Translated by Sean A. James

Translator's Introduction

Zheng Chaolin wrote the first of the three articles presented below sometime after he was released from prison in 1979. The second and third were written more than thirty years earlier, in 1946. They were published in the in the twice-monthly Trotskyist newspaper, *Xin qi* (New Banner), on 1 August and 16 August that year, as the penultimate and final parts of a series of seven articles. Parts one to four in the series had provided a general historical and theoretical background to the Chinese revolution; part five had attacked the Guomindang's concept of the revolution.

In his post-1979 article, Zheng gives us a brief but elegant recapitulation of the classic Marxist theory of revolution. Great revolutions, like the French Revolution and the Russian Revolution, are the result of the contradiction between outdated social relations and the developing productive forces. They transfer power from one class to another and fundamentally change the social structure. Such social earthquakes might be preceded or succeeded by minor tremors, such as palace or military coups, putsches, and so on but these comparatively trifling events cannot effect major social change and will, at most, transfer power from one stratum to another within the ruling class. Great revolutions cannot be artificially manufactured by 'heroes'. They are accomplished by entire classes entering the political arena *en masse*. Leaders may recognise the high and low tides of revolution and revolutionary parties may guide mass movements but cannot conjure them into being.

In the second article (part six of the series of seven) Zheng directs his fire at Mao Zedong's theory of New Democracy. New Democracy was Mao's version of the Stalinist two-stage theory of revolution, which in turn reprised the Menshevik conception of the Russian Revolution. According to Mao, the first phase of the revolution, during which at least some sections of the bourgeoisie will play a revolutionary role, will accomplish New Democracy or 'new capitalism' as Zheng derisively refers to it. Although the proletariat will play a leading role in this first stage, the revolution remains bourgeois-democratic in nature, resulting not in the dictatorship of the proletariat, but the joint dictatorship of 'all revolutionary classes'. Although Mao concedes that the first and second stages 'must be consecutive, without allowing any intervening stage of bour-geois dictatorship', he criticises those 'who are misled by the 'theory of a single revolution'' and rejects the 'utopian view' that the democratic and socialist tasks can be accomplished simultaneously, insisting rather that the socialist stage be preceded by a period of New Democracy. Zheng argues that Mao's the-ory will inevitably lead, in practice, to Communist submission to Guomindang ideology and leadership.

In the seventh and concluding article in the series, Zheng criticises the manner in which the Trotskyist majority leader, Peng Shuzhi, expounds the Trotskyist theory of permanent revolution. Zheng and Peng mutually accuse each other of failing to understand the theory and its application in China. In his report on 'Trotskyism in China', published in the July-August 1947 issue of *Fourth International*, Peng chastises Zheng and the 'New Flag' group:

> While we preached the elementary ideas of the Permanent Revolution, as a revolution starting from the democratic struggle to the goal of socialism, they condemned us as opportunists, because, according to their concep-tions, the Chinese revolution will be a Socialist revolution from the very beginning. 'Either Socialism or imperialism,' they proclaimed. Yesterday in a colonial war resisting imperialism, they took the position of defeat-ism – because the war was under the leadership of the Guomindang. Today when the Chinese people are only beginning to fight for element-ary democratic demands, they take a passive position – nothing less than socialism! As if the promised socialism would drop from the sky and does not grow out of the dirty ground of daily struggles. Everything is over-simplified and transformed into a lifeless abstraction.[1]

Zheng, on the contrary, argues that by suggesting the democratic tasks will pre-cede the socialist tasks, Peng upholds the notion of two-stage revolution in the same way that Mao's notion of a 'New Democratic' stage does. Such a concep-tion, he warns, will lead Peng and his supporters to oppose any revolutionary struggle of the workers or peasants that goes beyond democratic demands by threatening private property rights.

---

1 'Trotskyism in China – A Report (July 1947)', accessed March 12, 2020 www.marxists.org.

Discussion on Problems of Revolution (1979)

Translation source: 'Mu De (Zheng Chaolín): *Geming wenti mantan*'. https://www.marxists.org/chinese/zhengchaolin/marxist.org-chinese-zhengchaolin-1940.htm. Accessed 28 December 2019.

All of the problems of revolution we are discussing here are more historical than current, more theoretical than practical, and the scope is limited to the period before the Communist Party's 1949 seizure of political power. Even so, revolutionary theory remains the guide to revolutionary action, so even though this is an historical investigation, it still has unparalleled practical significance for the future development of the revolution.

First of all, we need to understand: what are the objectives of the revolution?

Revolution is the critical moment during the historical development from relatively lower social systems to relatively higher social systems, a juncture that cannot be by-passed. The development of human history is driven by the development of social productive forces. When the productive forces develop to a certain stage, human society forms certain necessary corresponding relations of production. The sum of these relations of production constitutes the social economy, and on the economic foundations is constructed the political, legal, religious, and ideological edifice. The economic foundations and the various superstructures constitute the social system. At first, the social system is compatible with the productive forces, and it can facilitate advances in the development of the productive forces. However, as the productive forces continue to develop, this compatibility gradually declines, and gradually the social system can no longer facilitate the development of the productive forces but will rather hinder it. As a result, social relations become fetters upon the productive forces, and a struggle develops between them. Finally, the productive forces break through these fetters, leaping forward to destroy the old social system and establish a new one. This is revolution. As the development of productive forces advances, the new social system again gradually becomes antiquated and a hindrance, at which point comes another revolution. And so it goes on. As far as human relations are concerned, revolution first of all represents the rise and fall of social classes. The dominant class of the old social system is overthrown, and one or more of the oppressed classes of the previous period rise to prominence in the new social system. In times of revolution, the normal, peace-time class struggle reaches a peak and arrives at the decisive battle. This is an overtly violent and ruthless life-and-death struggle, but it is inevitable.

In modern history we have seen many revolutions, from the sixteenth-century Dutch War of Independence to the more recent Spanish Revolution. According to their characteristics, we can generally divide the various revolutions of modern times into two categories: the bourgeois-democratic revolution and the proletarian-socialist revolution. The former destroys the feudal or pre-capitalist social system and replaces it with the capitalist social system; the latter destroys the capitalist social system and replaces it with a socialist social system. The former makes the bourgeoisie ruler of society, while the latter first makes the proletariat ruler of society, and then gradually abolishes all social class distinctions.

After a country has completed a revolution of one of these types, it is often supplemented by one or several relatively small revolutions, such as the French revolutions of 1830 and 1848. This type of revolution does not change the social system but rather improves that social system; it does not overthrow the domin-ant class, but rather substitutes one stratum within it for another. Such revolu-tions are of relatively minor significance, and are often referred to as 'political revolutions', as opposed to the above-mentioned 'social revolutions'. From this it can be seen that a revolution's fundamental purpose is to change the social system. Even a political revolution can take place only after a country has had a successful social revolution: only after the social system has been fundament-ally transformed can it have any significance.

Secondly, we need to understand: who is carrying out the revolution?

Revolution is not the undertaking of a few heroes: it is an undertaking of the masses. Revolutionary and non-revolutionary periods are clearly distin-guished: in a non-revolutionary period, the destiny of the state is in the hands of a number of so-called politicians – some of them are emperors, kings, prime ministers, chancellors, generals, while others are presidents, premiers, secret-aries, congressmen and women, or political party leaders – in short, those who profess to govern the country in the name of God or public opinion. In times of revolution, it is the broad masses of people that directly intervene in national affairs, and the masses, with their collective action, grasp the state's highest level of power directly into their own hands. In those times, there are, of course, also politicians and representatives of the masses who execute this highest level of power, but they are simply carrying out the will of the masses. If incom-petent, they can be recalled by the masses and their positions immediately filled by other representatives. So if the masses stand outside the halls of power and only a few politicians implement various reforms from the top down, no matter how virtuous they are, no matter how good the reforms are and how effective they are, they still cannot be called revolutions – at least not what we would call a revolution.

The masses mentioned above naturally include the military but certainly not just the military, no matter how many troops there are. It is a common occurrence in history that organised and armed troops under the command of an officer directly intervene in national affairs. These officers naturally call this a revolution and others may too, but if they are not part of a broader and deeper mass action coordinated with real mass action such military actions cannot be called a revolution. What we call real mass action is the action of the masses of the class that occupies an important position in social production.

Finally, we should understand what means the revolution employs.

Although the revolution does not exclude peaceful means, it can never avoid violence; although aimed at construction, it cannot avoid destruction. A peaceful, bloodless, purely constructive 'revolution' is not a revolution. Revolution is in essence a 'sudden change' in social development. It is 'gradual change' that has accumulated to a point at which it must leap forward. 'Revolution' contains within itself the significance of 'violence', 'destruction', 'sacrifice', and 'bloodletting'. Without destruction there cannot be construction, and the destruction accompanying the sudden change is naturally shocking and violent in nature. To summarise, here is a clear definition of revolution:

Revolution is the violent action of the masses, directly intervening in national affairs to destroy or change the old social system and replace it with a new one.

According to this definition, anything done to maintain the old social system cannot of course be called a revolution. Anything that relies not on mass action but on professional politicians or purely military action cannot of course be called a revolution. All rejection of violence, opposition to destruction, or advocacy of peaceful construction can certainly not be called a revolution.

Discussion on Problems of Revolution (1946, Part Six of Seven)

Translation source: Mu De, 'Geming wenti mantan (6)', Hong Kong, *Xin Qi* (1 August 1946).

The Communist Party's theoretical understanding is borrowed from Mao Zedong. Mao writes that the Chinese Revolution must be divided into two stages. The first stage is bourgeois-democratic in nature. As for completing this stage, '[i]f the Chinese bourgeoisie can fulfil this responsibility, no one will be able to withhold his admiration; but if it cannot do so, the responsibility will inevitably fall upon the shoulders of the proletariat'.[2] After it is complete, this stage 'is def-

---

2   Mao 2005 [1940], p. 340.

initely not, and cannot be, the establishment of a capitalist society under the dictatorship of the Chinese bourgeoisie but will result in the establishment of a new-democratic society under the joint dictatorship of all the revolutionary classes in China'.[3]

The two quotations cited above need explaining.

Concerning the question of the leadership of the Chinese Revolution, the Communist Party, or at least Mao Zedong's faction, did not dare to firmly assert, as the Trotskyists did, that it belongs to the proletariat. Mao Zedong still believes that the bourgeoisie has leadership potential, if it 'can fulfil this responsibility'. Since the bourgeoisie is both revolutionary and vacillating, in theory, it can also occupy a position in the future 'joint dictatorship of several revolutionary classes'. In practice, the Communist Party would join the Guomindang government, submit to Guomindang leaders, and embrace Guomindang ideology. This would represent a simple submission to bourgeois leadership of the revolution. But I will simply point out one thing. Regarding the leadership question, I have already said enough above, so there is no need to discuss it further. As for the post-revolutionary society, since it is not socialist, it must be capitalist. Later, I will argue that so-called 'New Democracy' is actually capitalism, or 'new capitalism', as some Communist Party members have frankly acknowledged.

First, I will refute the Communist Party's 'theory of two-stage revolution'. In his pamphlet, Mao Zedong devotes a special chapter to justifying this theory and to opposing the so-called 'theory of a single revolution'. He believes that the 'theory of a single revolution' has two types: 'malicious' and 'non-malicious'. The former is propagated by people in the Guomindang. They believe that 'the Three People's Principles' apply to all kinds of revolutions.[4] I have already said that the Three People's Principles do not go beyond the scope of capitalism, nor do they encompass socialist revolution. Apart from this, Mao Zedong here refutes the words of Guomindang members and directs his reply to Guomindang members. This is not my concern here. On the other hand, it is worth transcribing what he says in opposition to the 'non-malicious theory of a single revolution':

> But there are other people, apparently with no evil intentions, who are misled by the 'theory of a single revolution' and the fanciful notion of 'accomplishing both the political revolution and the social revolution at

---

3   Mao 2005 [1940], pp. 337–8.
4   Mao 2005 [1940], p. 348.

one stroke'; they do not understand that our revolution is divided into stages, that we can proceed to the next stage of revolution only after accomplishing the first and that there is no such thing as 'accomplishing both at one stroke'. Their approach is likewise very harmful because it confuses the steps to be taken in the revolution and weakens the effort directed toward the current task. It is correct and in accordance with the Marxist theory of revolutionary development to say of the two revolutionary stages that the first provides the conditions for the second and that the two must be consecutive, without allowing any intervening stage of bourgeois dictatorship. However, it is a utopian view rejected by true revolutionaries to say that the democratic revolution does not have a specific task and period of its own but can be merged and accomplished simultaneously with another task, that is, the socialist task (which can only be carried out in another period), and this is what they call 'accomplishing both at one stroke'.[5]

It is unclear exactly who these so-called 'non-malicious single revolution theorists' are. What exactly do they mean by 'accomplishing both the political revolution and social revolution in one stroke'? We are also opposed to the 'two-stage revolution theory', but I advocate not the 'theory of a single revolution' but the 'theory of permanent revolution'. The 'theory of permanent revolution', applied to China's specific conditions, means that no matter how the Chinese Revolution begins, if it does not develop towards a successful socialist revolution, it cannot be completed. In the course of the continuous development of this revolution, not only will there be 'no allowance for any intervening stage of bourgeois dictatorship' but no allowance either for the intervening stage of the so-called 'joint new-democratic dictatorship of several revolutionary classes'. China's unfinished bourgeois-democratic tasks cannot be independently completed beforehand within a given time but must be completed together with other tasks, that is, the socialist tasks. In other words, the tasks of the bourgeois-democratic revolution can only be accomplished in the course of the proletarian-socialist revolution.

Why is it absolutely necessary to divide the revolution into two stages? Why must one revolution follow another? Mao Zedong did not explain this point but simply advanced it as a proposition that needs no proof. In fact, it is similar to the proposition that the bourgeois revolution must happen under the leadership of the bourgeoisie. In general, this proposition is not a supra-historical

---

5   Mao 2005 [1940], p. 349.

law but is determined by history. Under certain historical conditions it is valid, under others it is not. After the October Revolution in Russia, and in the present conditions in China, this law does not hold. Before the twentieth century, bourgeois revolutions were, of course, under the leadership of the bourgeoisie. The Mensheviks turned this fact into a supra-historical law, and therefore advocated that the Russian Revolution would take place under the leadership of the bourgeoisie, so they gave to the bourgeoisie the power that the proletariat had seized, believing that in 1917 there was no hope of success. In the same way, previous revolutions were necessarily divided into two stages and could only proceed from one revolution to the next. However, since the Russian Revolution of 1917, the situation has changed. Was the Russian Revolution clearly divided into two stages? No, it was not. Did it first complete the bourgeois-democratic revolution and only then begin the proletarian-socialist revolution? No, it did not.

The Russian Revolution in 1917 proceeded as follows. In February, the proletariat and soldiers rose up, overthrew the monarchy, and then handed power over to the liberal bourgeoisie. In the villages, peasants responded to the urban movement, rising in struggle against the landlord class. But from February to October, the land problem was not resolved, and other tasks of the bourgeois-democratic revolution also remained unresolved. In those eight months, the revolution deepened and widened and the bourgeois regime was in constant turmoil. Politically, economically, and socially, there was not a moment of stability. In October, the proletariat seized power and established the proletarian dictatorship. In the cities, workers' supervision of production rapidly turned into confiscation of all of the capitalists' property, while in the countryside, the struggle of all peasants against the landlords rapidly turned into the struggle of the poor peasants against the rich peasants. As a result, the land problem was resolved.

If the nature of a revolution is determined only by the change of political regime, the 1917 Revolution had two stages. Indeed, after the bourgeoisie seized political power, eight months passed before the proletariat seized power. But in general, the nature of a revolution is determined not by the change in regime but rather by the tasks it resolves. The Communist Party has always determined the nature of revolutions in this way. This means that the Russian bourgeois-democratic revolution was not completed before October. Rather, it was completed after October, that is, after the dictatorship of the proletariat had been established. This bourgeois-democratic revolution (which mainly consisted of resolving the land question), was not completed in the wake of the proletarian-socialist revolution (which brought about of public ownership of the means of production), but at the same time. So the revolution cannot be divided into two stages. One revolution does not follow on from another; rather, they are intertwined and interdependent. In short, this process of permanent revolution cannot have a 'fairly long' intervening stage of 'New Democracy'.

If this is true of the Russian Revolution, then it is even more so of the Chinese Revolution. In terms of regime change, the Chinese bourgeoisie had, no later than after the victory of the Northern Expedition, seized full political power. In terms of resolving tasks, national independence and the agrarian revolution not only cannot be resolved by the bourgeoisie but also cannot be resolved by the proletariat within the bounds of the democratic revolution. To resolve these tasks, the proletariat must both establish the dictatorship of the proletariat (or the dictatorship of the proletariat leading the poor peasantry, which means the same thing) and, at the same time or even sooner, expropriate Chinese and foreign bourgeois property, proclaim public ownership of the land, form a union with other workers' states, and so on. In short, the tasks of the bourgeois-democratic revolution can only be accomplished in the course of the proletarian-socialist revolution. These revolutions do not progress from one to the other; rather the two revolutions are intertwined and interdependent and cannot be separated. There is no intermediary New Democratic stage to speak of.

Does this need to be expressed more clearly? In that case, let's look carefully at Chinese national independence and the agrarian revolution, the two main so-called bourgeois-democratic tasks. What we call national independence does not simply mean formal independence. It does not mean being listed as one of the world's four or five strongest countries following the Sino-Japanese War or after the end of the Second World War. Nor does it mean, after throwing off Japanese oppression and gaining independence, immediately becoming a vassal of the United States. True national independence means throwing off the shackles of world imperialism. However, China is unlike other colonies. China is the safety valve of the entire imperialist system. If other colonies were to gain independence, the imperialist system could still survive. If China were to gain independence, however, the imperialist system would be fatally wounded. So the imperialists will do everything they can to prevent that happening. Such a huge task cannot be resolved by the bourgeoisie, but neither can it be resolved by the Chinese proletariat alone. The Chinese proletariat must rely on the forces of world revolution to stamp the Chinese Revolution with proletarian-socialist revolutionary characteristics. In this way, it will join up with and become part of the world revolution.

What we refer to as the agrarian revolution is also not the same as the one that happened in the now advanced countries, where it was directed only against feudal landlords. The Chinese bourgeoisie is inextricably linked with the landlord class. Far from supporting the peasants against the landlords, it will support the landlords against the peasants. The agrarian revolution is thus directed against the bourgeoisie itself. The development of this revolution cannot be accomplished until the poor peasants occupy the rich peasants' land in the countryside and the workers expropriate the capitalists' factories in the cities. But this task, historically associated with the bourgeois-democratic revolution, must also be completed by the proletarian-socialist revolution.

After refuting the 'two-stage revolution theory', the Communist Party's views on other questions regarding the revolution are easy to criticise.

The Communist Party imagines that the bourgeoisie can lead or participate in leading the Chinese Revolution. This is wrong.

The Communist Party still defines the Chinese revolution as bourgeois-democratic in nature. This is wrong.

The Communist Party still believes that after the Chinese Revolution, it will be necessary to go through a fairly long New Democratic stage before the proletarian-socialist revolution can be carried out. This is also wrong.

Discussion on Problems of Revolution (1946, Part Seven of Seven)

Translation source: Mu De, 'Geming wenti mantan (7)', Hong Kong, *Xin Qi* (16 August 1946).

Among our fellow advocates of the theory of permanent revolution is one faction that disagrees with our perspective. Their formula is different from ours.

One of their representatives wrote:

> The significance of what we call the present Chinese revolution's permanence focusses on the first point: the problem of the democratic revolution 'transforming' into the socialist revolution. The core essence of this problem of 'transformation' is the proletariat's seizure of power, the proletarian dictatorship. This 'dictatorship' on the one hand is the outcome of the democratic revolution, and at the same time is the beginning of the socialist revolution, the product of the development of the revolutionary transformation (See the discussion bulletin, 'The Current Situation and the Tasks of the Opposition', p. 1).[6]

---

6   Peng 1982 [1933] p. 47.

This formula, like Mao Zedong's formula, also distinguishes two different stages of the coming Chinese Revolution: the democratic stage and the socialist stage. The difference is that Mao Zedong believes there will be a 'fairly long' New Democratic interval between the two stages, and this formula regards the dictatorship of the proletariat as the 'key turning point' in the transition between the two stages. As the former stage is completed, the second stage immediately begins.

We oppose Mao Zedong's formula, not only because he envisions a fairly long New Democratic stage but also because he divides the revolution into two stages; and not only because he divides the revolution into two stages, but also because he insists that the democratic tasks and the socialist tasks must be completely separated and cannot be achieved simultaneously.

According to the theory of permanent revolution, the completion of the democratic and socialist tasks cannot be separated chronologically in the course of the revolution. These two tasks must be completed simultaneously after the establishment of the dictatorship of the proletariat.

According to the theory of permanent revolution, the entire revolutionary process cannot be divided into two different stages, as though the democratic revolution could be finished in the first stage and the socialist revolution will commence in the second stage. In fact, well before the democratic revolution is finished, the socialist revolution will have started. Indeed, the socialist revolution will have begun a long time before the democratic revolution concludes.

According to the theory of permanent revolution, there is no 'key turning point' between the democratic revolution and the socialist revolution. The Communist Party cannot use the dictatorship of the proletariat as this 'key point' because the democratic revolution cannot simply be completed by the establishment of the dictatorship of the proletariat. Rather, the democratic tasks of the revolution will not be completed for a long time after the establishment of the dictatorship of the proletariat.

I will cite the facts of the Russian Revolution to demonstrate these points. Was the Russian democratic revolution completed when the proletariat seized power in October? No, at that time it was absolutely not completed; rather, its resolution was just beginning.

For at least half a year after the October Revolution, the proletarian regime was still resolving democratic tasks. At the end of the Russian democratic revolution, there was no 'special phenomenon of quantitative transformation between the two revolutions, that is, a tumultuous turning point' (see page 5 of the same book).[7] The democratic tasks in Russia were accomplished in passing,

---

7   Peng 1982 [1934] p. 80.

in the course of completing the socialist tasks, and it was done in such an unexceptional way that there was no special phenomenon of quantitative transformation.

So although the formula cited claims to be a theory of permanent revolution, it really has nothing in common with permanent revolution. Rather, it is no more than a variant of Mao Zedong's formula.

That formula, in order to insist that democratic tasks and socialist tasks cannot be completed simultaneously but must be divided into two distinct stages to complete its objectives, doggedly attacks the notion that 'the third Chinese revolution will include socialist characteristics from the beginning'. It claims that, in the first stage of the revolution – the stage before the establishment of the dictatorship of the proletariat – democratic tasks can be put forward, but socialist tasks absolutely cannot be.

It says: 'The slogan of socialist tasks must be put on the agenda after the proletariat seizes power (or perhaps the following day)' (see another discussion bulletin, 'The National Assembly and Soviets', p. 11).

It does not acknowledge that the 'dictatorship of the proletariat' is itself a socialist task. From the beginning, the revolution must address the needs of the proletariat's seizure of power; thus, from the start, the revolution has socialist characteristics. It also fails to acknowledge that the Chinese Revolution in its first stage must shake up the capitalist system of private property. In the countryside, it must call for the confiscation of landlords and redistribution of their land to the peasants, and also for the confiscation of land from the rich peasants and its redistribution to the poor. In the cities, whether we want it or not, the issue of workers' management of production will very soon be upon us. Anyone opposed to the revolution being socialist from the very start will inevitably oppose any slogan and action against the system of capitalist private property and thus weaken any efforts to seize power – and, as a result, bring ruin upon the revolution.

For the same reason, the formula in question attacks the notion that 'China's democratic tasks can only be accomplished in passing in the course of carrying out the socialist revolution'. It argues that the democratic tasks must be separated from the socialist tasks, and that they must be completed independently. It does not recognise that these two tasks are intricately intertwined and cannot be completed separately. In short, the completion of the democratic tasks is unthinkable until the proletariat establishes its dictatorship, for their completion relies on the establishment of the proletarian dictatorship and they are completed in passing in the course of the socialist revolution.

Those who advocate the theory of permanent revolution necessarily believe that (1) the third Chinese revolution will be socialist in nature from the beginning, (2) China's democratic tasks can only be accomplished in passing in the course of the socialist revolution, and (3) the democratic revolution and socialist revolution are intricately intertwined and cannot be separated. Conversely, those who assert that (1) the beginning of the Chinese Revolution must not be socialist in nature, (2) the democratic tasks cannot be achieved in passing, and (3) the socialist revolution can only begin after the democratic revolution is completed (regardless of whether they consider the proletarian seizure of power to be a 'key turning point'), whatever they want to call themselves, they cannot call themselves 'permanent revolutionists' because the three points they insist on are precisely what the theory of permanent revolution opposes.

We alone have determined that the Chinese revolution will be proletarian-socialist in nature, and that it will be so from the beginning.

Of those who fundamentally oppose this conception of the revolution I would ask: do you think the objective conditions for socialist revolution in China have already matured?

Taking China alone, there is no doubt that the objective conditions for socialist revolution have not matured. However, what sets us apart from other factions is that we do not look at the Chinese Revolution from the perspective of China in isolation; rather, we look at it from an international perspective. Taking the world as a whole, the objective conditions for socialist revolution matured long ago. In 1917, Lenin also regarded the Russian Revolution in this way. He insisted that the Russian revolution was socialist in nature. Does this mean that the objective conditions for socialist revolution had matured in Russia at that time? No! At the time, the Russian democratic revolution was not yet complete. However, although Russia by itself did not yet manifest the conditions for socialist revolution, the conditions for the dictatorship of the proletariat had already matured. The main Russian bourgeois-revolutionary institutions at the time had already created these conditions, and without the dictatorship of the proletariat, the democratic tasks could not be completed. Since the establishment of the dictatorship of the proletariat is essential for the development of revolutionary institutions, after its establishment it is also essential, like it or not, to move on towards socialist revolution. Whether or not the socialist revolution would succeed, and to what extent, would be decided not in Russia alone but, of necessity, internationally, at least by several of the most advanced countries. As in Russia, so too in China. The Chinese socialist revolution must implement the dictatorship of the proletariat and go down the road of socialist revolution. Only through world revolution can socialism be truly established.

Of those who do not oppose this view of socialist revolution but nevertheless insist that the first stage of the revolution is not socialist in nature we must also ask: do you think China's democratic tasks have been completed? Or do these tasks not occupy an important position in future revolutionary struggles?

No, China's democratic tasks have not yet been completed, and they will continue to occupy an important place in future revolutionary struggles. To say that the revolution will be socialist in character from the beginning is not to ignore or underestimate the democratic tasks. However, this assertion nevertheless emphasises that the democratic movement in the Chinese Revolution must, in order to acquire the necessary strength, be under the leadership of the proletariat, and the democratic tasks can only be completed after the establishment of the dictatorship of the proletariat. Furthermore, once the revolution has begun, it is not possible to avoid putting forward a number of demands that go beyond the scope of democracy and shake up the system of private property. Conversely, anyone who insists that the first stage of the revolution is not socialist in nature will tend at this stage to oppose raising demands that go beyond the scope of democracy or could shake up the system of private property. They believe that only after the establishment of the dictatorship of the proletariat ('or perhaps the following day') can such demands be made. However, if the revolution in the countryside does not, for the benefit of the poor peasants, oppose the rich peasants, and in the cities does not demand workers' control or management of production, then whether the dictatorship of the proletariat can be established and, consequently, whether the democratic tasks can be completed in China, will remain highly doubtful. Those who insist that the first stage of the revolution will not be socialist in nature will, on the positive side, at least tell people that China's democratic tasks have not been completed and that the democratic movement can also be very important for the revolution. On the other hand, they risk overlooking the fact that the democratic movement should be led by workers and that slogans and demands that go beyond the scope of democracy should be raised in a timely manner. The Chinese masses, however, are now awaiting the revolutionary party. They do not need to be reminded how important the democratic movement is. The masses recognise its fundamental importance and have already begun an extensive struggle for democratic demands. What the masses now lack is precisely people to explain how the democratic movement can achieve victory, and why achieving the dictatorship of the proletariat and a number of associated socialist demands is necessary to complete the democratic tasks. What the masses lack is the power of proletarian leadership of the democratic movement, wherein lies the future of socialism. Only those who have defined the Chinese Revolution as socialist in nature, and moreover, as socialist from the very start, are capable of giving the masses this direction.

CHAPTER 5

State Capitalism (1950)

Edited and with an introduction by Walter Daum

Introduction

Zheng Chaolin wrote 'State Capitalism' in 1950, soon after the Chinese Communist Party (CCP) had taken power. Until recently, the document was thought to have been lost.[1] A copy was found in China, and the discoverer translated it and sent to me in New York because he knew of my work on the Marxist theory of state capitalism.[2] He hoped the translation would lead to discussion and publication. I have lost contact with him, but including his work in this collection of Zheng's political and theoretical writings is an appropriate way to fulfil his intent.

This is a significant historical document. Zheng's central argument is that state capitalism is a phase of capitalism that follows after merchant capitalism, industrial capitalism and financial capitalism; and in particular that the so-called communist countries – including the Stalinist USSR after 1937, its Eastern European satellites and China after the 1949 revolution – were state capitalist societies.

Unlike most of his self-professedly more orthodox Trotskyist comrades, Zheng held that Mao Zedong's China was not a workers' state transitional to socialism. He referred to the revolution as a 'liberation' but held that it did not abolish capitalist relations. State planning and nationalised property can occur under state capitalism as well as under a workers' state and were already underway in China before 1949. Similarly, he argued that the USSR under Stalin was no longer a workers' state, having undergone a counterrevolution that overthrew the dictatorship of the proletariat created in 1917 and that culminated in 'the annihilation of the Bolshevik leaders in 1937'.

These propositions were perceptive, especially in hindsight. In the case of China, a few decades after the revolution the ruling party restored openly capitalist relations and created the world's largest super-exploited proletariat without a change in regime. The Marxist theory of the state implies that the

---

1 It is now available on the Marxists Internet Archive. See below for source.
2 See Daum 1990.

class nature of the state would have been some form of capitalism all along. In the case of the Soviet Union, in 1992 Zheng wrote a summary of the lessons of its collapse, pointing out that the change of state power 'from one "section of the bureaucracy" to another', a 'political revolution' that maintained the class nature of the state, did not confirm the Trotskyist theory that the USSR remained a workers' state. Had Trotsky lived, Zheng added, he 'would certainly not adhere to his "degenerated workers' state" theory.'

Like any theory, Zheng's is not above criticism. Despite his insights into the Stalinist counterrevolution in Russia and the non-proletarian nature of the Chinese Revolution, Zheng's reasoning, historically and theoretically, is weak on several scores. In this limited space, I will take up two that seem the most important.

1. Zheng's reason for denying that Mao's China and Stalin's USSR were workers' states was overly narrow, in that it was based exclusively on the absence of democracy. In his sketch of the history of the USSR, Zheng wrote that it was no longer a workers' state 'because the broad masses cannot enjoy democracy.' He contrasted this with the first years of the revolution under Lenin, when 'the labourers participated in the managing of production and in the drawing up of the plan' and 'the masses participated in free and direct elections to the soviets.'

But those democratic forms survived only briefly. Because of Russia's international isolation and economic backwardness, on top of the enormous destruction of industry and of the working class caused by foreign invasions and the civil war in the years after the revolution, the workers' institutions of government, the soviets (workers' councils), were decimated and essentially died. The lack of democracy in the early Soviet state, however unavoidable given the conditions, was a signpost of the revolution's degeneration and overthrow as well as an enabler of that process.

Zheng does not take up Trotsky's view that the Soviet workers' state survived in tenuous form because major gains the working class had won in the revolution remained, despite the loss of democracy. Zheng dates the final blow to the 'annihilation of the Bolshevik leaders' to the Great Purges of 1937: 'a whole era was needed to complete this gradual process,' when 'the bureaucracy went from being a servant of the masses to being their master.' That is well past the time when democracy was choked off. This suggests an alternative view: that the destruction of the last remnants of proletarian revolutionary consciousness in the ruling party was the last gasp of the workers' state.

2. In 1950 Zheng seemed to regard state capitalism as the most advanced form of capitalism, although not historically progressive in an age when socialism is on the agenda. He said (in section 3) that it can 'ease the contradiction between socialised means of production and private relations of production.'

By 'abolishing individual private ownership, [...] the centralised and socialised productive forces are used more efficiently than by old-style capitalism.'

This capacity applied to economically backward countries like China in their early years, when they swept away pre-capitalist vestiges and escaped from imperialist looting, thereby acquiring control over their own surplus value. But the capacity was short-lived. The ruling classes of both Russia and China came to recognise that their ostensibly socialistic state capitalism retained too many concessions to the working class (e.g., full employment and the 'iron rice bowl') to enable them to exploit labour efficiently. Hence the drive for devolution back towards traditional capitalist forms. China, through its present-day hybrid of state and private capitalism, dramatically advanced its economy not by expanding state ownership but by transforming hundreds of millions of peasants into migrant labourers subject to super-exploitation by Chinese and foreign capitalists. In his 1992 draft article Zheng noted that the rulers of the 'socialist camp' recognised that their 'special state-capitalist production method' had left them economically behind their Western and Japanese counterparts, in terms both of overall economic progress and their own 'material enjoyment.' So they strove to adopt traditional capitalist methods of production and exploitation.

In conclusion, Zheng's analyses both in 1950 and 1992 highlight his lifelong dedication to the interest of the working class in liberating itself from oppression and exploitation and becoming the master of society through socialist revolution. The 1950 document expresses the optimistic expectation that the working class and the increasingly proletarianised peasantry in China would grow both in numbers and consciousness: 'We will then be able to pose revolutionary questions on a higher historical plane.'

But one more thing has to be said. In 1992 Zheng concluded that a new revolutionary wave would 'not erupt on the edge of capitalism' as in 1917 or 1949 but rather at its centre, in Western Europe and North America. This prognosis is not being confirmed by historical events. The most rebellious proletarians have been in the countries of what Trotsky called 'uneven and combined development,' where workers face the most miserable living and working conditions that capitalism can impose – yet at the same time are concentrated in huge numbers where their class power can be wielded most effectively. China is the outstanding example. Its huge super-exploited working class is at the forefront of such eruptions. As Zheng wrote in 1950, that is where 'the contradictions will be sharper and harder to mitigate.' He concluded: 'Revolutionary Marxists ought to be preparing for this prospect.' His work was a huge step towards that end.

Translation source: Yu Feng (Zheng Chaolin) *Guojia zibenzhuyi*. https://www
.marxists.org/chinese/zhengchaolin/marxist.org-chinese-zhengchaolin-1950.
htm

State Capitalism

1.

The development of capitalism normally goes through the following stages:
merchant capitalism, industrial capitalism and finance capitalism.

Merchant capitalism emerged directly from feudal society. Feudal society is
a natural economy, as social production was for the producers' and exploiters'
direct use in consumption, and only the surplus was used for exchange. Initially, there is a direct exchange between the producers, and later exchange
takes place through a middleman (the merchant). The merchants gradually
accumulate capital and take up an important position in social production,
becoming a merchant capitalist class. Early on, a part of the merchant capitalist class starts to engage in credit and soon extends its reach to pawnshops,
private banks and banking houses, distinguishing itself from the common merchant. In Europe the people who engaged in this kind of activity were the Jews,
who were looked down upon. In China, however, the most adept were people
from the Shanxi region, who played this role for a few hundred years.

The demand for commodities increased and so the merchants sidelined into
industrial production. Initially such production was the handicraft industry of
the workshops, which later became machine industry, which is industrial capitalism. The merchants and some masters of the handicraft industry formed the
industrial capitalist class, while merchants operating the credit houses became
bankers. Their capital became banking capital.

Industrial capitalism is classic capitalism. It was this kind of capitalism that
was analysed by Marx in *Capital*. Generally speaking the features of capitalism are the features of industrial capitalism; the laws of capitalism are the laws
of industrial capitalism. To put it another way, these features and laws manifest themselves most clearly and purely under industrial capitalism. Previously,
these laws were set in stone, but in later capitalism they sometimes needed to
take a circuitous route to express themselves, or they expressed themselves in
a contradictory fashion.

For example, free competition is a feature of industrial capitalism. Not only
is there free competition between every kind of sector of production but also
between every enterprise within the same sector. A great many laws are determined by free competition. But free competition contains the seeds of monopoly,

and with time the monopoly emerges. On the one hand, the larger producers swallow up the smaller ones, and on the other, the role of banks increases. Industrial capital and banking capital combine to form finance capitalism. The industrialists and the bankers become the finance-capitalist class. A minority of trusts monopolises both national and world markets. It was this kind of capitalism that Lenin analysed in his book *Imperialism*. Whatever differences there are between capitalism in the epoch of Marx and the epoch of Lenin, the latter still based his work on the laws of the former and developed them from there. Some features of industrial capitalism faded with the arrival of the era of finance capitalism, lost their significance, or were limited to partial phenomena. Finance capitalism displayed a great many new characteristics that industrial capitalism had never exhibited. Some of these new features of finance capitalism were noticed and even pointed out by Marx and especially by Engels, but a satisfactory analysis still had to wait for Lenin and his peers.

Lenin called imperialism 'the highest stage of capitalism,' and what he meant was that finance capitalism could not develop any further, and that any further development would be socialism. The October Revolution verified Lenin's position, namely, that finance capitalism was preparing the material conditions for socialism by prompting the revolution's outbreak and success, for socialism could now be built on a world scale.

Finance capitalism is the fusion of industrial and banking capital. Several financial magnates form organisations such as syndicates, trusts, cartels, concerns, etc., swallowing up or controlling those smaller industries. Here the state apparatus appears to act on behalf of the capitalist class, especially the finance-capitalist class. In the capitalist epoch the state is the 'executive committee' of the capitalist class, as Marx said at the time. But in Marx's day, the state still appeared to be neutral, standing above classes, because at that time free competition dominated in everything, production had its own laws, and little state intervention was needed. The state, representing the interests of the capitalist class as a whole, did its best to avoid intervening in the free competition within the capitalist class. Each capitalist figured the less the state intervened, the better. But with the coming of the epoch of finance capitalism the role of the state grew. Now the state not only took a firmer stand on the side of the capitalist class to repress proletarian revolt but also stood on the side of the minority of capitalist magnates to repress the small and medium-sized capitalists. Here the state is simply the 'executive committee' of a minority of capitalist magnates, their tool of repression.

The state is a tool of the capitalist magnate but it is not the capitalist magnate itself. Political power serves economic power but they are two separate entities.

But in the aftermath of the defeat of the global revolutionary wave that began with the October Revolution, state power suddenly achieved an unprecedented scope. This is commonly called 'totalitarianism.' The state intervenes in everything. The state is not merely a tool to be used but is the user. Political and economic power are combined.

As in the epoch of finance capitalism, monopolies continue to drive out free competition, large-scale production continues to drive out small-scale production and production continues to centralise and concentrate, but now production is centralised and concentrated in the hands of the state. Large-scale production is undertaken by the state, or the state annexes the large producers and monopolisation becomes state monopolisation.

2.

Finance capitalism is the fusion of industrial and banking capital, but in this new phase finance capital and the state apparatus are fused. The most obvious feature of this new phase is that the state and capital combine as one. Naturally there are other features, but those features are either secondary or derive from this, so if we are to give this new phase a name then 'state capitalism' is the most appropriate.

Unfortunately, the term state capitalism is an old designation, and yet everything that we have said about it is new, in that it is a newly developing phase of capitalism. No matter how appropriate, using an old designation for a new phenomenon always brings with it the possibility of misunderstanding, because everything that was said about it in the past was about a phenomenon of another kind or kinds.

The term state capitalism has been used for a long time, but its meaning in the past was different in every way. For the moment, we won't use the terminology of capitalist scholars but merely that of Marxism. Marx and Engels have already used this designation, but at that time it was merely used for those industries (the post, the telegraph, the railroads, etc.) where the term privately-run was inappropriate. Lenin and Bukharin also used this designation, but at the time it merely referred to the military advantage gained by the state possessing and controlling the production apparatus in wartime. When we use this term now, however, it designates the fact that: the state and capital have become one; political and economic power have become one; the state owns all or most of industry (regardless of the character of the industry); and that ownership is non-provisional.

Since state capitalism is capitalism developing further to a new phase, we call this phase 'state capitalism,' just as in the past we spoke of merchant capitalism, industrial capitalism and finance capitalism in general. The merchant-capitalist class is made up of merchants; the industrial-capitalist class is made up of merchants and industrial craft masters; finance capitalism is made up of industrialists and bankers. So what are the components of the state-capitalist class?

Generally speaking, the state-capitalist class is composed of the industrial bureaucracy and the state bureaucracy, and sometimes includes some capitalist magnates. The state accounts for 50 to 100 per cent of the means of production within the country, but the bureaucracy controls the state, while the majority of party members and upper and middle-level officials of the ruling party within the bureaucracy (the leading elements in the military, the unions, peasant associations, students' associations, women's associations, those in charge of the state organs, paid scholars, engineers, artists, musicians, opera and movie actors, etc.) all form a class that collectively owns the means of production.

There were many common points between successive forms of capitalism. In its transformation to a subsequent phase, the majority of former capitalists became a part of the newly dominant capitalist class. But there are few common points between the state-capitalist class and former capitalist classes. The traces of metamorphosis are not so evident, because the state-capitalist class is composed almost entirely of the industrial and state bureaucracy. In the previous forms of capitalism, the bureaucracy was normally a servant of the ruling capitalist class but was not the capitalist class itself. But this particularity stems from the particularity of state capitalism.

3.

In the late capitalist period all contradictions can be reduced to two fundamental contradictions: the contradiction between the socialised productive forces and the private relations of production, and the contradiction between the globalising market and the frontiers of the nation state. The only way that these two contradictions can be thoroughly resolved is through world socialist revolution.

Now that the first socialist revolution in the world has been defeated, these two contradictions have not only not been resolved but have intensified. Capitalism seeks to prolong its existence and cannot but reflect on how to mitigate these contradictions.

If we first take the second contradiction, capitalism seeks to broaden the scope of the nation state to the scope of a bloc of states. This tendency originated long ago. Initially, there were five or six blocs of imperialist powers with their corresponding vast colonies. Later this kind of form was inadequate, as these Great Powers attempted to form organisations encompassing whole continents (for example, Japan's East Asia Co-Prosperity Sphere, Germany's European New Order and the US's Monroe Doctrine). Finally, that is to say now, the world is split into two great blocs headed up by the US and the Soviet Union. Within each bloc, state boundaries have been somewhat broken down, customs barriers have been somewhat overcome, and what cannot be done within the scope of one nation can be done within the scope of the bloc. This eases the contradiction between the world market and national frontiers.

To return to the first and more important contradiction, the more capitalism develops the more the capitalist forfeits his 'productive function.' Initially the capitalist still administered or participated in the administration of his own production: one part of the capitalist's income was profit and another part was his 'salary.' Later, the capitalist entrusted administrative responsibility to high-level functionaries, namely, the industrial bureaucracy. The capitalist became a purely parasitic social organism who reaped the profits: ownership rights belonged to the capitalist, but because the rights to administration and use belonged to the industrial bureaucracy, production became more socialised. As user rights became more important than ownership, and as the role and status of the industrial bureaucracy increased, a socialisation of production resulted, and in turn nationalisation was inevitable: the industrial bureaucracy and the state bureaucracy began to combine, ownership and user rights became further separated, and the latter overtook the former. The bureaucracy enjoyed complete user rights and declared that ownership belonged to 'the state' and 'the people.' In fact, at that moment forms of ownership rights and stock interests still remained with the nationalised property of the former capitalists or fell into the bureaucracy's hands at the same time as user rights.

The bureaucracy forms a class, and this class as a whole is entitled to most or all of the means of production, but as individuals within the bureaucracy they can't privately own any means of production as individuals. Here we have private property as a class, yet no individual private property.

Not only did each kind of former capitalist class not have this particularity of the bureaucratic class, or state-capitalist class, but it is very hard to find even within the ruling classes of other former societies.

It may be very hard to find but it is not impossible. In theory, individual private property and class private property can be separated. In analysing society, Marxism paid much attention to class ownership of the means of production but little to individual private ownership of the means of production. In fact, wherever there is individual private ownership, there is also class private ownership, but if there is class private ownership this doesn't necessarily mean there is individual private ownership. Taking the Catholic Church of the Middle Ages as an example, the Church was a part of the landlord class. One third of all the land in France was Church property. The French prime minister was very often a cardinal, a leader of the Church. But the Church, not individuals within the Church, owned this one third of French land. The bishops enjoyed 'the supply system': they wore good clothes, lived in good homes, ate good food, travelled widely and enjoyed fine entertainment, etc. Not much different from the earthly nobles. The Church or certain parishes supplied all this. They could enjoy Church property as individuals but they could not privately own Church property. Only the Church itself could privately own this property. If the Catholic Church as a part of the feudal landlord class could maintain the system of private property as a class and yet abolish individual private property, then why couldn't we conclude that a part of the capitalist class (namely, the state-capitalist class) would be able to preserve private property as a class while abolishing individual private property?

Thus we can see that the newly emerging capitalism preserves the system of private property as a class, abolishes individual private property, and thereby eases the contradiction between socialised means of production and private relations of production.

But to dull the contradictions is by no means to resolve them. Under these conditions mitigating or postponing these two contradictions only makes them all the sharper.

4.

State capitalism is still capitalism but it is capitalism in its death agony. It cannot escape its ultimate destiny, though it can temporarily blunt the contradictions.

There are some who would use the term 'socialism' to refer to what we designate as a historical phase of state capitalism, but this is mistaken.

Socialism is a higher level of society than capitalism. Though in its initial period socialism cannot implement 'to each according to his needs; from each according to his ability,' at least material production ought to be more abundant than capitalism, human existence ought to be more comfortable and culture ought to be more brilliant. Although the state hasn't withered away, its repressive role would be quite mitigated. But today's 'socialist state' is quite to the contrary. The state apparatus is unprecedentedly strong. The proletariat as well as the common people are nowhere to be found within the bureaucracy and are deprived of every kind of liberty; daily necessities are still lacking; and the level of production still hasn't reached that of the capitalist countries. Referring to this kind of society as 'socialism' is to desecrate socialism.

There are others who argue that although this phase is of course not socialism, it has already emerged from capitalism and is a kind of society between capitalism and socialism. It has many names but the most familiar is 'bureau-cratic collectivism.'

Among other reasons for denying that this phase is socialist we note that many of the features analysed in *Capital* do not apply.

Certain features of a certain period, in the process of development, can change or decline or be superseded by other features. Even fundamental features such as free competition are superseded. It is a feature of capitalism but in the epoch of finance capitalism its antithesis, the monopoly, supersedes it and becomes a more important characteristic.

What then are the features that are common to every phase of capitalism? Bukharin explains in the *ABC of Communism*: 'Capitalism has three features: producing for the market (commodity production), the capitalist class mono-polises the means of production, and wage labour, which is based on the sale of labour power.'

Even if these three features are superseded by their antithesis, as when free competition is superseded by monopoly, we still should not rashly conclude that we have emerged from capitalism! But rather, that in this new stage these three features exist all the same but have merely changed their form. First of all, production goods still retain their character as commodities. There are people who for specious reasons explain that what is circulated internally is not a com-modity, but that by no means proves that the goods circulating in the world market aren't commodities. A country that has developed to this phase carries out trade with other countries in the world market. Whether a state is in this new phase or in an old phase, they all use commodities. Secondly, the means of production are still monopolised by a class and don't belong to the producers themselves, despite the difference between the new and old classes of capit-alists. Finally, society is still based on a work force that sells its labour. The labourer's standard of living is no doubt lower and the rate of exploitation is higher.

According to Marxism, we cannot conceive of some new stable form of soci-ety lying somewhere between capitalism and socialism, regardless of whether this form has a fine-sounding name or not. We believe that during the period between capitalism and socialism there is only a transitional period, which in the process of permanent revolution and the ongoing destruction of capitalist relations excludes any kind of stable form of society.

5.

Is what we refer to as a historical phase of 'state capitalism' maybe just a trans-itional period? Although it is not mature socialism, maybe it is at least socialism as it 'emerged from the womb of the old society,' or Marx's so-called lower stage of communism? Maybe those capitalist features are just unavoidable 'birth-marks of the old society' during the transitional period? This is a question that needs discernment.

Marx said: 'The first step of the proletarian revolution is converting the pro-letariat into the ruling class and conquering the democracy.' The proletariat will use its political rule to gradually seize all capital from the hands of the capital-ist class and centralise all the means of production into the hands of the state. The proletariat, with the ruling power organised in its hands, will move to build up the productive forces as rapidly as it can.

In 1917, the October Revolution happened in that way. The Russian prolet-ariat overthrew the rule of the aristocrats, landlords and capitalists, set up the dictatorship of the proletariat, nationalised the important means of produc-tion and started to administer a planned economy.

From the point of view of all that Marx said and the experience of the Rus-sian Revolution, we can view it from two sides: the political side, where the pro-letarian dictatorship conquered the democracy, and the economic side, with nationalisation and planning. These two sides constitute a whole and cannot be separated. With a proletarian dictatorship, the fact that temporarily there was no nationalisation or little nationalisation and planning was not a big deal because the dictatorship could hold out. Very soon, it would take the road of large-scale nationalisation and planning. But if there is nationalisation and planning yet no proletarian dictatorship then things are completely otherwise. Call it what you want but you can't call it socialism. Nor can you call it a trans-ition between capitalism and socialism because in theory and in fact capitalism itself can also carry out nationalisation and planning.

From a theoretical points of view, Engels said:

> [T]he transformation, either into joint-stock companies and trusts, or into State-ownership, does not do away with the capitalistic nature of the pro-ductive forces. In the joint-stock companies and trusts this is obvious. And the modern State, again, is only the organisation that bourgeois soci-ety takes on in order to support the external conditions of the capitalist mode of production against the encroachments, as well of the workers as of individual capitalists. The modern state, no matter what its form, is essentially a capitalist machine, the state of the capitalists, the ideal personification of the total national capital. The more it proceeds to the taking over of productive forces, the more does it actually become the national capitalist, the more citizens does it exploit. The workers remain wage-workers – proletarians. The capitalist relation is not done away with; it is rather brought to a head. But brought to a head it topples over. State

ownership of the productive forces is not the solution of the conflict, but concealed within it are the technical conditions that form the elements of that solution.[3]

In fact there is nothing new about a capitalist state carrying out large-scale nationalisation. The most remarkable case is the current post-war Labour government in Britain. Though the level of nationalisation there hasn't reached that of the process in Russia or the Eastern European states, its scope is so immense it has exceeded all expectations.

As for planning, it is closely linked to nationalisation. Although property belongs to a sole master, whether the state or a joint stock company, it belongs to a specific capitalist. It is always possible for the owner to institute planning within the scope of its entire industry.

Here we can see that basing the argument on whether or not there is nationalisation and planning is not enough to judge whether a state belongs to the transitional period or has already emerged out of capitalism. It is more important to know whether there is a dictatorship of the proletariat.

Nationalisation and planning under the dictatorship of the proletariat is a transitional economy. If there is nationalisation and planning but no dictatorship of the proletariat, it is still a capitalist economy or state-capitalist economy, unless it is the future higher stage of communism.

Now, how can we know whether this state is a proletarian dictatorship? A subjective standard is unreliable so we must rely on objective facts.

When most people talk about the dictatorship of the proletariat they usually pay attention to only one aspect, that of 'dictatorship.' Certainly, the proletarian dictatorship must be violent, deprive a minority of its rights to freedom, and repress some people. Of course, the democracy of the dictatorship of the proletariat and that of the bourgeoisie are counterposed: capitalist democracy is essentially a capitalist dictatorship. But this is only one side of the question. Originally Lenin stressed this aspect of the question in order to break the masses' illusions in bourgeois democracy. But Lenin didn't neglect the other side of the question, namely, that violence is only used against the oppressors and exploiters, the former rulers. They accounted for a tiny minority of the population of the country, while those who suffered their oppression and denial of rights and freedoms made up the vast majority of the labouring masses. They indeed enjoyed democracy under the proletarian dictatorship and, what's more, authentic democracy. Lenin said:

---

3 Engels 2010 [1892] p. 319.

The dictatorship of the proletariat, the period of transition to communism, will for the first time create democracy for the people, for the majority, along with the necessary suppression of the exploiters, of the minority.[4]

In fact, during the Lenin regime after the October Revolution, the Russian labouring masses did indeed enjoy democracy. The important industries at the time were taken over by the state: the labourers participated in the managing of production and in the drawing up of the plan. This is economic democracy. The masses participated in free and direct elections to the soviets, and the all-Russian soviet congress decided on government representatives and policy. This is political democracy. Because the means of production were seized from the hands of the landed aristocracy and the capitalists by the masses themselves, and the old regime was overthrown by the masses themselves, the new regime was the masses' own creation. The democracy the masses enjoyed was achieved by the masses themselves. It wasn't bestowed by any ruling party, but on the contrary the ruling party was brought to power by the masses themselves. Initially the Russian Revolution was practically unarmed or poorly armed and the Bolshevik Party was merely one of many parties supported by the masses, and within the soviets they were a tiny minority. It is only because they better represented the masses' interests that they gradually received the trust and support of the masses. From a minority in the soviets they became a majority and ultimately took power. In this situation in the epoch of Lenin it is indisputable that the Russian toiling masses enjoyed democracy. It was completely natural.

Even with nationalisation and planning, without a proletarian dictatorship capitalism still remains, so it is not a transitional period. Likewise, without democracy, without the vast labouring masses enjoying democracy (without political soviet democracy and economic management democracy), there is no proletarian dictatorship. If the means of production have all been nationalised and the state draws up and carries out a plan but the labouring masses don't enjoy democracy, how can we know if the state is of the majority or the minority? How can we know if the planned economy is in the interests of the majority or the minority? This democratic issue is not a simple formal question but is directly related to the issue of ownership of the means of production.

On the surface many similarities can be found between state capitalism and the transitional period. But just as appearance can be passed off as content,

---

4   Lenin 1960–78 [1917e] p. 468.

when the weeds destroy the lawn we must know how to distinguish the two, and the standard for discernment lies in this: do the masses really enjoy democracy or don't they?

6.

Indeed, for many years after the October Revolution Russia was a workers' state in a transitional period, although poorer than today. Although the degree of nationalisation and planning didn't reach that of today, it was indeed a proletarian dictatorship because the masses enjoyed democracy. There is no dictatorship of the proletariat today in Russia because the broad masses cannot enjoy democracy. Economically they can participate neither in administering production nor in planning, and politically they have no freedom whatsoever and the soviets no longer exist. The nationalised property in Russia today is in fact the property of the bureaucratic capitalist class, and the planned economy is in fact planned and implemented in the interests of the bureaucratic class.

In its transition from capitalism to a workers' state, Russia experienced a sudden change, where ten days were enough to 'shake the world.'[5] But the transition from a workers' state to a new capitalism, namely state capitalism, was gradual and needed more than ten years. Starting from the time of Lenin's sickness in 1923 to the annihilation of the Bolshevik leaders in 1937, a whole era was needed to complete this process. In it, the bureaucracy went from being a servant of the masses to being their master. The right to control production and to have political freedoms was gradually strangled by the bureaucracy. The whole generation of cadres that carried out the October Revolution gradually left the stage and was ultimately liquidated. During this process, on the surface the same system has continued pursuing the same Marxist-Leninism, but in fact it has undergone a great revolution, and the property of the already declining masses was seized and delivered into the hands of a privileged class. But this was an emerging privileged class and not the old privileged class.

We have followed this process with our own eyes from when it emerged and developed until it was completed, but in the past we thought it was nothing more than the growing bureaucratisation of the transitional workers' state founded by the October Revolution. We thought the soviet bureaucratic gang was merely a clique, a part of the proletariat; that bureaucratisation was merely a growth on the organism; and that Russia was still a workers' state, though

---

5   A reference to John Reed's classic book on the October Revolution, *Ten Days That Shook the World*.

deeply degenerated. We now think this is wrong. Although in the past we paid attention to the danger of capitalist restoration in Russia, we were merely watching for a counterrevolution encompassing the old landlords and capitalists or the kulaks and the Nepmen. We figured that capitalism could only be restored through the triumph of these two kinds of counterrevolution. We never imagined that the soviet bureaucracy itself could become a kind of capitalist class or could represent a kind of capitalism. When the bureaucracy seized the property of the masses, it didn't allow the kulaks or capitalists to get their fingers in the pie. Our mistake lay in this: in merely focusing on nationalisation and planning we neglected the masses' right to manage production and to exercise political liberties.

7.

In the Eastern European New Democratic states everything is nationalised, even 99 per cent nationalised, because everything is planned. But the broad masses have no right to manage production or exercise their political rights. These states, as well as current-day Russia, belong to the same genre, namely, they are all state capitalist.

But there are small differences within the larger similarities. First of all, they are different in origin. Russian state capitalism is a product of the counterrevolutionary degeneration of a transitional workers' state set up after the October Revolution, whereas in the case of the Eastern European states there was never any proletarian revolution. State capitalism in the latter states was the product of war and favourable conditions. Second, Russian nationalisation was a one-time expropriation of the property of the landlords and capitalists, an unequivocal liquidation of the landlords and capitalists. In the Eastern European states they merely expropriated the property of enemy states and local capitalist 'traitors.' They didn't set out to liquidate the landlords and capitalist class as such but merely to expropriate the property of a section among them that had cooperated with the enemy. The state capitalists and the private capitalists coexisted for a period, in accordance with the law of competition plus state intervention. The former gradually swallowed up the latter, and in the process the state sometimes offered 'compensation,' using stocks and other benefits to reward the former owners. This allowed the former owners to share in the profits of state capitalism and enter the state-capitalist class as a constituent. Finally, in comparing Russia and the Eastern European states, there is a great disparity in the magnitude of state power. With the exception of Yugoslavia, the Eastern European states were directly liberated by the Russian Red Army, so the relationship between Russia and these states is similar to that between an imperialist state and a colony.

Because there are important small discrepancies within the differences, the 'theory' of 'new democracy' was developed. There are people who say this theory was coined in China and made its way to Eastern Europe, but who invented it is not at issue. We simply want to point out: the meaning of the all-purpose new democracy in Eastern Europe is different from that in China. In China, new democracy and socialism are two different stages. During the new democracy stage you can't talk about the building of socialism: when the common programme was drafted, the CCP leaders even opposed writing about socialist perspectives. But in Eastern Europe the two meanings are inseparable: they call themselves new democratic states, or people's democratic states, but at the same time they boast that they are already constructing socialism. 'Socialism' represents nothing more than the fact that these states and Russia belong to a common genre. The 'new democracy' label, however, reflects the fact that these states after all share several important differences with Russia, not to mention with other advanced countries in the world. For example, Communist leaders in Japan, Germany, Italy, France and the US also flaunt new democracy. Certain elements within the Japanese Communist Party who called for carrying out a socialist revolution in Japan were expelled from the Party. The new democracy in these advanced countries simply reflects the demand to implement state capitalism, not by way of a proletarian revolution and a degenerating workers' state like the revolution that originally took place in Russia but rather by way of compromises with the former capitalist class, using means of 'compensation' to allow the former capitalists to benefit from state-capitalist profits, or by entering the state-capitalist class as a constituent. Or perhaps the phrase expresses their dependence on Russia for military protection or political leadership!

Russia and the Eastern European states constitute a bloc of states within which there is a relation of master to subordinates, a bloc of 'equals' within which some states give up a part of their sovereignty. And yet they still cannot combine to form a solitary state. If they are all building socialism then why do they preserve state borders?

We see that in every bastion of state capitalism there is a state-capitalist class. Between state-capitalist classes there remain intimate relations, but they still cannot become as one because there are clashing interests. Each state seeks to monopolise the right of exploitation of its own indigenous labouring masses, while the more powerful among them salivate at the prospect of enjoying the right to exploit foreign labouring masses. It is for this reason that there exist two kinds of tendencies within all the Eastern European state-capitalist classes. One faction is forced by circumstance to allow the Russian state-capitalist class to participate in the right to exploit the local labouring masses, the other refuses to grant this right and demands complete independence and an equal voice with the Russian capitalist class. The domestic political chaos within the East Europe states in the last few years derives from that urge, and that urge has a name: 'Titoism.'

Titoism only achieved success in Yugoslavia. In other Eastern European states, it came under heavy attack, and that is because the Russian Red Army did not liberate Yugoslavia. The state capitalist class in Yugoslavia didn't rely directly on Russian might to seize power, and the separatist faction within it suddenly emerged as predominant. The relationship of forces between the two factions within the other Eastern European states was completely to the contrary. Although in those states Titoism came under severe attack, it wasn't annihilated because the demand for independence (namely, the demand to monopolise the right to exploit the indigenous labouring masses) is the natural inclination of the indigenous state-capitalist class. When the anti-Titoist faction becomes fully-fledged, it will also take the road of its factional enemies.

8.

At this point China is engaged in new democracy. The CCP theorists strictly separate new democracy and socialism into two historical stages that absolutely cannot be combined. In the current stage they only allow party members to regard socialism as a distant dream, as an outlook, but not as a current task for discussion.

What the Eastern European theorists say about new democracy on this point is different. They are constructing socialism during the new-democracy phase. Yet this doesn't mean that the social nature of China and the Eastern European states is different. And it certainly doesn't mean that China intends to build socialism through a proletarian socialist revolution or that China is committed to liquidating the national bourgeoisie, won't make deals with them or won't adopt 'compensation' methods and let a section of the national bourgeoisie share in the interests of state capitalism or join the state-capitalist class as a constituent. And it doesn't mean that China won't rely on Russia for military defence and political leadership. This difference merely reflects the fact that the Chinese state capitalists hold a different ruling status: not only are they inferior to Russia but they are also inferior to the Eastern European states.

Currently, we still lack reliable statistics about the position occupied by the so-called publicly-operated economy of state capitalism within the Chinese economy as a whole. But we have statistics related to one particular region. After last year's liberation [of China by the CCP], a national capitalist organisation from Shanghai came back from a fact-finding mission to the Northeast and reported that, excluding the three important industrial cities of Fushun, Anshan, and Benxihu, the ratio of publicly-operated to privately-operated industries is 7 to 1, i.e., 87.5 to 12.5 per cent. If we include those three cities, the percentage must be a lot higher. On the commercial side, the ratio is 55 to 45 per cent. All in all, within the Northeast alone the position of state capitalism, though not as high as in the Eastern European states, is hardly inferior.

It is a pity we don't have these statistics. Let's play around with some old statistics. In an article by Xun Dixin on the direction of the Chinese economy based on an investigation in 1944, we find the following statistics: excluding the military-provisions industry, there is considerable public control in the central and provincial governments, the state shipping industry and the prefectures in the war zone: in the smelting industry publicly-owned capital exceeded private capital by 50 per cent, in the oil-refining industry by 13 per cent, in the textile industry by 23 per cent. In the machine industry state capital accounts for 70 per cent of privately-run capital; in the electric industry, for 60 per cent; in the paper industry, for 72 per cent; and in the cement industry, for 37 per cent. As for the proportion in the acid and alkali industry, the ratio of public to private capital is 8 to 1, but the strategic sites of the chemical industry are in fact in the hands of state capital, as the dimensions of certain chemical munitions factories exceed those in the private sphere in both their sum and their surplus. But arms production isn't included in these statistics. If we sum it all up, the relatively centralised public capital in the rear areas [not occupied by the Japanese] was proportionately much greater than private capital. To say the least, even though publicly owned capital in certain sectors was less than privately owned capital, the public sphere is quite centralised and its economic weight remains much more imposing by comparison.

This was the situation in the rear during the War of Resistance. After the victory the industries run by the Japanese and the collaborators were nationalised, so the proportion of publicly owned capital is naturally a lot higher. In his book *China's Four Big Families*, Chen Boda explains the situation of the post-war development of bureaucratic capital from every angle, including finance, commerce, industry, agriculture and culture. Using a May 1946 economic weekly, he roughly estimates: capital belonging to industries controlled by officials already accounted for more than 80 per cent of business capitalisation (though I doubt it)! Perhaps Chen Boda exaggerated a little, but even so his estimate favours our conclusion.

If it was that way before liberation, then what about after liberation? Although we don't have the statistics, we can imagine that the proportion of public capital would be more and not less. Not only were they public industries in the past but they remain so, and industries that in the past belonged to the four big families and other bureaucratic cliques have now been expropriated. We can imagine that the national railroads are no exception. With the exception of a small number of important mines still controlled by foreign capitalists, they have also been nationalised. There are hardly any privately run large factories in the steel-smelting industry, and the Central Textile Company's production exceeds the sum of all those in the private sector. The Commercial Trading Company and the Specialised Industry Company monopolise all the important trade. Financially, the state bank controls everything, and in the culture industry (films, news, publications) public capital now predominates.

Though there are no authentic statistics, we can say without exaggeration: within the entire country the publicly operated economy accounts for more than 60 per cent. In a word, this proportion is less than that in Russia and the Eastern European states.

If more than 50 per cent of industry is publicly owned or nationalised, then we believe this already constitutes a basis for state capitalism. In other words, from this point on it is possible to consolidate state capital with the fusion of political and economic power; it is possible for a new state-capitalist class to emerge to replace the former capitalist class; and it is possible to preserve private property as a class, abolishing individual private ownership. Not only is it possible but with such an approach the centralised and socialised productive forces are used more efficiently than under old-style capitalism.

9.

The development of Chinese capitalism (it is not a development of the productive forces, which is quite limited) passed in a very short time from industrial capitalism to finance capitalism and then to a state-run economy. Now a finance-capitalist class and a state-capitalist class have emerged in China. As such great changes have occurred since the defeat of the 1927 Revolution, fundamental questions need to be analysed anew by Chinese revolutionaries.

We now can confirm that China is not merely a typical capitalist society but a finance-capitalist society and a state-capitalist society.

So is China a colony or a semi-colony? For this we need to understand, in accordance with the normal definition, what constitutes a colony and what constitutes a semi-colony. A state that completely loses its political and economic independence we call a colony, like Korea under Japan or India under the British. If a state has formal independence but its economy is completely subordinated to the control of several great powers, and this control manifests itself as a consular jurisdiction, the right to control customs, military concessions and unequal treaties (China before the Second World War, Egypt, Persia), then these are semi-colonies. According to the broader definition, however, all countries that are politically and economically dependent could also be termed semi-colonies. Under the latter definition, not only were the

Latin American countries considered as American semi-colonies and the Eastern European countries as Western European colonies, but now even the old
imperialist states of France, Italy, the Netherlands, and Belgium are American
semi-colonies. If we consider China today as a semi-colony, then it's not by the
common definition but by the latter broader definition. If we were referring
to common, generic dependence, then the China ruled by the CCP would be
a dependency of the Soviet Union while the China of the latter Guomindang
period would be a dependency of the USA. This is similar to the relationship of
Czechoslovakia to Russia or France to America. Since we can't call Czechoslovakia or France semi-colonies, we should understand that China too cannot be
called a semi-colony.

Since China is not a semi-colony, what is the meaning of China's so-called
national independence? China already has the kind of independence that
Czechoslovakia or France has. If we still demand independence then it means
demanding independence from the Russian and American blocs on a capitalist
basis, which is impossible. Furthermore, it would mean demanding the carrying out of a socialist revolution in China.

So is China a semi-colony or not? Chinese society naturally has many 'semi-
feudal' or, if you like, pre-capitalist vestiges that are obstructing the development of the productive forces. The former capitalist class was unable and
unwilling to sweep away these vestiges. But these vestiges are no longer predominant in Chinese society, nor can they return. China is not a semi-feudal
society at all, and what's more the current state-capitalist class is willing and
able to sweep away these vestiges.

Sweeping away these vestiges is a task of the bourgeois revolution. We used
to think that the Chinese capitalist class, like its Russian capitalist counterpart,
could not complete this task. The further to the east one goes, the viler and
more slavish is the capitalist class with its intimate links with these vestiges,
and the more they fear the direct action of the toiling masses. This task must
be completed in the process of proletarian socialist revolution.

I don't think this view was wrong – on the contrary, it has been proved right
by the facts. The previous capitalist class in China could indeed not complete
this task. But the current situation is different. We have a new capitalist class
that can temporarily blunt this fundamental contradiction of capitalism. It can
use a new method, which corresponds to the development of the productive
forces and has no need to preserve or integrate these feudal vestiges. On the
contrary, it needs to liquidate the feudal landlord class and claim its entire legacy. In other words, it can carry out its land reform.

Land reform, historically speaking, means on the one hand eliminating the
feudal landlord class and, on the other, liberating the peasant. These two inter-

pretations were inseparable in the past. Historically, there were two fundamentally different modes of land reform, those of the French and Russian
revolutions. The former was carried out under bourgeois leadership and liquidated the feudal landlord class, liberating the peasant from the feudal land-
tenure system, recasting the peasant according to its own model. It transformed
the village economy into a capitalist economy in concert with the urban economy. The latter was carried out under proletarian leadership and not only
liquidated the feudal landlord class but also liquidated the capitalist landlord
class. It liberated the peasant from all systems of feudal land, using its own
model to recast the peasant. Even though the peasant became a petty capitalist, it made the rural economy cooperate with the entire transitional economy,
gradually assimilating the peasants into the working class in the common construction of socialism. They both liquidated the feudal landlord class and liberated the peasant. Naturally we are referring to the Russia of Lenin's time, not
that of a later period. In the Russia of the later period there was also assim-
ilation, but merely one of sharing the same fate as the worker in bearing the
exploitation and rule of the state-capitalist class.

In China today we can see that an ongoing land reform and the liquidation
of the feudal landlord class have practically already been achieved. We won't
even talk about the areas formerly liberated [by the CCP, before the victory of
the revolution at national level in 1949], where the land has already been distributed and the landlord class has already been liquidated. With respect to the
liquidation of this former class, of course, we have nothing to feel sorry about
and hope for its complete annihilation as soon as possible.

But who has inherited the property of this old class? Is it the peasant? No! It
is the state! Its current assets and provisions and agricultural taxes flow into the
state treasury. The land has been distributed to the peasant or will be distributed to the peasant, but the peasant must hand over provisions and agricultural
duties. In the past, the peasant had to turn over a part of his earnings from the
harvest to the landlord and another part to the state, with nothing to spare.
Now the peasant rents land belonging to the state. What they handed over to
the landlord as ground rent in the past has now changed in the sense that it is
handed over to the state.

In the not too distant future, after collectivisation has been carried out, the
land will be used collectively and the peasants will be industrialised. At that
point, it will be more obvious that the peasants are wage labourers, just like the
workers.

After China's current land reform, the peasants will not be able to exploit
their plots of land like after the French Revolution, nor will they be able to follow the workers in being masters of the state, as after the Russian Revolution.

China's feudal landlord class has been liquidated but the Chinese peasant has not achieved liberation.

But the feudal landlord class in China has after all been liquidated, as has the feudal mode of exploitation. From this day forward Chinese society more clearly reveals its capitalist nature. Thus the character of the Chinese Revolution has been simplified. From the beginning China's third revolution will be all the more a proletarian socialist revolution.

10.

Although the development of the productive forces has been quite slow in China, although it has encountered all kinds of obstacles and there are numerous pre-capitalist vestiges, Chinese capitalism has already gone through all its stages.

If we leave aside the commerce of the old society and start from when the sea lanes opened, we can say that it was then that China developed merchant capitalism. And if we ignore Li Hongzhang, Zhang Zhidong and other officials [of the late Qing Dynasty involved in attempts at industrial reform], China began developing industrial capitalism at around the time of the First World War. In the latter period of the Guomindang regime, taking war preparations and the war of resistance as a starting point, the rich and powerful family clans centralised production and developed finance capitalism. Now we have state capitalism.

The latter period of the Beiyang warlords and the pre-Guomindang regime represented the industrial and commercial capitalist class, namely, the national bourgeoisie; the latter Guomindang regime represented finance capitalism; the current CCP regime represents state capitalism. After finance capitalism developed in China, the national bourgeoisie could no longer play a leading role. It simply attached itself to a wing of the finance-capitalist class or the state-capitalist class to scramble for the crumbs. On the one hand it used the Guomindang, the democrats, the Youth Party and the Democratic Socialist Party to support the Guomindang regime, and on the other it used the democratic revolutionaries, the Democratic League and others to support the CCP regime. In China today only the finance-capitalist class and the state-capitalist class can vie for power; the other capitalists can only follow suit. The finance-capitalist class has been defeated and its power has already been reduced to one province [Taiwan] and a few islands off the coast. It would be very difficult for it to retake power on the mainland, and it is possible that its remaining power will be smashed. But it has the international finance-capitalist class as a backer, and this waning capitalist class is dissatisfied with the new regime in all respects and nurtures hopes in the old regime. Unconscious elements within the labouring masses also nurture these hopes, but the conscious ones are opposed to it, and moreover should oppose the retaking of power by the Guomindang, which represents the finance-capitalist class.

The class interests represented by the parties enumerated above are easy to understand. But how can the proletarian party understand the CCP? Does it also represent the interests of a faction of the capitalist class? This point must be explained further.

From the time the CCP was founded to when it led the 1925–27 revolution and went into the countryside and took up arms against the Guomindang, it always remained a proletarian party. No matter what kind of leftist or rightist mistakes the CCP committed, it fought in the interests of the proletariat and struggled against the bourgeoisie. After it shifted the great bulk of its forces from the city to the countryside, the CCP at least represented the peasants and the ordinary petty bourgeoisie. It did not and could not represent the ruling capitalists because the capitalist class at that time had already found the Guomindang to be a reliable representative. Moreover the capitalists hated the CCP.

But Japan invaded the Northeast of China [i.e., Manchuria] and the nation encountered serious difficulties; China underwent a great change. On the one hand, the Japanese finance capitalists made the Northeast a colony and strove to open it up for cheap labour, expropriating all of the capitalists' property. At the same time they also invested capital there, and within a short time the productive forces boomed. But Japan adopted state-capitalist measures to open up the Northeast, and a significant amount of production was concentrated in the hands of the Japanese state. Political and economic power was combined. The Northeast became nothing more than a big trust where everything belonged to the Japanese state.

Although the Japanese state itself is owned by Mitsui, Mitsibushi, and other financial groups, the Chinese state, in preparing for war, also concentrated production, and went from industrial capitalism to finance capitalism. Although production was being concentrated in the hands of the four big families, the process was carried out rapidly because it met with little resistance. This process was so successful that in a short time it exceeded that of the advanced countries. And here arose a problem: with production so concentrated, how on earth would adopting the mode of finance capitalism be more favourable? Wouldn't it be better to adopt the mode of state capitalism? The four big families naturally adopted the mode of finance capitalism but they could no longer help but overstep finance capital, and adopted several state capitalist measures. So we can see that finance capitalism was by no means the best mode. And apart from the four big family clans, there were others who proposed adopting the mode of state capitalism.

After the CCP completed its Long March to northern Shaanxi and settled down, its leaders had time to consider various fundamental questions. The process of transformation that had begun in Russia in 1923 was drawing to an end. Wasn't the CCP a member of the Third International? Didn't the Third International call on all Communist Parties to look up to the Russian party? Didn't the Russian system prove to be more effective than finance capital in dealing with highly concentrated production? Why not adopt this system for a united China after victory in the war? The CCP leaders considered the outcome and determined to go down this road, whereupon they brought forward the theory of new democracy. With themselves and the Party as the nucleus, they set about forming a state capitalist class.

There are many people who have tried to elucidate why the Guomindang was defeated and why the CCP won the Civil War, but none have come up with a satisfactory reason. Yet we believe the outcome of that war is easy to explain: under the conditions of such concentration, state capitalism was after all superior to finance capitalism.

11.

In as much as the state-capitalist class can complete the tasks of the bourgeois democratic revolution, would it be true to say that it plays an objectively progressive role in history?

Generally speaking, accomplishing the tasks of the bourgeois-democratic revolution is naturally objectively progressive, but society has already entered the era of the proletarian socialist revolution. And if the proletarian socialist revolution is sacrificed to completing the bourgeois-democratic revolution, there is nothing progressive about it.

The historic role of the state-capitalist class is not the same as that played by capitalism in its early period. Just as with finance capitalism, large-scale production swallows up small-scale production, trusts centralise the production of the scattered remnants, monopoly supersedes competition and a partial plan supersedes the rampant anarchy. Finally, national production is concentrated into the hands of the ideal aggregate of the capitalists (the state-capitalist class). This is certainly not a progressive role, but it does prepare the conditions for the future construction of socialism.

The October Revolution triumphed during the phase of finance capitalism, but it succeeded in a relatively undeveloped state of finance capitalism. So after it broke up the old state and set up a new one, the revolution was presented with more difficult problems, namely, how it could concentrate scattered production. This problem aggravated the revolutionary crisis and ultimately ruined the revolution.

But if a socialist revolution succeeds during the state-capitalist phase, the problem of how to concentrate production will already have been resolved before the revolution. The problem of how to break up the old state and construct a new one will perhaps be more difficult, but once resolved the revolution will be successful. Then it will be enough to declare that all state-owned property truly belongs to the labouring masses and that political and economic democracy have truly been achieved.

State capitalism could be compared to a machine. The machine helps the capitalists to exploit the workers. It throws many craft and industrial workers out of work and starves them. It sucks their blood and sweat and leaves them shirtless, but the machine can develop the social productive forces and push society forward. In one period in the past [Luddite] workers destroyed the machines. But the workers' movement really only needed to seize the machines from the hands of the capitalists. Similarly today, we don't want to oppose or obstruct the progressive aspects of nationalisation and planning under state capitalism. We just want to seize the nationalised property and planned economy from the hands of the state capitalists and declare that it all truly belongs to the labouring masses.

The socialist revolution is like the Titans of the Greek myth: beaten down they cannot die; they get up again but only stronger. That's why we are optimistic.

12.

For the moment, assuming that a third world war does not happen, and that the world revolution doesn't break out, the Chinese proletariat and poor peasants will continue in their unconscious and impotent state. State capitalism may develop smoothly, but the peasants will gradually be proletarianised and the city proletariat will increase in number, its quality will improve, its living conditions will become more concentrated, its consciousness will achieve greater definition. We will then be able to pose revolutionary questions on a higher historical plane. By that time the contradictions will be sharper and harder to mitigate. Revolutionary Marxism ought to be preparing for this prospect, and in the meantime no revolutionary crisis can be squandered.

CHAPTER 6

Poems on Political Themes (1958–90)

Translation and explanatory notes by Gregor Benton

Translator's Introduction

The Chinese Trotskyist leaders were not alone in writing poetry in the classical style – dozens of generals and political leaders of the official party, above all Mao Zedong himself, were also poets. Among the Trotskyists, Zheng Chaolin was by far the most accomplished poet, and it could be argued that he was the best Red poet in all China. As long as he was free to engage in political activity, Zheng had no time for poetry, but his imprisonment after 1952 gave him the chance to return to his youthful habit. Jail could stop him making revolution, but it could not stop him making poems. In prison, he also wrote other works, including books that were confiscated and probably destroyed during the Cultural Revolution, but the poems could not be so easily blotted out. Zheng had a phenomenal memory and retained hundreds of poems in his head, starting with prison poems he had composed in the early 1930s and extending through the entire period of his incarceration. This retention was made easier by the strict rhyme schemes and regular metres of the classical poetry Zheng espoused. So even when denied pencil and paper, he could continue to compose poems that he was later able to retrieve from memory. He often shared his poems with other Trotskyist and non-Trotskyist prisoners, some of whom were also poets. Even during his years in solitary confinement he engaged poetically with absent, dead or imagined interlocutors, modelling his work on classical archetypes in the form of matching poems and taking part whenever possible in poetic exchanges. His poetry has the same technical and formal properties and belongs to the same poetic world as Mao's, but it inhabits a quite different spiritual and affective world. It is quiet and gentle, whereas Mao's is loud and grandiloquent. Many of Zheng's poems dwell on personal loss and disappointment, but he also sometimes tackles political topics, as in the poems in this selection. When doing so, he usually cloaks his dissident opinions in cryptic language to fool the prison censor, using classical allusions to hint at the inevitability of great changes ahead – when seas will yield to mulberry fields and mulberry fields to seas, when Mount Meru hides mustard seed and mustard seed hides the mountain, suggesting that even tiny things can harbour limitless possibilities including the promise of great upheavals.

How the Mighty Fall

The poem begins by reminding readers of the rapid collapse of the Qin and the
Sui, the shortest-lived of China's main dynasties and the most authoritarian.
Mao Zedong explicitly modelled himself, in part, on the first emperor of the
Qin, Qin Shi Huangdi, who burned books and buried scholars alive. While Mao
lay dying in 1976, demonstrators in Tian'anmen Square in Beijing raised the call
to 'overthrow Qin Shi Huangdi', meaning Mao and his supporters in the 'Gang
of Four'. The poem repeats a theme, illustrated with terms and phrases drawn
from Buddhist and Daoist dialectics and classical writings, that is a constant in
his poetry: political power is transient, strength can turn quickly into weakness
and weakness into strength. It can be read as a hidden warning to the overween-
ing Mao.

> In antiquity Ying Qin,
> in middle antiquity Yang Sui –
> here today, gone tomorrow.
> Think of the quelling of the six states,[1]
> the repelling of the Hu, the drive against the Yue;[2]
> the merging of north and south,
> the opening of the borderlands.
> Earthshaking and all-powerful,
> they lash the planet –
> who dares stand up to them?
> But in the twinkling of an eye
> war smoke billows
> from the collapsing beams and pillars.
>
> Sewing the wedding robes for others,[3]
> I hear them talk for hours,
> praising the Han and Tang.
> I watch the Ying clan build its nest,[4]
> the Liu clan take up residence;[5]

---

1 The Qin waged wars of unification against the other six main states in what became China.
2 The Yue and Hu were non-Han peoples.
3 The sewing image was often used by thwarted officials forced to work for others.
4 The Ying clan is Qin Shi Huangdi's clan, in the Qin Dynasty.
5 Liu Bang founded the Han Dynasty.

Yang planting trees outside the door,[6]
the Li tribe lazing in the shade.[7]
Consider the West,
where Alexander
failed to secure the realm.[8]
Look closer then to now,
where Emperor Na and Kaiser Xi[9]
attest to life's highs and lows
as the sea yields
to mulberry fields
and the trees to seas.[10]

Training Monkeys

Here, the poet has fun at the expense of his jailers. He gives the background in a footnote: 'Zhuangzi [a Daoist sage] said, 'The Master lives in the mountain forest and eats chestnuts.' He also said, 'The monkey trainer gives [the monkeys] chestnuts.'' Zhuangzi explained:

A monkey keeper gave the monkeys chestnuts. He said: 'I'll give you three in the morning and four at night'. The monkeys were angry. The trainer said: 'Alright, I'll give you four in the morning and three at night'. The monkeys were now happy. Without changing either the name or the reality of the amount, he accommodated the monkeys' feelings.

The monkey trainer is Bolshevism (in its Stalinist garb) and Maoism: Stalin and Mao fooled the people by juggling statistics. Zheng is also reproaching himself for swallowing and helping to spread lies after his return to China from Moscow in 1924. The poet 'hides his status' both as a Trotskyist and as Zheng Chaolin, the man who, as an early leader of the CCP, knew its dirty secrets, like the immortal in the poem who had lived through all the dynasties.

---

6   Yang Jian founded the Sui Dynasty.
7   Li Yuan founded the Tang Dynasty.
8   Perhaps Zheng means that Alexander failed to prevent the dissolution of the Persian Empire.
9   Na is the character Zheng uses to transcribe Napoleon, Xi to transcribe Hitler.
10   The source of this metaphor about seas and mulberry fields was a work by the Eastern Jin Dynasty Daoist scholar and chemist Ge Hong.

As a young man and would-be star,
originally I aimed to storm the sky.
First I learned the art of training monkeys.
Then I assuaged their monkey feelings
with four chestnuts at first light and three at night.

Hiding my status,
I love to hum this well-turned phrase:
'Most of those mentioned in these annals were my friends,
but only half the facts are true'.[11]
With whom to share this saw?

Blind Man on a Blind Horse

This poem was written in October 1962, at the time of the Cuba crisis. Zheng knew from *Liberation Daily* that war was possible. The poem can also be read as an attack on Mao's mismanagement of the Chinese economy in the late 1950s and early 1960s. In a footnote explaining the language game Huan, Yin and Gu played in the fourth or fifth century, Zheng mentions that the players hid references to their own names in the epigrams they invented. This suggests that Zheng's use in the poem of the character for Mao, in its original meaning of 'hair' ('it scarcely sets his hair on end'), was a case in point.

What is the greatest wonder of the world?
Breadth of mind, so people say.
Consider: 'A blind man leaps without a moment's thought
onto the back of a blind horse
and plunges in the black of night
into a deep pool'.
That is surely dangerous?
But it scarcely set his hair on end.[12]
The man drowns and the horse drowns too –
but he remains alone in the dark, aloof.

---

11   The poet Qu Yuan described an immortal who attained the Way and lived through four
      Dynasties. Most great ministers of those times were his friends. He came to realise that
      many of the facts as reported in the annals were untrue. Zheng aims to alert readers to the
      true facts about the Chinese Communist Party, through whose history he had lived.
12   Mao ('hair') retains his composure while everything around him is collapsing.

A runaway train
and a drunken driver –
expect havoc!
Or a ship in a storm at sea
and a demented helmsman.
Think of the thousand passengers –
should they not also have their say?
Prepare for a shock:
dark clouds collect,
the Divine Land
will slide into the sea.[13]

When *Yin* Attains Its Limit

Zheng Chaolin and the Chinese Trotskyists were 'netted in one fell swoop' on 22 December 1952 – by a grim irony, the winter solstice, when the period of light is shortest and the night longest. Seven years later, on the anniversary of the arrest, Zheng notes that it is again midwinter, when *yin* attains its limit. But he goes on to remind himself that the day will lengthen and daylight will, in time, prevail.

The light today dies soonest,
tonight's the longest night.
Looking back to seven years ago,
I recall the night that broke our hearts in two.[14]

When *yin* attains its limit, *yang* begins to grow,
and heat and cold eventually swap place.
The years spin at an ever quicker pace,
and I plough my lonely furrow.

---

13   This line is modelled on one from Liu Yiqing's *Shishuo xinyu*: 'Causing the Divine Land to plunge into ruin for a century'.

14   This line draws on a *ci* edited by Zeng Zao.

A Revolution without Breaks or Interruptions

Zheng summarises his understanding, from a Trotskyist angle, of the course of
the Chinese Revolution after 1921. The revolutionary high tide in was reversed
by Chiang Kai-shek's attack on his erstwhile Communist allies in April 1927.
Zheng notes that the Chiang 'bandits' were wrongly taken by the Communists as 'in-laws' during the First United Front (1924–27), forced on them by
Moscow. The argument in 'court and commonality' is a hidden reference to the
Stalin-Trotsky split, during which Trotsky called for a return to Marx's teachings. When Zheng wrote this poem, probably at around the time of the Great
Leap Forward of 1958–61 or in its immediate aftermath, China's rural and industrial economy had begun a steep decline after a short-lived 'high tide'. The
second stanza talks about the course the Chinese Revolution should have followed after Chiang's betrayal: a revolution without breaks or interruptions, one
that would not pause for protracted periods at the discrete 'stages' that under-
pinned Stalin's and Mao's strategy. Does Zheng's comment have a further, hidden meaning? Starting in the late 1950s, Mao and his supporters began emphasising the need for an 'uninterrupted' or permanent revolution. In prison, Zheng
saw that Mao had changed his tune, though he probably had little confidence
that Mao knew the words to it. He could not resist sneaking into the poem's
cryptic last two lines a reminder that the Chinese Trotskyists had put forward
the same strategy at the time of their Founding Congress, in 1931.

> The tide is sucked back down the stream.
> Painful years
> for workers and peasants everywhere,
> with blood-stained snowflakes swirling in the gale.
> The fruit will soon be gathered in –
> but thieves will rally in the dead of night
> to plunder the peasants' fields and homes.
> Drawing lessons from the bitter past,
> I detect a deviation from the old true path:
> welcoming bandits
> as if they're in-laws.
>
> An argument splits court and commonality.
> A loud voice calls
> for a return to the essential teachings
> of Lenin, Marx, and Engels:
> a revolution without breaks or interruptions,

until the building's up and ready.
A different tune but sung with equal skill, for China's sake.
The scales have dropped from people's eyes,
but however loud the song, few really know the words.
Thirty years
seem like a day.

Forever Dissident

Zheng wrote this poem after a prison visit by his wife, who had been ordered to persuade him to admit his guilt and undergo reform. Zheng told her that there were limits beyond which he could not go.

You kindly advise me to follow others' suit.
Though I would love to compromise,
there is a gulf that I can never cross.
Seemingly just inches wide,
actually it reaches for a thousand miles.
It is the gulf between a human and a beast.
Should I drink the sweet and not the bitter cup,
I would disgrace my father and my mother!
And even if I crossed this gulf,
my mind would be forever dissident.
Do you not see some old acquaintances of mine
bending their heads low
and saying yes when so required,
but all to no avail?
Like me, they spent these thirteen years in jail,
hungrily looking upwards at the swan
that wings its way across the sky –
where is the leniency?

The Waxing and the Waning Moon

Writing in 1961, Zheng plays on the waxing and waning of the moon to describe his release under the Nationalists and his reunion with his wife in 1937, followed fifteen years later by his return to jail under the Communists.

'When autumn starts, the heat begins to die'.
At noon, the heat retains its fire.
At first light, and at last, small breezes stir,
while in the trees cicadas chirp.

Twenty years ago today and four,
at around this same time of the year,
the moon was full and I stepped out of jail –
who would have thought that after waxing it would wane again?

Memorial to Ding

In prison under Mao, Zheng celebrates his love for Trotsky in a poetic rebus
he wrote after reading in the Chinese press that Khrushchev had proposed
building a memorial to the victims of Stalin's terror; and that the Fourth International had written to tell Moscow that Trotsky's name should be on it 'in gold
letters'. The Chinese character *ding* 丁 is close in shape to the Western letter
T, and Zheng uses it to stand for Trotsky. The prison authorities failed to see
through this thin disguise.

The north wind gusts, the snowflakes dance,
vast buildings tower along the way.
Red flags on rooftops dapple white,
crowds surge like tides through subway gates.
This stubborn shade, this wisp of smoke,
will face God with its granite brain:[15]
clutching fresh blooms it treads the snow,
enquiring of each passer-by,
'Where is the grand memorial?'
When last here, I was very young.
Bullet scars could still be seen
around the university.
Yet people rose above the mean
and narrow streets to dwarf the gods.
Now poverty has given way
to affluence, unlettered night

---

15   Mao Zedong said of his opponents: 'Let them go to see their God with their granite brains'.

to dawning of the lettered light.
Sapling of my youth, you've grown
into a tree where people take
shade from the sun and pick fresh fruit;
those who planted it are dead,
the earth beneath is stained jade green.[16]
See, the marble comes in sight
clean and white as frozen fat.
Flowers bedeck the steps and plinth.
With spinning eyes I scan the stone
line by line for words of gold.
Framed in the blurred names' giddy ring,
whichever way I look I see
nothing but *ding*, *ding*, *ding*, and *ding*.

But for His Unyielding Character

Zheng wrote this in response to a poem presented to him on his birthday by his Trotskyist cellmate Yu Shouyi. Yu had advised him in his poem to plead guilty to political crimes. Zheng used the poem 'to respond to Yu's advice'.

1. Happily, he eats the maggots on the plum-tree by the well.[17]
2. Spurning the dates and clinging to the withered tree, he holds fast to his purity.[18]
3. In the Tianlu Pavilion, he treasures the ancient bamboo slips.[19]
4. Under the Fengbo Pavilion, his outstanding work expires.[20]
5. In the Western Hills, ferns feed men of virtue and integrity.[21]

---

16 Chang Hong was a high official killed by a prince in Shu. His blood changed from red to emerald, whence the saying that the blood of those wrongly killed turns green.

17 Chen Zhongzhi was an aristocrat from Qi who starved to death in order to remain 'clean'.

18 Bao Jiao, a recluse of the Zhou Dynasty, opposed government corruption and chose to live in the mountains, eating nothing he had not grown himself and wearing only clothes woven by his wife.

19 Liu Xiang was an official of the Han Dynasty stripped of office for remonstrating with the Emperor. He was famous for collating bamboo slips and silk scrolls in order to establish sound texts of Confucian and other writings.

20 Yue Fei was killed in the Fengbo Pavilion in Hangzhou.

21 Uncle Yi and Uncle Qi were princes of the Shang Dynasty. After the Shang's fall and the transition to the Zhou, they fled to the mountains, where they died of starvation.

6.   Orchids lack the soil in which to nourish errant thought.[22]
7.   Scratching your hoary head, you find your aspirations turn to
      nought.[23]
8.   The Park Gate inmates praise the ancient sages' style.[24]

Intoning History

Zheng said of these three poems: 'They use the past to satirise the present. The
first poem is ostensibly about Qin Hui,[25] actually it's about Stalin. The second
poem is ostensibly about the 'party stele' set up in the Northern Song Dynasty
at the time of the struggle between the new party and the old. At the time, the
new party was in power. Its supporters ... raised a stele on which they engraved
the names of the members of the opposition, and they called them 'the party',
the 'bad people'. Later, when the situation changed, the stele was destroyed. The
people named on it became 'good people' and their descendants were glorified.
The third poem is about corruption'.

> Chancellor Qin did not plan far ahead.
> He weeded out dissidents and killed the pure.
> Alive, much power rested in his hands:
> dead, he was judged to rate the headsman's blade.
>
> Warnings of the ups and downs at court are hard to find,
> but don't forget the towering party stele:
> raised to list dissidents accused of crime,
> toppled to right a wrong, forever and throughout all time.
>
> Console the people by punishing the bad, rise up among the wormwood
>   groves[26] –
> a general owes his victory to ten thousand bleaching bones.

---

22   Xie Ao and Zheng Sixiao were late Song Dynasty poets who mourned the fall of the Song
      and refused to serve under the new Mongol Yuan Dynasty.
23   Zheng borrows part of a line from Du Fu, who wrote: 'Leaving the gate, you scratched your
      hoary head / as if having failed in your lifetime aims'.
24   Park Gate was what the prisoners called the prison.
25   Qin Hui (1090–1155), a chancellor of the Song Dynasty, was despised as a traitor for his part
      in executing Yue Fei, a patriotic general.
26   Zheng borrowed the wormwood image, symbolising a wild place, from Chen Zi'ang.

I have not yet seen the common people sleeping in the rice-straw
    bowers,
but I've heard the new elite is raising canopies and towers.

The Waking of the Insects

This poem is rich in political imagery and implications – the revolutionary tide
at ebb (after 1927), unrealised hopes, doctrinal consolation and the hint of a
new spring.

Hurtling nonstop to my demise, remembering my spring –
what point is there in digging up the buried texts?
'Ox-Demon's writings mourned Li He,
a shovel borne upon a deer-drawn cart interred Liu Ling'.[27]

Woken insects ride the wind,[28]
can truth be grasped from what our fathers preach?[29]
The ebbtide etched deep marks while dropping down the beach –
as dying fishes stranded in a drying rut spout damping jets,[30]
still we discuss the sacred texts.

Requesting Criticism from Comrade Xie Shan

The Monkey King, Sun Wukong, born from a magic stone, is a main character
in the sixteenth-century novel *Journey to the West*. Supernaturally strong, he
knows seventy-two transformations and commands the elements. He defeats
Heaven's army and creates havoc. But although he can somersault around the
earth, he cannot escape the Buddha's palm. Even when he thinks he has leapt
to the farthest boundary of Heaven, the Mountain of the Five Elements turns
out to be the Buddha's fingers.

---

27   Cao Xueqin (1715–1763), author of *Dream of the Red Chamber* and of these two lines, ad-
     mired Li He. Cao avoided a 'living death' – turning into a careerist without conscience or
     integrity – by spurning rank and fame. Like the poet Liu Ling, he disdained etiquette and
     drank heavily. Liu Ling practised nudity and was followed around by a servant carrying a
     bottle of wine for him to drink and a shovel with which to bury him when he fell dead.
28   The weather is getting warmer, spring is about to start.
29   A reference to Kong Li, Confucius's only son, to whom he passed down instructions.
30   A classical idiom that describes stranded fishes moistening each other with water jets.

Soon ninety, but still basking in life's spring,
aspiring to be a second Monkey King.
Wielding a golden rod to put the Sky God's court to fright,
smashing the network, setting the whole world to right!

I calmly withstand the raging flames in Taishang Laojun's stove,[31]
but how to escape the Buddha's palm?
Seek quiet and isolation in the Mountain of Five Elements
and, after a long hard journey to the West, bear back the sacred texts.

Reflections on a Tour of the Historic Site of *The Bolshevik* Editorial Department

In the mid 1920s, Zheng Chaolin edited *Guide Weekly*, which became *The Bolshevik* in 1927. After his release from prison in 1979, Zheng was often consulted by scholars about Party history in the 1920s, of which he was by then a rare survivor. This poem describes his lively encounter with historians during a tour of his old workplace.

An old man up against a younger throng
of sage and virtuous questioners whose shining spears
and armoured horses clash and clang ding-dong.

As with each dying day my old friends pass away,
I watch the sunset flood the painted tower with light.[32]
'Washed by the moon, an overpowering sight!'[33]

A Response to Rong Sun (27 January 1988)

Rong Sun said that even in the winter cold the earth spins on and told Zheng not to be so glum, to which he answered:

---

31   Sun Wukong the Monkey King burned in the stove of Taishang Laojun, the supreme Daoist deity, for forty-nine days and became even stronger as a result.

32   The painted tower can refer to a boudoir in which a heroine lives. Here, it might symbolise Zheng's wife Liu Jingzhen, who died in 1979.

33   A line from a poem by Li Yu, to whose tune the present poem was written.

Immediately the blooming ends, new life begins again,
in shoots and leaves formed in the snow.
Gradually on the pond the dream of spring awakes.
The willow lightly casts its scent.
Cuckoos call the peasants to the fields,
which turn to green with shoots of rice.
The seasons follow their eternal wheel,
how many turns can an ailing man behold?

A Reply to Comrade Xie Shan (16 February 1990)

On 4 June 1989, less than a year before Zheng wrote this poem, pro-democracy
protests in Beijing and other major cities met with a brutal military crackdown. However, upheavals in Eastern Europe excited Trotskyists throughout
the world. Would they lead to socialism and democracy? This exchange of
poems conveys Zheng's mixed feelings. In it, they invoke a poem by Xin Qiji
voicing his anxiety at the fate of the Southern Song Dynasty, under hostile pressure at the time.

The *yang* is low, the *yin* is vigorous,
the day is cold and swept by storms,
and grey beards turn to white.
Who still remembers darling spring?
The old regret it to their dying day.

When will spring return and where to ask?
It's said that day by day
she's drawing closer.
My thoughts turn this way and then that,
good news is hard to count on.

Xie Shan's Original Poem

Zang and Gu both lose a sheep – who will find it first?[34]
Time presses,
as our hair turns grey.

---

34   Zhuangzi says Zang and Gu both lost a sheep. Zang had been reading bamboo tablets, Gu
      had been engrossed in a game. The sheep are hard to find, along forking roads. 'Nowhere

It is unbearable to recall old times.
Once old, you no longer bear the grudge.

Don't say that Heaven is too high to ask.
When winter passes,
spring will not be far behind.
'In the vicissitudes of life, my mind's set on an even course'.[35]
Tides ebb and flow at the appointed hour.

has there been anyone who has not under [the influence of external] things altered [the course of] his or her nature. Small people for the sake of gain have sacrificed their persons; scholars for the sake of fame have done so; great officers, for the sake of their families; and sages, for the sake of the kingdom'. This story is used to describe unintended consequences and complicated choices.

35   A line from Gong Zizhen that Zheng Chaolin used in Poem 61.

CHAPTER 7

Chen Duxiu and the Trotskyists (1980–1)

Translated by Gregor Benton

Translator's Introduction

Zheng Chaolin's memoirs, completed in 1945 but not at the time published, were unearthed from a government vault in 1979, shortly after Zheng's release (after twenty seven years) from gaol under the CCP. Sometime in 1979 or 1980, several copies of the manuscript were mimeographed in Beijing under the title *Zheng Chaolin 1945 nian huiyi lu* ('Zheng Chaolin's 1945 memoirs') for distribution as reference material among Party historians. In 1986, after sitting for several years on the manuscript, Chinese Communist officials finally authorised its publication, in an edition restricted to privileged categories of officials and researchers. In 1986, Beijing's Xiandai shiliao biankan she ('Association to edit and publish materials on contemporary history') published a printed version under the title *Zheng Chaolin huiyi lu* ('Zheng Chaolin's memoirs'), with this appendix commissioned by Party historians and written by Zheng. The appendix comprises a special study on Chen Duxiu's relationship to Trotskyism. On December 11, 1987, Zheng explained in a postscript to the English translation of his memoirs the circumstances under which he had composed the study on Chen Duxiu: 'I wrote the appendix 'Chen Duxiu and the Trotskyists' at the invitation of a certain research institute in 1980, shortly after I had regained my freedom. At the time, public opinion tended to make a distinction between Chen Duxiu and the Trotskyists. People said that Chen Duxiu was a good man whose good name should be restored, but they made no evaluation of the Trotskyists. So the aim of this long article is to show that Chen Duxiu and the Trotskyists cannot be dealt with separately'.

Chen Duxiu and the Trotskyists

(1)   *From Moscow Group to Chen Duxiu Group*
          The Cadres Who Returned from Moscow in 1924

1924 was an important year in the history of the CCP. It was the first year of formal cooperation between it and the Guomindang. Early on in 1924, the Guomindang, with the Communist Party's help, convened the First Reorgan-

isation Congress; several Communist Party leaders were elected onto the Guomindang's Central Executive Committee; the Huangpu (Whampoa) Military
Academy was started up; Soviet political and military advisers started work;
Guomindang branches in most places came under Communist control; the
urban labour movement, which had become passive after the strike of February 7, 1923, livened up again; and Communist activity developed on an unprecedented scale. Even more cadres were needed to carry out Party tasks. To meet
the need, the Moscow branch of the CCP dispatched back to China a number of
Chinese comrades studying at Moscow's KUTV. They returned in batches; all in
all they accounted for more than half the original number of Chinese students
at KUTV. Of those who stayed behind, some switched to the Military Academy
and others were preparing to return to China after a further six months.

The first batch returned before the 1924 summer holidays; the second set out
from Moscow during the summer holidays; during and after the summer holidays, right through until the spring of the following year, people trickled back
to China in smaller groups of two and three or four and five, or even singly.

All those who returned in 1924 or in the spring of 1925 took up high office
in the Party. Peng Shuzhi sat in on the Central Committee as head of the Propaganda Department and attended all its meetings. Though he hadn't been
elected onto it by the Third Congress, he assumed the same powers as one of
its normal members: he interviewed cadres and issued directives; even Deng
Zhongxia behaved respectfully in his presence, not to mention Zhuang Wengong, Secretary of the Shanghai District Committee. As for Chen Yannian, just
a few days after arriving in Shanghai he was sent to Guangzhou to be Secretary of the Southern Regional Committee. Yin Kuan, who had returned before
the summer holidays, had earlier gone to Shandong to be Provincial Secretary there. Zhao Shiyan, who had come to China on his own, took charge of the
Northern Regional Committee in Beijing. This Committee was nominally under
Li Dazhao, but Zhao Shiyan did the actual work. Wang Ruofei didn't get back
until early 1925, whereupon he was quickly appointed as Secretary to the Provincial Committee in Henan. Wang Zekai was sent to Anyuan to lead the Party
there. Luo Yinong at first came to Shanghai but later went to Guangzhou and
later still went to Beijing to run the Party school and to train cadres; finally, in
late 1925 or early 1926, he came back to Shanghai to become Secretary to the
Jiangsu-Zhejiang Regional Committee. Chen Qiaonian, who got back in early
1925, helped Zhao Shiyan on the Northern Regional Committee. Ren Bishi, like
Peng Shuzhi in the adult Party, sat in on the Central Committee of the Youth
League immediately after getting back to China, without having been elected
to it. Xue Shilun at first worked as Treasurer and Secretary to the Central Committee in Shanghai, but he was not up to it, so he was sent to Hunan to help

Li Weihan; Ren Zuomin took over his old jobs. Zheng Chaolin was appointed Secretary to the Central Committee's Propaganda Department, where Zhang Bojian, who had gone back from Moscow before the summer holidays, was already working. Many of the other people who returned from Moscow were assigned to the labour movement; later Wang Yifei, Yan Changyi, and others returned to China after having studied military science in Moscow and some of them were assigned to the Party's Military Committee.

The students who returned to China from Moscow in 1924 (including the first half of 1925) were united as one and worked in close concert. They had received a common schooling, and just before returning they had received special training; their views on the theory of the Chinese Revolution and on methods of work were in close accord, as if printed from the same font. Party cadres and members from before 1924 looked askance on us and dubbed us the 'Moscow people'. At first sight this was a neutral appellation, but secretly it reflected a mood of dissatisfaction among cadres and comrades from before 1924, who thought that these people had come to occupy a special position in the Party and formed a virtual clique. There had already been one such virtual clique in the Party – Zhang Guotao's 'National Trade Union group'. Li Longzhi (who later changed his name to Li Lisan), Liu Shaoqi, and Xiang Delong (who later called himself Xiang Ying), all three of whom had worked in the labour movement in the South, didn't belong to the 'National Trade Union group' so they were more prepared to cooperate with the 'Moscow people'. Li Weihan, the Provincial Secretary in Hunan, had returned to China directly from France, without passing through Moscow, but he, too, counted as one of the Moscow people. Zhang Tailei and Qu Qiubai, on the other hand, were not members even though they had been in Moscow. Later, they gradually became hostile to the Moscow people.

The 'National Trade Union group' and the Moscow group were virtual cliques. The former had united around Zhang Guotao and Luo Zhanglong, Zhang's right-hand man. It derived its solidarity from personal and work relationships; its solidarity could hardly be said to be grounded in theory or principle. Needless to say, the 'workerist' views that Zhang Guotao developed in the early period of the CCP were not entirely without relevance to his group's coherence. The Moscow group, however, was united mainly on the basis of theory and principle, though at the same time personal relationships also played a role in it.

The theory of the Moscow group was called 'the theory of national revolution'.

'The Theory of National Revolution'

In early 1924 – at the earliest in the fourth quarter of 1923 – comrades in the Comintern's Far Eastern Bureau and leaders of the CCP's Moscow branch met frequently to discuss the theory of national revolution. I knew about this, though I never attended any of the meetings, nor do I know who did. Naturally, Luo Yinong and Peng Shuzhi attended, but whether anyone else did I don't know. The outcome of these meetings was the 'theory of national revolution'.

The content of the theory is set out in Peng Shuzhi's programmatic essay in *New Youth Quarterly* no. 4, which was specially devoted to 'national revolution', and in the political resolution passed by the Fourth Congress and drafted by the Comintern representative Voitinsky. The two documents are the same. That's not surprising, for the 'theory of national revolution' was worked out jointly by leaders of the Comintern's Far Eastern Bureau and of the Moscow branch; or rather, it was worked out by the Comintern and embraced by the leaders of the Moscow branch.

I haven't seen those two documents in fifty-five years, and for the moment there's no way in which I can borrow them to read, but I still recall their general drift. Basically, they promote two arguments: China cannot carry out proletarian-socialist revolution without first going through national revolution, i.e., bourgeois-democratic revolution; and the proletariat must strive for the leadership of the national revolution.[1]

This was a new theory in the history of the CCP. We know that before the CCP's First Congress everyone viewed the Chinese Revolution as similar in character to Russia's October Revolution. I have to hand a copy of the 'Manifesto of

---

1   After finishing the first draft of this section, I managed to borrow the two documents concerned. Peng Shuzhi's article says: 'National revolution is the only way out'. Peng asks: 'Why does the Chinese working class not make this revolution its own class revolution – the proletarian revolution?' He gives three reasons, the second of which is that national revolution is 'the only road along which the Chinese proletariat can go forward to proletarian revolution'. After analysing China's bourgeoisie and China's proletariat, Peng concludes: 'So the Chinese working class is the natural leader of the Chinese Revolution'. The resolution that Voitinsky drafted for the Fourth Congress also stresses that there can be no talk of proletarian revolution without first going through national revolution, and that after the victory of national revolution the question 'whether or not there must first be a period of bourgeois democracy before going on to proletarian revolution' can only be answered in the light of the proletariat's level of preparation and the world political situation. The resolution also says: 'National revolution can only succeed if the most revolutionary proletariat is in the leading position'. In those days people stressed the proletariat's leading role in national revolution, but they denied that the Guomindang was a bourgeois party. Peng said: the Guomindang is 'built on the lumpenproletariat, for example bandit armies'. Voitinsky said: the Guomindang is a 'multi-class party'. [Note by Zheng Chaolin.]

the CCP', published in November 1920,[2] which says: 'The first step toward realising our ideal society is to eradicate the present bourgeois system. That can only be done by forcefully overthrowing the capitalists' state'. It also says:

> The Communist Party will lead the revolutionary proletariat to struggle against the capitalists and seize political power from the hands of the capitalists, for it is that power that maintains the capitalist state; and it will place that power in the hands of the workers and peasants, just as the Russian Communists did in 1917.

I also have a copy of the programme approved by the First Congress, which describes its aim as 'to overthrow the bourgeoisie with the revolutionary army of the proletariat and to re-establish the state on the basis of the toiling classes, until class differences are extinguished'. In sum, before and at the First Congress there was no theory – not even a glimmering of one – about first having to complete bourgeois-democratic revolution before starting proletarian-socialist revolution. After the First Congress the question of cooperating with the Guomindang was raised. It was discussed at the Second Congress and again at the West Lake Conference, and the Third Congress decided to join the Guomindang. But it was raised as a tactic, in terms of how can we even more quickly and effectively develop the revolutionary movement and Party forces.

But after the decision to cooperate with the Guomindang had been taken and implemented and after the alliance between the Guomindang and Russia, when the Soviets sent advisers to China plus funds and weaponry to help the Guomindang, the old tactical formula was no longer enough and the question had to be reframed in strategic terms: the old line of 'Guomindang-Communist cooperation' had to be replaced by one grounded in principle and basic Marxist theory. Thus was born the 'theory of national revolution', with its emphasis on the need to complete bourgeois-democratic revolution before going on to proletarian-socialist revolution. Were there grounds for such a theory? Yes, people cited the theoretical disputes in Russia before the Revolution as a basis for it. But they avoided talking about the actual course of events in 1917, for that showed that the Russians had already carried out the proletarian-socialist revolution even before completing the bourgeois-democratic one, that bourgeois-democratic revolution in Russia was completed as a by-product of proletarian-socialist revolution.

---

2   Even before the First Congress, which met on July 23, 1921, a 'Manifesto' was drafted in November 1920 and published on November 7 in the inaugural issue of the underground monthly *Gongchandang* ('Communist').

The second main argument connected with the 'theory of national revolution', i.e., that the proletariat must strive for leadership, is clearly subsidiary and, from a Marxist point of view, cosmetic. Before the revolution Lenin's idea that the proletariat must lead Russia's bourgeois revolution was premised in the belief that Russia's bourgeoisie had already forfeited its revolutionary role. How could the view that China's bourgeoisie still had a revolutionary role to play, that it should be richly aided with funds, weaponry, and advisers, and that the Communist Party should even be made to join the Guomindang as a wing of it – how could this view be reconciled with striving for proletarian hegemony in the revolution? Striving for proletarian hegemony was mere cosmetics, as the comments of senior members of the CCP clearly show. Peng Shuzhi, who imported the theory to China, said that hegemony over the revolution 'naturally' belonged to the proletariat so there was no need to strive for it; Qu Qiubai exposed this belief of Peng's in his pamphlet *Against Peng Shuzhiism*. According to Peng there was no bourgeoisie in China, just the ghost of one. When Mao Zedong wrote his 'Analysis of the Classes in Chinese Society' in March 1926, more than a year after the proclamation at the Fourth Congress of the 'theory of national revolution', he didn't say anything about the proletariat leading China's other classes. The present version of that article in Mao's *Selected Works* says that 'the proletariat is the leading force in the revolutionary movement', but the sentence was added later, when the *Selected Works* were edited for publication, and cannot be found in the 1926 text.

In late 1924 or early 1925, the CCP officially proclaimed 'national revolution' as the guiding theory for the entire revolutionary movement. The actual course of the Revolution of 1925 to 1927 showed this theory up as bankrupt. We who had been in Moscow studied this theory before returning home, and we all complied with it: it was the banner behind which we united. That it had been exposed as bankrupt implied the dissolution of the Moscow group.

The Central Force in the Party

The Moscow group was not tangible but it undeniably existed. The Moscow branch was originally led by three people, Luo Yinong, Peng Shuzhi, and Bu Shiqi. In early 1923, Bu Shiqi went back to China, leaving Luo and Peng in charge. After cooperation between the Guomindang and the CCP had been formally implemented, the 'theory of national revolution' formally launched, and the order sending comrades back to China formally issued, the Moscow branch decided that Luo Yinong would stay on to continue to lead it and that Peng Shuzhi would go back to China to join the Central Committee of the CCP and at the same time rally and lead the returning cadres, i.e., the so-called

Moscow people. Why didn't Luo go instead of Peng? I don't know. I was never told the reasons for that decision.

In early 1925, not long after the Fourth Congress, Peng Shuzhi fell ill with typhoid fever after editing the 'Lenin' number of the first issue of *New Youth Monthly*. Luo Yinong, who had just got back from Moscow, came to the Propaganda Department to see us. He was sitting beside Peng's bed. I happened to be standing there, and some of the things he said attracted my attention. I remember them to this day. The gist of his remarks was that we should form a central force in the Party so that we would be in a position to control the rest of it.

The actual situation in the Party at that time was like this. The batch of cadres who had returned to China from the Soviet Union all supported Peng Shuzhi and Luo Yinong. (The exception was Jiang Guangchi, who had opposed Luo and Peng in Moscow; after getting back to China he supported not them but Qu Qiubai, but the rest of the Moscow people opposed Jiang.) These cadres now occupied important positions in the Party. As long as they got on well with Chen Duxiu, they could control the feudal lords by using the emperor's name and so take over the Party's commanding heights. And that's more or less what happened.

Had Luo and Peng decided on such a plan before going back to China? Obviously not, or Luo would have had no need for his bedside talk with Peng. But the general tendency was there, even in Moscow.

It's worth noting that after Luo had spoken, Peng hummed and hawed and did not come out clearly in support of the proposal; but nor did he come out clearly against it. With the benefit of hindsight, I would judge Luo's comments as follows.

Peng Shuzhi was unlikely to oppose the idea of uniting the Moscow people around Chen Duxiu and using Chen's name to control the 'feudal lords': of setting up a central force in the CCP to control the rest of it. The reason he didn't actively support Luo's proposal was certainly not because he was against it, and even less so because he supported the prohibition on factions passed at the Tenth Congress of the Russian Communist Party. It was simply that he planned to keep the leadership of the Moscow group for himself rather than share it with Luo Yinong. In Moscow Luo played first fiddle and Peng second. On the surface they cooperated well together, but I'd already noticed that they had by no means completely merged. Luo invented for Peng the nickname Confucius, which caught on and still sticks. The nickname was meant to imply that Peng was a book-worm, that he'd read a lot, that he knew lots of theory, but that he was no good at doing things. Peng hated his nickname so we never used it to his face, but we did use it behind his back. Peng saw himself as China's Lenin, but in Moscow he had to yield to Luo. Back in China, where he was elected onto the Central Committee at the Fourth Congress, he joined the Presidium (later called the Standing Committee) and simultaneously ran the Propaganda Department. By then Peng's position was higher than Luo's. Luo was simply a cadre awaiting assignment. How did Peng manage to force Luo to share the leadership of the Moscow people? After their bedside talk, Peng decided to enter Baolong Hospital and arranged for Luo to move into the Propaganda Department building, where Luo slept on Peng's bed. Before going to the hospital Peng told me to lock his desk-drawer and not to let Luo rummage in it. I was surprised, but I did as he said. Later, on account of Chen Bilan,[3] Luo and Peng became enemies and stayed so. But that has nothing to do with what I'm now discussing, so let's stop talking about it.

As far as I remember Luo and Peng didn't mention Chen Duxiu in their bedside talk. But they didn't need to. In Moscow, if we were discussing the Central Committee of the CCP or the Party leadership, we had only Chen Duxiu in mind. Li Dazhao followed Chen in everything. We never mentioned the names Zhang Guotao, Qu Qiubai, Cai Hesen, or Tan Pingshan. In those days the leader cult had started up in the Soviet Union and the Soviet Central Committee was instilling it into the Party membership and the people. We worshipped Lenin as the supreme leader of the Soviet Republic – and in China we worshipped Chen Duxiu. But in Moscow the cult of Chen Duxiu meant something other to Peng and Luo than to the rest of us. Peng in Moscow saw himself as the Chinese Lenin, but he had to yield to Luo. Back in China in the autumn of 1924, he sneaked his way above Luo, but he still had to yield to Chen Duxiu. The only reason he clasped Chen's leg was so that one day he could replace him.

There were five members of the Standing Committee (or Presidium) after the Fourth Congress, namely Chen Duxiu, Cai Hesen, Zhang Guotao, Qu Qiubai, and Peng Shuzhi. At around the time of National Day[4] in 1925, after Cai had gone to Moscow to represent the CCP at the Comintern right up to the time when the Central Committee moved to Wuhan, it only had four members. I often sat in on its meetings. I used to hate Peng's performance at them. Almost every time he would first wait for Chen Duxiu to say what he thought and then – at great length and with much pedantry – supply additional arguments to back

---

3   Chen Bilan had been Luo Yinong's lover in Moscow, but she dropped him for Peng when they returned to China.

4   Then October 10 (the anniversary of the Revolution of 1911), now October 1 (the anniversary of the proclamation of the People's Republic in 1949).

Chen up. He used to speak at great length but no depth, so that the others in attendance became impatient at the loss of time, though Peng himself did not notice this. I must have betrayed my irritation and contempt, for Qu Qiubai – who was extremely sensitive – noticed it and told Jiang Guangchi. Jiang wrote it up in his novel *Des sans-culottes*,[5] where I make a shadowy appearance.

Needless to say, on several occasions at these meetings Peng expressed opinions that differed from those of Chen. He boasted to me once that at the meetings Qu Qiubai and Zhang Guotao used slavishly to follow the 'Old Man's' lead, and that only he Peng dared face up to Chen.

'Qiubai is simply a higher technician', he said. 'Guotao is simply a higher administrator'. What he meant was that only he, Peng, was a 'higher politician', i.e., a politician of higher quality.

We Moscow people, later to become followers of Chen Duxiu, were early on against Peng: we didn't wait until after the Fifth Congress to chime in with Qu Qiubai against him. Wang Ruofei, Chen Qiaonian, Ren Xu, He Zishen, and others all despised Peng Shuzhi. Perhaps Chen Yannian's opposition to Peng was a result of Borodin's influence. Luo Yinong had personal reasons to be against Peng. Ren Bishi and Xiao Zizhang, who worked for the Youth League, were probably swayed by Qu Qiubai and the Youth International, but that's another matter. We were opposed to Peng the man, not the 'theory of national revolution' he brought back from Moscow; and even less did we oppose Peng as a cover for attacking Chen Duxiu. Naturally, a minority, like Wang Zekai and Liu Bozhuang, supported Peng all along.

The Moscow Group Splits

After the Fourth Congress, the development of the Chinese Revolution was accompanied by splits in the Moscow group. Luo and Peng's plan was to use us as a central force with which to take over the entire Party, but as the Party grew the Moscow group – contrary to general expectations – split apart and was defeated and destroyed.

The first people to split away were those in the group under Chen Yannian. Chen Yannian (Secretary of the Southern Regional Committee), Mu Qing (head of the Organisational Bureau), and Huang Guozuo (alias Huang Ping, head of the Propaganda Bureau) had all returned from Moscow, where they had studied and supported the 'theory of national revolution'. But not long after Chen Yannian and others began working in Guangzhou, they became involved in the struggle between Borodin and Chen Duxiu, supporting the former against the

---

5   Reprinted in Jiang Guangchi 1983, pp. 189–270.

latter. Borodin was a senior adviser to the National[6] Government; perhaps he also represented the Comintern. Whatever the case, he meddled in the affairs of the CCP. He directly led the Party's Southern Committee regardless of the opinion of the Central Committee of the CCP and did his best to control Party work – at least where the 'national revolutionary movement' was concerned – across the whole of China. In so doing he encroached on the competencies of the official Comintern representative, Voitinsky. Before Chen Yannian took up his post in Guangzhou, in the summer of 1924, Borodin instigated Qu Qiubai (then staying in Guangzhou) to deal with the Guomindang in the name of the CCP, but many of Qu's speeches and actions did not tally with the Central Committee's position. Chen Duxiu and Cai Hesen in Shanghai were very angry about this, and in the name of the Central Committee ordered Qu to leave Guangzhou and return to Shanghai, which he did, leaving scars on his mind. Chen Yannian went to Guangzhou in the autumn, whereupon Borodin instigated Chen Yannian instead, regardless of whether the actions he encouraged Chen to undertake accorded with the wishes of the Central Committee. I know little about the struggle between Borodin and the Central Committee in Shanghai, for the issues in it were never publicly aired. All I know is that on one occasion when Chen Yannian came to Shanghai to deliver a report to the Central Committee, he stayed at my place and told me that Borodin had told him that the Central Committee in Shanghai only knew the slogan 'Workers of the world, unite!' What Borodin meant was that the Central Committee in Shanghai only knew how to mouth principles, and was incapable of flexibly applying them. But Chen Yannian didn't say exactly what principles were at stake. Borodin had arrived in China before the Comintern's Far Eastern Bureau had settled on the 'national revolution' formula, with which Voitinsky (who brought the idea to China) instructed the Fourth Congress. I'm not saying that Borodin didn't know about the theory, just that 'politicians' like Borodin put no price whatsoever on principle or theory and were only good at political conspiring. He behaved quite wilfully in Guangzhou, and paid not the slightest attention to the views of either the Shanghai Central Committee or Voitinsky, who was the official Comintern representative in China. Every time Borodin and Chen Duxiu clashed seriously, the Southern comrades led by Chen Yannian backed Borodin. In this way the Moscow people in Southern China set up their own banner under the leadership of Chen Yannian.

The second group to split away from the Moscow group were leading members of the Youth League. The Youth League turned against Chen Duxiu much

---

6   I.e., the Government of the Guomindang in Guangzhou.

later than the Guangdong cadres. I can't say for sure when the split began, but it was probably not until 1926. After the Fourth Congress of the CCP, the Youth League also held a Congress and changed its name from Socialist to Communist. At the same time Ren Bishi took over as its General Secretary from Zhang Tailei. The plan stemmed originally from Moscow: Peng Shuzhi, too, knew about and agreed with it. By 1926, the Youth League had gradually turned against Chen Duxiu, chiefly under the influence of the internal struggle in the Soviet Party. The Soviet Youth League (or Komsomol) did not agree with the Comintern's China policy and was especially opposed to Voitinsky, the official Comintern representative in China. According to Komsomol leaders, Voitinsky was an 'opportunist' and a 'rightist'. I don't know too clearly on what actual issues they opposed him. In 1923, the Trotsky opposition incited the Komsomol against the leading triumvirate in the Soviet Party, namely Zinoviev, Kamenev, and Stalin. But Trotsky was overthrown and the Komsomol, too, was purged. By 1926, it was apparently no longer in a position to oppose from a Trotskyist point of view the China policy of the Central Committee of the Soviet Communist Party and of the Comintern. But it's a fact that the Komsomol leaders opposed Voitinsky and through him Chen Duxiu, who was supposedly under his influence. After the controversy in the Chinese leadership about the Northern Expedition, Qu Qiubai joined the Komsomol in opposing Chen.

Qu Qiubai and Zhang Guotao both supported Chiang Kai-shek's Northern Expedition. Zhang was a well-known schemer and intriguer, but even so his skills as such fell short of Qu's. At the Central Committee meeting where the Northern Expedition was discussed, Zhang clashed frontally with Chen Duxiu but Qu – who supported the Northern Expedition no less than Zhang – pretended to comply with Chen. From then on, Qu plotted against Chen from behind the scenes. Whether Zhang did, too, I don't know, but I do know that Qu Qiubai did. In the second half of 1926, he said he was ill and stopped attending Central Committee meetings or working for the Party. Wang Ruofei, head of the Central Committee's Secretariat, early on became aware of what was happening. One morning in late autumn, while I was still asleep, he came to drag me from my lair and take me to Ximen Road where Qu lived. As we entered the upstairs room, Qu was sitting squarely at his desk working on an article. When he saw us he seemed a bit embarrassed. We exchanged a few words with him and then left. On the way back neither of us said anything about the incident, nor did we need to. It turned out that Qu wasn't ill but was working hard on an article that he didn't want anyone else to know about. It remained a mystery until the spring of 1927 in Wuhan, when it became clear that he had been writing up his pamphlet *Against Peng Shuzhi-ism*. Apart from that he had been inciting people against Chen Duxiu. These people included Ren Bishi and Xiao Zizhang, who had returned from Moscow to work in the Youth League, and others like He Chang and Lu Dingyi who had never been in Moscow. All this happened behind the backs of Chen Duxiu and Peng Shuzhi. Qu never argued his positions openly at a meeting of the Central Committee.

There must also have been a third group of Chen Duxiu supporters who turned against Chen because of mistakes they detected in the way the leadership conducted actual struggles, but I can't say exactly who they were.

Those of us who continued to support Chen learned early on to despise Peng Shuzhi as mean, dull-witted, vain, and unable to work together with other people. I wasn't the only one who thought like this. So did Wang Ruofei, Chen Qiaonian, Zhao Shiyan, and above all Luo Yinong. Whenever Peng's name came up, none of us liked to continue talking. But we all clearly distinguished between Peng and Chen Duxiu; we thought it was unseemly the way Peng always clung to Chen's leg.

The struggle against Chen broke out at the Fifth Congress. After Wuhan had fallen to the Northern Expedition, many senior officials of the CCP began to congregate there. People like Zhang Guotao, Tan Pingshan, Zhang Tailei, Li Lisan, Liu Shaoqi, Mao Zedong, Qu Qiubai, Luo Zhanglong, and Cai Hesen all went there. I can't say exactly when each arrived, or from where. All I remember is that Qu Qiubai left Shanghai for Wuhan after the defeat of the second Shanghai insurrection in February 1927. Chen Duxiu and Peng Shuzhi, who were on the Standing Affairs Committee, stayed in Shanghai. Chen was still the Party's General Secretary, but Qu Qiubai, Zhang Guotao, and Tan Pingshan reestablished the Central Committee in Wuhan and started issuing directives.[7]

---

7   Some people disagree with me on this. They say that the Wuhan Central Committee was set up on the basis of a resolution passed by a plenary session of the Central Committee and that it was merely an accident that Chen and Peng stayed behind in Shanghai; their presence there did not imply that there was still a Central Committee in Shanghai. But they have been unable to find this resolution. I, on the other hand, have found the necessary evidence to support my own contention. A recently published speech by Roy in Wuhan (not included by Roy in his book but published by Bakulin, the Russian minutes-keeper) says quite clearly:

When the Comintern Executive reached Hankou, there were actually two Communist centres in existence in China: one in Shanghai (representing the Central Committee) and another in Hankou (representing certain members of the Central Committee). The Hankou centre demanded the immediate convening of a congress of delegates on the grounds that there was a leadership crisis and the leadership had to be replaced. They expressed universal dissatisfaction with the Central Committee. (See *Guowai Zhongguo jindai shi yanjiu* ('Foreign research on modern Chinese history'), No. 6, 268.)

This is definitely reliable, for Roy was leader of the Comintern delegation. He must have known whether the Central Committee had resolved to move from Shanghai to Hankou. His speech was made on May 12, 1927, i.e., several days after the Fifth Congress. According to Roy,

For a while there were two Central Committees: the one in Wuhan lacked a General Secretary, but it dealt with the Central Committee of the Guomindang in the name of the Central Committee of the CCP; Chen Duxiu, acting on behalf of the Central Committee in Shanghai, issued a joint declaration with Wang Jingwei, who had just got back from Moscow. It was not until just before April 12, 1927, at around the time of Peng and Chen's departure for Wuhan, that the Shanghai Central Committee went out of existence.

By the time that Chen and Peng arrived in Wuhan, Qu's pamphlet attacking Peng had already appeared, and so had Mao's 'Report on an Investigation of the Hunan Peasant Movement'. The mood against right-opportunism had already been manufactured in Wuhan. I delayed leaving Shanghai for Wuhan until late April; when I arrived I went straight to the Central Committee offices to see them. The Central Committee was housed in a three-storey foreign-style building with the guard-room and the canteen on the ground floor, the conference room on the first floor, and the living quarters of Chen Duxiu, Cai Hesen, and Peng Shuzhi on the second floor. After chatting for a bit, we went downstairs to eat. Present were Chen, Peng, Cai, Huang Wenrong, and I. I can't remember whether Chen Bilan and Li Yichun attended. While we were still eating, Peng mentioned Qu's pamphlet. He addressed Chen Duxiu, probably with a request for support in a counter-attack against Qu, I can't remember exactly. Cai Hesen merely smiled. Chen said sternly, 'You're you, I'm me'. Chen had no intention of cooperating with Peng in an inner-Party struggle, so Peng had no choice but to fight alone. He stepped up work on his counterblast to Qu.

By that time Qu Qiubai, Zhang Guotao, and Tan Pingshan controlled the Central Committee. They used to caucus before it met to harmonise their views. They distributed tasks and chimed in with one another at the meetings, so their views always ended up by winning out. Peng Shuzhi was like a pathetic daughter-in-law – whatever he did, he was in the wrong.[8] Chen Duxiu become a puppet of the Qu-Zhang-Tang troika and implemented its decisions. Needless to say, the members of the troika also harmonised their views in advance with Borodin.

The Comintern wanted to replace Chen Duxiu as General Secretary, but soundings showed that his prestige was too high for that to happen easily.

---

the Shanghai centre was the Central Committee; it was not simply that one or two of its members had been left behind. As for the Hankou centre, it merely represented 'certain members of the Central Committee', and moreover was opposed to the Central Committee. [Note added by Zheng Chaolin in the early 1980s.]

8   Daughters-in-law were commonly abused, especially by mothers-in-law, under the traditional Chinese family system.

What's more, it was hard to know who to replace him with. At one point, the Comintern leaders settled on Tan Pingshan, but Qu and Zhang also considered themselves in contention for the post. Chen Yannian's name came up too, but he refused. Some people said that he was not against replacing Chen Duxiu, but that he simply didn't want to succeed him personally.

So at the Fifth Congress the Comintern representative and the Qu-Zhang-Tan troika adopted the tactic of isolating Chen: they kept him on, but they got rid of all those who supported him. On the day the Congress opened, Luo Zhan-glong, head of the Hubei delegation, proposed a slate of names for the Congress Presidium. Chen was on it, but none of his associates was. On the final day of the Congress, when the elections for the Central Committee were about to take place, this Presidium put forward another slate that like the first one had Chen Duxiu on it but none of his supporters. After the slate had been put forward, Roy stood up in the name of the Comintern and proposed adding the names of Peng Shuzhi and Luo Yinong to it. Congress agreed, but afterwards the new Central Committee immediately sent Peng to Beijing, Luo Yinong to Jiangxi, Wang Ruofei to Shanghai, Yin Kuan to Guangdong, and me to Hubei. In short, we were not allowed to remain on the Central Committee. The only exception was Chen Qiaonian, who became Secretary of the Central Committee's Organ-isational Bureau.

By the way, here's an interesting anecdote. Although Li Weihan wasn't among those people who had been in Moscow, like them he had in the past suppor-ted Chen Duxiu. During the Congress he at one point told Wang Ruofei that the other leaders were applying the trick known as 'removing the emperor's entourage'. It was not difficult for him to see what was really going on during the inner-Party struggle. I got this by hearsay, from Wang Ruofei. But after the Congress, Li resolutely opposed Chen.

By then the 'Moscow group' was no longer in existence. There were people who had returned from Moscow, but there was no 'Moscow group'. Those who stuck by Chen Duxiu, whether or not they'd been in Moscow, were known as the 'Chen Duxiu group'.

(2)   *From Chen Duxiu Group to Trotsky Group*

The Chen Duxiu Group after the August 7 Conference

Today everyone says with one voice that Chen Duxiu was removed as General Secretary at the August 7 Conference. But actually, he stepped down. I've always said so. Recently while re-reading Cai Hesen's *Dang de jihui zhuyi shi* ('History of opportunism in the Party'), I came across a passage that said that sometime early in July Borodin had passed on a Comintern directive ordering Chen Duxiu and Tan Pingshan to go to Moscow and Qu Qiubai and Cai Hesen to go to Vladivostok, and that 'the next day Duxiu stopped attending to his duties'. So Chen Duxiu himself relinquished the General Secretaryship a good month before the August 7 Conference.[9]

Perhaps the August 7 Conference formally removed Chen from his post? No, it didn't. I was at the August 7 Conference. I heard Qu Qiubai read out the 'Letter to Comrades' and I heard other people deliver speeches. They all criticised past opportunist errors. Doubtless their criticisms were aimed at Chen Duxiu, but from start to finish no one at the Conference so much as mentioned his name, let alone resolved to sack him. The recently published collection of essays by Cai Hesen[10] includes a transcript of his speech to the Conference. In it he declares his support for the new line and criticises the old opportunist line, but he, too, fails to mention the name Chen Duxiu.

In the two months or more between the Fifth Congress and the August 7 Conference, the balance of power on the Central Committee changed greatly. The Qu-Zhang-Tan alliance had already come apart. Qu Qiubai now occupied the leading role, Zhang and Tan had marched South with the Ye-He army, Borodin had gone back to Russia, Roy and Voitinsky had resigned, and the 'prodigy' Lominadze had arrived in China to replace them. Even more remarkably, the ex-Chen Duxiu-ite Luo Yinong, who had been transferred from his old

---

9   It was not until after I had finished writing this draft that I came across a quotation from Zhang Guotao's *Memoirs* saying: 'On July 14 Mr Chen Duxiu was also in a secret hideout from which he did not emerge'. The person who quotes this added: On July 15, Chen Duxiu sent a letter of resignation to the Central Committee. He said: 'On the one hand the Comintern wants us to carry out our own policy, on the other it won't let us withdraw from the Guomindang. There really is no way out, I really can't continue my work'. He asked the Central Committee of the CCP to relieve him of his post as General Secretary.

      The author of this article gives no source for Chen's letter of resignation, so we don't know whether he or she is quoting directly from the letter or from some other document. If the quote is reliable, it proves even more surely that it is nonsense to claim – as people have been doing for decades now – that the August 7 Conference sacked Chen. Huang Jieran says that when Li Weihan went to Chen's secret hideout and told him that the Central Committee had already removed him as General Secretary, Chen was furious. That can't be true either. If he resigned himself, why would he get furious? It is clear from all this that Chen's resignation was mainly in protest at the Comintern's decision not to let the CCP withdraw from the Guomindang. [Note by Zheng Chaolin.] Here Zheng has obviously forgotten Chen Duxiu's 'Appeal to All Comrades of the Party'. In it Chen wrote: 'From the beginning I could not persistently maintain my opinion; but this time I could no longer bear it. I then tendered my resignation to the Central Committee. My chief reason for this was: The International wishes us to carry out our own policy on the one hand, and does not allow us to withdraw from the Guomindang on the other. There is really no way out and I cannot continue with my work' (Evans and Block, eds, 1976, p. 604).

10   *Cai Hesende shierpian wenjian* ('Twelve articles by Cai Hesen').

post as Provincial Secretary in Jiangxi to do the same job in Hubei, rose on the eve of the August 7 Conference to become a member of the all-powerful Standing Committee[11] while simultaneously retaining his Hubei post. Luo was extremely capable, and in such critical times his support could hardly be dispensed with. But this is only an apparent explanation. I later heard that Luo had written to Zhang Guotao from Jiangxi saying that he would no longer back Chen Duxiu but would carry out the line of the Fifth Congress. This is hearsay and I have not yet been able to confirm it, let alone to see the letter. But I tend to think that it is the true reason for his sudden rise.

Luo Yinong lacked followers and in Shanghai he relied on the Chen Duxiu people. While he was Secretary in Hubei both Liu Bojian (the head of his Organisational Bureau) and Zheng Chaolin (who continued to run his Propaganda Department) were Chen Duxiu supporters; Ren Xu, the head of his Peasant Department, who had worked in Mao Zedong's Peasant Training Institute in Guangzhou, also became a Chen Duxiu-ite shortly after his transfer to Hubei. About one week after the August 7 Conference the Central Committee replaced Liu Bojian in Hubei with Chen Qiaonian and Zheng Chaolin with Hua Lin (also a Chen Duxiu supporter). Zheng Chaolin was switched back to the Central Committee, where he was assigned to revive the publication of *Guide Weekly*, which had been suspended for a long time.

Just imagine: at around the time of the Fifth Congress the Central Committee did everything in its power to exclude followers of Chen Duxiu, but after the August 7 Conference they had to be allowed back onto the same body that had campaigned against them. But it's not really so surprising. Chen Duxiu himself was no longer a member of the Central Committee, and Luo Yinong was no longer a Chen Duxiu-ite but a semi-Chen Duxiu-ite. Luo had no following, nor did Qu Qiubai; of the three members of the Standing Committee, only Li Weihan had a 'following' that had escaped with him to Wuhan from Hunan, but the Central Committee could not be kept going exclusively by Hunanese. For example, they couldn't revive *Guide Weekly*. In July Zhang Guotao had proposed getting Shen Yanbing to revive it, but Shen had a family to support. After the August 7 Conference it occurred to them that I could do it, for I was still a bachelor; what's more, I had experience in publishing. So they brought me

---

11   Before the August 7 Conference, Luo was simply a member of the Central Committee, but after the Conference he was promoted into the Politburo. When the Central Committee moved back to Shanghai, Luo was still a member of the Politburo. He became a member of the Standing Committee of the Politburo in late 1927 or early 1928. He had already attended meetings of it even before then. The Standing Committee consisted of Qu Qiubai, Li Weihan, and Su Zhaozheng. [Note added by Zheng Chaolin in 1990.]

back to work in the Central Committee. In late September, when the Central Committee transferred back to Shanghai, I was formally appointed editor of the Party journal.

In Shanghai the Central Committee had originally appointed Deng Zhongxia as Secretary of the Jiangsu Provincial Committee, but the cadres of the Committee were Chen Duxiu supporters who ignored Deng and listened only to Wang Ruofei. 'I'm only Deputy Secretary!' Deng complained to the Central Committee shortly after its transfer to Shanghai. What he meant was that real power in the Provincial Committee belonged to Wang Ruofei. Not long after that, he left the Jiangsu Provincial Committee.

Yin Kuan in Guangdong was unable to cooperate with Zhang Tailei, so he returned to Shanghai; the Central Committee made him Provincial Secretary in Anhui. He Zishen ran the Hunan Provincial Committee's Organisation Department and became its Secretary after Mao Zedong went up the mountains. The Hubei Committee was made up exclusively of Chen Duxiu supporters. In Beijing Peng Shuzhi took the post vacated by the death of Li Dazhao. And so on, and so forth.

Wang Ruofei worked out a plan to get Chen Duxiu back onto the Central Committee, but nothing came of it. The first obstacle was the Comintern. It was precisely the Comintern, precisely Stalin, that forced Chen Duxiu to 'throw away his official's hat' in early July, 1927; Chen had no choice but to resign as General Secretary (or, as Cai Hesen put it, to 'stop attending to his duties'). So the Comintern wouldn't have let Chen Duxiu return as General Secretary. In the summer of 1927, the Chen Duxiu people could never have been defeated in the inner-Party struggle but for the intervention of the Comintern. The second obstacle was the Guomindang's White terror, as a result of which Chen Qiaonian and Luo Yinong had been seized and martyred. Luo was a 'semi-Chen Duxiu-ite' who at the time was sitting on the fence. If conditions had been right, he might have approved of Chen Duxiu's return to power and backed him from his position on the Standing Committee as Director of the Organisation Bureau. The third obstacle was Chen Duxiu himself. He was completely passive, and had no wish to take up work again after having just given it up. Lots of people went to talk with him, but as soon as politics came up he'd change the subject. For example, when Luo Qiyuan tried to discuss inner-Party matters with him, he took out his scheme for spelling Chinese characters and started asking Luo how you said this character or that character in Cantonese. He later said that at the time he had been pondering basic questions in the Chinese Revolution, including how much responsibility he himself should take for the defeat. He weighed the issues over a long period of time, but was unable to resolve them. On occasions he raised criticisms of various policies then being pursued by the

Central Committee. He recorded them in letters, but needless to say the Central Committee was not prepared to accept them.[12] He knew that Wang Ruofei and Chen Qiaonian were working hard on his behalf, but he did nothing to encourage them, nor did he forbid them to do what they were doing. Some people thought that he was only pretending to be passive, and that he was secretly masterminding Wang and Chen's campaign. I disagree, but I, too, find it hard to explain why Chen had become so passive. Facts show that he could again become active once he had finished pondering the issues. In the second half of 1929, he was helped to do so by Trotsky's articles. He then came out resolutely against Stalin, against the Communist International, and against the Central Committee of the CCP.

In the face of these three obstacles, the Chen Duxiu-ites under the leadership of Wang Ruofei were doomed to failure.

Under the Politburo Elected by the August 7 Conference

The Central Committee elected by the August 7 Conference moved back to Shanghai in late September. Qu Qiubai and Luo Yinong were still very respectful toward Chen Duxiu. Two or three days after arriving in Shanghai, Qu went to visit him; his attitude toward him was the same as it had ever been. I don't know what they talked about. At that time Huang Wenrong was still living in Chen's house as his private secretary; he, too, didn't tell me what they talked about. All I know is that Chen handed Huang back to the Central Committee, and Qu accepted him. A few days after that Luo Yinong also went to visit Chen; needless to say, he, too, behaved respectfully. Chen got Huang to make a record of his conversation with Luo, but I haven't seen it. Not long after that, Huang was assigned to help me set up the editorial office of the Central Committee organ. In late December Luo Yinong came and asked me to invite Chen to stay in my

---

12   Chen's letters of November 11 and 12 and of December 13, 1927, are still extant, together with two replies by the Standing Committee. Chen's correspondence with the Standing Committee was greater than just these few items. According to his letter of August 5, 1929, to the Standing Committee, at around the time of the Guangzhou Insurrection he 'wrote several letters to the Central Committee that did not avoid taboo subjects'. 'The Central Committee not only paid no attention to the opinions I raised in my letters but spread them round as if they were jokes'. That reminds me of something that Chen once told me. The reason he stopped writing to the Central Committee born from the August 7 Conference was because Chen Qiaonian told him not to, on the grounds that the Central Committee was making jokes about his letters. It was not until July 28, 1929, after he had basically become a Trotskyist, that he wrote three letters on the subject of the Chinese Eastern Railway. The Central Committee born of the August 7 Conference considered his letters to be a 'joke': the Central Committee elected by the Sixth Congress considered them to be 'counterrevolutionary'. [Note added by Zheng Chaolin in 1980.]

house (i.e., in the editorial office) for three days so that he and Qu could have a discussion with the Old Man. On December 24, Huang hired a car to bring Chen over. Chen slept in Huang's room. That evening I organised a dinner for Chen, Qu, Luo, Wang Ruofei, and some other guests. The next day Qu and Luo had their talk with Chen. I had some private business, so I did not attend. On the fourth day Huang took Chen back home.

One day while we were chatting, Qu told me that the Old Man had said that if we had decided earlier to quit the Guomindang and carry out land revolution, he would have acted on the decision. Qu went on to express strong opposition to Chen's statement. I seem to remember that he asked me what I thought, but I said nothing.

The Standing Committee appointed Qu Qiubai, Luo Yinong, Deng Zhongxia, Wang Ruofei, and Zheng Chaolin to the editorial board of the Central Committee organ, with Qu Qiubai as chairman. I only recently saw the document, dated October 12, 1927, in which this decision was recorded. I'd always thought that I was editor and Qu was the bridge between us and the Standing Committee, that he represented the Standing Committee on the editorial board and told us what it thought and told it what we were doing. Clearly I remembered wrong. There's no mistake about the document. I must have known about it, but I'd completely forgotten. The editorial board was a fiction, it never met even once. Qu and Luo represented the Central Committee, Deng and Wang represented the Jiangsu Provincial Committee, and I did the actual work. Shortly after his appointment Deng left the Jiangsu Provincial Committee. He never once came to my house. Luo and Wang often used to come, but not for the editorial board.

The new organ no longer used the name *Guide Weekly* but called itself *Bolshevik*. I wrote an article for the founding issue titled 'What Next for the Chinese Revolution after the Betrayal of the Revolution by the Guomindang?' The article concluded that the revolution had already been defeated, and that we would have to start again. After it came out, no one discussed it with me, but I myself discovered that my own viewpoint directly contradicted that of the Central Committee, i.e. of the Comintern. It turned out that the Central Committee, i.e., the Comintern, not only did not recognise that the Chinese Revolution had already been defeated but concluded that it was still in spate, and that the tide had risen even further. I delivered myself a private warning: in future write fewer articles on policy. No one pointed out that my article ran counter to the Comintern line, and no one even noticed that it did. Wang Ruofei – not because he had noticed the article, but simply in the course of an idle conversation – once told me that he'd gone to see the Old Man with He Zishen and the Old Man said: Look, the British, US, and French troops stationed in Shanghai are withdrawing in batches, do you think that the imperialists would do that if the tide of the Chinese Revolution were still rising? Wang told me that it was as if Chen's comment had suddenly jolted him awake. I thought to myself, so the Old Man thinks the same as me, that the Chinese Revolution has already been defeated.

I invariably asked Qu Qiubai to write the *Bolshevik* editorials, for as a member of the Standing Committee he was familiar with Party policy. But for some reason he was too busy to attend the editorial conference that planned *Bolshevik* No. 11, so the task devolved on me. The Guangzhou Insurrection had just ended, so I called my editorial 'Long Live Soviet Power'. I said in it that China had only two possible futures: either a 'Great Dragon Empire' under the dictatorship of the warlord Zhang Zuolin and a Guomindang Republic under the dictatorship of the bourgeoisie, or a Soviet Republic under the dictatorship of the proletariat. There was no third way. The editorial got me into a lot of trouble. About a fortnight after it came out, at a meeting of the editorial board, Qu Qiubai reported that according to Li Weihan speaking at a meeting of the Standing Committee, Zheng Chaolin's editorial was at odds with Comintern policy; our slogan was 'workers and peasants' democratic dictatorship', not 'dictatorship of the proletariat'. So Qu wrote an editorial for *Bolshevik* No. 14 rectifying my mistake. He energetically explained that the Soviets set up during the Guangzhou Insurrection were a 'workers and peasants' democratic dictatorship', not a 'proletarian dictatorship'. After that I stopped writing editorials, and I generally did my best to write as little as possible. But my heresy as yet found no echo in the views of Chen Duxiu. Quite the contrary. Later, after we came into contact with Trotsky's writings, I immediately agreed with Trotsky's views on the nature of the future Chinese revolutionary state, but Chen Duxiu stood out against Trotsky on this point for quite some time.

After Qu Qiubai had returned to Shanghai from Wuhan, the first time he visited Chen Duxiu he asked him to write some articles for the forthcoming Party journal. Far from refusing, Chen sent me numerous items for his 'Inch of Iron' column, all of which I published, in issue after issue. They're in the recent reprint, you can read them for yourselves. He wrote them under the name Sa Weng, meaning 'Old Man Sa'.[13] I guess he wanted to say by using that name that he'd never again play any role in the leadership of the CCP. Apart from 'Inch of Iron', he also wrote some ballads satirising the Guomindang. Each issue of *Bolshevik* contained one or more of these space-fillers. They were omitted from the reprint series, but I still remember a few lines from one of them:

---

13   *Sashou* means to relinquish or let go one's hold.

The Three People's Principles are a muddle.
The Five Rights[14] are a mess.
Education that conforms to Party propaganda is tyranny.
Under military rule, only warlords have a say.
In the period of tutelage, the bureaucrats hold sway.
The period of constitutional rule is far, far away.[15]

Later, I can't remember when, he stopped writing 'Inch of Iron', and the verses stopped even earlier. I never learned what he thought of the various issues of *Bolshevik* that came out.

In the first six months after the move to Shanghai, three people were very friendly to me: Qu Qiubai, Luo Yinong, and Wang Ruofei. All of them wanted to win me over, but I kept a certain distance from them. I knew about Wang Ruofei and Chen Qiaonian's campaign, but I took no part in it. Wang never tried to force me to join them. He knew I'd never gang up with anyone against Chen Duxiu. Not long after the Central Committee elected by the Sixth Congress had returned to Shanghai from the Soviet Union and started work, Wang Maoting, Secretary of the Yunnan Provincial Committee, came to see me on his way back from Moscow and handed me a letter written in invisible ink. Wang Ruofei had asked him in Moscow to give it to me and to tell me how to make the characters appear. I got the two necessary chemicals and mixed them according to Wang Maoting's prescription. I made the characters appear and handed the letter to Chen Duxiu, for it was addressed to him. Wang Ruofei had asked the Central Committee to pass the letter on to Chen Duxiu through ordinary channels, but knowing that that would not happen, he had made an invisible copy of it and asked Wang Maoting to deliver it into my hands. All I remember about the letter is that it reported on the proceedings of the Sixth Congress and Wang Ruofei's own reactions to it, and that it mentioned Qu Qiubai's 'Zero International' and Cai Hesen's *History of Opportunism*, both of which it called 'shameful documents'. Wang Ruofei told Wang Maoting to ask me to send him Chen's reply written in the same invisible ink. I was prepared to do so, but after Chen had read the letter his face registered not the slightest reaction, and he did not reply. The reason I recount this incident is because it shows that Wang Ruofei trus-

---

14   Sun Yat-sen's 'Quintuple Constitution' was based on the five principles of administrative authority, i.e., judicial authority, legislative authority, executive authority, authority for conducting civil service tests, and authority to censor.

15   Sun Yat-sen had predicted that the Nationalist Revolution would go through three stages: military rule; political tutelage, i.e., rule by the party on behalf of the people; and, finally, democratic constitutional rule.

ted me completely, and it also shows that at that time Chen Duxiu was still not prepared to take an active part in the struggle.

Under the Central Committee Elected by the Sixth Congress

In September 1928, the Central Committee elected by the Sixth Congress took up its official duties in Shanghai. The General Secretary Xiang Zhongfa was a puppet: real power was in the hands of Cai Hesen, who ran the Propaganda Department. According to reports, before returning to China Cai had asked Qu Qiubai who should edit *Bolshevik*. Qu recommended that I be kept on to do so. I worked under Cai just as I had previously worked under Qu, but I got on with him less well than I had with Qu, though we still managed to push our way forward. That didn't last for long, however. Very soon Cai was toppled and replaced by Li Lisan. I was even less happy about working together with Li Lisan, for he was openly opposed to Chen Duxiu and knew I was a Chen supporter. We not only got on badly: we were downright hostile to one another. There were several instances of friction between us. At a meeting of the editorial board I asked Li to find someone more suited to the job. To my face he refused to let me go, but behind my back he sought the opinion of Qu Qiubai, then in Moscow. Qu decided to send Wu Jiyan back to replace me. As an interim measure Li appointed Pan Wenyu, who had already got back from Russia, to take over from me. So I quit work and lived idly. Chen Duxiu told Peng Shuzhi that if Qu Qiubai had been on the Central Committee in Shanghai, Zheng Chaolin would never have ended up in such a way.

While Li Lisan held power, that was exactly how followers of Chen were dealt with. Sharing my idleness were Yin Kuan, who resigned as Provincial Secretary in Anhui; Peng Shuzhi, who resigned as Provincial Secretary in Zhili;[16] Wang Zekai, who'd been active together with Wang Ruofei at the Sixth Congress and had been kept out of a job by the Central Committee; Liu Bojian, who had escaped from Hubei, where he had been Provincial Secretary, to Shanghai, but was kept idle by the Central Committee; and Ren Xu, who was in the same boat as Wang Zekai.

I and Jing moved out of the Central Committee office and went to stay with Cai Zhende. Zhang Yisen, the wife of He Zishen, was living in the small room with her baby daughter, not yet weaned. He Zishen himself had been sent to Shandong on Party business, though the Central Committee had at the same time warned the Provincial Committee in Shandong not to ask him to do any 'political work'. Not long afterwards something went wrong in the Provincial

---

16   Present-day Hebei.

Committee and He Zishen was arrested and thrown in prison. Cai Zhende was at that time a member of the Jiangsu Provincial Committee. Starting with the Jiangsu-Zhejiang Regional Committee, most cadre members of the committees at all the different levels in Shanghai were Chen Duxiu supporters. After the Sixth Congress, when Wang Ruofei was detained in Moscow, Li Fuchun took over from him as Secretary of the Provincial Committee in Jiangsu and his followers were gradually replaced by Li's friends; the only two to survive were Cai Zhende and Ma Yufu.

In early 1929, the Jiangsu Provincial Committee and the Central Committee clashed. There was a struggle, and the Jiangsu Committee even declared its 'independence'. I forget what the conflict was about, but it was personal rather than political. Li Lisan and Xiang Ying on the Politburo had both worked in the labour movement. In 1924, when I had first got back to China, Li was in charge of the labour movement in West Shanghai and Xiang in East Shanghai. They vied with one another to see who could achieve most. Li Lisan won, and became leader of the Shanghai General Labour Union. At some point, ill will grew up between them. By this time, after the Sixth Congress, Xiang was on the Politburo but his power and status were below Li's. I seem to remember that after the Sixth Congress Xiang Ying at first took over as Provincial Secretary in Jiangsu and it was not until later that Li Fuchun got that job. Xiang Ying incited Li Fuchun and the Jiangsu Provincial Committee against Li Lisan. He Mengxiong, head of the Organisational Department of the Provincial Committee in Jiangsu, also joined in the campaign. They asked Cai Zhende and Ma Yufu to see if Chen Duxiu was willing to help them. They especially needed help on the propaganda side, for they lacked people who could write. He Mengxiong said: get Zheng Chaolin. Cai Zhende heard him say this, and told me. Li Fuchun came personally to visit me. At that time I was living in the house of Li Minzhi. Li Fuchun told me about the conflict and said he hoped that I would help the Jiangsu Committee. I said I would. But he added that later he wanted me to take over as head of the Propaganda Department on the Jiangsu Provincial Committee. I took unkindly to that, and did not respond. During those days we Chen Duxiu supporters (Peng Shuzhi, Liu Bozhuang, Wang Zekai, Zheng Chaolin, Cai Zhende, and Ma Yufu) gathered at Cai Zhende's place to hear Cai's report on the conflict and to draft some necessary documents. In the end, the Jiangsu Committee lost its struggle after Zhou Enlai took measures against it. He called together comrades from all over China then in Shanghai for a meeting that passed a resolution reproaching the Jiangsu Committee in the name of the entire Party throughout China; at the same time the Politburo met and a majority jointly attacked Xiang Ying. So Xiang and Li Fuchun had no choice but to abandon their positions. The Jiangsu Committee was reformed, whereupon

Cai Zhende and Ma Yufu, the two Chen Duxiu supporters who were Wang Ruo-fei's friends on the Committee, withdrew from it.

During this conflict Chen Duxiu neither egged us on nor held us back. It is especially noteworthy that this time there was no choice but to allow Peng Shuzhi to join in the campaign. A year earlier, when Wang Ruofei and Chen Qiaonian were campaigning on behalf of Chen Duxiu, there was no question of letting Peng join them, and even less of letting him lead them. But now Chen Qiaonian was dead and Wang Ruofei was under detention in Moscow. Cai Zhende, Ma Yufu, and Zheng Chaolin despised Peng, but Wang Zekai and Liu Bojian supported him, so we had little choice but to let him join our campaign.

After Cai Zhende and Ma Yufu had withdrawn from the Jiangsu Provincial Committee, the Committee continued to provide for their livelihood and let Cai live in one of the furnished houses at the disposal of the Committee. Cai invited me and Jing to go and live with him. We moved there in mid February.

The Chen Duxiu Supporters' Leap to Trotskyism

Cai Zhende and his wife lived on the first floor of a three-storey building and Jing and I lived on the top floor. He Zishen's wife Zhang Yisen lived in the smallest room with her newborn daughter. Ma Yufu often used to drop in for a chat.

After the defeat of the Jiangsu Committee, the Chen Duxiu supporters' campaign against the Central Committee was exposed. Why were we against the Central Committee? From my own point of view there were four main reasons. First, the reproaches made at and after the August 7 Conference against the Central Committee represented by Chen Duxiu were unfair. The defeat of the revolution wasn't Chen's fault. Chen was simply carrying out the line of the Fourth Congress. Second, after the defeat had happened, the August 7 Conference denied it and claimed that the revolution was on the crest of an even higher wave, so the Central Committee called for insurrections and many lost their lives in vain in armed risings, without benefiting the revolution in the slightest. Third, there was no democracy in the Party, and senior cadres were split into numerous unprincipled warring cliques pursuing private ends. Fourth, the Party's various leaders were not acting in an upright way: they were base in character and morals. And so on, and so forth. Perhaps the other Chen Duxiu supporters saw things differently. In short, the issues we raised in the course of this struggle were all quite narrow and rarely touched on points of high principle. It's a fact that we failed to grasp those fundamental questions of the revolution; save for Chen Duxiu, we knew very little about the reality of China. If we'd carried on like that, then even if the Central Committee had tolerated us instead of attacking us our little group would soon have vanished.

On March 18, less than a month after my wife and I went to live with Cai Zhende, officers of the Guomindang's Public Security Bureau came to arrest Zhang Yisen and in passing unearthed documents in the rooms of our two families, so we were all taken off to prison. Ma Yufu, who had just happened to drop in at that moment, was also seized.

The Military Committee of the Central Committee under Zhou Enlai did everything in its power to rescue us, and some social contacts of mine and Cai Zhende's helped too, so except for Zhang Yisen, who spent several months in gaol, the rest of us left the Garrison Headquarters' detention centre at Longhua on April 29.

After we'd moved and settled down, Yin Kuan dropped in on us one day. Yin was meant to have visited us on the day we were arrested, but for some reason he hadn't come, so he'd escaped the misfortune that befell the rest of us. Now he started coming regularly again. Probably in mid or late May 1929, he brought some unusual mimeographed documents for us to see, documents of the Trotskyist Opposition in the Soviet Union. They were poorly translated and poorly mimeographed, but still they were intelligible. Yin Kuan had obviously been affected by them. He excitedly introduced them to us. I can't remember which documents they were, and whether he brought them separately or in one go, but they immediately gripped me. I had known that there was a fierce struggle going on in the Soviet Party, and that at first the Trotskyist Opposition had opposed the faction in power, consisting of Zinoviev, Kamenev, Bukharin, and Stalin; and that later Zinoviev and Kamenev had somehow allied with the Trotskyist Opposition against Bukharin and Stalin, who in the meantime had taken over. But I didn't know what the issues were, or even that they extended to the question of the Chinese Revolution. But now I had the documents in my hands. It turned out that Trotsky had publicly pointed out long before the defeat of the revolution that the Comintern's basic line on the Chinese Revolution was wrong, and that after the defeat of the revolution he had publicly pointed out that Bukharin and Stalin should take the blame for it. It also turned out that Trotsky had pointed out even after the Wuhan debacle that the Chinese Revolution had already been defeated. This was exactly what Chen Duxiu and his followers thought. We immediately embraced Trotsky's system of thought and steeped ourselves in his writings in order to discover on what grounds he had arrived at these two standpoints. They were not simply derived from his basic theory of 'permanent revolution'. He had analysed and quoted a large number of documents, including a copy of the resolution of the Jiangsu Provincial Committee drafted by Wang Ruofei pointing out numerous errors committed by the Central Committee of the CCP. Wang Ruofei had published this document in Moscow and the Trotskyist students there had translated it

into Russian for Trotsky. But it was very hard for us to achieve a thorough understanding of Trotsky's basic theory. In Moscow we (for almost of us who had now
become Chen Duxiu supporters were Moscow people) had studied Marxism
and Leninism, but not Trotskyism. We'd known for a long time that Trotsky had
a 'theory of permanent revolution', but we had no idea what it said. In the past
we'd also applied ourselves to questions like the nature of society, the nature of
the revolution, the motive power of the revolution, the object of the revolution,
the stages of the revolution, revolutionary strategy and tactics, the revolutionary state, and so on. But we'd studied them one by one, in isolation from one
another: we were unable to assemble such a wide range of topics into a single
whole, so the more we learned, the more muddled we became. Now, after studying the 'theory of permanent revolution', these topics suddenly sprang to life
and became linked together in a coherent system, so they were no longer confusing. After that I dropped the question of who was to blame for the defeat of
the revolution and whether the tide was high or low and went on to 'indulge
myself in abstract thinking', i.e., to study basic principles and the theoretical
aspect of how these various issues hung together.

Another issue that attracted my attention while reading Trotsky was his consistent opposition to the CCP's entry into the Guomindang. In 1922, in France,
when the branches of the Communist Youth Party had discussed this question,
I'd been against it and got into an argument with Yin Kuan, who was for it. As
for Peng Shuzhi, in Moscow in 1923, he enthusiastically supported entry.

We all quickly embraced Trotskyism. After discussing and exchanging ideas
for just a week or two, we basically became Trotskyists. But Chen Duxiu held
out for longer than the rest of us. At the same time as Yin Kuan gave Trotsky's
mimeographed articles to us (Cai Zhende and his wife Wang Shaohua, Zheng
Chaolin and his wife Wu Jingru, and Ma Yufu) to read, he also gave them to Peng
Shuzhi and his wife Chen Bilan, to Wang Zekai and his wife Du Lin, and to Liu
Bozhuang. The Peng and Wang families lived together in a house on Kunming
Road opposite the high wall of Ward Road Gaol where Chen Duxiu often used
to visit them. It was there that he read Trotsky's documents. He discussed them
with Peng Shuzhi, Yin Kuan, and Wang Zekai, and they convinced him. I personally did not take part in those discussions. We were not long out of gaol, and
Chen Duxiu did not come to visit me in that period, nor did I go to visit him in
his new house. Yin Kuan used to pass between my place and Peng's, so it was
mainly from Yin that I heard about the change in Chen's thinking.

After reading each of Trotsky's documents, Chen would raise a disagreement, and then they would argue with him; but by the next time he came he
would have abandoned his previous disagreement and would raise a new one
on the shoulders of their old argument. In the course of his gradual conversion

to their point of view, he had never once yielded to them in their presence, but next time he came face to face with them he would raise new differences on the basis of what they had previously told him. And so it went on. The person who put the most effort into winning him was Yin Kuan. But in the end, when it came to the question of the revolutionary power (should it be a dictatorship of the proletariat?), Chen was not persuaded, or at least not wholly persuaded. After Liu Renjing came back to China, and even when we and the other three groups were holding talks, Chen still didn't wholly accept Trotsky's views on the nature of this power.

In the course of this debate Chen not only spoke his views but also wrote them down in articles that he took along with him for Peng, Yin, and Wang to read. There were probably seven or eight such articles, all of which I read. None was published or kept, which is a pity, nor was a record made of the discussions. Otherwise we could have used it and the articles to trace the entire process whereby one of China's major modern thinkers came round to Trotskyism.

All this probably happened between the second half of May and the first half of July 1929. The reason I'm paying so much attention to dates and times is in order to dispel some current myths.

The most common myth is that Chen was unaware of Trotsky's views until Liu Renjing got back to China with a number of documents written by Trotsky, and that it was only then that Chen came under Trotsky's influence and became his follower. Actually, by the time that Liu Renjing met Chen Duxiu, Chen had already embraced Trotskyism (save for his above-mentioned reservations on certain theoretical questions). We followers of Chen Duxiu were by then even more resolutely Trotskyist. Liu Renjing reached Shanghai in September. He knew from the Chinese Trotskyist organisation that had returned to China from Moscow – he even knew it while he was still abroad, probably because Trotsky told him – that Chen Duxiu and his followers had already embraced Trotskyism. That's why he got someone to bring a letter to Yin Kuan and me asking us to visit him in a hostel in the French Concession. We spoke a common Trotskyist language. Later, when I took Liu Renjing to my home (on East Youheng Road) to meet Chen Duxiu, they, too, spoke a common Trotskyist language. Liu Renjing brought three documents with him back to China: one was the Draft Programme of the Chinese Bolshevik-Leninists, which Trotsky had specially written while Liu was a guest in Trotsky's house in Turkey; another, called 'Results and Prospects of the Chinese Revolution', was Trotsky's criticism of the part relating to the Chinese Revolution in Bukharin's draft programme for the Communist International; another was an article by Trotsky, titled 'The Chinese Question after the Sixth Congress', written after the Sixth

Congress of the Communist International. The two articles were very long and in Russian, as, too, was the draft programme of the Chinese Opposition.

Someone told me that Liu Renjing recently told a visitor from the Party History Department of one of the Beijing universities that the draft programme he brought back to China had already been translated into Chinese when it was handed over to Chen Duxiu, and that Zheng Chaolin later polished it for publication. That's possible, I can't remember. As for the two long articles, I remember clearly that we decided that Liu would translate 'Results and Prospects' and I would translate 'After the Sixth Congress'. The two translations formed the text of the second volume of *On the Question of the Chinese Revolution*. (The first volume consisted of the earlier articles by Trotsky that had come into our hands; it was published before Liu Renjing returned to China.)

Then there's Pu Qingquan's[17] theory. Pu says that Chen Duxiu first learned about Trotsky's views from his (Chen's) nephew Wu Jiyan. According to Pu, Wu came to see Chen Duxiu and us at the end of 1929, after he'd been unmasked as a Trotskyist, sacked from his post, and expelled from the Party. That was even longer after Liu's return to China. By then Chen Duxiu no longer needed a Wu Jiyan to show him Trotsky's writings. Before his expulsion Wu had been Secretary of the Central Committee's Propaganda Department and wouldn't have dared have dealings with his uncle or with us.

Then there's Peng Shuzhi's theory. Peng says that he got hold of 'Results and Prospects' and 'After the Sixth Congress' from some Trotskyist students who had returned from Moscow and showed them to Chen. What actually happened is that Yin Kuan got them from Wang Pingyi,[18] Yin gave them to Peng, and Peng gave them to Chen. Peng deliberately obscured Yin's link in the chain; what Peng showed Chen was not the two long articles but a number of shorter articles, i.e., those collected in the first volume of the Chinese edition of *On the Question of the Chinese Revolution*. The two long articles weren't translated into Chinese until after Liu got back from Europe. The story of how the two volumes were prepared and published is sufficient to refute Peng's theory.

Apart from this there are various other rumours, but what I've just said is the truth, and whatever does not accord with it should be rectified.

---

17   Alias Pu Dezhi, who was arrested together with Chen Duxiu and held in the same prison. In 1952, Pu was arrested by the CCP together with all the other Chinese Trotskyists, but he capitulated and was released. He wrote a long article called 'Chen Duxiu as I knew him' in *Wenshi ziliao xuanji*, no. 71, published by Zhongguo wenshi chubanshe for the National People's Political Consultative Conference.

18   A student returned from Moscow. See Sheng 1971, pp. 171–2.

All of us Chen Duxiu-ites became Trotskyists, but our motives, goals, and emphases were by no means identical. Roughly speaking, we were of two main sorts. One stressed the practical movement and recognised that given the defeat of the revolution, we should now conduct peaceful and legal campaigns, deeply enter into the masses, strike roots there, oppose the Central Committee's ill-omened armed struggle, and wait until the mass movement revived before preparing to take up arms again. Absolutely no one proposed disbanding the underground Party. So the charge of 'liquidationism' bandied about by the Comintern and the Central Committee was simply slander. The *liquidateurs* in Russian revolutionary history proposed disbanding the underground Party, for in French *liquider* means to disband or dissolve. It's a commercial term. If a company or an enterprise goes bankrupt and closes down, it 'goes into liquidation'. The words 'liquidate' and 'liquidator' entered our language through Japanese. What is it that's liquidated? The underground Party is liquidated, i.e., disbanded. So if no one proposes disbanding the Party, then it's wrong to start calling people 'liquidators'. Some Trotskyists of this variety opposed discussing theoretical questions concerning the nature of society, the revolution, and the state, and wanted to confine discussion to questions concerning practical activity and the practical struggle. The second sort stressed theory; they wanted to discuss basic issues of the revolution. But like the first sort, they were not against practical activity. One of the biggest differences between the Chinese Revolution and the early Russian Revolution was that the Russians had only set up their Party after extensively debating and quarrelling about basic issues of the revolution, and continued to do so even afterwards. So the Russian revolutionaries had already clarified these issues in the course of their revolutionary activity, and they all had their own ways of looking at things. The Chinese Revolution was not like that. There was no clear and wide-ranging theoretical struggle before the founding of the Party, nor afterwards either, when we hurled ourselves into the raging fire. For theory we relied on foreign comrades and the Comintern: we trusted them to solve our problems for us. This may be why the CCP was repeatedly defeated. The emergence of Trotskyism in China might have provided an opportunity for steeling revolutionaries in polemic and increasing their knowledge of theory, but unfortunately by that time the Comintern and the CCP were in the rough grip of Stalinism, so the opportunity was missed and only a handful of revolutionaries got a thorough theoretical training.

The intellectual preparation for China's proletarian revolution was far inferior to that not only of Russia's proletarian revolution but also of China's own bourgeois revolution. The polemics waged between reformists and revolutionaries before the Revolution of 1911 shook the whole country, that goes without saying; before the Coup of 1898, there were even violent theoretical disputes between conservatives and reformists, between the Orthodox Confucianists and the Modern Text School. In the course of the polemic, both sides relied on their own resources to resolve the various theoretical issues in dispute, and certainly neither of them looked abroad for help, from organisations or individuals. The proletarian revolution is of course world-wide, unlike the bourgeois revolution, which is contained within national boundaries, so the theoretical struggle on a world scale can more or less be substituted for that in one country; but that by no means dispenses with the need for theoretical struggle within the state where the revolution is occurring.

In this theoretical struggle Chen Duxiu was active, conscientious, and persistent, quite the opposite of his previous self. Many people had misunderstood his previous apathy. They had thought that he was just pretending, that he was deliberately letting Wang Ruofei campaign on his behalf while he hid behind the screen and pulled the strings. Others thought that he was genuinely apathetic about the revolution and about politics, that he had completely lost heart and given up. But now it can be shown that both suppositions were wrong. Between July 1927, when he 'stopped attending to his duties', and May 1929, when he first came across Trotsky's writings, Chen was passive because he had not yet thought through to the end important questions of revolutionary theory; by himself he was not capable of resolving the weighty issues in the Chinese and world revolutions with which he was then wrestling. Those at his side, starting with Wang Ruofei, were unable to help him in this enterprise. Only Trotsky's articles could do that.

I don't have his 'Letter to All Party Comrades' to hand, nor do I have the statement 'Our Political Views' signed by 81 people. But I do have his 'Reply to the Comintern' dated February 17, 1930. In it he says:

> After the tragic and shameful defeat of the Chinese Revolution in 1927, for a while I was really at a loss as to what course of action to follow, since I myself bore a heavy responsibility for the defeat. So I spent almost a whole year personally reflecting on those events. Although I did not thoroughly grasp the lessons of the defeat in time, and failed to discover a new way forward, I am deeply aware on the basis of my own experience that this defeat was the inevitable outcome of the entire political line of the past period.

He also says:

Because of your deceiving ways and your blockade on the free passage of information, it was not until half a year ago that some documents by Comrade Trotsky on the Chinese question and some questions relating to the Soviet Union came into our hands. It was only then that we thoroughly and systematically understood the true source of the opportunism and adventurism perpetrated in the course of the Chinese Revolution.

He also says:

At present the main issues concerning the Chinese Revolution are: (1) Will the revolutionary power issuing from the future third revolution be a workers and peasants' democratic dictatorship or a proletarian dictatorship? (2) Should we now directly prepare an armed insurrection, or should we raise political slogans appropriate to a transitional period in the revolution (e.g. the call for a National Assembly), and struggle for democracy?

Trotsky's writings had a big impact not only on Chen Duxiu but on Communists and revolutionaries the world over. When Trotsky's 'Criticism of the Draft Programme of the Comintern' was handed over to the Sixth Congress of the Comintern, it was initially kept from delegates; it was only when some delegates demanded to see it that the Comintern, under the control of the Soviet Party, allowed three delegates from each country to read it, under the strict injunction to divulge its contents to no one. Many unprejudiced delegates – and even some prejudiced ones – were influenced by Trotsky's critique and changed their view of the man. According to what someone told me, the Chinese delegation appointed Qu Qiubai, Guan Xiangying, and another person (whose name I forget) to read it. As a result Qu wavered but soon steadied; Guan was even more strongly moved, but he, too, later steadied. As for delegates of other countries, I read in James P. Cannon's *History of American Trotskyism* that he and a number of other Americans at the Sixth Congress were swayed by what they read, stole a copy, smuggled it back to the US, and carried out Trotskyist activity inside the US Communist Party. When one of Cannon's comrades, a militant, heard that Cannon had gone Trotskyist, he travelled from the West Coast all the way to New York to win him back. When Cannon realised what the visit was about, he asked the man to sit down and read the English translation of Trotsky's 'Critique' for himself. He did so, and stood up beaming. He, too, had become a Trotskyist.

Let's now go from theory to action.

(3)   *The Trials of Chinese Trotskyism*
          Our Activities

The first thing we did was to get organised. We set up three branches and worked hard on our new Trotskyist thinking. Yin Kuan drafted a 'Propaganda Outline', which was very long and was mimeographed as a fat pamphlet that served as a basis for discussion in the branches and for outside propaganda. Doubtless Chen Duxiu and Peng Shuzhi read it and agreed to its contents before it was printed. I can't remember whether I did too. We also collected together the articles by Trotsky then in circulation and published them in a printed volume titled *On the Question of the Chinese Revolution*. It consisted of writings by Trotsky himself but included none of the unsigned articles by Trotsky's Soviet followers. It's possible that the Trotskyists who'd returned to China from Moscow asked us for the money to help them publish this book. Wang Pingyi and others read the proofs. I was an experienced proof-reader but they ignored me and gave the job to Wang Pingyi and others, who had no experience whatsoever. So the book was riddled with mistakes, which particularly saddened me. The articles were poorly translated, and some sentences were unreadable. If I'd been proof-reader I could at least have rendered the translation a little smoother, even though I had none of the original texts to hand. The book was not announced as 'Volume 1'. When Liu Renjing brought back the Russian texts of the two long articles to China, Liu and I translated them into Chinese from the originals, so the translation was far superior. We published it as the second volume of *On the Question of the Chinese Revolution*. When it was decided to go ahead with this second volume, I rather impolitely claimed the proof-reading for myself, so the result was also much better. Apart from that, we published a periodical that was mimeographed and had no name. I can't remember how many issues of it we brought out.

Chen Duxiu financed all these publications, both printed and mimeographed. At some point, the CCP had stopped paying Chen's living expenses, but he managed to raise some money from his social connections, including some to finance our political work. As for the rest of us, we, too, had to fend for ourselves. At first the organisation had kept me and Jing; but after we left prison in the spring of 1929, when I started translating for the Propaganda Department, I got paid by the word: if I translated nothing, I got nothing. Every time I delivered a translation to the Propaganda Department I was given something new to do. Later, either because I stopped translating or because they didn't need me anymore, this source of livelihood dried up. Fortunately the newly opened Hubin Bookshop, where Ma Renzhi worked as manager and Yang Xianzhen as editor, gave me some translating work to do, so I solved my problem. Ma Renzhi was from the same county as Peng Shuzhi, who told him about Trotskyism and won him over. But Yang was impossible to win. Not long afterwards he went to Northern China, and the Bookshop fell completely into the hands of Ma Renzhi.

Apart from written propaganda, we were also active as an organisation, and we won over various Party comrades to our side. Ma Yufu was especially active in work of that sort. He had been the person on the Jiangsu Provincial Committee responsible for labour movement cadres. He knew lots of worker comrades and leaders of branches with a large working-class membership. Though he'd already withdrawn from the Jiangsu Provincial Committee, he still had connections in the Party. He won over a whole branch attached to the newspaper workers' union and another in a silk factory; he also won over a large number of individual workers, including railway workers, tram workers, mill workers, print workers, and building workers; apart from that, he won over several cadres who had been working for long periods in Shanghai. Peng Shuzhi and Wang Zekai won over some members of the Party and the Youth League who had come to Shanghai from other parts of China.

Ma Yufu let Yin Kuan, He Zishen, and Zheng Chaolin deal with these various individuals and branches. I personally was assigned the newspaper branch and two worker cadres. Tu Yangzhi, secretary of the newspaper branch, was full-square with us, and two of his branch cadres also generally supported us. Tu called a plenary branch meeting in the great hall of an old-style house within the area of the Little North Gate. I attended this meeting, and at it I opposed the policies of the Central Committee from the standpoint of the Trotskyist Opposition. Some activists backed me up, but by no means all of the twenty-odd people in attendance did so. To consolidate our influence, Ma Yufu and I decided to take Tu and the two cadres to meet Chen Duxiu. We borrowed the house of Dong Tiejian, a comrade, for the meeting. I also took advantage of my wife Liu Jingzhen's contacts among the Yunnanese in Shanghai to hold discussions with some Yunnanese comrades, including one sent to Shanghai by the Provincial Committee in Yunnan to make contact with the Party centre. I also met regularly with a cadre active among print workers and another active among railway workers, and gave classes in their homes on revolutionary theory and politics. From my own small effort you can gather the extent of our activities as a whole in those days.

Our Expulsion from the Party

Precisely because we were so active, Chen Duxiu and the rest of us were expelled from the Party. A few days before that, the Central Committee arranged for a car to fetch Chen and take him to a certain place to meet a representative of the Comintern. The representative, who was seated behind a desk, behaved extremely discourteously. He spoke a few sentences to Chen. His attitude was appalling. An interpreter, whose attitude was equally bad, stood by his side and translated all this into Chinese. It was not at all like a discussion among comrades – more like an exchange between a judge and a convict. Chen turned on his heels and walked out, and so the meeting ended. A few days later *Hongqi* ('Red Flag') carried a statement announcing Chen's expulsion from the Party. As I remembered it, at first only Chen and Peng were expelled. But recently I saw the record of the expulsions; actually, only Chen was expelled by the Central Committee: Peng's expulsion, which took place at the same time, was carried out by the Jiangsu Provincial Committee with the assent of the Central Committee, along with that of Wang Zekai, Cai Zhende, and Ma Yufu. I carried on attending Yang Xianjiang's branch meetings, and at them I protested as a member of the Communist Party at the Central Committee's expulsion of Chen and Peng, on the grounds that it violated inner-Party democracy. After that, when I turned up as usual for a meeting of the branch, Yang Xianjiang politely greeted me and Jing and told us that the branch would not meet that day. Soon someone told me that I and Jing had been expelled, and that the resolution expelling us had been published in *Red Flag*. The charge against me was that I had incited members of the newspaper branch against the Central Committee, and that I had talked at Liu Shaoyou's home with the Yunnan delegate about my criticisms of the Central Committee. To this day I have not seen the resolution expelling us. I remember that before we were expelled, the Jiangsu Provincial Committee sent someone to talk with me and Jing. Those who came were Wang Kequan and Li Chuli. Li took the notes but didn't utter a word throughout the meeting.

The others were similarly expelled. The last batch of expulsions took place after the publication of the Manifesto signed by eighty one people. First the Central Committee published a notice in *Red Flag* asking certain comrades whose names were among the signatories to the Manifesto to say within a given number of days whether they had signed it themselves or someone else had signed it for them. They, too, were expelled, for they failed to make the required statements.

According to a recent account, Chen Duxiu was expelled because he wrote three letters to the Central Committee attacking its position on the Chinese Eastern Railway Incident. I've not seen the resolution on Chen's expulsion, so the only thing I have to go on is my own memory. True, the Central Committee of the CCP published a pamphlet with by a number of articles denouncing Chen and an appendix containing Chen's three letters on the Chinese Eastern Railway question. True, in 1931, Cai Hesen published an article called 'On Chen Duxiu-ism' which said that these letters clearly showed that Chen had gone over to the counterrevolution. But in November 1929, Chen was expelled for 'anti-Party activity', not for expressing 'wrong opinions' on the Chinese Eastern Railway question.

Those of us who had been expelled denied the validity of the resolutions expelling us. We protested, and continued to view ourselves as members of the CCP. Chen Duxiu published his 'Letter to all Party Comrades'; we published 'Our Political Views', signed by eighty one people (about a third of them invented). The two documents are still extant, and recently someone quoted from them in a study. I myself haven't seen them in fifty years, so I forget what was in them. Recently I came across Chen Duxiu's letter to the Comintern written in 1930. On February 8, 1930, the Politburo of the CCP told Chen Duxiu that the Comintern had telegraphed requesting him to go to Moscow to discuss the expulsions. On February 17, Chen replied to the Comintern letter.

The main thing is that we set up a formal organisation. We set up branches, we set up several district committees, we elected leaders, and we published *Proletarian* in a properly printed edition.

Our first leadership consisted of Chen Duxiu, Peng Shuzhi, Yin Kuan, Ma Yufu, and Du Peizhi, who was secretary of a branch of the CCP in a silk-factory in Shanghai that Ma Yufu had won over. In those days we copied the Central Committee's practice of promoting workers into leadership positions, so there were workers at every level of our organisation. Du Peizhi, who had been elected on the recommendation of Ma Yufu, attended two meetings of the Central Committee, both of them at my place. Later he was arrested and held in Nanjing. Ma Yufu flew into a panic, fearing that Du would reveal where we held our meetings, for after one such gathering Du had joked that he could 'easily get rich, all I have to do is tell the detectives of the Guomindang that they can arrest Chen Duxiu at such-and-such a time at such-and-such a place and I'll get a big reward'. We were on the point of moving house when Ma rushed in to tell us that Du had been shot in Nanjing. It turned out that he'd been arrested not on political charges but for armed robbery in a city on the Nanjing-Shanghai railway line. He'd been delivered to Nanjing where they'd shot him shortly afterwards. He'd not breathed a word about his political activity: he'd not sold out Chen Duxiu.

Du Peilin, the elder brother of Du Peizhi, remained a member of our organisation. I met him on one or two occasions. But just before the First Congress of the united organisation in 1931, I heard that he, too, had been taken. Three weeks after the Congress, when the first batch of our Central Committee members were arrested, I bumped into Du Peilin in the detention centre run by the Longhua Garrison Headquarters. He'd changed his name to Wang Qichang. It turned out that he, too, had been arrested in Shanghai for an attempted armed robbery. He introduced to me his accomplice, a man called Zhou, who he said was a Trotskyist sympathiser. He'd been planning to introduce this man to our organisation. Du Peilin was politically quite knowledgeable, and a good speaker. Whenever we discussed political questions with Communist Party members in our prison, Du would occasionally interject a few sentences. Later he was sentenced to seven years in gaol. After Wang Fanxi was released from prison, he met Du in Shanghai and had a talk with him in a tea-house. Wang tried to get Du to become politically active again, but he refused. In 1940 when I returned to Shanghai I once saw him walking along the pavement while I was riding in a tram.

After Du's exit from the leadership, Ma Yufu recommended that he be re-placed by Luo Shifan. Wu Jiyan was in charge of our Secretariat.

Proletarian was published in thirty-two mo format. We brought out two or three issues of it. I never wrote for it, though I had thought up its name, and I was responsible for putting the name in French just below the main mast-head. I also used to read the proofs. The printing factory was at the junction of North Zhejiang Road and Haining Road. One of our print-worker comrades, a man called Wang, had introduced us to it. It was just an ordinary printing factory, but when I delivered the proofs some of the workers recognised me and said hello. It turned out that in the old days they'd worked in the printing factory that I'd run for the Central Committee, and for some reason or other had ended up here. Comrade Wang was one of the two worker cadres I mentioned for whom I used to hold classes. I'd been to his home. He didn't know my address, but he had enough clues to find it if he had wanted to. *Proletarian* was raided while the third or fourth issue was in the press. The police traced it back to Comrade Wang, who was gaoled for six months. He didn't talk about us to his captors, but after his release he no longer sought us out.

We were active and organised in several factories and on several tram-lines in East and West Shanghai; and in the French Concession and Nantao we were active among some groups of intellectuals. We were also able to use our con-tacts with the Hubin Book Company. We had links with the Shenzhou Guo-guang Society and produced a magazine for it called *Dongli* ('Motive Force'), which Wu Jiyan edited. On several occasions we mobilised the entire organisa-tion to distribute leaflets.

But in that period we put most of our time and effort into campaigning to 'unite' with the other three Trotskyist organisations.

The Emergence of the Original Trotskyist Organisation and Its Later Schisms

We Trotskyists under Chen Duxiu were midway converts, the product of propaganda and activity by the original Chinese Trotskyist organisation, which had grown up in Moscow in 1927. I only know about its early period from hearsay, so there's not much that I can say about it. I can just talk generally about it, on the basis of what other people told me.

Moscow's Sun Yat-sen University was founded in the autumn of 1925. Its first principal was Radek, a leader of the Soviet Trotskyist Opposition; there were also a number of Oppositionists on its teaching staff. These people were active among Chinese students and helped them set up a Chinese Trotskyist organisation. That was in the heyday of the Chinese Revolution, when the eyes of revolutionaries all over the world were fixed on China and when the Chinese Revolution was one of the three main issues of controversy in the Soviet Party. The Oppositionists had pointed out early on that the China policy of the Comintern, under the leadership of the Soviet Communist Party led by Stalin, was wrong and would lead to the defeat of the Chinese Revolution. But the Stalinists persisted with their mistaken policy. The course of the Chinese Revolution vindicated the Opposition on all counts, which brought more and more members and supporters of the Soviet Party over to its side; among the Chinese students, too, it grew and grew, as did the self-confidence of its members. On November 7, 1927, the Soviet Opposition staged a demonstration against Stalin during the march-past on the occasion of the tenth anniversary of the October Revolution. There were demonstrations both in Moscow and in Leningrad, where Trotsky and Zinoviev personally participated. In Moscow some Chinese Trotskyists also took part in the demonstration.

After these demonstrations, Zinoviev and Trotsky were expelled from the Party one after the other. Probably at the same time, the Trotskyists at Sun Yat-sen University came further into the open and were deported back to China, where they organised along Trotskyist lines. Some continued to be active in branches of the CCP. The main Trotskyist activity was in Shanghai and Hong Kong. In Hong Kong some people were active in the Tai-ku Dockyards, where they succeeded in gathering a group of workers around them. In Shanghai they began bringing out a mimeographed publication called *Our Word*. (Before 1916, Trotsky had published a Russian-language journal in Paris called *Nashe Slovo* ('Our Word'), which some people translated into China as *Womende yanlun* ('Our Views'). I don't know why the members of the original Trotskyist organisation in China insisted on using the same name as Trotsky.) They translated and mimeographed Oppositionist documents and they also controlled a small bookshop called New Universe. Apart from the comrades who'd come back

from Moscow, quite a few comrades were recruited in Hong Kong and especially in Shanghai, most of them members of the CCP.

To lump together what I know from different periods, the best-known members of the Our Word group were Ou Fang, Shi Tang, Chen Yimou, Liang Ganqiao, Zhang Te, Lu Yiyuan, Zhang Shi, and Duan Ziliang.

These people still kept up secret links to the Chinese Trotskyists in the Soviet
Union, using the New Universe Bookshop as their correspondence address.

After the first batch of Trotskyist students had been deported, the Chinese
Trotskyist organisation in Moscow continued to exist and indeed to flourish.
Apparently at one time nearly half the students there were Trotskyists, including at KUTV and other colleges. There was even a Trotskyist (i.e., Liu Renjing) at
the Lenin Institute. They carried out their clandestine work most profession-
ally, and succeeded in maintaining their cover.

In 1929, word went round that a batch of students were to be sent back to
China to work for the Party. When the Trotskyists heard this, they met secretly
and discussed what their response should be. They decided that the comrades
who went back would continue to work for the official Party, and moreover
would strive to do so better than anyone else; but that they would do everything
they could to avoid being discovered, and await the chance to reform the Party
from within.

Quite a few of these people took up important jobs in the Party. Wu Jiyan
became Secretary of the Central Committee's Propaganda Department, Wang
Fanxi became an aide in the Organisation Department, Du Weizhi (i.e., Tu
Qingqi) took up some important post in the Central Committee, and Zhao Ji,
Liu Yin, and Pu Dezhi also worked for the Party after attending a training school.

But Liu Renjing came out openly as a Trotskyist. He returned to China
via Western Europe. He visited the Trotskyist organisations in Germany and
France, and in Turkey he stayed in Trotsky's home[19] for several days. He discussed the Chinese Revolution with Trotsky, who wrote the 'Draft Programme
of the Chinese Left Opposition' for Liu to take back to China with him and to
present for use as an internal discussion document. Once Liu Renjing had got
back to Shanghai, he started looking up old friends, for example Yun Daiying.
He told Yun that the Central Committee was bureaucratic, but Yun denied this
and demanded proof; he also said that if the Central Committee really was bureaucratic, then he (Yun) would join Liu in opposing it.

Liu Renjing already knew that we Chen Duxiu-ites had gone over to Trotskyism. Through intermediaries he sent a letter to Yin Kuan and me asking us to

---

19   Trotsky was exiled to Alma Ata in Soviet Central Asia in January 1928 and deported to
      Turkey in January 1929.

go and see him in a hostel in the French Concession. He warmly greeted us. In 1926, when he was working in the Central Committee of Communist Youth, I'd been quite close to him, and in the spring and autumn we'd often gone for outings together if the weather was nice. I'd given him a quilt with cotton wadding on the eve of his departure for abroad, and I'd invited him for a meal at the East Asia Restaurant. It was quite natural that we should greet each other with such warmth. I forget what he told us that day. Obviously we talked about how we had become Trotskyists. He also told us about his meeting with Yun Daiying (described above).

I don't know if it was on that day or another day that he arranged to meet Chen Duxiu at my place. At the time I was living on East Youheng Road. I went to his hostel to fetch him, while Chen Duxiu waited for him in my home. I remember that when we had almost reached my house, Liu Renjing nodded to someone coming in the other direction. I asked him who it was. He said it was Li Mogeng.[20]

When he met with Chen Duxiu there was no longer any need to discuss who was right, Stalin or Trotsky. Liu took out Trotsky's 'Draft Programme' and his two long articles, typed in Russian. I've already described how Liu and I arranged between the two of us to translate these documents into Chinese, and how we Chen Duxiu-ites published them as Volume 2 of *On the Question of the Chinese Revolution*.

Sometime after Liu Renjing's return to China the Trotskyist organisation in Moscow was unearthed, a list of names was found, and two hundred-odd people came to grief. According to reports, after Liberation[21] two or three of them returned to China from places of exile in Siberia. As for the Trotskyists who had already returned home, if their names were on the list then the Comintern or the Soviet Party informed the Central Committee of the CCP, which expelled the lot of them. It's said that Zhou Enlai told the better-known ones that if they admitted their mistakes and criticised Trotsky, they could stay in. No one took up his offer.

In normal times these people still hidden in the Party had kept up secret ties to the original Trotskyist group. After their expulsion, the handful of people around Wu Jiyan came over to the Chen Duxiu group, but the rest joined the original Trotskyist group. Wu and his people all signed the statement 'Our Political Views'.

---

20   An ex-student of Beijing University, and briefly a member of the early CCP.
21   I.e., after the proclamation of the People's Republic of China in 1949. Actually, these people managed to cross the border and return to China not after but before October 1949.

Shortly after the Trotskyists from Moscow expelled while still working in the Party joined the original Trotskyist organisation, conflict broke out in its ranks and some people split away from it. This was mainly due to the activity of Liu Renjing.[22]

Liu Renjing prided himself on being a veteran who had met Trotsky in Turkey and had brought Trotsky's 'Draft Programme' back to China. He despised the young leaders of the original Trotskyist organisation. They in their turn despised him. So they got into a fight. Liu Renjing then wrote a long article listing some peccadillos committed by these young leaders and incited some members of their organisation against them. Most of them had only got back to China in 1929 and had only recently been discovered and expelled. The main one among them was Wang Fanxi, who in those days called himself Wang Wenyuan. They brought out a printed journal called *Shiyue* ('October') and set up a new organisation. After that, a minority, actually, only four people, copied them and set up yet another organisation and yet another journal, called *Zhandou*. In those days we used to receive through the post copies of *Militant*, the newspaper of the Trotskyists in the USA. Actually, *Zhandou* is not the equivalent of this word in Chinese. *Zhandou* means 'combat', whereas the English word 'militant' means combatant or (in Party terms) cadre. (I'm too lazy to check whether this definition is actually given in the English dictionary.) Whatever the case, these four people – Zhao Ji, Liu Yin, Wang Pingyi, and Pock-Marked Xu – translated it as *Zhandou*, regardless of what it meant in English. I never saw any copies of *Zhandou*, so I don't know whether it was printed or mimeographed. Later some other people joined this small group, but it was not as big as the October group and certainly not as big as the Our Word group.

Though these three groups fought one another, they were unanimous in their attitude toward the Chen Duxiu-ite Trotskyists: they considered us as opportunists who had lost favour with Stalin and now wanted to climb back into prominence using Trotsky's name. All three groups wrote to Trotsky setting out their views on us. After we had formally set up an organisation, we, too, sent Trotsky a letter explaining our point of view and enclosing a translation into English of the 'Letter to All Party Comrades' put out by Chen Duxiu after his expulsion, together with the statement on 'Our Political Views' signed by eighty one people. As far as I remember, we didn't explain to Trotsky what our attitude was toward the original Trotskyist group in China. Not long after Liu Renjing and Wang Fanxi had organised the October group, for some reason or another Liu resigned from it and set up on his own. Later he published a journal

---

22   See Wang Fan-hsi 1991, pp. 132, 140, and 141.

called *Mingtian* ('Tomorrow'). He was Trotsky's 'correspondent' in China, so he often used to write to Trotsky and Trotsky to him. I don't know how he estimated us Chen Duxiu-ites in his correspondence with Trotsky, but I know at least a little about the exchange between the two men. In October 1929, still in the period before our expulsion, our branch secretary Yang Xianjiang ordered me to join a flying demonstration[23] in front of the General Post Office on North Sichuan Road. After I'd got rid of all my leaflets, I bumped into Liu Renjing, so the two of us pretended to be passers-by and watched what was going on. We saw several demonstrators being arrested, and some dustmen sweeping up our leaflets and stuffing them into rubbish-carts. I and Liu then went our separate ways. Liu wrote to Trotsky describing this demonstration. His aim was to denigrate it, and to show that it was not worth the sacrifice. But Trotsky wrote back disagreeing. He said that demonstrations of this sort served at least one purpose, which was to let people know that the CCP still lived.

Though we Chen Duxiu-ites and Liu Renjing were constantly in touch, we never discussed organisational questions. None of us thought of trying to draw him into our group, nor did he ever ask to join it. Under the circumstances, it is easy to see why. Nevertheless, some people say that after Liu Renjing got back to China he asked to be allowed to join us and to lead our Propaganda Department but that Chen Duxiu said no, whereupon Liu joined the Our Word group and began opposing Chen. That is not in accordance with the facts.

I deliberately use the word 'group' (*jituan*) rather than 'society' (*she*) to describe the organisations formed around *Our Word, October, Combat,* and *Proletarian,* for 'society' was what others called us, whereas we ourselves never referred to our organisations in that way; and in any case 'group' is a better description of them.

The Negotiating Committee

There were four Trotskyist organisations in China. How did they become one?

At first the Our Word group put forward the following condition. The Chen Duxiu-ite opportunists, including Chen himself, would only be allowed to join their original Trotskyist organisation singly, after individual vetting. As far as I remember, Chen himself never expressed an opinion on this, but Peng Shuzhi did. In Peng's opinion there was only one conceivable way of achieving unity. These students who had come back to China from Moscow, being young and inexperienced, should join our organisation, which was built around a nucleus of old men steeled in the Great Revolution. Yin Kuan, on the other hand, pro-

---

23   See Wang Fan-hsi 1991, p. 118 for a description of a flying demonstration.

posed all along that it shouldn't be a question of either us joining their organisation or them joining ours, but of a merger of the various groups after a period
of joint discussion. Yin Kuan had more contact than the rest of us with members of the other organisations, and at one time shared a house with Zhao Ji and
Liu Yin. He knew that neither of the above proposals would work. The various
concerned parties reported to Trotsky, who wrote back criticising the students
from Moscow for their attitude toward Chen Duxiu and his supporters. He
carefully examined the documents of the Chen Duxiu group and could find
nothing wrong with them in principle: the arguments advanced by the returned
students were mere nitpicking. Trotsky also said that Chen Duxiu knew what
revolution meant, which is not necessarily true of you young people. He proposed that we should first unite and then deal with the outstanding issues, for
differences in our theoretical approaches could best be resolved by discussion
within the framework of a unified organisation.

This letter had a big impact. The Our Word group had no choice but to back
down from its original proposal and to recognise that Chen Duxiu was also a
Trotskyist, on a par with them. The other two groups were naturally happy to
accept Trotsky's proposal. But the Chen Duxiu-ites (actually, Peng Shuzhi and
his followers) became arrogant. On the surface they recognised that the four
groups were equal, but in reality, they wanted the other three groups to unite
around the Proletarian group.

Each organisation nominated two delegates to the Negotiating Committee.
At first I had nothing to do with this body, so I can't say who represented the
other three groups. All I remember is that initially, the Our Word group was represented by Ou Fang (I forget who the second delegate was), and that after Ou's
arrest they were represented by Liang Ganqiao and Chen Yimou. The October
group was represented by Wang Fanxi and Song Fengchun or Pu Dezhi. The
Combat group was probably represented by Zhao Ji and Liu Yin. The Central
Committee of the Proletarian group formally nominated Ma Yufu and Wu Jiyan.

The negotiations had been going on for a long time, but they were making no
progress. On one occasion Wu Jiyan told me in the course of a private chat that
the delegates had obviously studied the mores of bourgeois parliamentarians,
arguing first about this, then about that, and making no headway whatsoever
on the central issue, which was how to unite. Since I had nothing to do with
these negotiations nor did I attend meetings of our Central Committee, I have
no idea what the arguments were about. But for Yin Kuan's intervention, the
wrangling might have gone on for ever.

At this point, I shall return for a moment to discuss dealings between us
Chen Duxiu-ites and Chen Duxiu himself. During the period of the Great
Revolution no one ever knew precisely where Chen lived. He always used to

come to us, never the other way around. Even Ren Zuomin, who was Party Treasurer and Secretary to the Central Committee, didn't know where Chen lived, with the result that at the end of 1925 or the beginning of 1926, there was a big scare for a while when Chen Duxiu suddenly disappeared. Chen had not been to Ren's place to attend to Party affairs for quite some time, everyone began to panic. For the time being there was nothing for it but to wait and see. We waited and waited, but still Chen did not show up. We began to think that the imperialists or the warlords had secretly kidnapped him or even killed him. Chen Yannian, who happened to be passing through Shanghai, looked up Wang Mengzou, owner of the Oriental Book Company, and pleaded with tears in his eyes for news of his father. The Oriental Book Company people said that they, too, had not seen Chen for ages. Previously Chen had made a habit of going to look up Wang Mengzou at the Book Company's editorial office on Chang-sha Road, which was where he got most of his news about events in society and politics. The employees there were absolutely reliable, but they, too, had not seen him for what was already a long time. We sent Gao Erbo, a member of Communist Youth, back to Songjiang to make enquiries. Chen Taoyi, the then Governor of Jiangsu Province, was from Songjiang, where his family had been on friendly terms with Gao Erbo's family for several generations. If Chen had indeed been secretly arrested, some information might have leaked out about it. But there was not a whisper to be heard. Instead, Chen Taoyi was roundly denouncing various malpractices of the warlords, especially sex scandals. As far as I remember, Sun Chuanfang was then Commander-in-Chief in Nanjing of the Five Provinces.[24] On one occasion, in the course of a chat in the Central Committee's Peasant Department or some other Department, I seem to recall that Zhang Guotao said that the situation was quite hopeless. He began to talk with me about Chen's life, and he ended up by remarking that if Chen, with all his talents, had chosen a government career, he would have gone right to the top, but instead he'd become a revolutionary, and now look where he was. Everyone thought that Chen was already dead. Ren Zuomin put a missing-person notice in *Republic Daily*, but to no avail. One day, however, Chen Duxiu suddenly turned up at the liaison centre run by Ren Zuomin. Every-one rushed in all directions to spread the news. Chen Yannian had already boarded a ship to leave Shanghai, so we sent someone to fetch him back ashore. What had happened? It turned out that Chen Duxiu had contracted typhoid fever and gone to hospital, where his mysterious lover had looked after him.

---

24   Sun Chuanfang appointed himself to this post after routing the Fengtian warlords in Octo-ber 1925.

He hadn't wanted us to know about his lover, who was still a secret. He told us that before going into hospital he'd already informed Ren Zuomin that he'd be absent for quite a while. He'd seen the notice in *Republic Daily* while he was in hospital, but he'd paid no attention to it, thinking that he would soon recover and be discharged. Everyone was very angry about this, though I don't know if anyone criticised him. After that he apparently allowed Ren Zuomin (but no one else) to visit him at home. I don't know if the same applied to Wang Ruofei after Ren quit his job and a Central Committee Secretariat was set up under Wang. Neither Ren nor Wang ever breathed a word about where Chen lived.

Before the three armed risings of 1927, Chen's home had apparently already broken up. A few days before the risings started, Chen went to stay in the Central Committee's Propaganda Department, where he held meetings and met cadres. He was there on the night of the rising too, receiving reports and issuing directives. I was among the people who transmitted messages for him. It was not until early April, after his joint declaration with Wang Jingwei, that he left the Propaganda Department and went to Wuhan.

In Wuhan he stayed on the second floor of the Central Committee office, with Huang Wenrong as his private secretary. After he had 'stopped attending to his duties' he went into hiding together with Huang somewhere in Hankou. After returning to Shanghai, he went to live in a three-storey house on Fusheng Road (to the North of Range Road). He lived on the middle floor, under Peng Lihe and his wife, who acted as his cover. Wang Ruofei had arranged the house for them. Lots of people used to go and see him there. After I'd returned to Shanghai and settled down, I, too, went to see him; after I'd got married I took Jing to meet him. I know for certain that the following people went to visit him: Wang Ruofei, Qu Qiubai, Luo Yinong, Chen Qiaonian, He Zishen, Peng Shuzhi, Wang Zekai, and Luo Qiyuan. Wang Mengzou was also a regular visitor.

In 1928, after the arrest of Luo Yinong, Peng Shuzhi urged Chen to move, but Chen stayed put. In 1929, after I and Jing had been arrested, Peng again urged Chen to move, and eventually he did, to a place still North of Range Road but nearer to North Sichuan Road. Afterwards, Peng explained to me that it wasn't because he didn't trust me, but because he feared that my wife would be unable to stand the test of prison. After my release I refrained from visiting Chen in case someone might be following me.

Actually, all this has nothing to do with my main present theme, but since it occurs to me I might as well say it, for in any case these anecdotes concern the life of Chen Duxiu.

After his relations with the Central Committee of the CCP had been disrupted, Chen Duxiu moved from his house on Range Road into a place in the Tilanqiao area, but without informing the Central Committee of his new address. As far as I know, in this period only Peng Shuzhi knew where he lived.

Probably sometime in the second half of 1930, Chen moved to the upper floor of a terrace house on Dent Road near Seward Road. By that time several people were able to visit him, in particular Peng Shuzhi, Ma Yufu, and Zheng Chaolin. Little Pan[25] was already living with him. I think it's here that they got to know each other. One day in 1931 while I was out walking near the Hongkou Market I bumped into him and we walked along together. I asked him how things were. He told me that there was a man living in the small room above his kitchen who had told Little Pan that he was in the Communist Party, so Chen intended to move out. I told him that he should do so without delay, but he said things weren't yet so serious. I said I'd help him move. After a while either he or I found an empty room above a tailor's shop at the end of a lane off Zhoujiazui Road near Alcock Road and rented it. I helped him hire a cart and move. After that, I was the only person who knew where he lived. Little Pan didn't even know my name, and used to call me 'Little Fatty'. After that I seem to recall that he moved to another room at the top of a house on the same lane.

Yin Kuan never once went to Chen's place. He was only able to meet Chen at Peng Shuzhi's place, with Peng invariably in attendance. Yin never dared say anything to which Peng would object. Peng was like Chen's 'manager'. On one occasion Yin apparently bumped into Chen on the street and arranged for him to go to Yin's home and meet some people who told him about what was going on in the Negotiating Committee. Chen learned for the first time that Peng Shuzhi and Ma Yufu had been keeping him in the dark. It turned out that on the question of unity Peng and Ma thought as one: that the other three groups should unite around the Proletarian group. Wu Jiyan, Secretary to the Central Committee, went along with them. They had stuck to their opinion, in complete violation of the principle that the four groups should be equal and kept the true facts to themselves whenever the Central Committee of the Proletarian group met.

Chen Duxiu could not agree with this. He clearly felt that we embodied lethargy and lifelessness, and he enjoyed the youthful spirits of the Moscow-returned students. Before this, he had met and talked with a group of these students. I forget whether he reported on this at a meeting of the branch or told me about it in private conversation, but whatever the case he described the emotions he had felt at the time. He said it was like meeting young people at the time of the May Fourth Movement in 1919 or at the time of the founding of the

---

25   Chen Duxiu's last 'secret lover'.

Communist Party. He'd felt that they were full of vigour and vitality, and full of hope. So I don't believe Pu Qingquan when he says that Chen Duxiu denounced these young Trotskyists as 'monkey pups still smelling of their mother's milk'. Pu doesn't say whether he himself heard Chen say this or someone else told him that Chen said it. Judging by what Chen told me at the time about his feelings, I can hardly believe that he entertained such thoughts and even less that he expressed himself in such hostile terms.

What Yin Kuan said made Chen very angry. At the next meeting of the Central Committee he raised the issue. Peng argued back, and the Central Committee split into two factions. Chen and Yin proposed negotiating on the basis of equality: Peng Shuzhi and Ma Yufu stuck to their original proposal, which boiled down to uniting around the Proletarian group. I don't know what attitude Luo Shifan and Wu Jiyan took. The outcome was victory for Chen and Yin, whereupon Ma Yufu and Wu Jiyan were recalled as delegates to the Negotiating Committee and replaced by Chen and Yin. After that there was an argument – and a fierce one – every time the Central Committee met, right up to the time of the Unification Congress. Later Ma Yufu stopped attending meetings of the Central Committee and He Zishen took over from Wu Jiyan as Secretary. He Zishen stood full-square with Chen Duxiu.

After the Proletarian group had changed its representatives, the work of the Negotiating Committee progressed smoothly. It had discussed theoretical questions before too, but in a nitpicking way. Now, everyone put forward their points of view in a calm and measured way, so that it was quite easy to reach common conclusions. There was a serious and businesslike discussion about preparing the Congress. The Negotiating Committee became a Preparatory Committee for the Congress, which drafted a set of resolutions for the Congress and in the process hit some controversies, mainly on the question of proletarian dictatorship and the call for a National Assembly, which two issues were basically resolved by the Negotiating Committee. Either at the same time or later, the question of the number of delegates was raised, together with concrete arrangements for the holding of the Congress. It was decided that the Proletarian group would take charge of arrangements and funding, and that each group would elect its own delegates on the basis of the size of its membership. The Our Word group and the Proletarian group were allowed an equal number of delegates; the October group was allowed a much smaller number; and the Combat group was allowed one delegate.

Ma Yufu withdrew from the Central Committee and became inactive. Peng Shuzhi, on the other hand, held out in opposition to everything that the Negotiating Committee decided, and even called it 'a conference of robbers out to divide the spoils'. Those who supported Peng didn't dare oppose Chen Duxiu, so they concentrated their fire instead on Yin Kuan. Yin had fewer followers than Peng. So Chen Duxiu and He Zishen decided to drag out Zheng Chaolin.

After becoming a Trotskyist, I observed discipline, obeyed the order to attend the meetings of a Party branch, gave classes to new recruits from the Party, and discussed with various comrades how best to attack the Central Committee of the CCP, but I took no part in the internal activities of our own organisation. By trade I was a translator and publisher, so I volunteered to translate things for the organisation. But I wrote no articles, engaged in no diplomacy, and fought for no positions. Zhao Ji and Liu Yin, who lived in the same house as Yin Kuan, reproached Yin for sealing them off from people and for not letting them meet other Chen Duxiu-ites. They especially said that they wanted to meet Zheng Chaolin, Cai Zhende, and Ma Yufu. Yin Kuan told me about this on several occasions, but I never went. Someone once told me that one day while a number of comrades were chatting together at Peng Shuzhi's place, Chen Duxiu commented that Zheng Chaolin lacked the 'desire to be a leader'. Yin Kuan countered that it wasn't the 'desire to be a leader' that Zheng lacked, but a sense of duty to the cause. What Yin meant was that the reason he was always running about was not because he wanted to be leader but because of his sense of duty to the revolution. I still don't know to this day whether it's sense of duty that I lack, or 'desire to be a leader'.

When I was finally 'dragged out' to work for the organisation, at first I was Secretary of the East Shanghai District Committee, as successor to Liu Bozhuang. Liu Bozhuang was a Peng Shuzhi supporter. There should have been three people on the Committee, but I only remember the railway worker Wang Zhihuai helping me, I forget who the third person was. In those days most of our membership was concentrated in East Shanghai, and most of our branches were the Party's old Chen Duxiu-ite branches. As far as I remember, there was no workers' branch as such, just a certain number of workers we'd come into contact with on an individual basis. The Our Word group also had an East Shanghai District Committee. The Unification Congress had not yet taken place, but the work of the Negotiating Committee was proceeding smoothly and a decision had been taken to merge the district committees of the different groups forthwith. I accepted an invitation to go for talks on cooperation to a primary school run by the Our Word group in East Shanghai. There were three members of the Our Word group present, led by Shi Tang. I'd often heard his name, but this was the first time I'd actually met him. He knew me, however. It turned out that he'd worked as Ni Youtian's apprentice in the Central Committee's printing factory, where I'd often had to go on business. Many people worked there, and though I didn't know them, they knew me. Shi Tang had been sent to Moscow either before or after the defeat to study at Sun Yat-sen

University. Within a short while this printing worker had excelled beyond all
expectations and become a well-informed and well-read cadre of the revolution. After unification he went to Guangxi to teach in a middle school where
he became very popular among the students, many of whom came to Trotskyism through him. But all that happened later.

Shi Tang asked me: 'Why did we not hear people talk about you more often?'
But what was so strange about that? I had no dealings with the Moscow-
returned students, I was not on the Negotiating Committee, I had not uttered
an opinion on unification, and though I'd said what I thought on some theoretical questions that were raised in the branch, I'd not talked about them outside
the branch. But now that I had become Secretary of the East Shanghai District
Committee, and was trying to implement cooperation at branch level, my name
was often in people's mouths.

I also ran the election of delegates to the Unification Congress for the East
Shanghai District Committee of the Proletarian group, so I was inevitably
drawn into the internal struggle. The person in charge of preparing wax stencils
and running the mimeograph was Wang Zekai's nephew Wang Fusheng. At a
meeting he opposed my arrangements for the election. His uncle, a Peng Shuzhi
supporter, had put him up to this. Wang had come to my place and argued with
me about unification, and we'd parted on bad terms. If the negotiations had
gone on any longer, Peng's supporters might have switched their sights from
Yin Kuan to me.

The violent conflict in the Proletarian group about unification and the election showed Peng, Yin Kuan, and Ma Yufu in their true colours. Their main
ambition was to become 'leaders' of the Chinese Trotskyist movement.

The Unification Congress

He Zishen was in charge of Congress arrangements. We rented a newly-built
two-storey lane-house in an alley to the North of Ward Road on Dalian Bay
Road. Wang Zhihuai and his wife and daughter lived downstairs as landlords,
and we pretended to rent the upper storey. We made a rule that from May 1 to
May 3, while the Congress was in session, no one save Chen Duxiu should be
allowed to leave the building.

The Proletarian group was represented by Chen Duxiu, Zheng Chaolin,
Wang Zhihuai, Jiang Zhendong, and Jiang Changshi; later, after a membership
count, we were allowed one more delegate, i.e., Peng Shuzhi. The Our Word
group was represented by Liang Ganqiao, Chen Yimou, Song Jingxiu, and two
workers from Hong Kong. The October group was represented by Wang Fanxi,
Song Fengchun, Pu Dezhi, and Luo Han. The Combat group had only one delegate, Lai Yantang.

There are two questions on which people's recollections differ. The first is whether Luo Han represented the October group or the Our Word group. I've always believed that he represented the October group, and so does Pu Dezhi in his recent memoir. But Wang Fanxi told me in a recent communication that Luo Han represented Our Word's Northern Region. If that's true, other things fall into place. The Proletarian group had six delegates, and the Our Word group should also have had six; but according to my list, it only had five. If Luo Han attended the Congress as a representative of the Our Word group, then that would make six.[26] As for the October group, it was much smaller than the other two, so it shouldn't have had four delegates; if Luo Han was actually an Our Word delegate, that would bring the October group down to three, which is more commensurate with their real size. The second question is whether or not Peng Shuzhi attended the Unification Congress. I've always thought he didn't, but other surviving attenders say he did.[27] It seems as though I must amend my opinion. My view that Peng did not attend is also influenced by another matter that I shall mention shortly, though this other matter does not necessarily prove that Peng was not at the Congress.

The Congress went on for three days. Apart from the elections at the end, it spent its whole time discussing resolutions, principally political ones, that had been drafted by the Negotiating Committee after a long and intense discussion. But this discussion had been quite different in character from that during the early stages of negotiations, which had been little more than an exercise in mutual fault-finding. This later discussion was premised in a sincere wish for unity. The Negotiating Committee had reached broad unanimity on the questions of proletarian dictatorship and the National Assembly. The same went for other resolutions on the labour movement, the peasant movement, women, youth, and so on, as well as on rules and regulations. The Congress did not only pass resolutions. When the political resolution came up for discussion, Chen

---

26   Wang Fanxi recently wrote to me about Luo Han's status at the Unification Congress. According to Wang, Luo represented the October group but had been elected by the North China organisation of the Our Word group. The apparent contradiction here arises from the fact that the North China organisation of the Our Word group had already split away at the Second Congress in 1929 and later became a founding unit of the October group. I never knew this. It is now clear to me that it was not excessive to award four delegates to the October group. Another thing I must amend is that there were four, not two, Hong Kong workers represented at the Congress. [Note added by Zheng Chaolin in the early 1980s.]

27   Wang Fanxi, however, was convinced that Peng didn't attend the Unification Congress, although he was elected as an alternate member of the Trotskyist Central Committee that issued from it.

Duxiu addressed the Congress about it in the name of the Negotiating Committee; others then got up and spoke or argued, but only about minor details that were easily resolved. The same thing happened when the other resolutions came up. All these resolutions fell into the hands of the Guomindang intelligence service and may be available in the Guomindang archives on Taiwan.

The Congress elected a Central Committee composed of members and alternate members. Everyone's agreed that there were nine members, but most people have forgotten about the two alternate members. Different people remember different names. For example, I remember the full members as being Chen Duxiu, Wang Fanxi, Zheng Chaolin, Chen Yimou, Song Fengchun, Pu Dezhi, Ou Fang, Wang Zhihuai, and a Hong Kong worker; and the alternate members as Song Jingxiu and Peng Shuzhi. They didn't include Luo Han.[28] So the following controversies arise. Was Luo Han elected to the Central Committee? Was Peng Shuzhi a full member or an alternate member? Was Ou Fang elected? I stick to my opinion that Luo Han was not elected; as for Peng, as far as I remember the two people (Peng and Liang Ganqiao) who came bottom got an equal number of votes, so there was a run-off that Peng won, as a result of which he was elected. Nine of the eleven successful candidates became full members and two (Song Jingxiu and Peng) became alternate members. Ou Fang was in Caohejing Gaol at the time, still alive. He was elected as a gesture honouring him.

On May 4, we rested for a day. On May 5, we held our first Central Committee meeting, at the same place. Chen Duxiu was made General Secretary, Chen Yimou took charge of the Organisation Department, Zheng Chaolin became head of the Propaganda Department, Wang Fanxi was appointed editor of the Party organ, and Song Fengchun took over the Secretariat. The same five people constituted the Standing Committee.

An incident took place at this meeting that left a deep impression on those present, and that most survivors of the meeting still remember. I am referring to Peng's letter to Chen Duxiu. Peng, who had not originally been a delegate to the Unification Congress, had written a long letter to Chen Duxiu denouncing the Congress as a 'conference of robbers out to divide the spoils' and making other similar unpleasant allegations. After we'd all gone to start the Congress, he took this letter to the home of He Zishen (who was in charge of the Proletarian group's Secretariat) and asked him to give to Chen Duxiu. Peng didn't

---

28   After posting off this manuscript, I had second thoughts, so I'll mention my new theory just for reference. Seven full members and two alternate members were elected, i.e., nine people were elected and the two who came bottom were made alternate members. Ou Fang and Wang Zhihuai weren't elected. [Note by Zheng Chaolin.]

know where Chen lived, so he had no choice but to deliver it in this way. I don't know when He Zishen actually handed it over to Chen, but at the first plenary session of the Central Committee held on May 5 Chen produced it and as far as I remember someone read it out aloud. Chen then asked Peng if he still stood by the letter. All eyes turned to Peng, who sat there blushing violently and unable to utter a single word. If it had been Yin Kuan, he'd have bluffed his way out of it with some plausible-sounding argument. I suddenly began to feel sorry for Peng and said 'Let's not take this too far'. After all, it's no fun to watch someone speechless and squirming with embarrassment. Later Chen Duxiu told He Zishen what had happened, and He Zishen then told me off for being too soft: he said it could lead to bungles. He said that if Peng had won the upper hand, Peng would never have shown mercy. He Zishen was right, of course. I remember this incident clearly, but at the same time I have no clear recollection of Peng attending the Unification Congress, which is why I originally thought that Peng only came to Dalian Bay Road when the plenary session of the Central Committee was held on May 5.

The plenary session instructed Chen Yimou (head of the Organisation Department) to merge the branches of the four organisations as soon as possible and assigned Wu Jiyan, Zhao Ji, and Yan Lingfeng to the Propaganda Department. A decision was taken to call the Party journal *Huahuo* ('Spark') and to rush out the first issue. Finally, the Central Committee sent a letter to Comrade Trotsky reporting on the Unification Congress. I remember that Wang Fanxi wrote the letter and the rest of us all signed it. Now that Harvard University has opened Trotsky's letters archive, one day someone will probably unearth it.

I can't remember what happened between May 5 and May 21. I forget whether I stopped being Secretary of the East Shanghai District Committee, and if so, who replaced me. In those days my main visitors were Wang Zhihuai and Song Jingxiu. Song made a point of talking to me about Ou Fang, who he said should be promoted into the leadership as soon as he was released from prison. One day Wang told me that Ma Yufu wanted to know where Wang lived and where I'd moved to so that he could pay me a visit, and that he'd told him, which I said was all right. I wasn't the slightest bit vigilant at the time. Naturally, I didn't agree with Ma's attitude to unification and I disliked his inactivity, but it never occurred to me that he'd betray us. Peng Shuzhi moved from the house he's been living for quite some time to a place on Route Père Robert in the French Concession and told lots of people, including Ma Yufu, his new address. Ma Yufu, too, often used to visit him there. I was the only person Peng didn't tell. I didn't tell him when I moved, either.

Sometime between May 5 and May 21, we held a meeting of the Standing Committee to assess the draft of the first issue of *Spark*. I remember I had written an article for it on the Spanish Revolution. We decided to hold a rather bigger meeting on the 22nd. On the 21st, I held a meeting at my place about propaganda work. That afternoon Wu Jiyan, Zhao Ji, and Yan Lingfeng were all there. Yan, who was from Fuzhou, wasn't in any group at the time, having declared that he'd only join after they united. He I'd heard about him, but I'd never met him. He told me that before he'd left China for the Soviet Union, he'd heard me give a lecture at Shanghai University. In 1926, the Jiangsu-Zhejiang Regional Committee had frequently assigned me to give lectures at Shanghai University. These lectures weren't part of the formal curriculum, and took place in the evenings. Crowds of people used to attend them, including many who weren't students. I wasn't the only one who used to give them.

I forget what we decided at this meeting. I had a plan to make a study of actual issues in China and of Chinese history. It was easy to talk about Marxism, even though our knowledge of it was still quite limited, but whenever we got round to discussing China's 'national characteristics' we could only come up with commonplaces. At that meeting we could have done no more than talk about this plan, there was no discussion or decision.

We Are Arrested

After the meeting Zhao left, but Wu and Yan stayed behind for a game of mahjong that our landlord came up to join. I'd been there less than a month, so with that many visitors it was wise to play a game of mahjong to allay any suspicions that my landlord may have entertained. He was called Zheng, like me, and was twenty-odd, from Ningbo. He worked for an insurance company and was a member of the Merchants' Volunteer Corps[29] that the police used to call out when necessary to help maintain public order.

Just as the game was underway, Peng Guiqiu came rushing up and asked me if Yu Mutao knew where I lived. I quickly steered him out onto the sun terrace and quietly asked him what had happened. He told me that Yu had turned informer, that that evening at ten o'clock people would be arrested, and that I should flee. I told him that Yu didn't know my address. Peng Guiqiu then left, and after we had finished playing mahjong Yan Lingfeng left too, but Wu Jiyan and his wife stayed. I told them what Peng Guiqiu had said. They agreed that since Yu Mutao didn't know my address, we were safe, so they stayed in my place while I went to tell other people what had happened. I first went to Chen Duxiu's place. I was the only one who knew where he lived. We decided to scrap

---

29   The Merchant Volunteers were an armed organisation financed by wealthy businessmen and, reputedly, by foreign interests.

the meeting planned for tomorrow, and that he wouldn't go to Dalian Bay Road. I then went to Peng Guiqiu's place, where I met Xie Depan. There I learned that Peng Shuzhi had told Xie to bring me the news of the impending raid, but that Xie had sent Peng Guiqiu instead. It turned out that the story about Yu Mutao had been guess-work on the part of Peng Shuzhi. That there would be a raid at ten o'clock that night was a fact, but the rest was inference. Peng Shuzhi knew that the only unreliable person among those who knew his address was Yu Mutao, for Yu had recently asked Cai Yuanpei to write a preface for a book that Yu was about to publish. I now realised that the matter was not as straight-forward as I had originally thought. Perhaps the informer did know where I lived. Perhaps he even knew where the meeting was to take place.

I immediately went to see Liu Renjing, who lived close by. His wife, Lu Mengyi's younger sister, was already in bed, but Liu was still up. I told him what had happened, and he promised to get someone to go the following day to the meeting place and warn people. As I was walking home I had second thoughts, and went myself to the house where the meeting was to be held. The people inside were all asleep. They answered my knocking, and I told them what had happened. At the time I still thought that a raid was possible rather than certain, so I didn't insist that they vacate the building there and then. I told them that the meeting would not go through, but I failed to tell Song Fengchun to go that same night and warn Wang Fanxi and the others in West Shanghai. That was because of my general irresolution in the face of important events. I didn't think either to inform He Zishen, for very few people knew him, and all those who did were reliable. Had I done so, he was so vigilant and resolute that he would have proposed fleeing forthwith. When I got home it was already past midnight. Wu Jiyan and his wife were still there, but they, too, drew no new conclusions from the new information I gave them. They then went home. I thought to myself, since I had been emphatically instructed to flee, even though ten o'clock had long since come and gone, it would be best not to leave anything to chance. After a discussion, Jing and I started preparing to pack a few necessities into a small suitcase so that we could spend the night in a hotel. Just as we were packing, there came a knock at the door. It was a team of detectives from the Longhua Garrison Headquarters together with some Chinese and foreign policemen from Tilanqiao Police Station.

I and Jing, together with the maidservant who cooked for us, were taken by van to Tilanqiao Police Station, where we were put behind bars; the van then drove off again, to reappear not long afterwards with He Zishen and his wife. At that point, I realised that the informer was Ma Yufu. He knew where He Zishen lived, he knew where Peng Shuzhi lived, he'd recently found out where I lived from Wang Zhihuai, and he knew where the house was where the Congress had been held. Sure enough, the van soon reappeared with Wang Zhihuai and his wife and daughter, and with Song Fengchun and Jiang Changshi. None of us slept that night. The next morning sometime after nine the van took the whole lot of us to the Magistracy of the Settlement, where we were asked a few questions before being sent back to Tilanqiao. As we walked back in, we saw Chen Yimou, Wang Fanxi, and Pu Dezhi in the lock-up. It turned out that some policemen had stayed behind in the house where the meeting was to have been held, and when these people turned up as planned, they had been seized. Wang Fanxi had gone together with Zhang Te[30] (I don't know what the meeting was about). As soon as they entered, Zhang was snapped into handcuffs. Wang rushed out through the back door, and the policemen rushed out after him, so Zhang Te fled through the front door, still handcuffed. He took a rickshaw to Jiangwan, where he removed the handcuffs at a friend's house.

According to He Zishen, that very morning Chen Duxiu had gone to He's house, but at the mouth of the alley he had met the landlord, who informed him that He Zishen and his family had been arrested the previous night. That's more or less what did happen, but I don't know if He Zishen heard it from one of the other prisoners or just guessed it.

At Tilanqiao Police Station we were divided up into men and women. The men's lock-up was a big cell alongside a smaller one. One afternoon a lawyer came, accompanied by another person. A prisoner who some of us recognised as Lou Guohua was called out from the small cell. We understood from his conversation with the lawyer that on the 22nd he'd gone to visit friends on the Dalian Bay Road but unfortunately had knocked on the wrong door and been seized. He managed some firm for Yu Qiaqing; the man accompanying the lawyer was Yu's son. So he'd been locked up in a different place from us and handled differently. I realised that Liu Renjing must have told him to go to the place where he had been arrested and to tell the people there to flee. Later I found out that before doing so he'd shifted all the documents from his house and made preparations for the period after his arrest; only then had he gone to Dalian Bay Road to knock on that fateful door. He'd been a delegate for the Our Word group. His wife, also a comrade, had given birth on May 1, so he hadn't been able to attend the Congress and Song Jingxiu had filled in for him.

A few days later the entire case was sent for judgment to the courts in the International Settlement. Wang Zhihuai and his wife and daughter, my wife Liu Jingzhen, and He Zishen's wife Zhang Yisen were not extradited but kept in a

---

30   According to Wang Fanxi, Wang did not go to this place together with Zhang Te. Zhang had already been arrested and handcuffed when Wang knocked at the door.

lock-up attached to the courts (it was a month before they were released). Lou Guohua was remanded on bail of $10,000. The rest of us – seven in all, mostly under aliases – were extradited to the Shanghai Garrison Headquarters.

We were all bundled into a van and taken off to the White Cloud Temple at West Gate, where the detectives attached to the Garrison had their office. The boss, a man called Ma from Anhui, interrogated us individually. I told him I was Wang Jian from Ganzhou in Jiangxi.

'If you won't even tell me your right name, how do you expect me to do my job?' he said.

He kept on at me for quite some time and eventually began to threaten me with electric shocks, but still I refused to yield.

'Think of it from my point of view', he continued. 'All I want from you is your real name and an admission that you are a member of the Communist Party'.

As he said that, he dipped his finger in some tea and traced the name 'Zhongfu' on the table in front of him.

'Nor am I asking you about him',[31] he added. 'He's an old friend of mine'.

After that, I had no choice but to tell him my real name and that I was a member of the Communist Party.

Ma Yufu knew that only through me could Chen Duxiu be found. As soon as I had got through the door of Tilanqiao Police Station the Detective Sergeant there, a man called Wang Bin, had asked me to 'help out' by telling him where Chen lived. He asked the foreign police sergeant to use torture on me, but the man refused. The day we were extradited Wang Bin spread his hands and said that after so many days the bird would certainly have flown. Chief Detective Ma of the White Cloud Temple probably also calculated that even if I did tell them, Chen would by then have moved, so he might as well be kind to me.

None of the others save He Zishen had been arrested according to a special list of names, so the question did not arise whether the names they had given were true or false. The police at the White Cloud Temple took mug-shots of them and showed them to Ma Yufu. Naturally, he knew who they were, but the police didn't force him to put names to faces. He got He Zishen's family name wrong, and wrote it with another character that is pronounced similarly but in a different tone; and an official wrote the character *zi* as a *xian*, which looks quite similar. So Hé Zishen spent six years in gaol as Hè Xianshen. And that was lucky for him, because earlier he'd escaped from court-house custody in Ji'nan,

---

31   Zhongfu was one of the names used by Chen Duxiu. Like this man Ma, Chen was from Anhui.

and the Guomindang had put out a warrant for his re-arrest. If they'd found out who he really was, they might have sent him back to Ji'nan to be dealt with. Wang Fanxi, Pu Dezhi, and Chen Yimou didn't even say where they lived. They frequently felt the end of Wang Bin's rattan cane, but in the end he gave up on them.

We probably spent a week to ten days in the White Cloud Temple before being handed over to Longhua. Just before that, a detective told Jiang Chang-shi: 'You've got Ma Yufu to thank for this'.

A little over a month after we had reached Longhua, Lou Guohua turned up. He'd been bailed out all right, on a surety of $10,000 paid in by his friend. By then he believed that he was in the clear, so he attended court for the hearing, meaning afterwards to retrieve the $10,000 bail. But unluckily for him, in the meantime Wang Bin's people had searched He Zishen's house and unearthed a form that Lou had filled out at the time of the Unification Congress.

During our time at Longhua we were active in various ways, we had our struggles, and a number of interesting things happened, but I don't intend to talk about them here. I'll mention just one thing. A rumour reached us from outside that He Zishen and I were to be shot, but the others would be spared. In late October or early November I was called out for a mug-shot. Prisoners who'd been in Longhua for a long time knew that two or three days after that happened, you were invariably taken out and shot. I myself had seen the same thing happen on several occasions. But what could you do? 'An earthen pot will inevitably be broken on the well'.[32] However, the second day went by without anything happening, and so did the third, and so did a whole week of days. Finally, all seven of us were told to pack our things and attend court, where an official stood on a platform and read out our sentences from a notebook. I got fifteen years, He Zishen got ten, Pu Dezhi got two and a half, and the rest got six.[33] We were then sent to Caohejing Model Prison.

According to what others have told me, the reason I escaped the firing squad was because Xiong Shihui, Commander of the Shanghai Garrison Headquarters, was replaced by Dai Ji. Dai Ji was a general of the Nineteenth Route Army, which had just arrived to garrison Shanghai and was far more enlightened than the armies of Chiang Kai-shek's military clique.[34]

---

32   I.e., a revolutionary must expect to die for the revolution.

33   In the original text I mistakenly said they got five years. [Note added by Zheng Chaolin in 1990.]

34   In late 1933 and early 1934, this same army staged a rebellion in Fujian against Chiang Kai-shek and made friendly overtures to the Chinese Communists.

I don't intend to say anything about our odyssey through Chiang's prisons: how we went from Caohejing to Hangzhou, from Hangzhou to Suzhou, from Suzhou to Nanjing, and how we spent five years behind bars in Nanjing Gaol.

Finally, I should explain how it was that we knew that we would be arrested on the night of May 21. Our Comrade Ma Renzhi, manager of the Hubin Book Company, originally called Ma Shicai, had followed He Yingqin to Fuzhou at the time of the Northern Expedition. In Fuzhou he had carried out some revolutionary activities, and had worked together with Pan Gugong, a leader of the left-wing of the Guomindang in Fujian.[35] In 1929, when Pan escaped to Shanghai, the two met often. Most of the military judges at Longhua were Fujianese, and some were friends of Pan. Somehow or another Pan got wind of the arrests and informed Ma, who rushed by car to Peng Shuzhi's place on Route Père Robert to tell Peng. He then intended to drive over to my place to tell me, but Xie Depan happened to be at Peng's place, so Peng told Xie to take the news to East Shanghai. That's how things went wrong. Naturally, Ma didn't know that He Zishen and the people at the Congress building had also been targeted for arrest.

Things I Heard Said

I was in prison for the whole of the six years and three months between the night of May 21, 1931, when I was arrested, and the morning of August 29, 1937, when I was freed after the bombing of Nanjing.[36] I was not personally engaged in Trotskyist activity in that period, so I only know about it from hearsay. Some things I heard about while I was still in gaol, other things I only learned of after my release. I can't vouch for the accuracy of what follows.

While we were at Longhua, news filtered in that four members of the former Our Word group had issued a declaration breaking from Trotskyism and capitulating to the Guomindang. They were Liang Ganqiao, Zhang Shi, Lu Mengyi, and a fourth person whose name I forget. They'd quite simply gone over from revolution to counterrevolution, but they didn't serve up any comrades to the Guomindang as a 'gift on the occasion of a first meeting', so in that respect they did not quite sink to the depths of Ma Yufu. (Later, however, Zhang Shi and Lu Mengyi became leading members of Guomindang intelligence, and Liang Ganqiao became a leading anti-Communist under Hu Zongnan.)

It was hardly surprising that these four turned traitor. The Our Word group had originally opposed unifying with the Chen Duxiu-ites, and though Trotsky's

---

35 Of which Fuzhou is the capital.
36 By the Japanese.

letter had forced their hand, a minority of them were still inwardly opposed to it. The people around Ou Fang in the Our Word group were all right, but those around Liang Ganqiao were not. After Ou disappeared into gaol, Liang took over. His ambition was to become leader of the united Trotskyists, so that he could then indulge in his conspiratorial schemes. He planned to have Chen Duxiu elected General Secretary at the Unification Congress and then to send him to Turkey[37] so that he himself could take over, but things didn't turn out as he wished. He came bottom of the poll together with Peng Shuzhi in the election for the Central Committee, and he lost in the run-off. Peng's name stank in the nostrils of most delegates, but Liang's stank worse.

During the Congress, Wang Pingyi, a member of the Combat group, had to return to his home in Shandong after something came up. He returned to Shanghai after the Congress, and the people who were dissatisfied with its outcome disparaged it to him, so he declared that he would lead the opposition to it. I had heard about this even before our arrest. Sometime later Wang Pingyi, too, joined the Guomindang secret police and changed his name to Wang Bo-ping.

After our arrest some people in the Our Word group, including Zhang Te and Shi Tang, left Shanghai for Guangxi. In those days Guangxi was under Li Zongren and Bai Chongxi,[38] who were busy recruiting talent and going on about autonomy, for they planned to resist Chiang Kai-shek's Nanjing Government. Zhang Te was from Guangxi, though the others probably weren't. Zhang Te returned to Guangxi to become an official and participate in the internal struggles of the Guangxi clique; not long afterwards he abandoned Trotskyism. But some people, led by Shi Tang, went to become not officials but middle-school teachers, and they continued to propagate Trotskyist ideas both in the classroom and outside. They influenced no few of their students, who played an important role in a whole series of student movements in Guangxi. But Shi Tang and his friends never develop a Trotskyist organisation in Guangxi; on the contrary, they left the Trotskyist organisation. I only mention this in connection with the defection of Liang Ganqiao and the three others.

At Longhua we met up with seven other new Trotskyist prisoners. They were: Yin Kuan, Jiang Zhendong, Liu Yi, Song Jingxiu, and three others; all were held on a different block from us. According to what others have told me, there are two theories about these people. Yin Kuan says that when they realised that they were without a leadership, a number of them met together in a hotel on

---

37   Where Trotsky was.
38   Li and Bai were leaders of the anti-Chiang Kai-shek Guangxi clique.

Fuzhou Road to set up a new one, but unfortunately one of the people at the meeting was a spy who betrayed them. According to Song Jingxiu, however, there was already a new leadership and Yin Kuan's aim at this meeting was to set up a faction. So when Song learned about it he went to the hotel and urged Yin against this course of action, but unfortunately they were all arrested. I don't know who's telling the truth.[39] Subsequently Yin Kuan and Song Jingxiu were both sent to prison, but Jiang Zhendong, Liu Yi, and the other three were freed on bail. Later Song died in gaol, but Yin Kuan was bailed out when he fell ill, after which he failed to report back to prison.

I don't know when the leadership under Chen Duxiu was restored. After first we and then Song Jingxiu had been arrested, as far as I remember the only members – one full, the other alternate – left on the Central Committee were Chen Duxiu and Peng Shuzhi. Wang Zhihuai had gone to work as a labourer on the Zhejiang-Jiangxi Railway, Ou Fang had already died (in gaol), the Hong Kong worker had gone back to Hong Kong after the Congress, and though Pu Dezhi and Song Fengchun were already out of gaol, they were temporarily inactive. I don't know what activities this leadership engaged in. This was the period of the September 18 Incident[40] and the Battle of Shanghai,[41] so the country was in turmoil and conditions were ripe for revolutionary agitation.

In the late spring or early summer of 1932, Peng Shuzhi, Li Ji, Wu Jiyan, and Du Weizhi gathered briefly in Shanghai's Zhongshan Park for a meeting. After the meeting Peng and Li left by the back gate and Wu and Du by the front. Keeping watch at the front gate was Gu Shunzhang, who recognised Wu (though he didn't know his name) and arrested him and Du. They were handed over to the Nanjing Garrison Headquarters. Du Weizhi, a professor at Anhui University, phoned the principal of the University, Cheng Yansheng, and the Garrison Headquarters decided to send him to Anqing and hand him over to Cheng, whence he escaped back to Shanghai the same night. Wu Jiyan's cover eventually broke and he was sentenced to life imprisonment. A few years later his relatives got him out.

---

39   When Jiang Zhendong read this passage, he came up with a third theory. He said that
      the meeting was to set up a West Shanghai District Committee and that Song Jingxiu – a
      member of the revived leadership organ – was there on Peng Shuzhi's instructions. [Note
      by Zheng Chaolin.]

40   The seizure of Shenyang in 1931 by the Japanese, as a step toward occupying the entire
      Northeast.

41   On January 28, 1932, the Nineteenth Route Army successfully held out for more than a
      month against a Japanese attack on the land, on the sea, and in the air before a truce was
      declared and the Shanghai area was demilitarised.

In October 1932, I was in Nanjing's Central Military Prison. The man in charge of the Education Section in this prison was Shen Bingquan, a student of Hangzhou Law College and originally a member of the Communist Party who had been arrested on April 12, 1927, at Hangzhou. Somehow or another he'd ended up working for the Guomindang in this prison. Politics are a complicated business. Most people would call this man a traitor, and so did I at the time, but it's not true. In the Central Military prison he showed special consideration to political prisoners, particularly the better-known ones. When I was first in the South block of the prison, he got the Second Section to transfer me after a few months to the preferential treatment unit, where there were already two other political prisoners, both students of Nanjing's Central University, one a man called Yang Jinhao from Pudong, the other a man from Suzhou called Wang Chubao, the half-brother of Wang Rongbao. After we'd settled in, Shen Bingquan came to see us. He told us that the prison authorities planned to teach illiterate prisoners to read and write, so the three of us had been assigned to prepare a text-book. The other two thanked him and agreed to do so, but I kept quiet. This preferential treatment unit was alongside the prison sports ground, you could see it whenever you were let out for exercise. People used to say that Noulens and his wife[42] were at first kept here, though they were later moved to another place. In the summer of 1932, when I was let out for exercise on one occasion, I saw two political prisoners who were living in this preferential treatment unit, both of them members of the CCP who'd studied abroad, one called Chen Jiakang and the other Jiang Zemin.[43] We'd already met them at Longhua. They'd mended Wang Zhennan's car for him, so Wang Zhennan (who was Minister of Military Justice at the time) had instructed the prison authorities to send them to the preferential treatment unit. I could tell from the way that other prisoners talked whenever we were let out onto the sports ground that they heartily despised people who lived in the preferential treatment unit. After Chen and Jiang had left, Shen Bingquan managed to get me and the other two prisoners transferred there.

---

42   Hilaire Noulens and his wife Wandeli (a transliteration from the Chinese, perhaps representing her cover name, Marie Vandercruyssen) were said to be representatives in China of the Comintern's Far Eastern Bureau. They arrived in Shanghai in March and June respectively, and were arrested in the International Settlement in June 1931 and handed over to the Chinese authorities. They were tried by the High Court of Jiangsu Province and sentenced to life imprisonment, but were freed in September 1937, shortly after the Japanese invasion. Frederick S. Litten has written a manuscript titled 'The Noulens Affair'.

43   Jiang Zemin (written with the same characters) is also the name of the man who took over from Zhao Ziyang as General Secretary of the CCP after the June 4 Massacre in 1989, but this is a different Jiang Zemin.

During that period, one day a young political prisoner I knew came to see the doctor in the clinic on the other side of the sports ground. At the time I was taking a walk in front of the entrance to the preferential treatment unit. This young man told me, 'Chen Duxiu has been arrested'. His words struck me like a thunderbolt. On one occasion at Longhua I'd heard a rifle-shot from across the wall and realised that another political prisoner was dead. A few minutes later one of the guards, a man from Jiangxi, had stopped at the gate to our block to tell us that the man who had just died was an old man, a Communist Party leader. That, too, had given me a nasty shock, and it wasn't until later that I learned from another prisoner that the man they'd shot was Xiang Zhongfa. Now, in my preferential treatment unit, I hoped against hope that the rumour was not true. But the same day or the next, Shen Bingquan came to see us. He said with pretended nonchalance that Chen Duxiu was unlikely to die. I said instinctively that if he'd been arrested, I could see no reason why he wouldn't die. Shen Bingquan had thought that his words would startle me, and had never imagined that on the contrary my words would startle him. He asked me how I knew that Chen had been arrested. I can't remember how I answered. He must have thought that we political prisoners were extremely well informed. And so we were.

A few days later I wrote to Shen Bingquan requesting to be transferred back to the South block, and he had no choice but to accede.

While I'm on the subject, there's something else I ought to add about Shen Bingquan. In the summer of 1933, he again came to visit me in the South block. Without beating about the bush, he told me that he was responding to a request by my friend Hua Lin, who came from the same province as Shen, to show me special consideration. He told me that something had come up, and he asked me if I was interested. It turned out that the Military Court intended to appoint some people who knew foreign languages to translate foreign military law into Chinese for use as reference material in drafting a legal code for the Chinese military. The translators would be housed in the North block, and would spend their working day in the instruction rooms and return to their cells in the evening. Since I owed this chance to Hua Lin, I said I'd do it.

Later, my wife Liu Jingzhen came to see me and told me about Chen Duxiu's arrest. She said it was Xie Depan who had informed on him. I asked her whether he'd informed on him before or after his arrest. She said after.

At the time Jing was teaching in Shanghai. Each year during the summer and winter holidays she would visit me in Nanjing's Military Prison. She also visited me once or twice during term-time. Naturally, she also visited Chen Duxiu whenever she was in Nanjing. It wasn't until after my release that she told me that she had been in charge of liaison between Chen and the outside

world. She used to smuggle letters and documents of the Shanghai organisation to Chen, and to smuggle out articles and documents by him. Each time
she would hide these things in the bottom of a biscuit tin, underneath the bis-
cuits. She didn't necessarily read the documents, nor was she the only person
who worked for the organisation in this way. Because she did this work, Chen
Duxiu directed the organisation not to enrol her in any of its branches. I believe
that some Shanghai Trotskyist leaders went in person to visit Chen in gaol. The
articles contained in the mimeographed publications that we brought out in
that period, together with Chen's secret letters, which are still in existence, will
probably throw light on the nature of this liaison, and on the extent to which
Chen Duxiu had the Shanghai Trotskyist organisation under remote control in
those days.

After her arrest in 1952, Liu Jingzhen told the Government about her role as
link-woman in that period. She was freed in 1957. It's hard to believe that in 1968,
while she was under criticism in the Cultural Revolution, she was asked once
again to talk about the 'biscuit tin' episode, and her tricking of the Guomindang
dictatorship was used against her as evidence of 'counterrevolutionary criminal
activity'.

I don't know under what circumstances the Shanghai organisation was restored after Chen Duxiu's arrest. According to what I've heard, the main mover
was Chen Qichang, later assisted by Yin Kuan after he had got out of gaol; after
Yin's second arrest, Wang Fanxi got out of gaol and also helped. It was in this
period that the organisation was rent by a serious conflict.

At some point, a South African Trotskyist came to Shanghai to work as a
journalist. He was Deputy Editor of Shanghai's *China Weekly Review*, second
only on that publication to Edgar Snow. His name was Frank Glass, and his
Chinese name was Li Furen. Under his influence another left-wing newspaper
man in Shanghai, Yi Luosheng (Harold R. Isaacs), came over from the Third
International to the Fourth. These two both hoped to build the Chinese Trotskyist movement. They tracked down Chen Qichang, and at the same time they
tracked down Liu Renjing. Frank Glass gave Chen Qichang $300 to set up a
printing factory. It was a printing factory of a special sort: no machines but
just lead type, which you formed into bars, clipped into place, and smeared
with ink before printing.[44] At around this time Liu Renjing had brought some
young students to Shanghai from Beijing and had usurped the leadership of
the Trotskyist organisation. These people, having set up a Central Committee
formed by Si Chaosheng, Liu Jialiang, Hu Wenzhang, and Wang Shuben, with

---

44   C.f. Wang Fan-hsi 1991, p. 176.

Liu Renjing as General Secretary, got Frank Glass to support them. I believe he was even a member of this Central Committee. But Yin Kuan and Chen Qichang refused to recognise it, and were loath to hand over their 'printing factory'. A struggle ensued, on questions of both theory and organisation, and also on matters concerning people's private lives. I know nothing of all that, save that Chen Duxiu supported Yin Kuan and Chen Qichang, and that when Liu Renjing's Central Committee expelled Yin Kuan and Chen Qichang they expelled Chen Duxiu as well. Frank Glass backed all this. Chen Duxiu didn't trust Frank Glass. He said that that foreigner is an agent of the Settlement police, and told comrades not to pay any attention to him. Not long afterwards Liu Renjing's Central Committee was raided by the Guomindang and they were all arrested. From then on the only leadership in existence was that of Yin Kuan and Chen Qichang.[45]

The case of Liu Renjing and his supporters was handed over to the Nanjing Garrison Headquarters. Liu Renjing immediately turned traitor, so instead of going to gaol he was sent to the Suzhou Reformatory for a period of self-examination. The others – Si, Liu, Hu, and Wang – were not prepared to capitulate, so they ended up in gaol: Liu Jialiang got seven years, the rest got five. They were handed over to the Central Military Prison.

I met Si, Hu, and Wang there, but I never met Liu Jialiang, who was kept in the South block. Somehow they managed to persuade a fellow-prisoner who was a member of the CCP to explain about them to me. I didn't know this man, nor he me. He worked in the prison printing factory. The prisoners in the West block used to exercise in the area just in front of the printing factory windows. One day, I forget which year, but it was one or two years before the outbreak of the war with Japan, one of the prisoners working in the printing factory called me over to the window while I was out exercising. This man stood by the window and talked with me for a few minutes. He told me that there were four Trotskyists in the prison, that they had put up a good show while being held in the Nanjing Garrison Headquarters, and that they wanted to meet me but were afraid I wouldn't trust them, so they'd asked him to introduce them to me. Later, again while I was out exercising, a man came across and began walking alongside me. He told me that his name was Hu Wenwei (alias Hu Wenzhang); on another occasion, Wang Huating (alias Wang Shuben) also came

---

45   This paragraph is based on hearsay, and it may not all be true. At first Liu Renjing wasn't General Secretary. He was in Beijing, so the Central Committee was simply under his remote control. Some say that Si Chaosheng was General Secretary during this early period, others say Liu Jialiang was. [Note by Zheng Chaolin.]

across and started talking with me, and the same thing happened on several subsequent occasions. Hu and Wang told me about their struggle with Yin Kuan and Chen Qichang, and especially about the underground printing apparatus. At the time I thought it was a wrangle over a mimeograph. It never occurred to me that the so-called underground printing apparatus was in fact a 'printing factory'.[46] Wang Huating also told me about their analysis of the various classes in Chinese society. On one occasion when Si Chaosheng met me in the bath-house he talked with me at great length, not (like Hu and Wang) about the past but about the future. They heard from somewhere that I would soon be released, so Si proposed that I set up a magazine to propagate Trotskyist ideas. In the course of my talks with these three men I avoided voicing my own opinion. None of them tried to disguise their detestation for Liu Renjing.

Later, after I had got out of gaol, I heard that Liu Renjing had behaved quite shamelessly in the Reformatory, where he had become leader of the 'Students' Society' (or whatever the so-called autonomous organisation was called that the Guomindang political police set up for prisoners), with He Zizhen as his deputy. The two of them were one hundred per cent behind the Guomindang in its persecution of Communist prisoners. While I was in the Central Military Prison I came across an issue of the magazine put out by the Reformatory, in it an article by Liu Renjing praising Chen Lifu's theory of vitalism. (Another article by Peng Kang[47] was about Laozi. The magazine is probably available in some archive.)

Si, Liu, Hu, and Wang were also set free on August 29, 1937. They first stayed in a hotel in Nanjing for a while and only then went back to Shanghai. While they were in the hotel, Si said he didn't want to be a Trotskyist any more, but the rest continued to be active in Shanghai. They kept up their struggle against Chen Duxiu, and even denounced him as a 'Fuzhou Road prostitute'. Later Hu Wenzhang went to Manchuria to join an anti-Japanese army, and nothing more was heard of him. Liu Jialiang was seized and martyred in Vietnam.[48] As for

---

46   According to Wang Fanxi, the printing machine here referred to was left behind by Har-
       old Isaacs when he stopped publishing *China Forum* and went to Beijing to write *The
       Tragedy of the Chinese Revolution*. This machine was eventually sold to get some money
       with which to run the organisation. One or two years later, a new Provisional Committee
       was elected including Wang Fanxi, Chen Qichang, Yin Kuan, and Frank Glass. This new
       leadership decided to bring out an underground journal called *Douzheng* ('Struggle'), so a
       new machine was put together. It was very primitive, consisting of just two wooden frames
       into which type was inserted. This story is told in Wang Fan-hsi 1991, p. 176.
47   One of the Creation Society writers.
48   He was trapped by the secret service of the Vietcong together with some Vietnamese Trot-
       skyists in 1950, and died in prison shortly afterwards.

Wang Shuben, at the time of Liberation he died in the headquarters of the Sino-American Joint Mission[49] in Chongqing.

The printing press led to quite a storm. Either before or after Liu Renjing's usurpation of the leadership, a comrade working in the printing factory decided that he would expropriate the equipment for his own private ends and open a shop. Frank Glass then disguised himself as a British policeman and went by car, with Shao Lu acting as his chauffeur, to steal it back, with Little Zhao [Zhicheng] from the Telephone Company pretending to be his interpreter.

Chen Duxiu and Peng Shuzhi finally split in Tiger Bridge Prison in Nanjing. Pu Dezhi and Luo Shifan stood by Chen. Outside the prison, Yin Kuan and Chen Qichang also opposed Peng.

Apart from Pu Dezhi and Luo Shifan, four other people were arrested at the same time as Chen Duxiu and Peng Shuzhi. They were: Zeng Meng, He Zizhen, Peng Daozhi, and Song Fengchun. Not long after entering gaol, Zeng was freed through the intercession of former fellow-students of his from the Huangpu Military Academy after writing a letter of repentance. The others considered him a traitor. He Zizhen also got out, but via the Reformatory, where he behaved despicably. Peng Daozhi, Peng Shuzhi's younger brother, died in gaol of typhoid fever. Song Fengchun was also freed as a result of a campaign by people outside prison.

There's one other episode I'd like to recount concerning Chen Duxiu in gaol. Sometime in 1935 (the exact time would have to be checked) Mao Dun was responsible for editing a book called *Zhongguode yiri* ('One Day in China').[50] Through Wang Yuanfang he asked Chen Duxiu to record his activities, thoughts, and feelings on a given day. Chen agreed, and the ensuing record was published in *One Day in China*. Through some other person Mao Dun also asked Lou Shiyi,

---

49   A collaborative effort, between the CIA and Guomindang intelligence, whereby the former advised the latter in the use of modern techniques of surveillance, interrogation, and torture. The Centre's real name was the Sino-American Centre for Cooperation in Special Techniques (see Shen Zui and Wen Qiang 1984, pp. 71 ff.). Wang Shuben was killed by the Guomindang as part of its preparations to flee to Taiwan.

50   The advertisements calling for contributions to a record of one day – Thursday, May 21, 1936 – were in fact posted in the spring of 1936. The book was published in September 1936 in Shanghai by Shenghuo Shudian. The idea for the book came from the proposal by Maxim Gorky at the First Congress of Soviet Writers in 1934 for a book called *Den Mira* ('One day in the world'), eventually published (in Russian) in 1937. An English-language version of Mao Dun's book, one-fifth the size of the original and without Chen Duxiu's contribution, was published by Yale University Press in 1983 under the title *One Day in China: May 21, 1936*, translated and edited by Sherman Cochran, Andrew C.K. Hsieh, and Janis Cochran.

in the Central Military Prison, to do the same, which he did. I was one of the people he wrote about, though I'm not named as such. After the book came out, while I was still in prison, I saw it. Chen Duxiu's reflections brimmed with the spirit of internationalism, though he had usually spoken of the Chinese Revolution from the standpoint of China as a single country. His essay made a deep impression on me.

A Talk on the Eve of Our Separation in Nanjing

On July 7, 1937, the Lugouqiao or Marco Polo Bridge Incident took place,[51] marking the start of all-out war between Japan and China. By that time the Guomindang and the Communists had already formed their second united front. The Chinese Red Army had become the Eighth Route Army of the National Revolutionary Armed Forces and had set up an office in Nanjing. The Communists demanded the freeing of political prisoners and so did public opinion, but for a long a time before that a number of celebrities – old friends of Chen Duxiu – had been demanding Chen's release.

Before the Marco Polo Bridge Incident but after the establishment of the Eighth Route Army's office in Nanjing, Pan Hannian, a member of the office staff, had visited the Central Military Prison to see his cousin Pan Zinian. He told Pan Zinian that the Guomindang was still not prepared to free all political prisoners, and that it would only consider freeing prisoners if the CCP made a list of those it wanted released. Pan Zinian came back and reported on this exchange; I only heard about it indirectly. After a while Pan Zinian, who was serving life, was freed early. Only then can the question of a 'list' have come up, for if all the prisoners had been freed, there'd have been no need for one.

Some people said that the CCP asked the Guomindang to free a list of people including Chen Duxiu. I've never heard such a theory before, and common sense tells me that it's not true. Chen Duxiu was freed as a result of the campaign by those celebrities. It had nothing to do with the CCP. The formal procedure was that Hu Shi and Zhang Boling bailed him out. Some office of the Guomindang proclaimed that it had resolved to free Chen on bail because he 'loves his country deeply, and deeply regrets what he has done'. (Two days after his release, on August 25, Chen protested at this statement in a letter to the editor of Shanghai's *Shenbao* newspaper: 'A sincere patriot would not venture to brag about his love of country, and I know of nothing that I should regret'; 'I have done no wrong, so regret would have no object'.) In short, Chen Duxiu's release was not connected in any way with the CCP.

---

51   This act of aggression was staged by the Japanese at Marco Polo Bridge near Beijing.

Then there's the black propaganda of the Guomindang's dirty tricks department. According to one report, Zhou Enlai visited Chen Duxiu in gaol; according to another, Chen Lifu and Tao Xisheng greeted Chen Duxiu as he left the prison, Chen went to stay in the Guomindang Central Committee's guest house, Chen Lifu invited Chen Duxiu to dinner on the evening of his release, and at the banquet Chen Duxiu made a tearful speech of thanks. This is all mischievous fabrication. Zhou Enlai never visited Chen Duxiu in gaol and when Chen walked free it was his student Chen Zhongfan (then Director of Jinling University's Literature Department) who personally fetched him from gaol and put him up in his house in Yinyangying. As for us Trotskyists in the Central Military Prison and Tiger Bridge Prison, our release, too, had nothing whatsoever to do with the CCP. By August 13, the war had already reached Shanghai, and by August 15, Nanjing was being bombarded from the air. The Guomindang was preparing to abandon Nanjing, so it put into operation a regulation commonly used in bourgeois countries whereby in times of war the gaols are emptied and the prisoners dispersed. The great majority of the prisoners – political, common, and military – were released. Pu Dezhi, Luo Shifan, and Peng Shuzhi were freed in late August. Luo and Peng immediately went to Shanghai, Pu immediately returned to Anqing. He Zishen, whose original sentence had been shorter than mine, was freed about one week earlier than me and went to Tiger Bridge Prison to visit Chen Duxiu; he also met Pu, Luo, and Peng there. Chen Duxiu arranged for He Zishen and for me and my wife to go to Jixi in Anhui to stay for a while in the house of Wang Mengzou, owner of the Oriental Book Company. Without waiting for me to leave gaol, He Zishen was taken by my wife Liu Jingzhen to the Science Book Company in Wuhu.[52] I wasn't released until August 29, whereupon I immediately went with Jing to Chen Zhongfan's two-storey foreign-style house in Yinyangying. Downstairs was a guest-room and a dining room; upstairs was the main room, where Chen Duxiu and Little Pan were staying. Chen Zhongfan had already sent his dependants back to his native place in Yancheng, and he himself had moved into the upstairs side room. When I and Jing arrived, Chen Duxiu and Little Pan were temporarily away, so we waited for them in the main room. Pan came back first: Chen Duxiu didn't get back until the afternoon. Several groups of guests called in on him, and he received them in the downstairs guest-room. I and Jing went out to buy some bread and cakes for our supper. That night we slept on the floor in Chen Duxiu's room, and early next morning we set out for Wuhu.

---

52   The journey from Nanjing to Jixi passes through Wuhu. The Science Book Company was owned by Wang Mengzou. He Zishen went there to await Zheng Chaolin's release.

When we went up or down the stairs, we often saw Chen Zhongfan come out of his room. Chen Duxiu hadn't introduced us to him by name, he'd simply said that we lived in East Nanjing and had fled here to escape the bombing. Whenever Chen Zhongfan met Chen Duxiu he would stand respectfully by, in the manner of an old-style student in the presence of his teacher. On Chen Duxiu's bedside table I saw a *wuyangufeng*[53] that Chen Zhongfan had newly written for his old teacher. Part of it used the story about the divine dragon, and how you could see its head but not its tail, to praise Chen Duxiu.

In the evening I chatted with Chen Duxiu, who already knew my views[54] on the war from He Zishen. Naturally, he disagreed, but that evening he deliberately avoiding mentioning them. He merely showed me the theses he had composed in gaol. I studied them carefully, but I, too, disagreed with him. For the most part I can no longer remember what they said, but one still sticks in my mind. It said that for the time being we should have an 'armistice' with the Guomindang. I especially disagreed with that one, and read it but said nothing. He knew why. So we didn't talk any further about our estimate of the war and our attitude toward it. Instead we talked of other things, among them the question of the CCP. By then I opposed the CCP, not just generally but from a whole number of theoretical and practical angles. My opposition had been especially heightened by the recent Moscow trials, for in my opinion the CCP breathed out of the same set of nostrils as Stalin on this question.[55] I knew from Chen Duxiu's past attitude and from the tone of voice he adopted that evening that he, too, opposed the CCP. I crystallised my attitude to the CCP in the form of a question. I asked Chen Duxiu: Will the CCP disband wholesale and enter the Guomindang? No, he said, after a moment's thought: if they were to do that, they would no longer be in a position to play out their reactionary role to the end. He put special emphasis on the word 'reactionary'. It was completely obvious to me from his reply that he was even more opposed to the CCP than I was. So all the talk then by the Guomindang and the Communists about Chen wanting to start working again for the Communist Party was pure fabrication. Today people are still peddling the same rumours. Some people even claim that Chen said to Dong Biwu 'Of course I want to start working again for the Communist Party'. Others say that in 1938 in Wuhan every time he spoke Chen said that 'the Party's line and policy is completely correct' and that 'we resolutely support Party policy'. But in truth Chen opposed the CCP

---

53   A classical poem with five words in each line.
54   According to Zheng Chaolin, the war between China and Japan was from the very beginning an integral part of the imminent world war, so he opposed supporting it.
55   Actually, Mao Zedong privately criticised the Moscow trials.

even more thoroughly than I, the only difference being that at that time he didn't oppose the proposal for an alliance against Japan between the Party and the Guomindang. He had his own view of this proposal, which by no means boiled down to the view that 'the Party's line and policy is completely correct'. Chen Duxiu's subsequent speeches and actions right through until his death are all explicable in terms of what he told me that evening about his attitude toward the CCP.

We also talked of other things, but I only remember one of them, namely that I would take responsibility for finishing the translation that Pu Dezhi and Luo Shifan had begun in Tiger Bridge Prison of Trotsky's *Revolution Betrayed*.[56] The original text was in English. I took it and the draft translation with me to Jixi and after I'd completed it and checked it through, I posted it to Shanghai to be published. I believe that Chen Duxiu had given my wife the original book and the draft translation even before my release from gaol. I still remember Chen's evaluation of the book. He said it was not only a book written in opposition to Stalin and to the Soviet Union as it had then become but one that further developed the Marxist theory of the state.

That was the last time that Chen Duxiu and I met and talked.

The next morning I and Jing left Chen Zhongfan's house and went to the Railway Station outside Nanjing's Zhonghua Gate to catch the train to Wuhu. Chen Duxiu escorted us to the door and waved goodbye as we disappeared in rickshaws.

We corresponded with Chen Duxiu a few times after reaching Jixi. Probably some of his replies are still in existence.

After I parted from him I heard only indirectly about his life and thought in Nanjing, Wuhan, Chongqing, and Jiangjin, so I'd best leave to others the job of describing it.

(4)   *Trotsky's Theory of Permanent Revolution*
It's impossible to write a memoir of the Chinese Trotskyist movement or of Chen Duxiu's relationship to that movement without talking about the theoretical debates within Chinese Trotskyism. And in the final analysis it's impossible to talk about those debates without going back to Trotsky's theory of permanent revolution.

---

56   Called in Chinese *Suliande xianzhuang yu qiantu*, ('The Soviet Union now and in the future').

Trotsky's Estimate of Chen Duxiu

I once heard Liu Renjing say that while he was staying with Trotsky in Turkey the two men talked about Chen Duxiu. Trotsky highly estimated Chen Duxiu's talents as a revolutionary, but he said that Chen was no theoretician. Later, when Liu Renjing turned against Chen, he told people what Trotsky had said. Naturally, he put the emphasis on Chen Duxiu not being a theoretician rather than on him being a revolutionary, thus making Trotsky's comment seem derogatory. But in my opinion it was simply a statement of fact. The crucial question is what Trotsky meant by 'theoretician'.

By it he meant people like Marx and Engels and like Lenin, or at the very least people who were well versed in the writings of Marx and Engels and of the thinkers whose ideas Marx and Engels borrowed in the course of elaborating their theoretical system. Such people were not only good at theory but were also good at embedding theory in real conditions and using it to explain real conditions, and also at supplementing and even revising it on the basis of practice whenever it broke down. Clearly Chen Duxiu did not meet the requirements for a 'theoretician' of that sort.

But that doesn't mean that he was in no sense a theoretician. In preparing and enacting the Revolution of 1911, in opposing Duan Qirui and leading the New Culture Movement, in setting up the CCP, and in leading the Revolution of 1925–7, he advanced original theories and wrote theoretical essays. Looking back on his life as a revolutionary, it is evident that during each of its successive periods his acute vision enabled him to grasp the main elements in the objective situation and to propose policies for dealing with it. Before the Revolution of 1911 he realised that 'reform and modernisation' were no longer enough and that what was needed was 'revolution', so he stopped supporting Kang Youwei and became a 'rebel'. After the defeat of the Revolution of 1911 and of the Second Revolution,[57] he realised that the New Army, the secret societies, and

---

57   Although the Revolution of 1911 was started by members of the Guomindang (then called the Tongmenghui), power over the new government fell into the hands of Yuan Shikai. Yuan commanded strong armed forces and would not tolerate the armed forces – weak as they were – influenced by the Guomindang in the Southern provinces. So he threatened to eliminate them. When they became aware of his plans they took preemptive military action, in July 1913, but they were defeated by Yuan in September of the same year. These events were called the 'Second Revolution' to distinguish them from the 'First Revolution' of October 1911. At the time Chen Duxiu was very active in Anhui province, and played a small role in these events, as a result of which he almost lost his life. It was precisely from this 'Second Revolution' that Chen concluded that pure military actions without mass support were bound to fail. So he broke with China's traditional way of rebellion. [Note added by Zheng Chaolin in 1990.]

armed activity were no longer the way forward, and that it was necessary to launch a direct onslaught on traditional morality and culture. So he set up a youth journal and attacked the doctrines of Confucius and Mencius that for more than two thousand years had ruled China. Unlike Kang Youwei and Liang Qichao, who carried out reforms under the cover of the 'Late Texts School' or Zhang Binlin, who did the same under the cover of the 'Old Texts School',[58] he preferred to assail Confucianism head-on. And he was right. The situation as it then was required precisely such an assault on the 'Confucian shop': neither the Confucius of the Late Texts School nor the Confucius of the Old Texts School were capable of mobilising young people. After the May Fourth Movement, Chen realised that cultural revolution by itself was not enough and that political revolution was called for, so he threw himself into building the Chinese Communist movement and gathered together like-minded people to found the CCP. From then on his views constantly diverged from those of the 'China experts' in the Comintern's Far Eastern section. In 1926, after the Zhongshan Gunboat Incident, he immediately proposed that the CCP withdraw from the Guomindang and cooperate with it from the outside, but those same 'China experts' disagreed. Constrained by discipline, he was unable to break completely and decisively with his opponents, as he had done with Hu Shi and his ilk in the later phases of the May Fourth Movement on whether or not to 'talk politics'.[59] After the defeat of the so-called 'Great Revolution' he clearly saw that the revolution had been defeated and that the blame for the defeat belonged to those self-same 'China experts' and ultimately to Stalin, who had usurped power in the Soviet Union. But he was unable to understand precisely why

---

58 The Late Texts School and the Old Texts School were schools formed in the Western Han dynasty (206–23 BC) in annotating the Confucian classics. Qin Shihuangdi, the First Emperor of the Qin dynasty, banned and burned the Confucian classics, but the Han dynasty, which replaced the Qin, rehabilitated and patronised Confucianism. Some surviving scholars wrote down the classics from memory. These texts with their annotations were later called the 'Late Texts'. Sometime during the reign of Emperor Jing (156–141 BC) a whole set of Confucian classics was accidentally discovered in the walls of the Confucius Family Mansion in Qufu in Shandong. These texts generally coincided with those rewritten from memory but the annotations were different; they later became known as the 'Old Texts'. From then on two schools formed around the two lots of texts, each school calling the other texts forgeries. In the late nineteenth century some scholars of the Late Texts School (the best known being Kang Youwei) saw an implicit theory with various progressive and even revolutionary implications in the annotations to the *Spring and Autumn Annals* (the only book attributed to Confucius) and used them as the theoretical basis for their reform movement.

59 According to liberals like Hu Shi, the student movement of 1919 was not political, nor should it be. They agreed with the signs hanging in the tea-shops: 'Don't talk politics'.

Stalin wanted to deny that the revolution had been defeated and why Stalin imputed to him the Party's past mistakes. He mulled these questions over in his mind for more than a year, but he was still unable to resolve them. It was not until mid-1929, when he read Trotsky's articles, that the scales finally fell from his eyes.

Considering Chen Duxiu's life as a whole, the reason he could grasp the main elements in the situation, make a correct assessment of it, and settled on appropriate policies for dealing with it was because he had a clearer vision than his contemporaries, but it was also because objective conditions had by that time ripened so far that the main elements in the situation were starkly visible. Before then even the clearest vision would not have helped: only a systematic grasp of theory and of Marxism would have illuminated their hidden contours. But Chen Duxiu lacked such knowledge: he frequently understood things correctly and grasped the main elements in the situation, but he was unable to analyse them from the point of view of systematic theory or to discern them in a situation that had not yet ripened.

However, that does not give us the right to denigrate Chen Duxiu's standing as a revolutionary. Though never a theoretician to match Marx, Engels, Lenin, or Trotsky, he can still be considered an outstanding revolutionary. Karl Liebknecht was a brilliant revolutionary, but he didn't understand dialectical materialism and was even against it. Plekhanov, on the other hand, though completely familiar with the theories of Marx and Engels, was blind to the objective situation. In a revolution you don't want people who know lots of theory but are blind to what's going on around them: better someone who is not well versed in theory but is alive to real events. The final judgment on a person can only be passed when the last nail has been hammered into his coffin lid. Our judgment on Chen Duxiu should be that he was a Communist revolutionary of the first water, a Marxist, a Chinese revolutionary thinker, and a theoretician – even if not on a par with Marx, Engels, Lenin, and Trotsky.

Theoretical Disputes within Chinese Trotskyism

From the moment when they first embraced Trotskyist ideas, the Trotskyists in China have been divided by numerous theoretical disputes, and perhaps they still are even to this day.[60]

---

60   Zheng Chaolin in Shanghai was not in a position to follow developments in the Chinese Trotskyist movement outside China, but his surmise was correct. The Trotskyist movement in Hong Kong is still split, and the lines of the split have their origin in the disputes of the 1930s and 1940s.

When we Chen Duxiu supporters first came across Trotsky's articles in May and June 1929, we did not become Trotskyists overnight. Our conversion must be considered as a process. The Chinese Revolution had already been defeated and the fault was Stalin's – we accepted these two points forthwith, for we thought the same. But there were other elements in Trotskyist theory that took longer to accept. One was the thesis that not feudal remnants but capitalist relations were predominant in China, that China had long been capitalistic, that China's backward rural economy was dominated by urban capitalism, and that Chinese society was already bourgeois; so the job of the Chinese Revolution was to expropriate the bourgeoisie, set up a dictatorship of the proletariat, coordinate with the revolution in other countries, and found a socialist society – in short, China's revolution (or rather, China's third revolution) would be proletarian-socialist. Only after a rather long period of reflection and debate did we each in our own time come round to this and other theses of Trotskyism. The speed and depth of conversion differed from person to person. Chen Duxiu held out longest and raised a host of differences in the course of his discussions with us (mainly with Yin Kuan and Peng Shuzhi). The debate was not just verbal but written, in the form of articles. Unfortunately these writings of Chen Duxiu have all been lost. According to what Yin Kuan told me, at the end of each separate discussion the Old Man would stick to his own opinions and oppose ours; but by the next meeting he would already have accepted our position and would raise new issues on the basis of it.

Finally, Chen accepted the thesis that Chinese society was already capitalist, that the cities controlled the villages, and that capitalism benefited from feudal exploitation. He made these views his own: they became a constituent element in his thinking. Using his rich knowledge of Chinese history, he explained the special function of Chinese commercial capital. He even used his philological knowledge of ancient Chinese to show that China had never known a slave society. This reminds me of an incident in late 1929, when Zhou Enlai and Xiang Zhongfa went to visit Chen in his house on Range Road. Just at that moment Peng Shuzhi came in. Chen's two guests got up, shook hands with Peng, and said hello. Peng then joined in the conversation. I don't know what they talked about, nor do I know the purpose of Zhou and Xiang's visit, but I do know either from Peng or Chen that at one point, there was a discussion about whether the towns dominated the villages or vice versa. As soon as Chen raised this question, Xiang replied without thinking that the villages dominated the towns. Zhou Enlai intervened in a conciliatory way to say that things were not quite so simple. Zhou Enlai, who knew more about society than Xiang, realised that Xiang was making a fool of himself. This incident happened just at the time when Chen Duxiu was coming over to Trotskyism. I don't believe that this was an expression of Chen's acceptance of Trotsky's analysis of the nature of Chinese society, for it's a truism that towns dominate villages, you don't need to be a Trotskyist to think that.[61] It was simply a temporal coincidence. But right up to his death Chen never completely accepted the Trotskyist thesis on the nature of the Chinese Revolution and of revolutionary state power. He broadly embraced it, but he did so reluctantly, and rather less than whole-heartedly. Even as late as 1939 in his reply to Trotsky's letter he still criticised some Trotskyist comrades for saying that China's third revolution would be socialist from the outset. Actually, the comrades who sustained this thesis had correctly grasped Trotsky's theory of permanent revolution, but Chen Duxiu failed to do so, right up to his death. There's a document (Chen's letter of August 5, 1929, to the Central Committee) in which Chen advances the thesis that the present Chinese Revolution is not bourgeois-democratic but what 'Lenin in Russia had called a 'democratic revolution of the proletariat and peasantry''. This shows that Chen had already embraced Trotsky's thinking but was still wavering on the question of the nature of the revolution. When on February 17, 1930, Chen replied to the Comintern's telegram inviting him to Moscow, he proposed a 'proletarian dictatorship' in opposition to the Central Committee's 'democratic dictatorship of the workers and peasants'. That means that he had already solved the problem of how to define state power and, consequently, the nature of Chinese society. Finally, by 1938, the only problem he had still not solved was whether or not China's third revolution would be socialist from the start.

---

61   To my surprise, today I came across a document that confirms this incident. On August 5, 1929, Chen Duxiu wrote in a long letter to the Central Committee:

> You ignore these evident facts, so that today you still overestimate the position of the feudal forces. Even a leading comrade on the Central Committee said to me recently in the course of a discussion about the relative weight of the bourgeoisie and the feudal forces: 'At present in the Chinese economy the villages dominate the towns'.

This is a reference to the incident I described; the 'leading comrade on the Central Committee' was Xiang Zhongfa. But after this passage in Chen Duxiu's letter, the editor of *Zhongguo geming yu jihuizhuyi* ('The Chinese Revolution and opportunism') adds the following note:

> Yet another fabrication. The Central Committee merely said that China was a backward agricultural country in which rural production exceeds urban production; naturally, the trend of development was for the towns to dominate the villages, there were no differences of opinion on that. But there can be no doubt that the villages are more backward than the towns, and cannot be considered on a par with cities like Shanghai and Hankou.

Probably Zhou Enlai didn't tell the Central Committee about Xiang Zhongfa's indiscretion, so this 'editor' arbitrarily accused Chen Duxiu of 'fabrication'. This document shows that Xiang and Zhou must have visited Chen before August 5, 1929. [Note by Zheng Chaolin.]

Yin Kuan and Peng Shuzhi, Chen's interlocutors in those days, also failed ever to understand Trotsky's theory of permanent revolution.

Yin Kuan opposed our raising the question of the nature of Chinese society and its revolution in discussions with other comrades in the branch before we were expelled from it. In his view it was enough to discuss issues like whether the revolution was in ebb or in spate, who was to blame for its defeat, and the need under present circumstances to conduct the struggle by peaceful and legal means. He thought that it was scholastic and harmful to discuss the nature of society and of the revolution. Yin Kuan was a good writer, but I forget whether he wrote any articles on systematic theory. His position suggests to me that he did not properly grasp what Trotsky's theory of permanent revolution meant.

I had an argument with Peng Shuzhi at one of our branch meetings at which Chen and Peng were both present. This is what I said. The Chinese Revolution is in essence proletarian-socialist. From a theoretical point of view, the past defeats happened because the Chinese Revolution was viewed as bourgeois. Actually, my remark was a mere commonplace. In June 1922 in Paris I had already held this opinion when I and many other comrades launched the Communist Youth Party. In 1921, the programme adopted by the CCP at its First Congress also embodied this thesis. It said:

> Our Party programme is as follows. (1) To overthrow the bourgeoisie with a revolutionary army of the proletariat and to rebuild the state with the toiling classes, until all class distinctions are abolished. (2) To introduce a dictatorship of the proletariat in order to achieve the goal of class struggle – an end to classes. (3) To destroy the system of bourgeois private property and to expropriate machines, land, factories, and the means of production, including semi-finished products. (4) To ally with the Third International.

Peng Shuzhi probably didn't know about this programme (I myself saw it for the first time only recently). At the meeting he argued against me, saying that China's third revolution would be socialist but that its second had still been bourgeois-democratic. He argued that the consciousness of the masses can decide the nature of a revolution, and that during the second revolution the masses had still not gone through this experience, so they lacked that consciousness. After the discussion, Chen Duxiu spoke. He chose his words cautiously, but their drift tended in the direction of Peng's position. We never resumed this discussion in the Proletarian group. Later, on the Negotiating Committee, Wang Fanxi drafted a document in which he said that 'the coming [third] Chinese revolution will be socialist in character from the very outset'.[62] This caused a commotion. Liu Renjing was the first to criticise this formulation, and apparently the *Proletarian* also published criticisms of it. I'd forgotten about this. Actually, Wang was quoting directly from Trotsky. In his article 'Summary and Perspectives of the Chinese Revolution' Trotsky said: China's third revolution will be forced from the very start to shake both the feudal and the bourgeois systems of ownership.[63] In short, Wang and I (at the time we still didn't know each other) at least had differences of a formal nature. Wang was only talking about the third revolution, whereas in my view the second revolution, i.e., that of 1925 to 1927, also should have been proletarian-socialist.

In the internal controversies of the Chinese Trotskyist movement Liu Renjing certainly played an important role, but I could never make out exactly what he thought. He was renowned for his fickle opinions and for skipping from left to right and back again. I can't say whether he correctly understood Trotsky's theory of permanent revolution. The reason I haven't mentioned him in this context is not because he later degenerated into a counterrevolutionary, a turncoat, and an agent of Hu Zongnan and the CC Clique.[64]

Our 1942 split[65] was also about the question of the nature of the revolution (though other issues also entered into it). It turned out that Peng Shuzhi denied the socialist character not only of the second revolution but also of the first stage of the third revolution. In his opinion the first stage of the third revolution was still democratic. Only after it was over would the revolution 'permanently' develop along socialist lines. Fifty years later, I don't know whether today's Peng Shuzhi has acquired a sounder grasp of Trotsky's theory.

---

62   See Wang Fan-hsi 1991, p. 143.

63   Trotsky actually said: '... the third Chinese revolution, despite the great backwardness of China, or more correctly, because of this great backwardness as compared with Russia, will not have a 'democratic' period, not even such a six-month period as the October revolution had (November 1917 to July 1918); but it will be compelled from the very outset to effect the most decisive shake-up and abolition of bourgeois property in the city and village' (Evans and Block, eds, 1976, p. 305).

64   According to one version, the ultra-conservative CC clique got its name from the Chen brothers, Lifu and Guofu, who directed the investigation division and the organisation department of the Guomindang respectively; according to another, it stands for 'Central Club'.

65   In 1942, the Chinese Trotskyists split into two organisations, each with each own publication. The Peng Shuzhi group continued to bring out *Douzheng* ('Struggle'); the group around Zheng Chaolin and Wang Fanxi started bringing out *Guoji zhuyizhe* ('Internationalist').

Trotsky's Theory of Permanent Revolution

I don't have to hand a copy of *Permanent Revolution*, which Trotsky finally wrote in 1928, nor of his 1905 version of the same thesis. These things are not available in China.[66] But I do have a 1922 version of it, quoted by Stalin in one of his attacks on Trotsky reprinted in Stalin's *Problems of Leninism*. My wife Liu Jingzhen gave me this book while I was still in gaol in 1964. It didn't 'reform' my thought, but it delivered into my hands Trotsky's famous formula, so that whenever necessary in gaol I could measure my ideas against it.

Here is the passage Stalin quoted in his article 'The October Revolution and the Tactics of the Russian Communists':

> It was precisely during the interval between January 9 and the general strike of October 1905 that the views on the character of the revolutionary development of Russia which came to be known as the theory of 'permanent revolution' crystallised in the author's mind. This abstruse term represented the idea that the Russian Revolution, whose immediate objectives were bourgeois in nature, would not, however stop, when those objectives had been achieved. The revolution would not be able to solve its immediate bourgeois problems except by placing the proletariat in power. And the latter, upon assuming power, would not be able to confine itself to the bourgeois limits of the revolution. On the contrary, precisely in order to ensure its victory, the proletarian vanguard would be forced in the very early stages of its rule to make deep inroads not only into feudal property but into bourgeois property as well. In this it would come into *hostile collision* not only with all the bourgeois groupings which supported the proletariat during the first stages of its revolutionary struggle, *but also with the broad masses of the peasants* who had been instrumental in bringing it into power. The contradictions in the position of a workers' government in a backward country with an overwhelming majority of peasants can be solved *only* on an international scale, in the arena of the world proletarian revolution.[67]

Clearly the Russian Revolution of 1917 unfolded precisely in accordance with Trotsky's formula of permanent revolution.

---

66 I am wrong here. Trotsky's *Permanent Revolution* was published in China while the Gang of Four was still in power. The volume included both Trotsky's 1928 book and his 1906 essay. But it was translated into Chinese as 'negative teaching material' and its circulation was restricted to senior Party members. [Note added by Zheng Chaolin in 1986.]

67 Stalin 1940, p. 92. The italics in this passage are Stalin's.

Here I should add that the differences and disputes that arose between Lenin and Trotsky before the Revolution of 1917 evaporated after it, when the views of the two men tended to converge.

When Trotsky first advanced his theory of permanent revolution in 1905, he argued with Lenin on a whole series of questions. Trotsky thought that in a backward country like Russia the bourgeois-democratic revolution could only be completed if the proletariat controlled the state, but if the proletariat did control the state, then the bourgeois-democratic revolution in Russia would burst its historically prescribed bounds: proletarian state power would encroach deeply not only on the feudal but also on the bourgeois property system. Lenin, on the other hand, believed that Russia's bourgeois-democratic revolution could not exceed its historically prescribed bounds, and proletarian-socialist revolution could only begin after bourgeois-democratic revolution had been completed. These two revolutions could not become intertwined. So Lenin insisted on the slogan of workers and peasants' democratic dictatorship, and opposed the slogan of proletarian dictatorship. Lenin frequently wrote on this question. I shall quote just one or two instances.

In Chapter 10 of *Two Tactics* he said:

> Our slogan – a revolutionary democratic dictatorship of the proletariat and the peasantry – [recognises] the incontestably bourgeois nature of a revolution incapable of *directly* overstepping the bounds of a mere democratic revolution ...[68]

In the same chapter he stressed that these two revolutions should not become confused and intertwined:

> To confuse the petty bourgeoisie's struggle for a complete democratic revolution with the proletariat's struggle for a socialist revolution threatens the socialist with political bankruptcy. Marx's warning to this effect is quite justified. The reason:
>
> In actual historical circumstances, the elements of the past become interwoven with those of the future; the two paths cross. Wage-labour with its struggle against private property exists under the autocracy as well; it arises even under serfdom. But this does not in the least prevent us from logically and historically distinguishing between the major stages of development. We all contrapose bourgeois revolution and socialist

---

68   Lenin 1960–78 (1905), p. 87.

revolution; we all insist on the absolute necessity of strictly distinguishing between them; however, can it be denied that in the course of history individual, particular elements of the two revolutions become interwoven? Has the period of democratic revolutions in Europe not been familiar with a number of socialist movements and attempts to establish socialism? And will not the future socialist revolution in Europe still have to complete a great deal left undone in the field of democratism?[69]

Here Lenin admitted that the 'the elements of the past become interwoven with those of the future', that 'their paths cross', but only in order to emphasise that their main and essential components should not be allowed to do so.

Lenin stuck to this opinion right through until 1917, on the eve of his return to Russia. On March 20 of that year, i.e., after Russia's February Revolution had already broken out, while preparing to return to Russia Lenin wrote in 'Letters from Afar':

With these two allies, the proletariat, *utilising the peculiarities* of the present transition situation, can and will proceed, first, to the achievement of a democratic republic and complete victory of the peasantry over the landlords, instead of the Guchkov and Milyukov semi-monarchy, and then to *socialism*, which alone can give the war-weary people *peace*, *bread* and *freedom*.[70]

Right up to that point, Lenin had insisted that socialist revolution could only start when bourgeois revolution ended. The two revolutions must not be confused. Their main and essential components must not become intertwined.

But after his return to Petrograd on April 4, his views on the nature of the Russian Revolution changed. First, he abandoned the call for a 'democratic republic' and started calling for a 'commune state', meaning that power must be placed 'in the hands of the proletariat and the poorest sections of the peasants'. Next, he started calling for the 'confiscation of all landed estates' and for 'the immediate amalgamation of all banks in the country into a single national bank, and the institution of control over it by the Soviet of Workers' Deputies'.[71] This means that he wanted simultaneously to carry out bourgeois revolution and socialist revolution, simultaneously to encroach on the feudal and bourgeois property systems. 'The Threatening Catastrophe and How to Fight it',

---

69   Lenin 1960–78 (1905), pp. 85–87.
70   Lenin 1960–78 (1917), p. 308.
71   Lenin 1960–72 (1917d). p. 23.

which he wrote five months later, put this same position even more clearly: 'We are living in the twentieth century, and power over the land *without power over the banks* is not capable of regenerating, rejuvenating the life of the people'. Here, the intertwining of the two revolutions is by no means just that of 'elements', but concerns components as important and fundamental as the expropriation of the land and of the banks.

Finally, a few months after the October Revolution, Lenin once again wrote (in 'New Times and Old Mistakes in an Old Guise'):[72]

> Was the revolution a bourgeois revolution at that time? Of course it was, insofar as our function was to complete the bourgeois-democratic revolution, insofar as there was as yet no class struggle among the 'peasantry'. But, at the same time, we accomplished a great deal *over and above* the bourgeois revolution *for* the socialist, proletarian revolution.

The revolution did not just go beyond its limit. Four years after the October Revolution Lenin said: The tasks of Russia's bourgeois revolution can only be resolved by proletarian-socialist revolution, and what's more the former will be resolved as a by-product of the latter. In 'Fourth Anniversary of the October Revolution' he said: 'We solved the problems of the bourgeois-democratic revolution in passing, as a 'by-product' of our main and genuinely *proletarian-revolutionary*, socialist activities'.[73]

Trotsky had only said that at the same time as encroaching on the feudal property system the revolution will encroach on the bourgeois property system. Lenin went one step further. He said that encroaching on the bourgeois property system was the main revolution, and encroaching on the feudal property system was a 'by-product' of this main revolution, that it was achieved in passing.

In short, after Lenin's return to Russia in 1917, there were no longer any differences between him and Trotsky on how the Russian Revolution would develop.

After Lenin's death, Joffe (the same Joffe who signed the joint manifesto with Sun Yat-sen),[74] a leader of the Trotskyist Opposition, committed suicide in the course of an intense struggle within the Soviet Party. Before doing so he wrote Trotsky a letter in which he recalled a conversation he had once had with Lenin

---

72   Actually, this article was written in August 1921; see Lenin 1960–72 (1921a), p. 22.
73   Lenin 1960–78 (1921), p. 54.
74   On January 26, 1923, Sun Yat-sen and the Soviet diplomat Adolf Joffe issued a joint manifesto which said that the Soviet system was not suitable for China and that the Soviet Union would help the Guomindang unify China.

where they had discussed Lenin's pre-1917 dispute on how the Russian Revolution would develop. Lenin had admitted that in the dispute Trotsky had been right and he himself had been wrong.

In 1917, Lenin and Trotsky jointly led the Russian Revolution to victory on the basis of the theory of permanent revolution. Thirteen years later, in 1930, Trotsky reflected on that revolution and elucidated its inner nature with the help of this same theory in his *History of the Russian Revolution*, which graphically explains the revolution. The book's main thesis is that the core of the Russian Revolution of 1917 was socialist but that it was wrapped in numerous democratic layers that first had to be peeled away before its true nature was bared.

Trotsky's theory of permanent revolution is inseparable from his 'law of combined development'. Lenin discovered the 'law of uneven development' and used it to explain a great many things. Trotsky invented his 'law of combined development' on the foundations of Lenin's discovery, and used it to explain even more things. Trotsky's law showed that a large number of so-called 'transitional' periods in history are not simply 'transitional' but constitute social systems in their own right. Past and future forms of development 'combine' their special characteristics and so develop into a system. For example, the system of 'autocratism' in modern European history produced by the 'combination' of certain special features of capitalism with others of feudalism can endure for a comparatively long time and sustain its own special politics, culture, and thought. 'Tsarism', the system that ruled Russia in the late nineteenth and early twentieth centuries, was not only 'transitional' but formed a rather integrated system in its own right, its special characteristic being that capitalism controlled the state by making use of feudal exploitation and feudal methods of rule. It's precisely because capitalism and feudalism developed in combination that the Russian Revolution could not first topple and expropriate the feudal system of ownership but had simultaneously to topple and expropriate the capitalist system of ownership. Many historical and practical problems are easily solved using Trotsky's law of combined development.

Why did some Chinese Trotskyists, led by Peng Shuzhi, find it so hard to understand the theory of permanent revolution? Were they too stupid? Or were they just pretending that they did not understand it? Certainly they frequently paid lip-service to the theory, piously intoning that the revolution will develop 'permanently', that it must not stop after completing the bourgeois-democratic revolution, and that as long as the bourgeois-democratic revolution has not been completed all efforts must be bent toward completing it, so that the revolution that happens afterwards will have an initial bourgeois-democratic stage; and so on. In *Hongqi* ('Red Flag') No. 16 (1980) there is an article criticising Kang Sheng that quotes Kang's interpretation of the Marxist-Leninist theory of 'uninterrupted' revolution. Kang Sheng says that Marx' and Lenin's theory of uninterrupted revolution 'is mainly about the stage where democratic revolution turns into socialist revolution, and how it must not stop'. Peng Shuzhi's interpretation of Trotsky's theory of permanent revolution is the same.

There's an old saying that 'when a scholar returns after being away for three days, you will see a difference in him'. I've not seen Peng for more than thirty years: maybe he's changed his ideas in the meantime.

The 'National Assembly' Slogan

Another important dispute in the Chinese Trotskyist movement concerned the call for a National Assembly.

In 'The Chinese Question after the Sixth Congress' Trotsky said that a democratic movement should be carried out in China, around the call for a National Assembly; slogans calling for socialism, proletarian dictatorship, and Soviets should be relegated to general propaganda. This proposal of Trotsky's is inseparable from his appraisal of the Chinese situation at the time. As a realist, he considered that the Chinese Revolution had already been defeated, that the revolution was at a low ebb, and that the tactics adopted by revolutionaries in such circumstances must differ from those used while the revolution is in flood.

In his reply to the Comintern dated February 17, 1930, Chen Duxiu quoted Lenin to the effect that in a period of reaction

> the revolutionary parties had to complete their education. They were learning how to attack. Now they had to realise that such knowledge must be supplemented with the knowledge of how to retreat in good order.[75]

It is sheer common sense that in a period of reaction, when the revolution is at a low ebb, revolutionaries should change their tactics. The tactics adopted by the Bolsheviks in the years between the defeat of the Revolution of 1905 and the relaunching of the revolution in 1917 are a case in point. But Trotsky's suggestion that Chinese revolutionaries should call for a National Assembly and employ the tactic of a democratic movement provoked a violent dispute among Chinese Trotskyists. The dispute, at first internal, gradually became public. Deng Yanda, who was just setting up his Third Party at that time, sent a car to fetch Gao Yuhan for talks, after which Gao reported back to Chen Duxiu. I, too, knew about it at the time, and though I've forgotten most of it, one things sticks in my mind. Deng asked Gao why the Trotskyists called for a National Assembly

---

75   Lenin 1960–78 (1920), p. 28.

when they thought that the Chinese Revolution was proletarian-socialist. He didn't understand, just as he didn't understand why the CCP adopted the tactic of Soviets and armed struggle when according to them the Chinese Revolution was bourgeois-democratic. Actually, if Deng was clever enough to pose the question in this way, a moment's reflection should have told him the answer to it.

At their Sixth Congress the Chinese Communists reluctantly admitted that the revolution had been defeated and that it was at a low ebb, but in their heart of hearts they still believed that it was in flood or at the very least soon would be. Various measures that the Party took were premised in this belief. Otherwise how can we explain the so-called 'Li Lisan line' of late 1930 or the 'third left line' that ruled the CCP for four long years?[76] The tactics that the CCP followed in those years were tactics appropriate to a period of revolutionary high tide.

Even some Chinese Trotskyists believed that the revolution was still in flood. They were convinced by Trotsky's ideas on basic issues in the Chinese Revolution, but they did not accept his estimate of the situation in China. Before the unification talks started, I came across a mimeographed copy of *Our Word* on a bookstall at the intersection of North Sichuan Road and Range Road. Flicking through it, I noticed that the lead article stressed that the revolution was at high tide. Needless to say, people who believed that could hardly accept Trotsky's proposal for a National Assembly, and even if they did, it would be contrary to their convictions. They would attach all sorts of bizarre interpretations to the slogan. As far as I know, this view was not represented in the Proletarian group.

Some other Chinese Trotskyists believed that the next revolutionary high tide was distant and uncertain, that China's bourgeois state would probably enjoy a long period of stability, and that the present system of military dictatorship would gradually give way to parliamentary democracy, which in their view would be long-lasting. Naturally, these people, whose main representative was said to be Liu Renjing, welcomed the call for a National Assembly.

Between these two extremes came a variety of nuances. In short, most people did not grasp the need to distinguish between strategy and tactics, between propaganda and agitation, between the revolution in flood and at ebb. They thought that the call for a National Assembly was incompatible with the socialist character of the Chinese Revolution, and that this slogan and the slogan calling for Soviet state power were mutually exclusive.

---

76   The 'third left line' refers to the period from 1931 to 1934, when the leadership of the Party was in the hands of Wang Ming and Bo Gu; the Party's Maoist leaders consider this line to have been 'even more sectarian' than that of Li Lisan.

A large number of people wrote to Trotsky reporting on this controversy. I still remember one passage in Trotsky's reply where he warned against absolutely counterposing the two slogans. He said that generally speaking in a period of reflux we should use the National Assembly slogan to mobilise the masses and to bring on the high tide. But we can't rule out that with the masses on the rise and a National Assembly elected and leading the revolution, it might be possible in the name of the National Assembly to proclaim China a Soviet Republic!

Even today people still ask why Trotsky proposed calling for a National Assembly, and what role this slogan played in the history of the Chinese Revolution. I have already explained its active meaning; as for the actual role this slogan played in China's recent history, all I can say is that the Chinese Trotskyists, whose job it was to give full scope to the slogan in its positive sense, were in no position to do so, battered as they were from two directions at the same time: by the Guomindang, which was out to destroy their bodies, and by the CCP, which was out to destroy their souls. So the slogan was monopolised by the Guomindang, which employed it in its passive and counterrevolutionary sense.

(5)   *Chen Duxiu and the Trotskyists*
Was or was not Chen Duxiu a Trotskyist?

This is one of the hardest questions currently facing students of contemporary Chinese history and people who wish to study and grasp the present political situation in China. Chen's role in Chinese and world history can never be rubbed out. The old slanders against him cannot be upheld.

Just think of the picture of Chen Duxiu painted by several generations of political commentators! An opportunist who buried the Great Revolution, a renegade, a national traitor, a paid agent of the Guomindang, a counterrevolutionary, and so on. The founder of the CCP, elected its top leader at five successive congresses, was that sort of man? Some people even go so far as to claim that the leader of the May Fourth Movement of 1919 was not Chen Duxiu but someone else.[77]

Things only began to change in 1979, which was Chen's hundredth birthday and the sixtieth anniversary of May Fourth, after which the press began to recognise Chen's role in leading it. Around July 1 and October 1[78] of that year the press also started to recognise Chen's role in founding the CCP. The Museum of

---

77   For many years, the pretence was maintained in China that the May Fourth Movement was led by Li Dazhao and Lu Xun.

78   The anniversaries of the founding of the Party (in 1921) and the People's Republic (in 1949).

the Revolution in Beijing displayed his picture and the taboo on discussing the relationship between the Comintern and the CCP was broken. Historians began to reach new conclusions that were more in accordance with the facts. Articles began to appear in the open and the internal press[79] showing that when Chen Duxiu said in 1923 that China's bourgeois revolution would be led by the bourgeoisie, he was simply representing the Comintern's point of view; and that when in 1926 and 1927 the CCP was pursuing an opportunist line, it was also following Comintern directives. Later, during the War of Resistance to Japan, an article appeared in *Xinhua Ribao* ('New China Daily') accusing Chen Duxiu and Luo Han of coming to an agreement through Tang Youren with Japanese intelligence by which they would be paid $300 a month: but now evidence has been produced to reveal this as political calumny. In the past, people used to say that Chen's three letters to the Central Committee of the CCP about the Chinese Eastern Railway Incident proved that he had gone over to the counterrevolution, but now others are saying that in this controversy the Central Committee was wrong and Chen was right. As for the charge that he capitulated to the Guomindang, became an agent, and took money from Chiang Kai-shek, many, many people have now produced evidence to rebut it.

Finally, there is the question of the Trotskyists. The Comintern taboo has already been broken; but the taboo on Trotskyism remains, and people carry on repeating – as they have been doing for decades now – that the international Trotskyists and the Chinese Trotskyists are counterrevolutionaries. So how come Chen Duxiu, leader of May Fourth and founder of the CCP, got mixed up with this counterrevolutionary political organisation?

Some people say that he was only influenced intellectually by Trotsky, and that he didn't join the Trotskyist organisation.

Some people say that he joined the Trotskyist organisation but broke with it after the Guomindang arrested him.

Some people say that after his release from the Guomindang gaol he declared that he was not a Trotskyist, i.e., that he broke with the Trotskyist organisation, and that after that there is no evidence that he had anything more to do with the Trotskyists.

Some people say that when he joined the Trotskyist organisation the Trotskyist question was still a contradiction among the people,[80] and that by the time the Trotskyists had become a bunch of murderers and foreign spies he had already broken with them.

---

79   The internal or *neibu* press is accessible only to privileged categories of people.
80   A Maoist expression, used in opposition to a 'contradiction between the enemy and us [i.e., the revolutionary people]'.

Some people say that he gave up his Trotskyist ideas a few years before he died.

And so on.

Naturally, there are also people who know full well that the Trotskyists are anything but counterrevolutionary and that Chen Duxiu's conversion to Trotskyism and his membership of the Trotskyist organisation were an organic outcome of his entire intellectual development. But they still don't dare say so in public.

In my view, there is no longer any need for me today to defend Chen Duxiu against the charge that he was an 'opportunist', that he was to blame for the defeat of the revolution, or that he was a 'counterrevolutionary', a 'renegade', an 'agent', a 'running dog of the Guomindang', and a 'national traitor'. I simply wish to explain the facts and meaning of his relationship to the Trotskyists, and to say that any attempt to research his life and thought that tries to bypass this relationship is as self-deceiving as the stupid thief who in trying to steal a bell plugs his own ears in the hope that no one will hear it ringing.

There is no way that Chen's membership and leadership of the Chinese Trotskyist organisation can be denied, or of denying that while in gaol he continued through secret channels to control that organisation. There are documents and articles to show that this is true. His declaration after leaving gaol that he no longer had dealings with the Trotskyist organisation was mere diplomatic verbiage. At that time he wanted to unite in the war against Japan democratic personages beyond the influence of the Guomindang and the CCP, so he wanted to avoid getting entangled at the outset in the Trotskyist question; in any case, by then the leadership of the Trotskyist organisation had been taken over by Peng Shuzhi, so Chen was not inclined to submit his statements and actions to its disciplinary constraints. But it is clear from contemporary sources that he had by no means left the Chinese Trotskyist organisation. His 1938 letter to Chen Qichang et al., which still exists, is enough to show that he still considered the Trotskyist organisation his own, that he looked upon Luo Shifan, Chen Qichang, Zhao Ji, and Han Jun as his own cadres, and that he only criticised them because he cared for them and for the Trotskyist organisation, even though he was not then working to revive Trotskyist organisation. In early 1939 or late 1938 the Trotskyist organisation sent Chen Qichang by devious routes from Shanghai to Jiangjin to meet Chen Duxiu, and to pass on Trotsky's advice to him to leave the country. Chen wrote a personal letter to Trotsky the tone of which showed quite clearly that he considered the Trotskyist organisation his own: the sharp criticisms he raised in it only showed that he still loved and cherished this body. Let's quote some passages from his letter.

The membership of the CCP is far in excess of ours, but they're just armed forces with intellectuals but without any working-class base at all. We have fewer than fifty people in Shanghai and Hong Kong, plus probably more than one hundred stragglers in other parts of the country.

Needless to say, we do not fool ourselves that we will grow quickly in this war, but if we had pursued more or less right tactics, we would not be in our present feeble state. From the very start our group tended toward ultra-left positions ... A small closed-door ultra-left organisation of this sort obviously stands no chance of winning members; and even if it did, it would be an obstacle to the further development of the Chinese Revolution ...

We should beware of perpetuating the illusion that we can only restart our activities after the recovery of territories now occupied by the Japanese. Even today, while Japan continues to occupy parts of our country, we should prepare forthwith to start work afresh, within the narrow space that remains open to us ...

If ultra-leftists who stay aloof from the masses and the real struggle ... continue to brag and pretend to be big leaders, to organise leadership bodies that lack all substance, and to found petty kingdoms for themselves behind closed doors and relying on the name of the Fourth International, they will achieve nothing beyond the tarnishing of the Fourth International's prestige in China.

Ask yourself, are those the words of someone who has placed himself outside the Chinese Trotskyist organisation?

At the time of the Hitler-Stalin Pact, Chen Duxiu became so angry that he said things in letters to his friends that went beyond the limit of what is permissible, but it would be wrong to take that as proof that he had broken with Trotskyism.

I have in my possession an article he wrote on May 13, 1942, a fortnight or so before his death. The article, called 'The Future of Oppressed Peoples', shows that he remained a Trotskyist to his dying day. Here are some excerpts from it.

So in my opinion, in a capitalist-imperialist world, no small or weak people can hope for a future so long as it tries only behind closed doors, relying only on its own small forces, to remove the reality of imperialist aggression. Its only hope lies with oppressed toilers the world over. The national question will automatically be resolved if the oppressed, backward peoples unite, overthrow imperialism everywhere, and replace the old world of international capitalism based on commodity deals with a new world of international socialism based on mutual help and a division of labour.

This passage shows that right up to his death Chen Duxiu continued to stand on the side of Trotsky's world revolution and rejected Stalin's idea of socialism in one country.

The article also says:

> Some people vilify the Soviet Union of the early period, whereas we support it; others flatter the Soviet Union of the later period, whereas we detest it. There's a very big difference between these two periods. In the former period the Soviet Union stood for world revolution; in the latter, for Russian national self-interest. Ever since the Soviet leaders first betrayed their own cause after the setback to the revolution in Western Europe and abandoned the policy of putting world revolution to the fore, replacing it instead with Russian national self-interest, clear-thinking people in all countries have gradually progressed from scepticism to disappointment; and though some still think that the hope for mankind lies with the Soviet Union, in reality they can only view it as one among a number of world powers. People who stubbornly insist on calling it socialist only besmirch the name of socialism.

This passage, too, supports Trotsky and opposes Stalin. The difference is that Trotsky still considered the 'Soviet Union of the later period' to be a 'degenerated workers' state', whereas Chen Duxiu denounced it point-blank as a one of the 'world powers'. It's a fact that the 'Soviet Union of the later period' had already degenerated into 'social-imperialism'; it had started to degenerate from the time of Stalin onwards.

So Chen Duxiu remained a Trotskyist till his dying day, from both an organisational and a theoretical point of view.

Looking back, the main 'injustices, frame-ups, and mistakes'[81] were the show-trials of the 1930s, which practically wiped out a generation of revolutionaries. Even today the victims of these trials are treated with contempt. First they must be rehabilitated.

---

81   A phrase often used in China in the wake of the Cultural Revolution to describe the 'fascist lawlessness' of the 'Gang of Four'.

Needless to say, I am not speaking from a juridical point of view. Only a Soviet court, under the control of the Communist Party, can judicially rehabilitate these victims – the so-called 'Trotskyites', 'Zinovievites', and 'Bukharinites'. I am speaking only from the point of view of historical fact. From the point of view of history, i.e., from the point of view of the overwhelming majority of know-ledgeable people in the world, these victims have long since been rehabilitated. Just a short time ago the new Pope John Paul II rehabilitated Galileo, but for the past several hundred years there can hardly have been anyone still convinced by the charges against Galileo. Today probably only a handful of people in the world still believe the Moscow verdicts against the 'Trotskyites'.

A footnote in Mao Zedong's *Selected Works* quotes Stalin as follows:

In the past, seven or eight years ago, Trotskyism was one of such polit-ical trends in the working class, an anti-Leninist trend, it is true, and there-fore profoundly mistaken, but nevertheless a political trend ... Present-day Trotskyism is not a political trend in the working class, but a gang without principle and without ideas, of wreckers and diversionists, intel-ligence service agents, spies, murderers, a gang of sworn enemies of the working class, working in the pay of the intelligence services of foreign states.[82]

Stalin said this in 1937, in the period of the Moscow show-trials. But on what grounds did Stalin claim that the Trotskyists were 'agents, spies, murderers'? True, Vyshinsky, who was in charge of investigations, came up with all sorts of 'criminal evidence', but this 'evidence' has already been systematically rebutted by the Dewey Committee. This Committee published two volumes of findings to show that the charges were groundless, and it declared Trotsky innocent. Dewey apart, other evidence has accumulated over the past forty or more years that I would like to mention.

According to Stalin, Trotsky's two biggest crimes were to assassinate Kirov and to spy for the Gestapo in order to help plot Germany's invasion of the Soviet Union.

First the assassination of Kirov. Even at the time Trotsky came up with evid-ence to show that Stalin himself killed Kirov to frame the then Opposition, but this evidence did not have much impact. More than twenty years later, Stalin's successor Khrushchev, at the Twenty Second Congress of the Commun-

---

82   Quoted in Mao Tse-tung 1967 (1935), p. 177, fn. 31. (This note has been removed from the current edition of Mao's *Selected Works*.)

ist Party of the Soviet Union, proved that Kirov had indeed been killed by Stalin. Recently twenty letters by Stalin's daughter Svetlana were published in China. In one of them Svetlana denies Khrushchev's allegation and says that Kirov was killed not by Stalin but by Beria. Whatever the case, in today's world, including in the Soviet Union, no one – or at least hardly anyone – any longer believes that Kirov was killed by Zinoviev and Trotsky.

Stalin also killed Tukhachevsky, Blücher, and two other Red Army generals on trumped-up charges of having secret dealings with the Nazis and plotting to betray the Soviet Union. But at the Twenty Second Congress Khrushchev declared these allegations, too, to be Stalin's fabrications. Stalin had first forged them and then surreptitiously leaked them to President Benes of Czechoslovakia. Benes, believing them to be true, secretly informed Stalin, who imposed death sentences on the basis of them.

This is just one piece of 'evidence' among many. After the Second World War, when the Allies tried the Nazis for war crimes at Nuremberg, some well-known people led by H.G. Wells wrote to the Tribunal asking it to produce from among its vast files evidence of Trotskyist collaboration with the Nazis. It couldn't.

For the time being I'll restrict myself to just these three points. There is a mountain of evidence to show that the charges levelled against the Trotskyists at the Moscow show trials were groundless, and another mountain of evidence produced by the Dewey Committee. Today researchers can investigate whether or not this evidence substantiates Stalin's charges against the Trotskyists.

As for the Trotskyist organisation in China, there is ample evidence to clear its name. It has already been shown that Chen Duxiu and Luo Han did not act via Tang Youren as paid agents for Japanese intelligence, but the strange thing is that people still believe that the Chinese Trotskyists did. It has been proved that Chen Duxiu was not a Guomindang agent or a running dog of Chiang Kai-shek, but people still think that the Chinese Trotskyists were. The charges against Chen Duxiu were unable to stand up under scrutiny. But what is the evidence against the organisation of the Chinese Trotskyists? Can it stand up under scrutiny?

We commemorate Chen Duxiu, this outstanding figure of modern Chinese and world politics. In commemorating him, we Trotskyists are stirred deeper than other people. We recall that for a while he was General Secretary of our organisation. We consider this an honour.[83]

---

83   This extra section was written thirty five years after the memoir proper. The two parts of
      this book frequently overlap and repeat one another; not surprisingly there are discrepan-
      cies between them, for an interval of so many years places an inevitable strain on human
      memory. I'll let them stand as they are. [Note added by Zheng Chaolin after reading the
      proofs of the Chinese edition of his memoirs, to which this study is a supplement.]

Appendix: Chen Duxiu Had No Wish to Rejoin the CCP on Leaving Gaol

Translator's note

This article was completed on August 10, 1981, two years after Zheng Chaolin himself had emerged from twenty-seven years in prison under the Chinese Communists and while he was under Party supervision and denied access to the archives. On the basis of the scant documentation available to him he builds a strong case for 'historical truth' and against received opinion regarding Chen Duxiu's view of the Communist Party in 1937. I translated the article from its unpublished manuscript version, titled 'Chen Duxiu chuyu hou jue wu fuhui Zhonggong de yuanwang' ('Chen Duxiu definitely did not wish to rejoin the CCP after leaving prison'); at some point, it was published under the same title in Zhongbao yuekan (Hong Kong).

Just as many people claim that Chen Duxiu was dismissed as General Secretary [of the Communist Party] by the August 7 Conference [of 1927], so for several decades now people have been saying with one voice that after his release from a Guomindang gaol in 1937, Chen expressed a wish to return to the Communist Party; but Mao Zedong raised three conditions and wanted Chen publicly to repent his errors, which Chen did not do, so Chen did not rejoin. Not only Communist Party members say this; so do some democrats, and they have even been joined by the ex-Trotskyist Pu Qingquan.[84] In his article 'Chen Duxiu as I knew him',[85] Pu ascribed the following words, told in reported speech, to Chen: 'I definitely want to return to Party work'. In this way, Pu 'proves' the groundless rumours of that period. But when he was a Trotskyist, Pu gave no credence to these rumours. I shall clarify this question by discussing a few facts.

I myself have never believed these rumours, and I always considered that they were not worth discussing. In recent years, however, more and more people have started doing research on Chen Duxiu, and nearly all of them believe the rumours to be true. The time has therefore come to clarify the matter and save from further error those who now and in the future engage in research on Chen and on this period in Chinese history.

---

84   I.e. Pu Dezhi.

85   Pu Qingquan 1980. Pu's article was reprinted in four instalments in *Zhongbao yuekan* (Hong Kong), also in 1980.

No, between leaving gaol and dying, Chen never entertained the idea of rejoining the Communist Party. The idea never once occurred to him after he had embraced Trotsky's proposals and worked in the Trotskyist organisation.

Personally, I have not the slightest doubt of this. I do not need to consult a single document or fact; I base my conclusion solely on his usual conversations with us [before we went to prison]. On September 29, 1937, the day I was released from prison, I went to stay at his residence and had a talk with him. Our talk proved to me that he had not changed; as a result, I am even more firmly convinced of my opinion on this matter.

But I cannot expect to convince others to share my firm belief simply by referring to conversations that Chen had with several of us before going to gaol and to a talk he had with me on the first night after my release. Elsewhere, I have already explained on the basis of our conversation that evening that after leaving prison in 1937 he had not the slightest intention of rejoining the Communist Party. Here, today, I do not intend to base my argument on that talk, because it can convince only me. Instead I shall provide more objective evidence.

The best proof that Chen Duxiu expressed no wish to rejoin the Communist Party after leaving gaol in 1937 can be found in Chen's own words. In Hankou in [March] 1938 he wrote an open letter to *Xinhua ribao* in which he said: 'According to Luo Han, they still hope I will rejoin the Party'.[86] In other words, he himself did not hope to 'rejoin the Party', but the Communist Party hoped that he would, and moreover had dropped Luo Han a hint along these lines.

Let us see what light Luo Han's famous 'open letter'[87] throws on this question. In August [1937], after the start of the battle for Shanghai, Luo Han came to Nanjing. Chen Duxiu was still in gaol at the time, and Luo did not visit him. He went directly to the Eighth Route Army office at Fuhougang in search of Ye Jianying.[88] At the time of the Northern Expedition, Luo had been 'Party representative' (or 'director of the political department') of the Fourth Army of the [Guomindang's] National Revolutionary Armed Forces, at the same time that Ye Jianying (if my memory serves me rightly) was its chief of staff. The two men were naturally close to one another. Luo Han had two aims in going to the Eighth Route Army office: first, to ask the Communist Party to do what it could to get the Guomindang to release political prisoners, including Chen Duxiu and the other Trotskyists still in gaol; and, second, to repeat the old pro-

86   Chen Duxiu 1980 (1938).

87   On April 24–5, 1938, Luo Han published an open letter to Zhou Enlai and others in *Zhengbao* ('Upright Daily'). See Feigon 1983, p. 223, fn. 73.

88   The Eighth Route Army was formed in 1937 on the basis of the old Red Army; Ye Jianying was the Communist Party's representative in Nanjing.

posal of 1932, when the Trotskyist organisation had formally suggested bilateral cooperation with the Communist Party against Japan. In 1932, the Communist Party had ignored the proposal, but now that it was working together with the Guomindang against Japan, Luo Han, acting in his personal capacity, revived the proposal. This shows that Luo Han's proposal referred to the question of the Trotskyists and the Communist Party working together against Japan, and not to the question of Chen Duxiu or other Trotskyists 'rejoining the Party'. Luo Han spoke very clearly about this to Ye Jianying in Nanjing and to Lin Boqu[89] in Xi'an, and Ye and Lin heard very clearly what he had to say. Luo Han declared several times that he represented only himself and not the Trotskyist organisation or Chen Duxiu. Lin Boqu said: 'Since you are only setting out your own views, in a personal capacity, and do not enter into discussions in a representative capacity, things could as well be settled by radio communication'.

Even so, [the Communist leaders in] Yan'an did not completely believe what Luo Han said, and still thought that he was representing Chen Duxiu. They therefore set three conditions for Chen's 'capitulation'. That is to say, even though the two sides would be merely cooperating, Chen would still have to repent his errors and oppose Trotskyism. It is also possible that Yan'an actually thought that Chen Duxiu had sent Luo Han, to discuss not just cooperation but 'rejoining the Party'. All these things passed through a series of lips and finally reached the conclusion that Chen Duxiu would repent his past errors and return to the Party ranks. (During a talk between Wang Ruofei and Luo Han, Wang said something about sections of the Third International not admitting members of the Fourth International; this remark was precisely a reference to this question of 'rejoining the Party'.) Chen Duxiu did not repent, whereupon the rumour-mill again began to grind: Chen Duxiu had been unable to accept the three conditions, so he had not been allowed to rejoin the Party.

From what I have said above, we can see that all this talk about Chen Duxiu wanting to rejoin the Party or go to Yan'an is Communist Party propaganda without any basis in fact.

Some people might, of course, object that I base my argument solely on letters of Chen Duxiu and Luo Han, that I have absolute faith in their veracity, and that I completely ignore Communist Party documents that provide evidence to the contrary.

Regarding such documents, I have access only to Ye Jianying, Bo Gu, and Dong Biwu's letter to *Xinhua ribao*.[90] I don't even have the other articles pub-

---

89   Lin Boqu (1896–1960) was a veteran Party leader.
90   Bo Gu (1907–46), the alias of Qin Bangxian, had been acting General Secretary of the

lished in *Xinhua ribao* on this question. So I can quote only from Ye, Bo, and Dong's letter.

This letter was written in reply to Chen Duxiu's open letter to *Xinhua ribao*. It says: 'At the beginning of September, after his release from gaol, Chen entrusted Luo Han to talk with us, and told us that he wanted to return to work under Party leadership'. This statement can, of course, be interpreted as meaning that 'Chen wished to rejoin the Party'. There is a difference between this statement and what Luo Han said in his 'open letter'. Luo Han declared that he was acting on his own account, whereas this letter says that he was representing Chen Duxiu; Luo Han said that he had gone to negotiate cooperation, this letter says that he transmitted Chen Duxiu's wish to return to work under Party leadership. So who is right and who is wrong? I believe Luo Han to be right, since he gives dates. He went to Nanjing to talk to Ye Jianying in August [1937], before Chen Duxiu had left prison; he left Nanjing for Xi'an on August 30, arrived in Xi'an on September 2, met Lin Boqu on September 3, received Yan'an's three conditions on September 10, and returned to Nanjing on September 15, by which time Chen had already left for Wuhan. In the week from August 23, when Chen left gaol, and August 30, Luo Han did not meet Chen Duxiu. This is understandable, since he did not know where Chen lived. I was at Chen's house the whole of August 29, day and night; I did not meet Luo Han, nor did anyone else mention him.

Ye, Bo, and Dong's letter goes on to say:

> After Luo had left Nanjing, Chen also sent Mr Li xx [i.e. Li Huaying[91]] to hold talks: Mr Chen had already broken decisively with the Trotskyists, and urgently wanted to meet us. We took the view that this would be difficult, since Chen had not publicly set out his political position. Mr Li xx said: what Mr Chen wants is precisely to explain his political position to us, so Bo Gu and Ye Jianying met Mr Chen. We requested him to explain his attitude to the anti-Japanese national united front and to leave the Trotskyists ... Afterwards, Chen again sent someone to say that because Li xx had been at the meeting, Chen had found it difficult to speak freely,

---

Chinese Communist Party from 1932 to 1935. Dong Biwu (1886–1975) was a veteran Communist, and became a Central Committee member after 1945. The two men were members at the start of the war of the Party's Changjiang Bureau, set up to represent the Party and lead its work in central and southern China. The letter by Ye, Bo, and Dong referred to here is reprinted in Zhang Yongtong and Liu Chuanxue, eds, 1980, pp. 235–6. See Feigon 1983, p. 223, fn. 73.

91   The given name was added by Zheng Chaolin; it is not clear who Li Huaying was.

> so he asked to see [Ye] Jianying a second time. At the meeting, Jianying asked Mr Chen publicly to express to the entire nation his opinion on three points ... [Dong] Biwu too met Chen in Hankou to urge Mr Chen to fulfil these three conditions.

These three meetings all ended inconclusively. Even more noteworthy, in the course of them Chen Duxiu expressed no wish to 'rejoin the Party'. So apart from the opening sentence about Chen wanting to 'return to work under Party leadership', what other support does this letter provide for the claim that Chen wanted to 'rejoin the Party'? (As I have already explained, even this sentence is unreliable: Luo Han had not met Chen in Nanjing, so there was no way that he could have received a commission from him.)

What is more, the claim that Chen wanted to 'return to work under Party leadership' is open to another explanation: the 'united front' entailed various groups and parties working together with the Communist Party yet outside the Party, but it also entailed these groups and parties 'working under the leadership of the Party'. Ye, Bo, and Dong deliberately used this ambiguous formulation in their letter, and for the following reason: neither Chen Duxiu nor Luo Han had spoken of 'rejoining the Party', so if Ye, Bo, and Dong had said 'Chen wants to come back into the Party and work under the leadership of the Central Committee', their statement would have had no basis in fact.

If Zhang Guotao's memoirs are to be believed, Yan'an discussed Chen Duxiu's case in terms of 'cooperation' and not of 'rejoining the Party'.

Recalling the Politburo Conference of December 1937 in Yan'an, Zhang notes a speech by Wang Ming:

> We can cooperate against Japan with anyone except the Trotskyists. Internationally, we can cooperate with bourgeois politicians, warlords, and even anti-Communist executioners, but we cannot cooperate with the followers of Trotsky. In China, we can cooperate with Chiang Kai-shek and his anti-Communist special agents, but we cannot cooperate with Chen Duxiu.

Finally, I would like to mention the attitude of the Trotskyist cadres, who were concentrated in Shanghai. At that time, Peng Shuzhi's supporters and his opponents were equally dissatisfied with Chen Duxiu's activities in Wuhan.

But they only opposed Chen's wish to cooperate with the CCP and not his alleged wish to 'rejoin the Party'. They found it completely inconceivable that Chen would wish to 'rejoin the Party'. On November 21, 1937, Chen wrote to Luo Shifan, Chen Qichang, and Zhao Ji:

> About cooperating with the Stalinists, my view is that there's nothing wrong with it in principle, but at present its out of the question. To cooperate, both sides must have something to give; in addition, there must be some common activity that necessitates both sides getting in touch – yet at present such conditions do not obtain. Naturally it's crazy to talk of 'cooperation'; Luo [Han] didn't mention this matter to me, you have no cause to get oversensitive about it.

In other words, Chen Duxiu was not opposed in principle to cooperating with the Communist Party against Japan, but saw such cooperation as conditional on our having a certain strength, and on the necessity of constant contacts with the Communist Party arising from the anti-Japanese activities. At the time, that condition was absent, so Chen opposed cooperating with the Communist Party. So he would have been even less likely to want to 'rejoin the Party'. If those 'oversensitive' individuals had suspected that Chen was inclined to 'rejoin the Party', rest assured that they would have raised a great hue and cry.

Chen Duxiu's letter proves even more conclusively that Luo Han's actions in Nanjing and Xi'an were his own personal initiative. After he had met with a rebuff and gone to see Chen, he 'never talked about' the cooperation.

Whether we are dealing with big matters or small, we should always stick to the historical truth. Anything that does not accord with historical truth should be pushed aside, even though people repeat it as if with one voice. Some may consider that it is a minor question, not worthy of detailed study, whether or not Chen Duxiu expressed a wish to 'return to Party work' after his release from gaol. But in my opinion, from the point of view of the struggle of the Chinese Trotskyists, of Chen Duxiu's character, and of Chen's relationship with the Chinese Trotskyists, it is no minor matter, but one that requires thorough clarification on the basis of historical evidence.

CHAPTER 8

On Chinese Cadreism (1985)

Translated by Kevin Lin

Translator's Introduction

Zheng Chaolin and the Critique of Cadreism

In his unpublished manuscript 'Waiting for a Return to *Huilongwu*' (*Huilongwu* is the name of the 'ancestral mountain' of his family), completed at the age of eighty-four, Zheng Chaolin developed a systematic critique of 'cadreism' in order to understand the failures of the Soviet Union and Maoist China, as well as the direction of China's post-Mao capitalist development. While Zheng dated the completion of the manuscript to the end of 1985, the ideas informing his critique of cadreism have origins going back to his writings in the 1960s when Zheng and other Trotskyists were imprisoned in a Chinese jail.

In a personal essay written at the age of ninety, Zheng recalled the circumstances in which he undertook his analysis of cadreism:

> Starting in 1964, I was allowed openly to express opinions in jail, to write books, and to criticise current policies and theories. For from then on, I was allowed to form a study group with other prisoners arrested in connection with the same case, Trotskyists who, like me, had not yet been sentenced ... We studied so-called 'anti-revisionist documents', that is, the theoretical dispute between the Chinese and Soviet Communists. Afterwards, we each had to write a 'summary'. Although no one told us 'you may write whatever you like', I used the occasion to develop a comprehensive critique of the Stalinist system on the basis of the ideas that I had formed in the course of my isolated prison reflections. I decided to disregard any possible consequences. Finally, I wrote up my 'study summaries' into a book of eighty five thousand characters, which I called *Ganbu zhuyi lun* ('On Cadreism').[1]

This background is relevant because these ideas were first conceived in the intellectual and political context of disputes between the Stalinist Soviet Union

---

1 Zheng 2015, p. 1112.

and Maoist China in the 1950s and 1960s. They provided the foundation for Zheng's own independent historical comparison of the Russian and Chinese revolutions, and were intellectually and politically courageous.

In the present translated chapter of his manuscript, written twenty years later, Zheng's goal is not only to develop a critique of Stalinism and Maoism but to extend the theoretical framework to encompass China's market reforms, which had just begun at the time of his writing in the early 1980s. In his analysis, Zheng makes an important theoretical contribution, both dispelling any illusion about the nature of Stalinist and Maoist regimes that proclaimed themselves socialist and offering an incisive analysis of the nature of China's post-Mao transition.

So what is cadreism, and how does Zheng use this concept to criticise Maoism? Cadreism, an original concept at the heart of Zheng's radical critique, refers to a social formation in which cadres form a distinct social class with its own class interests separate from those of ordinary Chinese. In tracing the genealogy of this concept, Zheng notes that 'cadre' does not appear in any of the writings of classical Marxists. In his writings criticising the Stalinist Soviet Union, for example, Trotsky referred to 'bureaucrats'. It was, ironically, in Stalin's writings that the term 'cadre' first appeared. It was later adopted by Mao Zedong and the Chinese Communist Party, in a positive evaluation of the role of cadres. In fact, 'cadre' was derived from military terminology, meaning commanders, as opposed to ordinary soldiers. This was no accident. Zheng argues that in borrowing this military term, Stalin and Mao were not only making a distinction between cadres and ordinary soldiers but also laying bare their strategic reliance on military power and armed struggle rather than mass movements in advancing revolutions. Zheng believes that in the absence of a mass movement, an armed struggle could only create an undemocratic cadre class standing above the masses. In other words, cadreism means that cadres replace the masses as agents of revolutions.

Zheng makes clear that dependence on cadres has to be understood in the historical context of the retreat of world revolutions. He carefully draws on the historical comparison between the Russian Revolution and the Chinese Revolution, making critical distinctions between their revolutionary experiences. He argues that China never had a proletarian socialist revolution, unlike the Soviet Union. The cadre class in the Soviet Union was only formed after the October Revolution degenerated against the background of the receding tide of world revolution. In comparison, the formation of a cadre class in China preceded the Chinese revolution of 1949, as the tide of world revolution had already receded and the mass movement in China was not broad and deep enough to support a genuine socialist revolution.

The 1949 revolution was therefore not a socialist but a cadreist revolution: that is to say, a revolution led by cadres through armed struggle in the absence of mass movements, one that then created a society governed by the cadre class, in its own interest. In this system, the means of production were, nominally, collectively owned by the masses, but actually they were owned and managed by a cadre class. Not only was the Maoist cadreist system not socialist but it was, according to Zheng's analysis, a variant of capitalism, which Zheng refers to elsewhere as state capitalism.

This has important implications for understanding China's post-Mao reform. For Zheng, the market reform was not a regression from socialism to capitalism, because there never was socialism in China, but a transition from one variant of capitalism to another – from a restricted to an unrestricted form of capitalism. Why did this transition happen? Zheng believed that the cadreist system was fundamentally unstable, and that the cadre class was seeking a way out of its crisis. By introducing market mechanisms and foreign capital – and, in the process, relinquishing a measure of control over its collectively owned and managed assets – the cadre class hoped to create a mixed economic system that could maintain the rule of the cadreist system. More than three decades later, Zheng's analysis has proved prescient. We can see that such a trade-off has indeed succeeded in maintaining a system dominated by 'red capitalists', who have become wealthy.

An underdeveloped aspect of Zheng's critique is the nature of class relations in Maoist China. In focusing on the cadre class, Zheng left aside any analysis of its other social classes. Class is relational, and the cadre class exists in relation to other classes. What are the relations between the cadre class and other classes, such as the working class on whose behalf the cadre class claims to manage the means of production? Has conflict between them shaped the cadreist system? At various moments during the Maoist period and since, Chinese workers have directed challenges to their economic and political conditions either at the cadre class or, indirectly, at the cadreist system. How have these workers' struggles, and the threat of more, shaped class relations in China?

It would be wrong to see Zheng's critique merely as a historical curiosity. His ideas continue to have contemporary resonance. The emphasis on the centrality of mass movements and democracy, including the democratic election and recall of office holders, remains relevant to any contemporary effort at organising mass social movements in China and around the world. Revolutionaries, however dedicated, cannot substitute themselves for the masses and mass movements in driving revolutions and should not merely take state power on the behalf of the masses. The radical implication of Zheng's critique is nothing less than a call for the abolition of 'cadres' as a political category in the revolutionary movement. Zheng's life experience is a reminder of the human costs of failing to do so, for he and other oppositionists were persecuted, jailed or drive into exile by the cadreist state that he criticised.

At the end of the manuscript, Zheng reaffirms the importance of revolutionary theory. Zheng belonged to a revolutionary generation and tradition which, while clear-eyed about the true nature of Stalinism and the resilience of capitalism, looked forward optimistically to the possibility of a real socialist revolution emerging from a mass movement. He believed the task of revolutionaries is to use Marxism, not as an ossified orthodoxy but as a living theory in need of constant development and refinement, in order to understand the period we are in. This chapter offers a brilliant demonstration of this principle.

On China's Cadreism (1985)

China's current system is certainly cadreist. But China's cadreism has many important points of difference from the Soviet Union's cadreism.

First Comes the Cadre Class, Then Cadreism

The Soviet cadre class came into being after the tide of world revolution receded and the Soviet working class, having begun the transition from capitalism to socialism, was forced to retreat and await support that never came. A section of the revolutionary cadres degenerated into a cadre class. This class then transformed the retreat into a long-term system – cadreism. In China the situation was the opposite. Under the influence of the Soviet cadre class, the revolutionary cadres who survived the revolutionary defeat of the 1920s rapidly formed into a class. These cadres modelled themselves on the Soviet system following Stalin's usurpation of power. They looked to the Party and military leaders in the Soviet Union as models, and as a result introduced the social contradictions arising from the division and conflict between cadres and the masses.

When Marx, Engels, Lenin, Trotsky and their contemporaries analysed social composition and internal party structure, they did not (or did not often) mention 'cadres'. In an index of their works, we would find no, or very few, references to the term 'cadre'. There would be entries for 'professional revolutionary', 'activist', 'union bureaucrat', 'Party bureaucrat' but not to 'cadre'. Trotsky, in his later works, did not use the term 'cadre', preferring to use 'bureaucrat'. But in Stalin's works and in the international Communist publications of the 1920s and 30s, there are repeated appearances of 'cadre'. We see the juxtaposition between 'cadre' and 'masses', and the incorporation of the term 'cadre' into slogans and aphorisms. For example, Stalin said 'cadres determine everything!'

Usually, the existence of an object precedes the name representing it. A new object, when it first appears, is often given the same name as similar objects, or is given more than one name. Only after the characteristics of a new object become familiar to people would a single name or a new name be confirmed. The social elements that emerged in the Soviet Union after the receding of world revolution, and gradually occupied powerful positions, were at first called 'professional revolutionaries', 'activists' and other names. When, soon afterwards, these terms came to be considered inappropriate, they were renamed 'bureaucrats'; when this, too, was seen as inappropriate, people settled on 'cadres'. In fact, 'cadre' is an old name, borrowed from the military. It refers to 'commanders', as distinct from 'combatants', and includes all officers from company leaders to commandants. The Paris Commune abolished the standing army, and the commanders of the national guards were elected from among combatants and could be recalled anytime, so there were no cadres and no distinction or opposition between commanders and combatants. A 'cadre' is a commander in a standing army, appointed from the top and not elected. I do not know when the 'leaders' of the Party, the soviets, unions, and other mass organisations, who are not elected but appointed from the top, started to borrow 'cadre' from the military. 'Cadre' now means unelected public officeholders, a social element over and above the masses, people who become lifelong-tenured activists and constitute a class. It is no longer used in the sense of 'commander' in the military.

In the Soviet Union, the cadre element and cadre class came into being after the transitional system had degenerated into a cadreist system. The cadre class and cadreism were born at the same time and were mutually reinforcing. This was not the case in China. The Chinese Revolution began in 1925, after the Soviet degeneration, when Lenin had died, the Soviet Union's General Secretary Stalin had taken power, and the Soviet Union in fact had already instituted cadreism. By this time, the Soviet cadre class had already been formed, and had marginalised the leadership of the October Revolution and the dictatorship of the proletariat. But the masses in China (and other countries) saw the Soviet regime as the standard proletarian regime, and saw the system as constructing and achieving socialism. After the defeat of the 1925–7 Chinese Revolution, the base areas established during the rural armed struggles took the Soviet system as their blueprint, distinguishing between cadres and the masses. Unlike the Paris Commune and the early stages of the October Revolution where public office holders could be elected and recalled, the cadres were appointed, and the cadres and the masses became two different social elements. Cadres are necessarily cultivated and promoted from the masses. But once they have become cadres, they no longer belong to the masses. So while the social system in the period of rural guerrilla warfare cannot be called cadreism, a cadre class had already formed. The regime in the base areas at the time, could be called 'the regime of the cadre class'.

There was no attempt to hide the division between cadres and the masses. Before the Long March, during the guerrilla warfare in Jiangxi, Mao Zedong said

> large numbers of cadres are needed to extend the campaign of economic construction. This is not a matter of scores or hundreds of people, but of thousands and tens of thousands whom we must organise, train and send to the economic construction front. They will be the commanders and the broad masses the soldiers on the economic front.[2]

Here the relationship between commanders and combatants on the battlefield is used by analogy to describe the relationship between cadres and the masses in economic battles. Commanders are appointed, so are cadres.

When the Long March reached Yan'an, the number of cadres expanded and their distinction from the masses became more obvious. In the years of all-out Anti-Japanese War, when the base areas were small, the cadres' position was well above that of the masses. Mao Zedong said in May 1937: 'Our revolution relies on cadres. As Stalin said: "Cadres determine everything"'[3]

On this view, revolution does not rely on the masses but on cadres, and such cadres are not put forward by the masses.

In 1942, in the base area the division between cadres and the masses became even more obvious. In May of that year, Mao Zedong hosted the Forum on Literature and Art, when he discussed the question of cadres:

> The audience for works of literature and art consists of workers, peasants, soldiers and revolutionary cadres. There are students in the base areas, too, but they are different from students of the old type; they are either former or future cadres ... Take the cadres alone. Do not think they are few; they far outnumber the readers of any book published in the Guomindang areas. There, an edition usually runs to only 2,000 copies, and even three editions add up to only 6,000; but as for the cadres in the base areas, in Yan'an alone there are more than 10,000 who read books.
>
> Besides raising standards to meet the needs of the masses directly, there is the kind which meets their needs indirectly, that is, the kind

---

2   Mao 1975 [1933], p. 135.
3   Mao 1975 [1937], p. 291.

needed by the cadres. The cadres are the advanced elements of the masses and generally have received more education; literature and art of a higher level are entirely necessary for them. To ignore this would be a mistake. Whatever is done for the cadres is also entirely for the masses, because it is only through the cadres that we can educate and guide the masses.[4]

Here cadres and the masses are clearly distinguished, and cadres are clearly placed above the masses. Only through the cadres can we educate and guide the masses. The Yan'an of 1942 had 10,000 cadres. Unfortunately, I do not know the population of Yan'an or what percentage of the population were cadres.

At this time, the Chinese CCP was far from gaining state power. Although the cadres controlled the military and political power and the mass organisations in the base areas, they did not yet control economic power. Production and enterprise in the base areas was miniscule compared with areas controlled by the Guomindang.

In the fall of 1948, during the civil war, when the CCP was on the offensive and close to occupying the whole of the country, its Central Committee met in September to discuss the question of managing cadres nationally. After the meeting, Mao Zedong said in a circular:

The task of seizing political power throughout the country demands that our Party should quickly and systematically train large numbers of cadres to administer military, political, economic, Party, cultural and educational affairs. In the third year of the war, we must prepare thirty to forty thousand cadres of lower, middle and higher ranks, so that in the fourth year when the army advances they can march with it and bring orderly administration to newly liberated areas with a population of some 50 to 100 million. China's territory is very large, her population is very numerous, and the revolutionary war is developing very rapidly; but our supply of cadres is very inadequate – this is a very great difficulty. In preparing cadres during the third year, while we should rely on the old Liberated Areas to supply the greater part, we must also pay attention to enrolling cadres from the big cities controlled by the Guomindang. In the big cities in Guomindang areas there are many workers and intellectuals who can take part in our work and who have, generally speaking, a higher cultural level than the workers and peasants in the old Liberated Areas. We should make use of large numbers of working personnel from the Guomindang's

---

4   Mao 1967 [1942], pp. 71–2, 83.

economic, financial, cultural and educational institutions, excluding the
reactionary elements. School education in the Liberated Areas must be
restored and developed.[5]

This demonstrates that during the expansion from base areas to the entire
country, the already formed cadre class was too small. It had to be enlarged,
opening its doors and increasing its numbers in order to adequately 'guide' the
masses. The existing cadres were at the core of this expansion. In the newly
liberated areas they could assimilate cadres with a higher cultural level.

In the fall of 1948, the CCP was merely preparing to govern an area of 50–100
million people. By 1949, after victory in the Battle of Huaihai, it was preparing
to govern the whole of China. New guidance was issued regarding the cadre
question.

In sum, in China the appearance and expansion of the cadre class preceded
the capture of national power, the completion of the revolution and the formal
institution of the cadre system. The Chinese Revolution did not pass through
a historical stage like that between the October Revolution and the death of
Lenin. It did not experience the primary stage of the transition from capitalism to socialism. In this primary stage, there was no standing army, all public
office holders were elected by the masses, could be recalled at any time by the
masses, and were paid no more than the wage of an average worker. Even after
the formation of a standing army, where officers were paid higher wages, as
capitalist experts were, and election was replaced by appointment, people at
the time believed that it was a necessary but only temporary system, soon to
be abolished. The Chinese Revolution did not experience this primary stage of
transition.

The difference between the Chinese and Russian revolutions determined the
subsequent development of China's cadreism.

China's Cadreist Revolution

In China, victory was won by not an October-style revolution or a proletarian
socialist revolution, but by a cadreist revolution. This revolution started only
after the defeat of the so-called 'Great Revolution'.

A mass revolution took place in China between 1925 and 1927. Its momentum
was so massive that it earned the title of 'Great Revolution'. At the time, some
people said that this revolution could be compared to the French Revolution of
1789, or the Russian Revolution of 1917, and should be called the Great Chinese

---

5   Mao 1975 [1948], p. 274.

Revolution. But the so-called 'Great Revolution' not only failed but was humiliated. However, the designation of 'Great Revolution' has been preserved to this day. From a historical perspective, this revolution did not deserve to be called a 'Great Revolution'. How could it be compared to French Revolution of 1789, or the Russian Revolution of 1917? We should more properly call it 'the Revolution of 1925 to 1927'. But because 'Great Revolution' is used widely, we will continue using it.

The Chinese Revolution of 1925–27 was in fact an aborted revolution, a shadow of the October Revolution, destined to be aborted from the start.

In the 1920s, China was ripe for revolution. Capitalism had developed; feudalism or pre-capitalist social formations were in crisis, necessitating fundamental change. But as in Russia in the late nineteenth and early twentieth centuries, the capitalist class was unable to shoulder the task of this historical change, leaving it to the proletariat to lead. However, the proletariat would not restrict itself to the task of establishing bourgeois democracy. It had its own agenda – of socialist revolution. In other words, China too faced a permanent revolution – not the permanent revolution of the nineteenth but that of the twentieth century – Trotsky's permanent revolution. As Lenin said in 1922: the Russian bourgeois-democratic revolution is merely the byproduct of the Russian proletarian socialist revolution.

But Russia's permanent revolution succeeded, whereas China's failed. Why? There is an objective reason for this: the Chinese Revolution of the 1920s took place after the first international high tide of revolutions ignited by the Russian Revolution had receded. At the time of the Russian Revolution, the world was reborn in a revolutionary tide powered by the Russian Revolution, but it receded, leaving behind an isolated Soviet regime. By the time of the 1925 Chinese Revolution, the Soviet regime had degenerated into a regime of the cadre class. It controlled the Communist International, and the Communist International controlled the CCP. The revolution fermented by Chinese workers and peasants began under the leadership of the CCP. But the masses advanced beyond the control of the CCP by demanding land reform and the establishment of soviets. Since the objective conditions were not conducive to revolution, and the power of the masses was restrained by the Soviet cadre class, how could the revolution not fail?

The Chinese Revolution of 1925–27 was a ripple compared with the October Revolution, or rather, its shadow. Its defeat ended the first worldwide revolutionary tide led by the October Revolution.

The Chinese Revolution – the one that succeeded in 1949 – should be dated back to the failure of the Chinese Revolution of 1925–7. This new revolution was a cadreist revolution.

After the defeat of the 1925–27 Revolution, we were able to see in hindsight the ebbing of the first world revolutionary tide, and the failure of a new tide to arrive. But the surviving revolutionaries did not understand this at the time and continued to hope that a new revolution would arrive soon. They continued discussing the nature, method and model of the coming revolution. Chinese society was developing in the direction of cadreism. This, too, was a 'revolution', but one of a different kind.

Its most important characteristic is that it was an armed revolution, not a mass revolution. More accurately, it was an armed revolution supported by the masses. Mass revolutions like the Paris Commune and the October Revolution had long disappeared, in the wake of their defeats. The mass movements organised between 1925 and 1927 had also disappeared after their defeats, and could not be resurrected, at least not soon. We should reflect on a debate that preceded the revolutionary outburst of 1925: the Communists criticised the Nationalists, arguing that one of the most important reasons that Sun Yat-sen and his Party had failed to carry out a revolution despite decades of trying, is that they did not value the power of the masses but believed only in military power. It was due to a combination of circumstances, not a correct strategy, that the armed struggle waged by Sun Yat-sen's Xinhai Revolution overthrew the Qing Emperor in 1911 and established the Republic.

But the regime soon fell into the hands of the northern warlords, while the Guomindang more or less held power in Guangdong. At the time, its leader Sun Yat-sen still believed religiously in military power, siding with one southern warlord against another. Among the northern warlords, he sided with Duan Qirui and Zhang Zuolin against Cao Kun and Wu Peifu. The Chinese Revolution could never succeed using such methods. The Communists advised Sun Yat-sen to abandon his belief in military power and reform his Party so that it relied on the power of the mass movement, as had the Russian Revolution. Sun Yat-sen was not convinced. But given the Soviet Union's military and financial assistance, he pretended to believe that 'Russia is Our Teacher' and agreed to 'support the workers and peasants' and develop a mass movement. He started to reform the Guomindang, a corrupt party, with the assistance of Soviet advisors and the CCP. He allowed Communists to join his Party as individuals. But in his bones, he never abandoned the path of armed struggle. The reform of the Guomindang into a Soviet-style Party and the mass movement of workers and peasants were merely tools in the hands of his armed revolution. After the Party reform, Sun Yat-sen continued to focus on military opportunism, and allied with the Anhui and Fengtian factions of the northern warlords against the Zhili faction that controlled power. Right up to the moment of his death, Sun Yat-sen never believed in the revolutionary potential of the masses of workers and peasants.

History might be said to have proved that in the debate around the Guomindang's reform, Sun Yat-sen and his heirs' reliance on military power and the standing army in the course of making revolution was correct, and the Communists' reliance on the masses of workers and peasants was wrong. After all, the mass movement organised by the Communists during the May Thirtieth Movement of 1925 was not enough to defeat the northern warlords and the imperialists. The mass movement played second fiddle to the standing army trained by the Guomindang in the course of the Northern Expedition. The CCP took advantage of the Northern Expedition as an opportunity to organise and expand the mass movement, to promote armed unrest at the peak of the mass movement to grab power and create a situation like that of the October Revolution. But when the standing army, controlled as it was by the landed gentry and the capitalist class saw that the mass movement was threatening their very existence, they used the army to crush the mass movement. This led to the defeat of the revolution of 1925–7.

On reflection, this revolution was a ripple of the first tide of world revolutions set off by the October Revolution. The tide receded and the ripple died away. But immediately after the defeat, people were unable to see clearly what had happened. Some thought it was a mere setback. Others thought revolution was still rising. Still others thought that Sun Yat-sen had been right in the debate about the Guomindang's reform, that the CCP had been wrong and that the revolution had no choice but to rely on arms. But the powerful Hunan peasant army could not resist the onslaught of the standing army. In the autumn of 1917, the commander of Russia's standing army led an assault on the revolutionary masses of St Petersburg, but faced with the mass movement, the army fell apart even before it entered the city. The masses and their armed Red Guards, uniting with the revolutionary soldiers, occupied the Winter Palace. The attempt to bring the army back from the front to regain power was defeated by the masses outside the city. All this seems like a fairy tale! Now many have come to believe that mass movements are useless, or can at best fly the flag for a standing army. In other words, they believe that a struggle between a standing army and the impassioned masses will always result in the defeat of the masses.

This conclusion was drawn not only by Sun Yat-sen and his heirs. Even the surviving leaders of the CCP accepted it after the defeat of the revolution, when Mao Zedong came up with the slogan 'Political power grows out of the barrel of a gun'. In 1938, Mao Zedong reiterated the classic formula of armed struggle in 'Problems of War and Strategy':

> In China war is the main form of struggle and the army is the main form of organisation. Other forms such as mass organisation and mass struggle

are also extremely important and indeed indispensable and in no circumstances to be overlooked, but their purpose is to serve the war. Before the
outbreak of a war all organisation and struggle are in preparation for the
war ... after war breaks out, all organisation and struggle are coordinated
with the war either directly or indirectly.[6]

To subordinate the mass movement to armed struggle with such clarity was
unprecedented. Sun Yat-sen did so in practice but did not say so out loud. In
the same essay, Mao Zedong praised the 'militarism' (*zhanzheng zhuyi*) of Sun
Yat-sen and Chiang Kai-shek. He said, 'He [Chiang Kai-shek] has held firmly
to the vital point that whoever has an army has power and that war decides
everything. In this respect we ought to learn from him. In this respect both Sun
Yat-sen and Chiang Kai-shek are our teachers'.[7] The debate about the relative
importance of military struggle and mass movement during the reform of the
Guomindang was thus tacitly resolved: Sun Yat-sen and the Guomindang were
right, and the Communist International and the CCP were wrong.

The October Revolution relied on the mass movement, carried out armed
struggles at the peak of the mass movement, and won power on that basis. The
arms were in the hands of the masses, the Red Guards, like the National Guards
of the Paris Commune, not of a standing army. The first lesson that Marx drew
from the experience of the Paris Commune was the need to 'abolish the standing army'. The Chinese Revolution relied on an army that was not based in the
masses. In the autumn of 1928, Mao was leading the armed resistance being
waged in the Jinggang Mountains by survivors of the defeat of the revolution.
They were scheming to resurrect the revolution and produce a regime from the
barrel of a gun. Mao knew full well that the armed struggle was detached from
the mass movement. In November of the same year, he said in a report to the
Central Committee:

> In the past year we have fought in many places and are keenly aware that
> the revolutionary tide is on the ebb in the country as a whole. While Red
> political power has been established in a few small areas, in the country
> as a whole the people lack the ordinary democratic rights, the workers,
> the peasants and even the bourgeois democrats do not have freedom of
> speech or assembly, and the worst crime is to join the CCP. Wherever the
> Red Army goes, the masses are cold and aloof, and only after our propa-

---

6   Mao 1975 [1938] p. 221.
7   Ibid., p. 223.

ganda do they slowly move into action. Whatever enemy units we face, there are hardly any cases of mutiny or desertion to our side and we have to fight it out. This holds even for the enemy's Sixth Army which recruited the greatest number of rebels' after the May 21st Incident. We have an acute sense of our isolation which we keep hoping will end.[8]

These sentences show that Mao was relying on military power to carry out his new revolution. The army was not formed at a peak of the mass movement but at a revolutionary low tide when the masses were cold and aloof. But this did not represent a return from the revolutionary method of the Communists to that of the pre-reform Nationalists. Rather, this was the method of a cadreist revolution. Later, especially after the Mukden Incident, when the mass movement was rising, some connections were established between military activity and mass movements. But, objectively and subjectively, there could be no return to the mass-based armed struggle as waged during the October Revolution. Instead, as Mao Zedong explained, war was the main form of struggle, and the army was the main form of organisation. So was a mass movement deemed necessary? Yes, but only as an auxiliary power for the purposes of waging war. Before the outbreak of war, the mass movement must help prepare for it; during the war, it must support the war effort.

We can compare the Paris Commune and the October Revolution to see what method was used historically by proletarian socialist revolutions. Marx summarised three lessons from the Paris Commune. The first is to abolish the standing army. In the *April Theses* and other writings of the period, Lenin reiterated and emphasised Marx's point. The establishment of the Red Army in Russia represented a restoration of the standing army. The revolution had stalled, and in order to preserve the fruits of victory, a trade-off was needed. Only after Lenin's death and the degeneration of the revolution did Stalin proclaim that the Red Army was the pillar of the dictatorship of the proletariat. The standing army was not only restored but became a pillar. In China, the Red Army was established at the beginning of China's new revolution, and all mass movements were relegated to the role of accessories of the Red Army and its activities.

Marx's three lessons of the Paris Commune were all abandoned. Not only was the Red Army established, but it became the main form of revolutionary organisation, and war the main form of revolutionary struggle. Neither election

---

8   Mao [1928], pp. 97–8.

nor recall could be implemented. A non-standing army may implement election and recall, but the commander of a standing army, the Red Army, has to be appointed from above, and cannot be elected, or recalled by soldiers at any moment. The mass movement and its organisations, and any administrative and economic organisations outside the army, are accessories of the army. Their office holders can also not be elected or recalled by the masses. What about the third principle that all office holders should receive the wage of an average worker? Generally speaking, in times of struggle, in order to win, military cadres and administrative clerks share weal and woe. However, their livelihood is guaranteed. After taking power, even if their benefits were not significantly higher than those enjoyed by the masses, they benefited from privileges not shared by the masses, as did their children.

After the defeat of the 1927 revolution, objective conditions in China determined the method of struggle. This method, in turn, determined the outcome of the struggle. This led to the formation of a cadre class. The victory of the new revolution could only establish a cadreist social and political system.

The Internal Struggle and Development of Cadreism

The cadreist system, thus formed, can, in its early stages, only be a Stalinist cadreist system. The Stalinist cadreist system was a regression that came about during the transitional period after the October Revolution. It was a 'transitional' system, not from capitalism to socialism but from the transitional system as described by Marx and Lenin to a formalised cadreist system. One could not leap directly from the system created by Lenin and Trotsky to a formalised cadreist system. There had to be a process of transformation. It had, first of all, to preserve the socialist 'banner'. The 'Soviet system', even if not a socialist system, nevertheless had to demonstrate a determination to move towards socialism. Socialism had been firmly implanted in the hearts of people. The landed gentry and capitalist ownership had been abolished. So the new cadreist class could claim their ownership was 'socialist ownership' and hang out the banner of 'socialism'. In 1936, Stalin simply announced that the Soviet Union had achieved 'socialism'. More than a decade earlier, he had already announced the theory of 'Socialism in One Country'. The Stalinists had to do this, or the masses would not have consented. The masses had lost power, but they still mistakenly believed that the new system was advancing towards socialism – or had already achieved socialism. If the masses were to lose this illusion, the rule of the cadre class would be endangered.

The Stalinist cadreist system was to an extent consistent with combined development. The existence and development of public ownership, created by the October Revolution after abolishing the landed gentry and capitalist ownership, could be combined with the remnants of the feudal economy and Russia's backward capitalist economy. This combined system, after the tide of world revolution receded, developed a life of its own. During three decades of Stalin's rule, the Soviet Union not only survived but significantly developed its productive forces. This development was said to be the result of 'the superiority of socialism'.

After the Chinese Revolution of 1949, there was no other system to emulate than the Stalinist cadreist one. Why should this be a surprise? This system also developed China's productive forces.

But the combined system could not remain stable indefinitely. Even while Stalin was alive, his system was already unsustainable. He had to use terror to maintain his rule. The target of terror was, at first, the surviving forces of the October Revolution, and later, other factions within the cadreist class. It continued to use the charge of 'Trotskyism' against oppositions in the cadreist class. But even by carrying out historically unprecedented terror, Stalin was unable to eliminate opposition within the cadreist class, just as he could not entirely eliminate the legacy of the October Revolution. The opposition born of the October Revolution disappeared with the receding of the tide of world revolution. But the opposition that developed in the cadreist class was a new force that could not be eliminated. Reflecting on the history of his three decades in power, even if Stalin had not died his system would have needed reform and his rule would have had to be overthrown – unless he had been prepared to lead the reform himself.

The essence of the Stalinist cadreist system is an excessive emphasis on centralised planning and excessive regulation of the market mechanism. In capitalist society, as production becomes more centralised, centralised planning becomes possible. Engels once wrote that trusts are by nature planned. The October Revolution centralised all Russian production in the hands of the Soviet government. In theory, it could then have implemented the planning of production and phase out the market mechanism over time. This was done in the period of so-called War Communism. At the time, people thought this was a normal procedure. However, it failed. The New Economic Policy then replaced War Communism, and the latter was now said to have been an abnormal but necessary and exceptional measure during a time of war. When a city is besieged, all resources, publicly or privately owned, are confiscated for public use rather than traded at market prices. After the end of the Civil War, this system was abolished in favour of a market mechanism. Peasants were taxed but their grain was not confiscated. After paying their taxes, peasants were allowed to trade their grain freely. This helped them through the crisis. It also showed that the market mechanism was not so easily abolished.

People generally think that under Lenin and Trotsky the Soviet Union declared all means of production (factories and the land) to be publicly owned, but did not abolish the market mechanism. That was because land was only nominally owned by the state but was in fact tilled by peasants in individual households. After the collectivisation of the land, production, it was hoped, could be comprehensively planned, and the market mechanism set aside. That was how Stalin understood the situation, but he failed.

All factories, mines, railroads, ships, etc., as well as land, came to be owned by the cadreist class. Agriculture, handicrafts and so on were collectivised and managed by the cadreist class. In this situation, if it was still not possible to abolish the market mechanism, the responsibility could be laid on 'the encroachment of capitalism' and the receding tide of world revolution. After the first tide of world revolution receded, the Soviet Union, as the birthplace of world revolution, became an isolated island besieged by capitalist states. This led to the degeneration of the revolution from a socialist transitional system into a cadreist system, which determined the limits of production planning and the importance of market mechanism.

The market mechanism is a capitalist method of production, but a limited amount of planned production can also occur in capitalism. Engels said that there is also production planning within a trust. As capitalism develops, an entire country can become a trust, which will promote national production planning while retaining the market mechanism. The balance between production planning and the market mechanism varies depending on conditions.

The Stalinist cadreist system underestimated the necessary role of the market mechanism. The Stalinist system worked for a while, but eventually it ran into a wall. Some members of the cadreist class demanded reforms to put more emphasis on the market mechanism. The more these people were repressed, the stronger they became. They ended up overthrowing the Stalinist cadreist system.

When the Chinese cadreist revolution succeeded, there was only the Stalinist cadreist system to emulate. People believed that that system represented 'socialism'. Given that there was nothing else to emulate, they copied the entire Stalinist economic system. Although the Stalinist system was already displaying various negative features, and was attracting severe criticism, China still copied it.

Politically, Mao Zedong was dissatisfied with Stalin on the question of Sino-Soviet relations. Regarding the economic system, however, he continued to believe that the Stalinist system was predestined.

After Stalin's death, the internal contradictions within the Soviet cadre class were exposed. Some leaders of the CCP also became aware of the faults of the

Stalinist system and the need for change. However, Mao and his followers held firmly to the Stalinist system. The struggle within the CCP emerged from this confrontation. This struggle was intense while Mao still lived, and it continued after his death. It has still not yet ended [in 1985]. But the cadres opposed to Mao Zedong have obviously won.

China ahead of the Soviet Union

The Soviet cadreist system is today no longer Stalinist, but nor is it yet a classic cadreist system. There is a historical reason for this. As I said earlier, Soviet cadreism was a degeneration from the October proletarian socialist revolution. The propaganda and activities took root in people's hearts, and these glorious origins and their socialist legacy cannot be obliterated. Second, although the Stalinist cadreist system ultimately failed, it succeeded for a while and developed Russia's productive forces – this fact too cannot be erased. The burden of this historical legacy weighed heavily on the Soviet cadre class, so that it was unable to stride freely forward in the direction of a classic cadreist system.

The burden of historical legacy on the Chinese cadre class was much lighter. China did not experience a proletarian socialist revolution or a period of transition. China's Stalin never developed on a large scale the productive forces left behind in the China under Guomindang rule. The Stalinist economic system, as implemented by Mao, experienced repeated failures. Because of all these factors, China's cadre class was relatively unburdened and could stride forward in the direction of classic cadreism.

What is classic cadreism? It is collective ownership of the productive forces by the cadre class, as the basis of capitalist production.

The abnormal transitional Stalinist cadreism that China experienced was similarly based on collective ownership by the cadre class. Although Stalin did not entirely eliminate private ownership, he reduced it greatly. Mao also did his utmost to eliminate private ownership, but I lack the necessary statistics. However, in my opinion, even if he was less thorough than Stalin, he was not far off. Yet collective ownership by the cadre class without the complement of private ownership was demonstrably not working. Classic cadreism implements a model of capitalism that abides by the law of value and uses a combination of planning and the market mechanism. It not only allows for private ownership but makes private ownership necessary. In the Soviet-style Stalinist cadreist system, on the other hand, the market mechanism was excessively restrained and remained rudimentary. As a result, the economy suffered. In short, the cadreist system needs capitalist production, albeit in a restrained form. Without capitalist production, the cadreist economy is necessarily autarkic. Stalin experimented for decades with a cadreist system of this sort, and the experimentation continued under Mao. But it could not be sustained and had to be 'reformed'.

China strode ahead faster than the Soviet Union along the path of 'reform', and has become an 'open' economy, whereas the Soviet Union remains a 'closed' economy. Rural China has implemented a household responsibility system, while the Soviet Union is only beginning to do so. Why is this? Because the burden of the historical legacy is much lighter in China than in the Soviet Union.

Which Way Forward for China?

China is moving towards classic, complete cadreism. China did not have the Soviet Union's historical burden, and once it concluded that the Stalinist-Maoist cadreist system was not working, it readily abandoned it and strode forward in the direction of classic cadreism. This does not represent a regression from socialism to capitalism, for neither the Stalinist nor the Maoist system was socialist. Neither is the new set-up of One Country, Two Systems [devised in the early 1980s by Deng Xiaoping to describe the governance of Hong Kong and Macau after they became regions of China]. It is merely a transition from restrained capitalism to unrestrained capitalism. In this transitional period, both systems coexist but both are capitalist.

The difference between capitalism and cadreism is that capitalism is based on private ownership whereas cadreism is based on collective ownership (i.e. collective ownership of the means of production by the cadre class). Both systems are governed by the law of value. But capitalism, even if unrestrained, will also necessarily lead to the collective ownership of all the means of production by the capitalist class – not in form, but in substance. Engels wrote that when it comes to economic trusts, private production will disappear. He also said that economic trusts adopt elements of planning. Let us imagine: if the trusts are combined, would they not be the same as cadreism? In today's China, with its backward productive forces and in the face of competition with advanced capitalist countries, the state must manage capitalist production while at the same time maintaining collective ownership by the cadre class. If the latter cannot be maintained and the expansion of private economy is allowed gradually to replace collective ownership, 'restoration' will be complete: a regression from cadreism to classic private capitalism. But I think that this is unlikely, since capitalism today is also moving toward collective ownership by the capitalist class.

The leaders of the cadre class see clearly that collective ownership by the cadre class has to be maintained at all costs. But to maintain it, it must open up the closed system of cadreism. China has to take its place in the capitalist world market and must introduce foreign capital in order to develop its backward productive forces. To this end, it has to do away with the restraints on capitalist production and prioritise the market mechanism over economic planning. The planned economy cannot be completely abandoned because today's capitalism has already adopted elements of planning. Are collective ownership and the market mechanism (the law of value) compatible? They are not compatible under free capitalist competition, but they may be compatible under monopoly capitalism. When necessary, the cadre class might abandon part of its ownership of the means of production, but not all of it.

There is nevertheless a historical burden on the Chinese cadre class. The banner of 'socialism' remains, and socialism means public ownership. But public ownership implies a planned economy, and a planned economy must lead to China's closing off from the rest of the world. This so-called 'socialism' is no longer working and must be 'reformed', by maintaining collective ownership by the cadre class while introducing capitalist production. Because of this historical burden, the reforms have to proceed in stages, and their ultimate goal cannot be made fully public in advance. At first, opening up, i.e., increasing the volume of foreign trade, meets little resistance, because the Maoist system has already pushed the Chinese economy to the verge of bankruptcy. Implementing private ownership in the rural areas meets greater resistance. However, it is whitewashed as a Contractual Responsibility System, in which the land remains collectively owned but it is contracted out to peasants. The peasants hand over some of their produce to the rural commune, just as they did in the past to the landlords who owned the land. Next, the development of commodity production and the cultivation of a private economy are whitewashed by pretending that they are merely auxiliary. Finally, when it comes to the full implementation of capitalism, four Special Economic Zones were created, then fourteen cities and Hainan Island were opened up, as well as the Liaodong and Shandong peninsulas, then all coastal regions and finally the interior of the country. The scale of private business is not restricted. Private business people are allowed to run large factories. Foreign capital can set up joint ventures with Chinese enterprises and even set up their own businesses. This is the direction in which Chinese cadreism is heading. There is no guarantee that all the collectively owned enterprises will not be privatised, as under capitalism. The only hope that is that contemporary capitalism is busy concentrating private ownership into share-holding companies such as trusts. This shows that concentrated ownership is more conducive to production than individual ownership, and that collectively owned capitalist enterprises will not return to the individual ownership of the past. It is possible that the concessions to private ownership will grow, and that full privatisation will come about in the short term. All other things being equal, such a step would stabilise the cadreist system.

This is the true meaning of what China's cadreist class has been promoting in the 1980s under the slogan of 'structural reform'. It aims to create a social system consistent with the logic of development: a coordination of class-based collective ownership with production governed by the law of value. This constitutes a mutual compromise. Collective ownership makes some concessions to private ownership, while the system of production makes concessions to planning. As to the extent of the compromise, it will be determined by the balance of forces.

Cadreism in Other Countries

I have now finished analysing the Soviet and Chinese cadreism. I think my analysis is sufficient, and there is no need for another chapter on cadreism in other countries. If the world does not change unexpectedly, Soviet cadreism will also head in the direction of normal cadreism, i.e., capitalist production on the model of class-based collective ownership of the means of production. If this happens in the Soviet Union, other countries are even less likely to escape such a future – unless the world sees an unexpected change.

CHAPTER 9

The Young Karl Marx and the Theory of Alienation (1988)

Translated by Gregor Kneussel

Introduction by Gregor Benton

Despite decades behind bars, Zheng kept up a lively interest in new developments in Marxist thinking, and he was not shy of offering an opinion on them. One topic that attracted the attention of critical Marxists in the West starting in the 1960s and in China in the 1980s, after the death of Mao and Zheng's release from jail, was alienation and related concepts like humanism and species-being that had featured centrally in the thinking of the young Marx. Their emergence as a focus of critical thought in China was by no means new. In the early 1960s, the Marxist aesthetician Zhu Guangqian and the philosopher Ba Ren and others had already experimented with this novel form of Marxism, which had emerged after the discovery and rediscovery of Marx's early writings, first in the West and then in China. However, Zheng's attitude to the new humanist school of Marxism was not what one might have expected from a Communist who throughout his life had struggled against tyrannical authority in both its bourgeois and its Marxist guise and who was thoroughly imbued with the idea of socialism as true human liberation. Far from welcoming the new trend, Zheng criticised it as covert attack on the concept of class struggle and a way of using the immature theories of the young Marx to attack the old Marx, with whom Zheng continued to identify. Instead of viewing the publication in Chinese translation of Marx's juvenilia as an opportunity to attack Marxism's Stalinist perversion, as critical Marxists in the West and in China had done, he criticised them as a source of ideological confusion and argued that the mature Marx had abandoned the concept of alienation. Whereas other critics of Chinese state ideology under Mao saw humanism and associated concepts as a dagger with which to attack orthodoxy and a means by which to resolve the gathering crisis of Marxism in China and the world, Zheng called instead for a return to the fundamental principles of Marxism that Stalin and Mao had betrayed and traduced.

The Young Karl Marx and the Theory of Alienation (1988)

For a while now, 'alienation' and 'humanism' have been fashionable topics in Marxist circles. People are talking about these issues. In recent years, since China's 'opening', they have also spread to China, where they have attracted debates and controversies. At one point, the debate became rather fierce. Outside Marxist circles, some people have also discussed these issues, and some have used 'alienation' and 'humanism' to oppose Marxism. They think they are exposing contradictions within Marxism. Before the Second World War, Marxists did not talk about 'alienation', except in specialised debates on philosophical issues. 'Humanism' was mentioned occasionally, but it had not been mentioned at such a prominent level. Why has the trend suddenly changed in this way since the War?

Marx's Economic and Philosophical Manuscripts of 1844

In 1932, some manuscripts by Marx were published in Moscow. The manuscripts had no title – the current title was devised by the publishers because many of the manuscripts discuss economics and a few discuss philosophical issues. After the publication of the original German version, they were translated and published in Russian, French, English and other languages. In 1979, when the People's Publishing House in China published volume 42 of the *Collected Works of Marx and Engels*, a Chinese translation of these manuscripts was included.

Since the manuscripts were written in Paris, they are sometimes called the 'Paris Manuscripts' or part of the 'Paris Manuscripts', because Marx also wrote other manuscripts during his stay in Paris. These manuscripts were combined from three different sets of manuscripts, all written between April and August 1844, before Engels came to Paris to meet Marx. They are fragmented and incomplete.

These three manuscripts are obviously reading notes, or research notes, not a finished work. The editors of the German edition wrote: This is Marx's 'first economic work [*Arbeit*]' in the broadest sense of this term. Marx originally did not understand economics. In the preface to his *Critique of Political Economy* that came out later, he described the 'course of his studies' roughly as follows: When he edited the *Rheinische Zeitung* (1842–1843) and debated the forest thefts, the division of landed property, free trade, protective tariffs and other issues 'that are known as material interests' with the Governor of Prussia and other people, he encountered some difficulties and thus decided to study economic questions. And when the *Rheinische Zeitung* published statements on French socialism, he objected, because those philosophical articles were too superficial. However, he also felt that his previous studies had not equipped him to judge the rights and wrongs of French socialism, so when the Prussian government banned the *Rheinische Zeitung*, he grasped the opportunity to withdraw from public view and study economics. He said that he started studying economics in Paris.[1] These manuscripts are the most systematic and longest of the research notes he made in Paris, and Lenin said in his biography of Marx: 'Marx's journalistic activities convinced him that he was insufficiently acquainted with political economy'.[2] It wasn't that his knowledge was insufficient, but that when editing the *Rheinische Zeitung*, he had not yet crossed the threshold into studying economics.

Regarding economics, Engels was one step ahead of Marx. In his *Introduction to the Critique of Hegel's Philosophy of Right* published in the famous *Deutsch-Französische Jahrbücher* (February 1844), Marx wrote that in order to analyse civil society, you need to study economics. However, in the same issue, Engels already presented an article on an economic topic, *Outlines of a Critique of Political Economy*. Marx was immediately attracted to this article. These *Manuscripts* were written after the *Jahrbücher* came out, and the preface to the *Manuscripts* mentions this article by Engels; the preface to the *Critique of Political Economy* also mentions Engels's article, calls it 'a brilliant essay', and says: 'I maintained a constant exchange of ideas by correspondence' with Engels after its publication. In the first half of 1844, i.e. at the same time as writing the *Manuscripts*, Marx also wrote reading notes on this essay by Engels (see *Complete Works of Marx and Engels*, vol. 42; for Engels's article, see *Complete Works of Marx and Engels*, vol. 1). Engels may have been one step ahead, but he merely used Hegel's philosophy to make a critique of economics and had not reached the next stage in his studies. Later, in 1871, Engels himself said in a letter to Wilhelm Liebknecht that his essay 'is by now *quite obsolete* and full of inaccuracies'.[3] In 1871, not only the *Critique of Political Economy* but *Capital* too had been published. In 1844 Marx did not know about the theory of surplus value, and nor did Engels.

A person's reading, study or research notes are usually intended for subsequent development towards formal publication. Once the results of that research have been published, these notes are not worth preserving and can be destroyed by the author or passed on to his heirs, who in turn might be loath to destroy them. However, from such notes one can see how an author's thoughts develop. For example, if a set of clothes that a person wears when young is

---

1 See Marx 1987, p. 262.
2 Lenin 1974, p. 47.
3 Engels 1989, p. 136.

kept until he grows into adulthood, we can see how that person looked when he was younger, and when the clothes still fitted him. But when it comes to a great historical thinker like Marx, things are not the same. All the papers and writings he left behind should be published, so that people can study them. So the publication of the *Economic and Philosophical Manuscripts of 1844* cannot be faulted. When I bought volume 42 of the Chinese edition of the *Complete Works of Marx and Engels*, I had no intention of reading these *Economic and Philosophical Manuscripts*, since there were so many standard writings by Marx that had been discovered during his lifetime and after his death that I had not had the time to read even them, let alone read his notes. Finally, I did read them, and I read them closely over and over again. That is because after the Second World War, the *Manuscripts* suddenly became popular and played a major role in worldwide ideological and political struggles. What's more, here in China we had an ideological and even a political struggle over them. So it is impossible to study the *Manuscripts* on their own, separate from other reading notes by Marx. However, they are nevertheless reading notes, and if we study and discuss them today, we do so in order to explain why they play such an important role in modern ideological and political struggles, and how people sometimes misunderstand and misinterpret them.

Before we come to the main question, please indulge the following digression.

The term used in these *Manuscripts* by Karl Marx is *Nationalökonomie*,[4] which in the Chinese edition is consistently translated as *guomin jingjixue*. The preface to the *Manuscripts* mentions an article published in the *Deutsch-Französische Jahrbücher* that also has '*Nationalökonomie*' in its title.[5] By 1859 at the latest, when Marx published his famous *Critique of Political Economy*, the term he uses was *politische Ökonomie*, translated as *zhengzhi jingjixue*. In this article, I shall use the term *jingjixue* for both *Nationalökonomie* and *politische Ökonomie* when I quote from Marx.

Are 'national economics', 'political economics' and 'economics' different words for the same thing or different words for different things? Forgive my ignorance, but I've never heard an explanation of this problem. I do know the history of this problem, its origins and development.

When Yan Fu[6] translated Adam Smith's *Wealth of Nations* into Chinese, he translated it as *jixue*, but this term did not pass into general use. At the time,

---

4   German in the original.
5   Friedrich Engels: *Umrisse zu einer Kritik der Nationalökonomie*.
6   Yan Fu (1853–1921), a Chinese scholar and famous translator who set new standards for translation into Chinese.

there were more Chinese students in Japan than in Europe, and they brought back the term that had been coined in Japan, *keizaigaku/jingjixue*. This translation is actually irrational. In Classical Chinese, *jingji* is an abbreviation of *jing bang ji guo* ('to govern the country'), so *jingjixue* actually means 'politics' or 'political science'. If someone had a talent for *jingji*, that didn't mean that he had a talent for managing the economy but one for ruling the country. When Zuo Zongtang said: 'I ask you: can you govern the country well?' (*Wen ru jingji yi he ceng?*), he was ridiculing Zeng Guofan, saying that Zeng was incapable of ruling the country.[7] So the term *jingjixue* then coined does not make sense. However, it has been used in China for a long time and become established, so there is no need to change it.

In the 1920s, the Communist University of the Toilers of the East[8] in Moscow had a course on economics, that was called *politicheskaya ekonomiya* or (for short) *politekonomiya*, which was about the economic theories of Marx. In order to distinguish between 'proletarian theories' and 'bourgeois theories', the Chinese students used the word *jingjixue* ('economics') to refer to bourgeois economics and *zhengzhi jingjixue* ('political economics') to refer to proletarian economics. This is how the term *zhengzhi jingjixue* came about. However, as our understanding deepened, we started to realise that this distinction in our translation did not make sense: our textbooks were about 'proletarian economics', but they occasionally also mentioned 'bourgeois economics', and in Russian they used the term *politicheskaya ekonomiya* for both; it did not make sense to distinguish the class character in this way, so we just translated both as *zhengzhi jingjixue*, and this is how it continues to be done to this day. I can see no reason why this should change in the future.

So what is 'political economics'? If there is 'political economics' shouldn't there also be 'apolitical economics'?

In fact, in Britain this field of study was called 'political economy' from the beginning. As in Chinese, foreign words have both a common and a specialised meaning. The word 'political' is derived from the ancient Greek *polis*, i.e. 'city-state', referring to the ancient Greek states. The word 'economy' is also derived from ancient Greek, and originally referred to the economy of a single family or

7   Zuo Zongtang (1812–1885) and Zeng Guofan (1811–72) – two Chinese military leaders and politicians. From 1850 to 1961, Zuo helped Zeng crush the Taiping Rebellion, but they often had disagreements.

8   *Kommunisticheskiy universitet trudyashchikhsya Vostoka*, KUTV. This school was originally founded in 1921 to train non-Russian cadres from within the Soviet Union, but later mostly accepted students from China and several other Asian countries, many of whom later became leading figures in communist parties in their countries. Zheng Chaolin studied at KUTV.

household.[9] When this field of study emerged in the early seventeenth century, it was not about the economy of one family or household but that of the commonalty, the economy of society, or the economy of a country, and the word 'political' was put before 'economy' to indicate that its object of research was the economy of the commonalty. Here, this attribute means 'common' or 'public', not 'political'. Back then, the experts were aware of the specific meaning of this word. At the time when Marx was writing these *Manuscripts*, the Germans called this field of study *nationale Ökonomie* or *Nationalökonomie*, i.e., 'national economics', indicating that its object of research was the economy of the commonalty, the economy within a whole country. Later, however, backward Germany gradually caught up with Britain and France, cultural exchanges became more frequent, more foreign words entered the German language, and scientific terms were often borrowed directly instead of undergoing translation, so that by the 1860s, the Germans were also using the loanword *politische Ökonomie*. When Marx published his book in 1859, he called it *Zur Kritik der politischen Ökonomie* and not *Zur Kritik der Nationalökonomie*.

Although there were two different German terms for this field of study, they meant the same thing. When the *Manuscripts* were translated into Chinese, they should not have used the term *guomin jingjixue* ('national economics'), at least not without explaining whether it had a special meaning apart from *zhengzhi jingjixue* ('political economics').

Do you need further proof that 'national economics' is the same as 'political economics?' Well, Marx in his *Manuscripts* frequently mentions Adam Smith, Jean-Baptiste Say, David Ricardo, François Quesnay, J.-C.-L. Simonde de Sismondi, Constantin Pecqueur and others; in quoting them, he calls them *Nationalökonomen* and their field of study *Nationalökonomie*.[10] Marx quotes the article that Engels published in the *Deutsch-Französische Jahrbücher* as '*Umrisse zu einer Kritik der Nationalökonomie*', but in volume 1 of the Chinese edition of the *Complete Works of Marx and Engels*, the title is translated as *Zhengzhi jingjixue pipan dagang*.[11] Are these few examples not sufficient to prove that *guomin jingjixue* ('national economics') is the same as *zhengzhi jingjixue* ('political economy'), and that the subject of both is simply *jingjixue* ('economics')? To cut a long story short, in this article I shall use the term *jingjixue* ('eco-

---

9   from *oikos* 'household' + *nemo* 'to tend'.

10   In the English translation: 'political economists' and 'political economy'.

11   As in English, '*Outlines of a Critique of Political Economy*', and in Russian (the source of many translations of Marx's and Engels's works into Chinese), *Nabroski k kritike politicheskoy ekonomii*.

nomics') and not *zhengzhi jingjixue* ('political economy') or *guomin jingjixue* ('national economics'). Now I shall now return to the topic at hand.

The Historical Background to How the Manuscripts Became So Important

We are now in a situation where the first wave of world revolution that began with the October Revolution has subsided and a second wave is yet to be seen. We are in a non-revolutionary era that began before Lenin's death. The fate of Marxism in a non-revolutionary era is always different from its fate in a revolutionary era. People start thinking that Marxism is outdated and useless, that the defeat of the revolution is a failure of Marxism. Even if they don't want to abandon Marxism completely, they want to 'revise' it or 'complement' it. Historically, there is no lack of such precedents. The most obvious are the various theoretical struggles among Marxists that took place after the defeat of the 1905 Revolution in Russia. That was a failure of revolution in just one country. Today, we are faced with a defeat of the revolution throughout the world.

What is particularly confusing is that after the tide of world revolution subsided, Stalinism emerged in Russia, the birthplace of the October Revolution. It still pretends to be 'Marxist', but its words and actions are not in line with Marxism as we know it, and its reign of terror is horrifying. At the point when Marx's *Economic and Philosophical Manuscripts of 1844* first appeared, some Marxists used them to oppose Stalinism. They thought that the 'alienation' and the 'humanism' they talk about were something new, something that had not been broached before in Marxism as they knew it. The *Manuscripts* showed them another face of Marxism. The structures that Stalin imposed and that did not conform to socialism were actually an 'alienation' from socialism; we must 'sublate' this 'alienation', and only then can socialism be restored. Marx did actually speak about 'humanism' and Stalin's terror was definitely not compatible with 'humanism', so Stalinism obviously wasn't Marxism.

Such people make a distinction between the young Marx and the mature Marx. They want to use the young Marx to transform the mature Marx; they want to advance a new explanation of historical materialism and to re-evaluate *Capital* on the basis of the *Economic and Philosophical Manuscripts of 1844*. They say that the purpose of Marx was to liberate all humankind, that his philosophy is centred on humankind, that he advocated revolution and class struggle all for the sake of humankind, that you must use the idea of 'alienation' to analyse society, etc.

Others who have made a careful study of Marx's *Manuscripts* do not at all advocate using them to transform the theories of the mature Marx, but such people are in a minority.

Others still, people who take a reactionary position and have always opposed Marxism, use these *Manuscripts* of the young Marx to oppose Marxism. This further illustrates the negative role these *Manuscripts* have played against the backdrop of this era.

This is why we cannot ignore important works of Marx from his mature period. The *Economic and Philosophical Manuscripts of 1844* themselves make clear which position they occupy within Marx's entire corpus, and why it is not possible to use them and other works by Marx from the same period to 'transform or replace the works and theories of the mature Marx'.

No Marxism yet in 1844

In 1844, there was Marx but not yet Marxism. In 1844, Marx had just turned 26 and was a young man, but he was already a prominent thinker and political activist among the youth of his generation. In the 1840s, a bourgeois revolution was brewing in Germany. At the time, bourgeois youth (with Marx and Engels among them) were committed to making revolution. At the forefront were the 'Young Hegelians'. Hegel had died ten years earlier (in 1831), but his teachings dominated German thought. Marx was too young to have attended Hegel's classes, but when he started studying at the University of Berlin, he also became a Hegelian. He originally studied law and had planned to inherit his father's law office, but inspired by Hegel, he gave up law and began studying history and philosophy. His doctoral thesis was a philosophical study based on Hegel's theories.

Hegel's doctrine was the imperial philosophy of Prussian absolutism, whose rule it defended. By the 1840s, however, his philosophy had become incompatible with the needs of the time. The revolution required above all the destruction of the barriers raised by this conservative philosophy. The ideological activities of young people could not be confined within the scope of philosophy. The fermenting revolution required criticism of actual politics. And to criticise politics, one had first to criticise religion. Religion and politics were forbidden territory for German thinkers at the time, and forbidden territory for Hegelian philosophy too. The French Enlightenment philosophy of the eighteenth century and the subsequent Great Revolution had already broken into these two forbidden territories, but in Germany the barriers remained intact. However, the forces of revolutionary ferment gradually overcame the stubborn forces of conservatism. It is strange that this theoretical revolution was born from within Prussian imperial philosophy. Among the Young Hegelians, David Friedrich Strauss and Bruno Bauer, who both studied the Christian Bible, applied textual criticism to the stories told in the four Gospels, and proved that they were all forged, and that even the existence of Jesus was questionable. Thus they basically undermined the foundations of the entire edifice of Christianity, while still using the language of Hegelian philosophy. After Strauss and Bauer came Ludwig Feuerbach. He did not indulge in textual criticism of the Bible and the abstract disputes that followed on from that, but he directly explained what Christianity was and where it came from. So he could not but abandon Hegel's idealism and turn to the materialism that had long been popular in Britain and France. In 1841, Feuerbach published his most important work, *The Essence of Christianity*.

Marx was the youngest of the Young Hegelians, but he had a high reputation. His status was not inferior to that of Bruno Bauer, their best-known representative at that time. The *Rheinische Zeitung*, launched in 1842, hired Bauer as its editor-in-chief and Marx as its deputy editor; soon afterwards, Marx became editor-in-chief. This was shortly after *The Essence of Christianity* was published. In his later years, Engels recalled the changes in their thinking at the time:

> One must himself have experienced the liberating effect of this book to get an idea of it. Enthusiasm was general; we all became at once Feuerbachians. How enthusiastically Marx greeted the new conception and how much – in spite of all critical reservations – he was influenced by it, one may read in *The Holy Family*.[12]

Engels tells us in these few sentences that in 1844, one year before the two co-authored *The Holy Family*, Marx was still a Feuerbachian: he had abandoned Hegel but remained with Feuerbach. Marx embarked on a study of economics from Feuerbach's new perspective and wrote his *Economic and Philosophical Manuscripts*. At the time, there was of course no Marxism as yet. So when did Marxism emerge? In his later years, Engels said: 'This further development of Feuerbach's standpoint beyond Feuerbach was inaugurated by Marx in 1845 in *The Holy Family*'.[13] *The Holy Family* both enthusiastically embraced Feuerbach and began to move away from Feuerbach. *The Holy Family* merely 'inaugurated' the move towards Marxism.

From this, it can be seen that it is absurd to revise and transform Marxism using research notes written by Marx when he did not yet have his own point of view, or to use them to oppose the splendid works that he wrote later, by which time Marxism had matured.

---

12   Engels 1989, p. 364.
13   Engels 1989, p. 381.

The Theory of Alienation Is a Token of Marx's Immature Period

Marx only started studying economics in Paris in 1844. He knew French at the time, but he did not understand English (rather, his English was not yet very good), so instead of reading the works of the British economists in the original, he read them in French translation.

He was, after all, no specialist and studied economics as a philosopher, a Hegelian philosopher; he also studied it because he had felt that he lacked knowledge of this field in regard to the political struggle. From the very beginning, he studied it with a critical eye. Marx abandoned Hegel's idealist system at this time, but he did not abandon Hegel's dialectics. He wanted to establish his own point of view in economics, to introduce dialectics into economics, and – in short – to criticise economics. He understood from the very beginning that economics was a field of the bourgeoisie, as he had learned from Engels' *Outlines of a Critique of Political Economy*, if he had not yet discovered it for himself. At the very beginning of the first manuscript, three large sections – 'Wages of Labour', 'Profit of Capital' and 'Rent of Land' – distinguish the three major classes of 'civil society'. This is the language of an economist. Marx first saw that the division of the three major classes had neither existed since time immemorial nor were going to exist throughout eternity. Under the heading 'Rent of Land', in addition to excerpts from the works of economists, he advanced many arguments, including his main conclusion, that 'Rent of Land' will be incorporated into 'Profit of Capital' and the landlord class will be incorporated into the class of capitalists.

However, in these *Manuscripts* Marx did not yet establish his own point of view (as he did in the later *Critique of Political Economy*). Instead, he resorted to the theory of alienation.

When he wrote these *Manuscripts*, he did not forget the argument he had had with his former close friend Bruno Bauer. In the preface to the *Manuscripts*, he attacked Bauer without naming him:

> Whereas the uninformed reviewer who tries to hide his complete ignorance and intellectual poverty by hurling the '*utopian phrase*' at the positive critic's head, or again such phrases as 'quite pure, quite resolute, quite critical criticism', the 'not merely legal but social – utterly social – society', the 'compact, massy mass', the 'outspoken spokesmen of the massy mass', this reviewer has yet to furnish the first proof that besides his theological family affairs he has anything to contribute to a discussion of worldly matters.[14]

---

14   Marx 1975, pp. 231–2.

Bruno Bauer broke into the forbidden territory of criticism of religion. He was progressive, but he confined himself to the criticism of religion, beyond which he was not able to venture even one step, and thus he failed to keep up with the times. He also dealt with questions of 'worldly affairs' or 'civil society' in a theological way – no wonder Marx despised him.

However, Marx himself, in the year that he was writing these *Manuscripts*, criticised economics using the philosophical method rather than the methods of theology.

He also said in the same Preface: '[P]ositive criticism as a whole – and there-fore also German positive criticism of political economy – owes its true found-ation to the discoveries of *Feuerbach*'.[15] This is not to say that Feuerbach wrote a work that criticises economics. It is only to say that to criticise economics, you have to take Feuerbach's philosophy as the basis. He added in the Preface: 'It is only with *Feuerbach* that *positive*, humanistic and naturalistic criticism begins'.[16] This simply meant that at the time Marx did not yet have a philosophy of his own and was criticising economics on the basis of Feuerbach's 'positive, humanistic and naturalistic' philosophy. What is so strange about this? Didn't Engels say in his old age that in those years, '[e]nthusiasm was general; we all became at once Feuerbachians'.[17] Engels also said that Marx at the time still had 'critical reservations' about Feuerbach. However 'in spite of all critical reserva-tions',[18] Marx still accepted Feuerbach's philosophy on one basic point.

One of Marx's 'critical reservations' was that he thought that Feuerbach only resolved the contradiction between God and man but not that within human society, and that he did not understand this contradiction. Marx thought that he should do the work that Feuerbach had failed to do. This was at most an admonition of Feuerbach, not a transcendence of him, for he still praised Feuerbach for resolving the contradictions between man and God and the method he had adopted to do so, namely, the theory of alienation.

Marx accused Bruno Bauer of using empty 'phrases' to 'discuss worldly mat-ters'. Marx himself had carefully and meticulously studied 'worldly matters' and their theoretical expression, economics. But in 1844, the first year of the 'inaug-uration' of his studies, he had as yet obtained no results. He had not yet grasped the methodology of research. He had to resort to the theory of alienation. Feuerbach's theory of alienation had solved the contradiction between God and man, so why shouldn't he use this theory of alienation to resolve the con-

---

15   Marx 1975, p. 232.
16   ibid.
17   Engels 1989, p. 364.
18   ibid.

traditions within 'civil society'? In the *Manuscripts*, after studying the three major classes and the three different types of 'income', he therefore devoted much space to the theory of the 'alienation of labour'. He says:

> The worker becomes all the poorer the more wealth he produces, the more his production increases in power and size. The worker becomes an ever cheaper commodity the more commodities he creates. The *devaluation* of the world of men is in direct proportion to the *increasing value* of the world of things. Labor produces not only commodities; it produces itself and the worker as a *commodity* – and this at the same rate at which it produces commodities in general.
>
> This fact expresses merely that the object which labor produces – labor's product – confronts it as *something alien*, as a *power independent* of the producer. The product of labor is labor which has been embodied in an object, which has become material: it is the *objectification* of labor. Labor's realization is its objectification. Under these economic conditions this realization of labor appears as *loss of realization* for the workers; objectification as *loss of the object and bondage to it*; appropriation as *estrangement*, as *alienation* ...
>
> All these consequences are implied in the statement that the worker is related to the *product of labor* as to an *alien* object. For on this premise it is clear that the more the worker spends himself, the more powerful becomes the alien world of objects which he creates over and against himself, the poorer he himself – his inner world – becomes, the less belongs to him as his own. It is the same in religion. The more man puts into God, the less he retains in himself.[19]

This passage is quoted from the section on estranged labour in the *Manuscripts*. There is much more in that section that is worth quoting, but there is no need at present. The original text can be found in the *Complete Works of Marx and Engels*.

From the last few sentences in the passage quoted, it is clear that Marx's theory of the alienation of labour follows Feuerbach's theory of religious alienation in all respects.

Marx also said: 'Man is a species-being' (*Gattungswesen*).[20] These are precisely the words of Feuerbach. Since man exists as a 'species', and since he lives

---

19   Marx 1975, pp. 271–2.
20   Marx 1975, p. 275.

the life of a 'species', the contradictions of the society of the human species are secondary and cannot be compared with the contradiction between God and man. Feuerbach does not deny that there are contradictions between humans, but he believes that these contradictions are accidental, not inevitable, and that the life of humans as a 'species' is harmonious. Marx's comments in the *Manuscripts* are not that much different from Feuerbach's. The alienation of labour described by Marx is neither the alienation of the labour of one person nor the alienation of the labour of one class but the alienation of the labour of the human 'species'. When describing the alienation of labour, he always talks about the alienation of the labour of 'the worker'; after emphasising that '[m]an is a species-being', he describes how 'man' comes to alienate his labour. 'The object of labor is ... the *objectification of man's species-life*'.[21] Society's class division is the result of the alienation of the labour of the human 'species'. 'An immediate consequence of the fact that man is estranged from the product of his labor, from his life activity, from his species-being, is the *estrangement of man* from *man*'.[22] That is to say, first there is the alienation of the 'species' and then there is the alienation of human from human. '[W]ithin the relationship of estranged labor each man views the other in accordance with the standard and the relationship in which he finds himself as a worker'.[23] That is to say, as a 'species-being', every human is a 'worker'.

So where do the landlords and capitalists come from? 'If the product of labor is alien to me, if it confronts me as an alien power, to whom, then, does it belong?'[24] Marx gave the answer himself: it doesn't belong to the gods and can only belong to 'man himself', 'only man himself can be this alien power over man'.[25]

This is how Marx explained the contradictions within human society. He also brought the contradiction between God and man down to the contradiction between man and man. He said that 'religious self-estrangement necessarily appears in the relationship of the layman to the priest, or again to a mediator'.[26]

Marx's 'estrangement of man from man' does not mean class struggle, but it is the result of the alienation of the labour of the human 'species'. In short, Marx at the time had not yet come to see that '[t]he history of all hitherto existing

---

21   Marx 1975, p. 277.
22   ibid.
23   Marx 1975, p. 278.
24   ibid.
25   ibid.
26   Marx 1975, p. 279.

society is the history of class struggles'.[27] This idea cannot be derived from the theory of alienation. 'Private property ... results by analysis from the concept of alienated labor, i.e., of alienated man, of estranged labor, of estranged life, of estranged man'.[28] The concept of 'private property' that Marx wrote about explains all categories of economics. He said that 'on the one hand [private property] is the *product* of alienated labor, and that on the other it is the *means* by which labor alienates itself, *the realization of this alienation*'.[29]

Marx thus thought that he had fully understood the science of economics. He concluded: 'This exposition immediately sheds light on various hitherto unsolved conflicts'.[30]

Fortunately, Marx later on discarded the conclusion he reached in the *Economic and Philosophical Manuscripts of 1844*; otherwise, he would have continued to advance it.

Had he established his critique of economics on the basis of the theory of alienation, no matter whether the whole system was right or wrong, it could not be understood, it would not be convincing, and it would be impossible for the masses to grasp.

The Mature Marx Abandoned the Theory of Alienation

In philosophy, a discourse of 'alienation' has existed since ancient times. But it was only Hegel who elevated 'alienation' to a principle and developed it to its fullest. However, there are only two instances in which the theory of alienation has been successfully applied. One is the example that Hegel himself gave. He applied the theory of alienation mainly in *The Phenomenology of Spirit* and *Science of Logic*. He set the 'absolute idea' as the ontology, and the 'absolute idea' was alienated to become nature; nature itself continues to develop and reaches the spirit through various stages. The spirit finally realises the 'absolute idea', thus sublating alienation and returning to itself. The other example is from Feuerbach, who used the essence of religion in order to criticise it. In his *Essence of Christianity*, he started from man, i.e., from man as a 'species-being', and reached the conclusion that the other world, the other side, or God, and everything that relates to god, is nothing but an alienation of the essence of man. For example, Christians use bread and wine as sacred objects during mass. After being blessed by a priest, the bread given to the believers to eat is said to be the flesh of Jesus, and the wine given to the believers to drink is said

---

27   Marx and Engels 1976, p. 482.
28   Marx 1975, p. 279.
29   Marx 1975, p. 280.
30   ibid.

to his blood. Feuerbach thinks that bread and wine are used as sacred objects simply because food and drink are indispensable material conditions of human life.

After warmly welcoming Feuerbach's doctrine, Marx went on to apply the theory of alienation to study 'civil society', and as a result wrote the *Manuscripts*. However, Marx failed in his attempt.

In 1845, just one year after writing the *Manuscripts*, Marx adopted a critical attitude towards Feuerbach. He wrote out his critique in eleven items, not for publication but for his own future use. These are the *Theses on Feuerbach* that Engels found and later published.

In the *Manuscripts* he used the concept of alienation to analyse the contradictory nature of the labour of the modern working class because he had not yet conceived the theory of surplus value. Once he discovered surplus value, he was able to explain capitalist labour more fully, and no longer had to resort to alienation.

The thesis most relevant to our discussion is the fourth:

> Feuerbach starts out from the fact of religious self-estrangement, of the duplication of the world into a religious world and a secular one. His work consist in resolving the religious world into its secular basis. But that the secular basis lifts off from itself and establishes itself as an independent realm in the clouds can only be explained by the inner strife and intrinsic contradictoriness of this secular basis. The latter must, therefore, itself be both understood in its contradiction and revolutionised in practice. Thus, for instance, once the earthly family is discovered to be the secret of the holy family, the former must then itself be destroyed in theory and in practice.[31]

This thesis affirms Feuerbach's achievements, that is, how he resolved the religious world into its secular basis. This thesis at least does not deny Feuerbach's achievement in the theory of alienation. The critique simply blames Feuerbach for not further criticising the secular basis. Compared to Engels's criticism of Feuerbach in his later years, Marx's statement here is rather superficial. This also shows that at the time Marx had only made the first step towards breaking from Feuerbach. But we can see from this thesis that Marx himself had made great progress compared to the previous year. Now he emphasises the secular basis, that is, the 'civil society' studied in economics, the 'inner strife'

---

31   Marx 1976, p. 7.

and the 'intrinsic contradictoriness', and, even more importantly, he no longer talks about 'estranged labour' and no longer uses the theory of alienation to clarify 'civil society', so it is no longer the alienation of the labour of man (as a species-being) that has produced the capitalists but the 'strife' and 'contradictoriness' between capitalists and workers that is a *fait accompli*. None of the eleven theses, except for the fourth thesis referring to Feuerbach's 'religious self-estrangement', mention 'alienation'.

Also relevant to our discussion is the sixth thesis:

> Feuerbach resolves the essence of religion into the essence of man. But the essence of man is no abstraction inherent in each single individual. In its reality it is the ensemble of social relations.
>
> Feuerbach, who does not enter upon a criticism of this real essence, is hence obliged:
>
> 1. To abstract from the historical process and to define the religious sentiment [*Gemüt*] by itself, and to presuppose an abstract – isolated – human individual.
> 2. Essence, therefore, can be regarded only as 'species', as an inner, mute, general character which unites the many individuals in a natural way.[32]

This also represents progress compared to the previous year. The previous year, when writing his *Manuscripts*, Marx had also argued that 'man is a species-being', and used this as a basis to explain the alienation of labour. He had expressed not the slightest disagreement with Feuerbach's proposition. But now he completely rejects it. This also means that he denied Feuerbach's 'humanism'. We shall explain this point in more detail later.

Engels said that these eleven *Theses* contained 'the brilliant germ of the new world outlook'.[33] Engels thought that *The Holy Family*, which Marx wrote in the same year, not only showed Feuerbach's influence on Marx but marked the beginning of Marx's development beyond Feuerbach.

The words 'inaugurate' and 'germ' indicate that in 1845, Marx had not yet formally shaped his 'new world outlook' and had not yet completely 'developed beyond' Feuerbach, but later, in cooperation with Engels, he continued to progress, completing the entire course from the old worldview of classical German philosophy to the new worldview that bears his name.

---

32   Marx 1976, pp. 7–8.
33   Engels 1990, p. 520.

As a politician and revolutionary, Marx applied 'empirical criticism' instead of simply using empty 'phrases' or abstract principles, like Bruno Bauer. He delved into the 'civil society' of his time, studied economics and socialists' theoretical reflections on that society, and uncovered 'surplus value'. This was a great discovery. Engels likened Marx's discovery of surplus value to Antoine-Laurent Lavoisier's discovery of oxygen (see the preface to Volume II of *Capital*).[34] Just imagine what modern chemistry would be like without the discovery of oxygen! Similarly, without the discovery of surplus value, the science of 'critique of economics' could not have been established. And the critique of economics could also only reach the level of the masters of utopian socialism, i.e., it could not pin down and mount a critique of the crucial points of economics, it could only resort to moral preaching about 'humanism' and 'justice' etc., and moral preaching cannot touch even a hair of economics.

After Marx thoroughly studied the various economic facts of 'civil society', he found that all commodities have a certain value. In the final analysis, they are exchanged with each other for equal value. Only one commodity is an exception: 'labour'. The value of labour is determined by the value of the means of subsistence used to produce it, that is, the labour required to produce those means of subsistence. However, capital uses wages (i.e., means of subsistence) to buy labour, which is not an equivalent exchange. Other commodities cannot add to the value of anything: only this special commodity, labour, can produce additional value. In addition to compensating for the value of the means of subsistence given by the capitalists, the workers also do unpaid work. The value created by this unpaid labour is 'surplus value'.

After the discovery of surplus value, all the controversial issues in economics can be solved, and the three major sources of income – wages, profits and land rent – as well as other economic categories have a new meaning and receive new interpretations.

It is not the theory of the alienation of labour but the theory of surplus value that 'immediately sheds light on various hitherto unsolved conflicts'.[35]

Having discovered surplus value, Marx abandoned the 'theory of alienation', at least in practice.

My conclusion may raise objections: One could argue that the alienation of labour and surplus value are not contradictory. Marx said in the *Manuscripts*: 'How, we now ask, does man come to alienate, to estrange, his labour?'[36] When

---

34   Marx 1997, p. 19.
35   Marx 1975, p. 280.
36   Marx 1975, p. 281.

Marx later discovered surplus value, he found out exactly how labour is alienated; and Marx later did not completely dismiss 'alienation', for the word 'alienation' appears in a few places in *Capital*.

This objection is untenable. It is true that I have not been able to find a clear declaration by Marx that Feuerbach's theory of alienation cannot not be applied to the study of 'civil society', in the same way that Marx declared quite clearly that Feuerbach's understanding of the nature of man as a 'species-being' was wrong. Perhaps 'alienation' is mentioned in several places in *Capital*. I don't need to present those 'few places' in *Capital* for research and explanation. I will simply say that in the *Manuscripts*, Marx mentions 'alienation' numerous times and bases his whole critique of economics on the theory of alienation, while in *Capital* there are only a few mentions of 'alienation'. He doesn't really say that 'surplus value' is a specific mode of 'alienation', does he?

More importantly, not only did Marx no longer use the theory of alienation to clarify economic questions but he dismissed Feuerbach's use of alienation to clarify religious issues. Engels in his *Ludwig Feuerbach* used Marx's historical materialism to explain religion without resorting to alienation at all, that is to say, he did not regard God as an alienation of man or God's world as an alienation of man's world. At first, however, Marx and Engels warmly welcomed Feuerbach's theory of religious alienation.

Engels said in *Ludwig Feuerbach*: 'Religion arose in very primitive times from erroneous, primitive conceptions of men about their own nature and external nature surrounding them'.[37] So religion is obviously not an 'alienation' of human nature. When primitive society gave way to class society, all classes used religion as a weapon in their struggles.

> In the Middle Ages, in the same measure as feudalism developed, Christianity grew into its religious counterpart, with a corresponding feudal hierarchy. And when the burghers began to thrive, there developed, in opposition to feudal Catholicism, the Protestant heresy, which first appeared in Southern France, among the Albigenses, at the time the cities there were in their heyday ...
>
> The ineradicableness of the Protestant heresy corresponded to the invincibility of the rising burghers. When these burghers had become sufficiently strengthened, their struggle against the feudal nobility, which till then had been predominantly local, began to assume national dimen-

---

37   Engels 1990, p. 394.

sions. The first great campaign occurred in Germany – the so-called Reformation. ...

The forcible measures of Louis XIV only made it easier for the French bourgeoisie to carry through its revolution in the irreligious, exclusively political form which alone was suited to a developed bourgeoisie. Instead of Protestants, freethinkers took their seats in the national assemblies.[38]

These words by Engels are part of an overview of Marx's historical materialism. It can be seen that Marx and Engels did not develop Feuerbach but went beyond him, and in particular abandoned Feuerbach's theory of religious alienation. Only then did Marxism come into being.

Can we not conclude from this that Marx had already abandoned the general theory of alienation?

I would never have imagined that this old tool that Marx abandoned more than one hundred years ago would, in recent years, be picked up again as a magic weapon.

On Humanism

Another tool that Marx discarded was 'humanism'. Today, some people use the word 'humanism' (which occurs in a few places in the *Manuscripts*) to advance the view that Marxism is based on 'humanism', that only later did Marxists advocate class struggle, or even that it was only Stalin who practised that kind of terror, and that all of this is a violation of Marx. Thus they use the young Marx to explain or even to transform the mature Marx. They draw their conclusions from the *Economic and Philosophical Manuscripts of 1844*.

Here are the few places in the *Manuscripts* that mention 'humanism':

A quote from the Preface: 'It is only with Feuerbach that positive, humanistic and naturalistic criticism begins'.[39] This means that 'humanistic criticism' began with Feuerbach.

A quote from the section on Private Property and Communism: 'This communism, as fully developed naturalism, equals humanism, and as fully developed humanism equals naturalism'.[40] Some people today use this sentence to claim that Marx believed that communism was the same as humanism. In fact, although Feuerbach is not mentioned here, these are still the words of Feuerbach: Feuerbach saw the human species as a part of nature, so humanism is, in the final analysis, naturalism.

---

38   Engels 1990, pp. 394–6.
39   Marx 1975, p. 232.
40   Marx 1975, p. 296.

Another quote from the same section: 'Thus society is the complete unity of man with nature – the true resurrection of nature – the accomplished naturalism of man and the accomplished humanism of nature'.[41] This means the same as the section quoted above, i.e., humanism is naturalism.

A quote from the section on Critique of Philosophy: 'Here we see how consistent naturalism or humanism is distinct from both idealism and materialism, and constitutes at the same time the unifying truth of both. We see also how only naturalism is capable of comprehending the action of world history'.[42] Here, Marx says: humanism is consistent naturalism. Here, too, it can be seen that Marx was, at the time, philosophically still a complete Feuerbachian, because Feuerbach denied that his philosophy was materialism or idealism and claimed that it was naturalism or humanism.

Another quote from the same section: '[A]theism, being the supersession of god, is the advent of theoretical humanism, and communism, as the supersession of private property, is the vindication of real human life as man's possession and thus the advent of practical humanism, or atheism is humanism mediated with itself through the supersession of religion, whilst communism is humanism mediated with itself through the supersession of private property'.[43] Here, too, 'humanism' is raised to the level of a philosophical principle, and it is a philosophical principle of Feuerbach.

These are all the sections of the Manuscripts that mention 'humanism' (if I haven't missed any). From all of these passages we can see that Marx takes 'humanism' as a philosophical principle, as a philosophical principle that is on the same level as idealism and materialism. In the Chinese translation of the *Complete Works of Marx and Engels*, the word *rendao zhuyi* is used to translate this term. Is that an appropriate translation? The common understanding of this word in China is that it means compassion, mercy, saving lives, treating people humanely, and so on. In short, in our language, *rendao zhuyi* is understood as a virtue, as a property of ethics.

I happen to have the original German version of the *Economic and Philosophical Manuscripts of 1844*. I searched for the German original of the word that is translated into Chinese as *rendao zhuyi*. In German it is *Humanismus*. The term *Humanismus* also has other Chinese equivalents, namely *renwen zhuyi* and *renben zhuyi*. These terms refer to a trend of thought that emerged during the Renaissance and advocated a human-centred approach as opposed to the medieval god-centred approach to issues. This trend emerged at the

---

41   Marx 1975, p. 298.
42   Marx 1975, p. 336.
43   Marx 1975, p. 341.

time of the development of capitalism and finally took shape as the French Enlightenment in the eighteenth century. It encompassed various tendencies and factions, the common basis being that it was human-centred. Generally speaking, Feuerbach's philosophy can be classified as part of *Humanismus*, but it did have its particularities. His philosophy played a prominent role in the history of philosophy, not just because of its generality but because of its particularity. Feuerbach himself would call his philosophy *Anthropologismus*, a word derived from the Greek root *anthropos*, while *Humanismus* comes from a Latin root. Both roots mean 'person', so *Anthropologismus* is *Humanismus*. Feuerbach preferred the former in order to highlight the fact that his philosophy is different from general 'humanism'. Feuerbach particularly emphasised that 'man is a species-being'. In order to make that distinction, I use the word *Anthropologismus*, which should be translated into Chinese as *renlei zhuyi*.

Naturally, the idea of *Humanismus* that took off in the Renaissance was also translated as *rendao zhuyi*. As a literal translation, this is not wrong, but given the usual meaning of this word in Chinese, it is not appropriate.

As a result, the 'humanism' in Marx's *Manuscripts* (assuming that *rendao zhuyi* is an inappropriate translation) cannot be used to counter Stalin's terror. Using humanism in its common Chinese meaning to counter Stalinist terror is weak and ineffective.

Marxists did not oppose the Red Terror of 1793 in France or the Red Terror of 1918 in Russia, because it advanced history. However, they opposed the White Terror that followed the Thermidor after the revolutions in France and in Russia, as instances of historical reaction.

In 1845, two years after he had written the *Manuscripts*, Marx clearly abandoned Feuerbach's 'anthropologism' or 'humanism' in his *Theses on Feuerbach*. Marx criticised Feuerbach's philosophy, saying that he resolved the essence of religion into the essence of man, but he regarded the essence of man as an abstraction inherent in each single individual and had failed to understand that it is the ensemble of social relations. So Feuerbach erroneously assumed an abstract and isolated human individual, and he erroneously assumed the essence of man as 'species', an internally voiceless and undifferentiated commonality.

After rejecting the idea that 'man is a species-being', how can anybody continue to talk about 'humanism?'

This so-called 'humanism' that is currently on everyone's lips is being used by people out to transform or complement the Marxism that was established by Marx in his mature period.

Conclusion

It cannot be denied that today Marxism is in crisis, we are in a period in which all kinds of 'Marxism' appear and all kinds of strange 'theories' are propounded. Some people want to supplement Marx, to transform Marx, to use the young Marx to reject the mature Marx, and so on. For the time being, I can see no way out of this crisis.

But the crisis must be resolved, and to resolve it, we must rely on Marxism.

First, there is a crisis of Marxism only because we are in a trough between two waves in world revolution. We have ridden for too long in this trough and cannot see the masthead above the next wave. But we can only use Marxism to study and explain why this ebb has persisted for such a long time.

Second, during this prolonged period of ebb, the established capitalist countries have not only been stable but are even prospering. It is said that the inventions of science and technology during the two decades either side of the mid-1970s surpassed those of the previous two thousand years. This, too, can only be studied and explained using Marxism. During the same period, a series of self-styled 'socialist' countries have been coexisting peacefully with established capitalist countries and have also enjoyed stability, prosperity, and technological development. This, too, can only be studied and explained using Marxism. These phenomena are related to the prolonged ebb, and may determine the way in which the second wave of world revolution arrives.

Finally, the second revolutionary wave will inevitably raise doubts. When the time comes, a new way must be taken, a new way must be proposed, and new questions must be asked. Not only when the time comes, but now – we must affirm the fundamental principles of Marxism, and we must also examine whether certain non-fundamental principles are out of date and need amending. Amending certain non-fundamental outdated principles will not harm Marxism. In 1872, a quarter century after the *Communist Manifesto* was written, the two authors of the *Manifesto* wrote a preface to the new German edition of the *Manifesto* in which, apart from affirming that 'the general principles laid down ... are, on the whole, as correct today as ever', also announced that some details might be improved and that 'this programme has in some details become antiquated'.[44]

Partially revising some basic principles in accordance with changes in the objective situation is part of the actual meaning of Marxism. However, to understand clearly the arguments that Marx advanced during the explorations of his youth, arguments that he himself later discarded, and then to pick up

---

44   Marx and Engels 1988 pp. 174–5.

these arguments in order to revise the theoretical system that Marx established during his mature period, i.e., the system of Marxism – that is not permissible.

What is 'alienation'? What causes 'alienation'? There has been no convincing explanation. There is no need to explain Hegel's use of 'alienation'. He said that the 'absolute idea' was alienated to become nature, and nobody demanded that he explain how the 'absolute idea' can be 'alienated' to become nature because nobody asked what the 'absolute idea' is. Later, Engels asked where the 'absolute idea' can be found. When Marx and Engels were 'young Hegelians', they would not have asked that question. How strange it is that an abstract thing 'abstractly' changes into an 'alienated thing'. But Feuerbach said: if man alienates to become God, then you have to explain why a natural thing would 'alienate' into a non-natural thing. But at the time Feuerbach's 'theory of alienation' caused classical Germen philosophy to make the transition from idealism to materialism, it functioned as a 'liberation', so there is no need to study this in depth. Later, Engels abandoned the theory of 'religious alienation' and used historical materialism to explain how religion emerged and developed. In 1844, Marx used the theory of 'alienation' to explain the contradictions of 'civil society', so it was even more necessary for him to explain why labour is 'alienated'. Marx continued his research and discovered surplus value, and at that point he abandoned his theory of the 'alienation of labour'.

'Humanism' – i.e., *rendao zhuyi*, the usual translation of this word in Chinese – is even less settled. The 'humanism' mentioned in Marx's *Manuscripts* would be best translated as *renwen zhuyi, renben zhuyi*, or *renlei zhuyi*, that is, 'humanism' as a worldview. The *Manuscripts* do not talk about 'humanism' as ethics. Marxists never advocate cruelty against people, disregarding people's suffering, or treating people as anything less than human. However, in a class society, Marxists attach great importance to class struggle. For the benefit of the vast majority of people, minority reaction can be suppressed, and in order to extend benevolence to the majority, the reactionary minority can be treated ruthlessly. This idea does not violate 'humanism' as an ethical concept. As for 'humanism' as a worldview, Marx abandoned it a year after he had written the *Manuscripts*, when he criticised Feuerbach.

To sum up, using the theory of 'alienation' and 'humanitarianism' to oppose Stalinism is weak and ineffective. To describe as 'alienation under socialism' phenomena such as cadres enjoying privileges and using their positions for personal gain, the absence of laws that you can rely on or the presence of laws that you cannot rely on, individuals shirking their responsibility and people condemned to powerlessness, you would first have to determine that the social system established under Stalinism is 'socialism'. As for 'humanism': even if the 'humanism' that Marx talks about in his *Manuscripts* actually is some kind of ethical 'humanism', it would still be pointless, for the Stalinists could not care less about that idea.

During this revolutionary ebb, we must prepare revolutionary theories for the inevitable second wave of world revolution. There is much to be done. Clarifying the ideological confusion caused by the publication of Marx's *Economic and Philosophical Manuscripts of 1844* is part of that work.

CHAPTER 10

Reflections on the 1989 Tian'anmen Incident (June 20, 1989)

Translated by Tsim Shum Kow, edited and introduced by Owen Miller

Editor's Introduction

Zheng Chaolin wrote this article two weeks after the violent suppression of the Tiananmen uprising in June 1989. He had been out of prison for 10 years and China's 'reform and opening' process had been proceeding for even longer. Zheng was 87 and living in Shanghai, but he was as politically engaged with current events as he had ever been. As he emphasises in the opening lines of this article, his aim, as ever, was to understand the current events and, ultimately, to point the way forward for fellow Communists. Naturally the article itself was never published in the PRC, though it was eventually published in Hong Kong in 1998 by Cosmos Books.

The analysis in the article is built upon ideas Zheng had developed over four decades, both in and out of prison. Key among these ideas are the concept of a 'cadre class' or bureaucratic ruling class, which had de facto ownership of the means of production, and the idea of the 'Stalinist model of capitalism', which at other times Zheng referred to as 'state capitalism'. These concepts allow Zheng to place the events of June 1989 within the context of broader processes that had been happening in the 'socialist' bloc since the Second World War and within the even broader context of capitalist society as a whole.

In the first part of the article, Zheng explains what he means by the Stalinist model of capitalism: a society that cannot be socialist because there are still commodities, classes and states, and workers' democracy is non-existent. Instead, the 'cadre class' of high officials is firmly in control of the means of production. He emphasises – and this is a theme of the whole article – that the Stalinist version of capitalism has fallen decisively behind the 'traditional' form of capitalism because it is less efficient, although he does not expand on exactly why this might be. The fact that Stalinist capitalism is losing in the competition with traditional capitalism means that reforms and economic liberalisation are unavoidable in China and in countries such as the Soviet Union and Poland. This gives rise to the contradiction that Zheng places at the centre of his analysis: political reforms have lagged behind economic ones because the ruling 'cadre class' has been unwilling to share political power with the new private capitalists. But the logic of the economic reforms leads to popular demands for political reforms, reforms that will erode the very basis for the survival of the cadre class. Zheng then poses the question: 'Can it [the Chinese ruling class] find a solution to this fundamental contradiction?'

With the benefit of hindsight we can say, more than thirty years on, that the Chinese ruling class has found a way to solve this contradiction, even if the solution is improvised and fundamentally unstable. China's hybrid form of capitalism is now hugely wealthier and more complex than at the time Zheng was writing, and the new Chinese working class has begun to demonstrate its power; but private capitalists have not demanded full democratic rights and the CCP has remained firmly in control. Zheng himself may not have predicted this but his insights into the current situation would no doubt be as penetrating as those he provides in this article.

One further aspect of this article is worthy of note from our current perspective. Zheng sees the period during which he is writing as the 'nadir' between two waves of international socialist revolution; a first wave that came to an end with the defeat of the Chinese Revolution in 1927 and a second wave that is yet to come. While Zheng's temporal perspective on socialist revolution is impressively long, from our perspective in the third decade of the twenty-first century it is hard to know whether the nadir has yet been reached. There have been many false dawns for the global advocates of a truly Communist society, including the fall of the Stalinist states that came so soon after Zheng wrote this article; but, as yet, the 'second wave' has not begun. Perhaps we can draw strength from Zheng's conviction that, however long it takes, the next wave of international socialist revolution will come, simply because the crises of capitalism are many and irremediable.

Translation source: *Shishi yu huiyi*, vol. 2, pp. 375–84.

Reflections on the 1989 Tian'anmen Incident

There is a famous line from Spinoza: 'Do not weep. Do not wax indignant. Understand'. So many people have quoted it that it has become a cliche. But I still need to quote it today because it is particularly relevant to this article. Witnessing this still ongoing revolution, we cannot laugh of course. However, grieving is of no use to the thousands of lives that have been sacrificed. The most important task is to understand: why did this revolution happen? Was it inevitable? What are the consequences now it has failed?

1.   *The World Has Two Models of Capitalism*

Today's world belongs to capitalism. There are many backward countries or regions where pre-capitalist social formations still exist, but these societies have already been dominated by capitalism and will be completely assimilated to the capitalist system sooner or later. Apart from these social formations, there are around ten self-acclaimed 'socialist' countries within which capitalism has been, according to them at least, eliminated. The fact is, however, these nation-states are just a different form of capitalism. Socialism has not yet appeared anywhere in the world.

For the sake of distinction, let's name these ten or so countries 'Stalinist capitalist states' and the rest 'traditional capitalist states'.

Why are these Stalinist countries not 'socialist'? According to Marx's definition in *Critique of the Gotha Programme* and Lenin's identical definition in *State and Revolution*, socialist society has no commodities, commodity exchange, classes, or states. When Stalin declared that the Soviet Union had achieved 'socialism', or when Leonid Brezhnev pronounced that the Soviet Union had reached the stage of 'advanced socialist society', or when Mikhail Gorbachev proclaimed 'the primary stage of socialist society', the term 'socialism' does not coincide with Marx and Lenin's original definition. The same criticism can be applied to China's declaration that it has achieved the 'primary stage of socialist society'.

If we take one step back, can we say the Stalinist model (Stalinism) is neither socialism nor capitalism, but a transitional period between capitalism and socialism? No. Although Lenin once stated that the transitional stage contains both socialist and capitalist elements, the regime during this stage must be a dictatorship of proletariat which sees the gradual expansion of socialism while capitalism diminishes to its eventual demise. Seen from the present, the regimes of the Stalinist countries are hardly dictatorships of proletariat; on the contrary, their capitalist elements, instead of diminishing, grow day after day.

If it is neither a socialist nor a transitional state, it must be capitalism.

From a Marxist perspective, if state monopolies continue to grow, at a certain point the Stalinist form of economy would appear. That is, a minority of capitalists in a given country could join forces to take over the state and nationalise the entirety of the means of production in the name of the state. This system is still capitalism but not far away from socialist revolution. This is the result of the progress made by capitalism. However, today's Stalinist system is a result of an ebbing international revolution and the compromises made by an economically backward Russia where a socialist revolution took place, and nationalisation of the means of production as well as a transitional system was implemented. The state claims to be 'a dictatorship of the proletariat' but is, in fact, a dictatorship of a section of the population, the cadre group (or class). It is claimed that the means of production are owned 'collectively' but actually they are owned by this cadre group (or class).

The Stalinist model of capitalism, in its early period before WWII, was still efficient enough to compete with the traditional model of capitalism or even surpass it, for which reason it was seen as 'socialism'. However, after WWII, the situation changed. The Stalinist system could no longer keep up with the traditional capitalist system.

2.   *The Fundamental Contradictions of Countries under the Stalinist Form of Capitalism*

Countries under the Stalinist form of capitalism began to put forward 'reforms' as they lagged far behind the traditional capitalist countries in terms of economic efficiency. The first item proposed was naturally economic reform, that is, how to surpass traditional capitalism in economic efficiency. This meant switching from a closed economy to an open one; respecting the law of value; producing and exporting commodities to compete in the world market; attracting foreign investment; abolishing some collective property and expanding some private ownership. The last ten years of reform in China have been exactly within this range. It is undeniable that the Chinese economy has grown and people's lives have improved during this decade.

However, according to historical materialism, economy, politics and ideology are tied together. In the ten years of Chinese economic reform, we cannot say politics and ideology did not change at all, but compared to economic reforms, change in this area was minimal and therefore insufficient. This is exactly where the problem lies. Policymakers were aware that in order to achieve economic growth, it was necessary to sacrifice part of the vested interests and tolerate private capitalists sharing in the profits brought by 'collective' property. Nevertheless, they did not know that, in order to further economic development, it is necessary to implement political and ideological reforms: that is, to share their political power with the private capitalists. Maybe they were conscious of this issue but still chose to maintain the dictatorship and further delay political reform. This possibly endangered the very existential basis of their social group or class, because they were not willing to concede their long reign as the single dominant power over other classes.

Political reforms (as well as ideological reforms) must be carried out along with economic reform, sometimes even before it. For example, in Gorbachev's Soviet Union, the economic reforms were not as thorough as China but the political reforms were ahead of China's. Whether the political reform can proceed smoothly, then, depends on the actual struggle.

Here lies a fundamental contradiction found in all the Stalinist countries. Today, these countries are all in desperate situations, and thus reforms are imminent. First of all, reform means abolishing the Stalinist model and (re)adopting the traditional model of capitalism. Reforms were first carried out in the realm of economy. However, at a certain point, it is necessary to incorporate political reforms into the economic ones. After political reforms, there is no turning back: it is no longer enough to partially restore private ownership, it is now necessary to privatise all the remaining so called 'common property'. The reforms, in effect, destroyed the basis of existence for that particular social group or class discussed above. This class emerged under the Stalinist model of capitalism, without which it becomes a tree without its root or a river without its source. It will struggle to survive no matter what it does. Today, it has to reform only to the degree that it does not risk its very survival. It is now exploring the extent of this limit. Can it find this borderline? Can it find a solution to this fundamental contradiction?

Chinese policymakers thought economic reform without political reform would provide a solution. Economic reform can be furthered, which means privatising more state enterprises. Political reform, on the other hand, is stalled at the stage of empty slogans like 'democratisation' without any real reforms materialising. However, the current political reform, from the objective requirements reflected by the masses, can no longer remain at the stage of minor compromises or empty slogans concerning democratisation. Today, after ten years of economic reform in China, the necessary political reform is a change 'from a one party to a multi-party system'. But this is something that is not accepted by the ruling social group.

The multi-party system, party politics, and parliamentary elections are the peak of traditional capitalism as they are in congruence with the system. This does not mean traditional capitalism can only have this form of democratic politics. In history and in actuality, we have seen examples of despotism and dictatorship: from Mussolini's Italy and Hitler's Germany, to Marcos's Philippines and Park Chung-hee's South Korea. However, these are, after all, not conventional. In an ordinary setting, in order to build a traditional capitalist economy, orthodox capitalist politics, that is, parliamentary democracy, needs to be established. This democracy should certainly be a 'capitalist democracy', in other words, this means the 'liberalisation of the capitalist class'. But in China, on the one hand, reform and development of a commodity economy, that is, implementation of capitalist economy, is required; while on the other, the 'liberalisation of the capitalist class' is opposed. This brings to mind the Chinese proverb: 'to expect a horse to run fast and without feeding it'.

Here, I would like to raise another issue. The term 'Socialist Democracy' is very popular now. However, just like the term 'socialist commodity economy', this phrase itself does not make sense. What on earth is a 'socialist commodity economy'? There is no such thing as 'socialist democracy' either. The concept of 'socialism' includes 'democracy' therefore there is no need to flag democracy as a separate category. Could there be such a thing as 'undemocratic socialism'? If people living under a self-proclaimed 'socialist' system still demand 'democracy' it can mean only one thing; that this so-called 'socialism' is a sham, a counterfeit. Struggling for socialism is the same as fighting for democracy. The Stalinist countries are exactly this kind of fake and counterfeit 'socialism', a system that refuses to give in or pains itself to allow democracy. This demonstrates that this type of society is divided into classes; an exploitative ruling class and an exploited ruled class.

In a genuine rather than counterfeit socialist society, why would so many people demand a multi-party system, competitive elections, and freedom of speech and association? Today, the demands that people raise are, of course, for a capitalist democracy and the liberalisation of the capitalist class.

What the Chinese people are now demanding is precisely this kind of democracy and freedom. What China's rulers are refusing to hand over is exactly this kind of democracy and freedom.

The fundamental contradiction China's rulers are dealing with right now is this: since the Stalinist model of capitalism no longer works, adaptation to traditional capitalism is unavoidable. However, once the transition to traditional capitalism goes past a certain point, that is, once the advice of economists about restoring private ownership has been followed and the people's demands for a multi-party system have been accepted, the foundations of the social class they represent will be lost. This June Revolution erupted from this fundamental contradiction.

3.   *Relevant Examples from the Reforms in Hungary and Poland*
Now that the revolution has been violently suppressed, does this mean the fundamental contradiction is solved? That is to say, that the ruling group, from now on, can continue to exist as the economy grows? Can violence provide any solutions to fundamental problems?

Engels wrote three chapters on 'Force' in *Anti-Dühring*, which explore the historical function of 'force':

> [A]fter the political force has made itself independent in relation to society, and has transformed itself from its servant into its master, it can work in two different directions. Either it works in the sense and in the dir-

ection of the natural economic development, in which case no conflict arises between them, the economic development being accelerated. Or it works against economic development, in which case, as a rule, with but few exceptions, force succumbs to it.[1]

The Chinese authorities have resorted to violence to crack down on the masses demanding democracy. Is this consistent with economic development, or against economic development? We should, of course, 'settle accounts after the autumn harvest'.[2] Let's see if the use of force is accelerating the economy or is itself crushed by economic pressures. Using a similar methodology to Engels, let's try to predict the future.

Among the dozen or so Stalinist countries, China is not the first one to suppress people's democratic demands with violence. In the autumn of 1956, as Hungarian and Polish people had already realised the Stalinist regime was bankrupt, they demanded reforms – first of all, political reforms, in other words, democracy. The Polish uprising in Poznań was soon crushed. The Hungarians instigated an even larger scale uprising, leading to paralysis in the Hungarian army, which was unable to crackdown on the protests. The masses then established a revolutionary regime headed by Imre Nagy, which was crushed by the Soviet military. A leader from the Hungarian Communist Party then took over the government from the Soviet military while Nagy was arrested and executed. Janos Kadar, who was only recently deposed, ruled Hungary for 33 years with the support of the Soviet army. Force did succeed in suppressing revolutions in Poland and Hungary but it did not solve the underlying problems. Poland has been in a mess until now, while Hungary under Kadar experimented with reform and some traditional forms of capitalism early on, which caught the world's attention. However, the reforms were restricted to economics with the country remaining Stalinist politically and this led to the failure of economic reform. In recent years, among all the voices demanding reform in Stalinist countries, only the Polish and the Hungarians learnt the lesson of the 1956 revolution: political reform is indispensable. In these two countries, there was also a social group that dominated the regime and rejected the multiparty system, but then realised that the multi-party system cannot be avoided. Without political reforms, the economy will not advance, which means the state will ultimately fall into bankruptcy, and the cadre group will not be able

---

1 Engels, 2010 [1878] p. 170.
2 A Chinese idiom. Here its meaning is double-edged. In the first instance, it means appraising an event's aftermath; in the second, it obscurely refers to the incessant crackdown all over the country following the main events on Tian'anmen Square in Beijing.

to maintain its system of collective ownership. Under popular pressure, Communist parties in these two countries had to acknowledge the multi-party system. A Hungarian Communist Party leader made the promise that the party would stay out of office if it failed in future elections while the Polish Communist Party acknowledged that it had lost the elections and agreed to stay in office with the opposition party.

This reflects what Engels said, force that violates economic development, will eventually collapse.

4.   'Opportunist Officials'[3]

As has been noted above, the fundamental paradox currently confronting China, along with the other dozen or so Stalinist countries, is that on the one hand it has to abolish the Stalinist model of capitalism and implement traditional capitalism while on the other it has to limit these reforms so that the ruling class supported by the Stalinist model will not lose the basis for its own existence. Transition to a different model of capitalism is necessary for economic development. In the current situation, further economic development actually requires even more thorough reforms of the economic model, in short, it is now necessary to restore private ownership as well as multi-party politics. This is where the obstacle lies: since the ruling group refuses to proclaim its own death sentence, there is no way out. The question of the moment is: is it economic development that determines the survival of the class or the other way around?

As Marxism has taught us, productive forces determine productive relations, with some exceptions in certain situations where productive relations can interfere with the productive forces and obstruct their development. In other words, a revolution is bound to occur. Revolutions are prone to fail but will eventually overcome the obstacles and clear the way.

The Chinese ruling class defeated the revolution this time, but it still needs to reform and continues to set a limit to reforms in order to secure its own existence. Will they eventually be able to find the right limit line between reform and the status quo?

The cadre group will strive to maintain its existence and not allow the reforms to cross this line of life and death. But would the ruling class realise if its line of defence were to be breached? Surely it must have realised what

---

3   The original Chinese word is *guandao*, a term that emerged in the reform of the 1980s. It refers to politicians or people with a political background manipulating this advantage for economic purposes and private gain. During the protests in 1989, 'down with opportunist officials' was a major slogan.

will happen to it if it fully restores private ownership and liberalises the capitalist class. When that happens, those who are in power today will cease to exist as a class. However, they will continue to exist as individuals, who can even remain in power on the condition that they also become members of the capitalist class, based on private ownership. Thus, they have to 'get ready for the rainy day',[4] that is, they have to try to acquire as much as they can while the current so-called 'collective' ownership system[5] is in the process of collapsing.

There are some historical examples of this. Primitive communist society, which was based on real collective ownership, grew economically to the degree that it had to adopt private ownership. The first group that owned private property was precisely those who were in power in the primitive commune: the chief of the clan, the leaders of the army and other people with influence. They 'abused their authority for personal gain'; they made personal gains during the process of the reform.

In late feudal society, there had long been a system of private ownership. However, there were also some remnants of public ownership. Everyone in a village had the right to use the common property of the village, such as forests, pastures, fishponds and rivers, regardless of their social status as landlords or peasants. As the commodity economy developed, these common lands became valuable and thus landlords and churches, in short, whoever had power in the village, sought to 'abuse their authority for personal gain' and take possession of the commons while prohibiting other villagers from using them.

Although private property had existed for thousands of years in China, public property never disappeared and collective ownership was preserved in some cases: for instance in the form of common clan property, common temple property, guild property, the property of benevolent associations and other similar organisations. These sorts of organisations were administered either by someone elected from the clan or group or in some cases everyone took a turn in administration, providing periodical accounting reports to the collective. As this form of collective property gradually disappeared, it was these administrators and influential people in the collective who gained the most. They were again 'abusing their authority to make personal gains'.

By citing these examples, I am not saying the privatisation in today's Stalinist countries is the same as what happened to the remnants of collective ownership in primitive or feudal societies. However, the transition from pub-

---

4 A Chinese idiom meaning to get ready or take measures for when a disaster occurs.
5 De facto ownership by the cadre group or bureaucracy.

lic ownership to private is the same, and, in both cases, the people already in power have always acquired the most during this transition.

There are many people discussing 'opportunist officials', but none from the perspective that these 'opportunist officials' are mainly the relatives or children of high ranking officials or even high officials themselves. In short, they are influential or powerful figures in the ruling class. They realise that Stalinist capitalism will eventually concede its throne to traditional capitalism, that is, private ownership will inevitably be restored. When that happens, law abiding and righteous cadres will never be able to compete with capitalists, old and new. Thus it is necessary to gather and scavenge enough capital for the future while they are still in positions of power.

Marx's *Capital* is about how capitalists use their capital to extract surplus value from workers and then expand their capital through accumulated surplus value. This all takes place according to economic laws. But where does the initial capital come from? Is it accumulated 'fairly' according to economic laws? No. Marx wrote a chapter on primitive accumulation in the first volume of *Capital* in which he showed that capitalists' initial accumulation of capital was never done 'fairly' following economic laws, but through violence, fraud and other non-economic and 'unfair' means. As Marx states, the accumulation of initial capital is 'written in the annals of mankind in letters of blood and fire'.[6]

I do not mean that China is still at the stage of primitive accumulation today. Rather, what I want to say is that, in the coming traditional model of capitalist society, the capital gathered by the 'profiteers' has indeed been written in the annals of China's last ten years with 'letters of blood and fire'.

5.   *The International Climate*

When we think about today's 'international climate', we can say: today is the nadir between two waves of international revolution. The first international revolution began with the victory of the 1917 Russian Revolution and ended with the defeat of the Chinese revolution in 1927. The second wave of international revolution has not yet arrived and when it will arrive is unknown. But it will certainly come.

We can only speculate about the 'climate' at this nadir of world revolution. This 'climate' is: two different models of capitalism (the traditional and Stalinist models of capitalism) coexist, compete with each other, and struggle

---

6   Marx, *Capital* vol. I, chapter 26. (https://www.marxists.org/archive/marx/works/1867-c1/ch26
      .htm)

against each other. The winner has now been revealed: the Stalinist system has failed. The self-proclaimed 'socialist' countries, one after another, have abandoned the Stalinist-style economy and restored the traditional economic system, however, they have done this without a willingness to give up Stalinist politics. This is where the dilemma lies and where the whole 'unrest' originates. Is this 'unrest' or 'rioting' being spread unintentionally? This depends on whether decision makers learn anything from history. Polish and Hungarian decision makers were originally not willing to abandon Stalinist politics but the lessons of 1956 forced them to agree to a multi-party system this year. This recent 'unrest' in China was clearly the result of not learning from the historical examples of other countries.

The Hungarian 'riot' of 1956 is recognised as a 'people's revolution' by the Hungarian government today. This current 'riot' in China is also a 'people's revolution' and will be recognised as such by future Chinese policy makers. However, this kind of revolution is not part of an international wave of socialist revolution but a revolution of traditional capitalism replacing Stalinist capitalism.

In the traditional capitalist countries, there is also unrest and even rioting, but only among those countries that are lagging behind, in Latin America, the Middle East and southern Africa. There is no unrest the in developed countries.

This is not to say capitalism is immortal. Capitalism has developed from the stage of monopoly to state monopoly, then to the stage of transnational corporations. Crisis is permanently embedded in the capitalist system. Economists have tried many methods to save it from its demise, but they only provide temporary solutions. Capitalism will eventually be replaced by socialism. When advanced capitalist countries start to revolt, it means that the second wave of international revolution is beginning.

But for now, in a situation where two models of capitalism coexist, the traditional model, no matter how crisis-prone it is, is still better than the Stalinist model. The Stalinist economic system has gone bankrupt while the traditional capitalist economy can still generate new productive forces. We have seen several examples of divided nation-states, with the Stalinist model on the one side and the traditional model on the other. When they are compared, one side develops slowly or not at all while the other develops rapidly.

Both models are capitalism, so why insist on a failed model and refuse the successful one? The 'model' I am referring to here includes both economic and political aspects. Clinging to Stalinist politics, while practising the traditional model of capitalism, will ultimately bring unrest and revolts.

All the above is said to those in power. As for people who advocate for international socialist revolution, for Communists, something else should be said. We believe – not the kind of belief based on faith but that supported by scientific analysis – that a new wave of international socialist revolution will inevitably come. A new society is bound to arise, with neither commodity production nor monetary transactions, neither class nor state. We need to prepare for this revolution; and in the meantime, we must participate in the current struggles and fight for the interests of the exploited and the oppressed.

June 20, 1989

CHAPTER 11

The October Revolution, Thermidor, and the Stalinist Mode of Capitalism (1991)

Translated by Yang Yang

Translator's Introduction

Zheng Chaolin developed his ideas on the nature of the 'socialist' states that emerged in the aftermath of the October Revolution over a period of decades. In his 1950 pamphlet *On State Capitalism* he characterised both the Soviet Union and the new CCP regime in China as state capitalist. Forty-one years later following the collapse of the Soviet Union and its East European clones he reexamined his views and wrote the paper we publish here.

In his 1950 pamphlet Zheng described four stages of capitalism – merchant capitalism, industrial capitalism, finance capitalism and state capitalism. He believed that Stalinist Russia was a state capitalist society in which private property continued to exist but was collectively owned by a new ruling class of bureaucrats. Their relationship to this property might be compared with that of the medieval Catholic clergy to the Church's wealth. At this time, we should remember, Zheng believed state capitalism was a more advanced form than finance capitalism. China's 'New Democracy' was simply a new edition of the Soviet system. The victory of the CCP over the Guomindang confirmed his view that state capitalism represented the latest and highest form of capitalism.

Zheng did not agree with the Menshevik view that the October Revolution took place too soon. But he also differed from Chinese comrades who, following Trotsky, maintained that the Soviet Union and China were deformed workers' states. His views at this time resembled those of Tony Cliff and Max Shachtman.

Inside and out of prison, Zheng continued to study world events and in 1991 he systematically recorded his reflections on the dramatic collapse of the Soviet Union and the East European 'socialist' states. He insisted that the collapse did not signify the failure of socialism since these states had never been socialist. In his *A Self-Description at the Age of Ninety*, he reflected:

> Seventy years ago, one process took place; now, seventy years later, the opposite process has taken place. What does this fact signify? Most say that it is an expression of the bankruptcy of socialism. But that is wrong.

It is merely an expression of the bankruptcy of Stalinism, of the doctrine of socialism in one country. We Trotskyists alone in the world have dared – and with justification – to reach this conclusion, for we alone over the last several decades have maintained that socialism cannot be built in one or a few countries. We have never conceded that the system realised in the Soviet Union or the other 'socialist states' is socialist.[1]

But the collapse of 1991 also forced him to reexamine his earlier belief that state capitalism represented a higher and more advanced form of capitalism than finance capitalism. After all, an earlier, more traditional form of capitalism had triumphed over the supposedly more advanced form. At the age of 91, he set out to retrace the history of Stalinist state capitalism from its origin in the aftermath of the October Revolution to its eventual demise. After re-reading Lenin, Trotsky and Luxemburg and observing the events of the late 1980s and early 1990s, he developed his own views as to how the Stalinist model emerged and why it eventually collapsed.

Like his fellow Chinese Trotskyists Wang Fanxi and Peng Shuzhi, Zheng never conceded that the October Revolution was wrong or undertaken prematurely. He remained convinced that it was an opportunity to initiate a world socialist revolution.

Zheng compared the performance of the two competing modes of capitalism – the traditional mode of capitalism in the advanced Western countries and the Stalinist mode of capitalism in the Eastern so-called 'socialist' countries. He concluded that in different periods each model may outstrip the other. During the cyclical downturn of the Great Depression, the Stalinist model outperformed the Western model. But during the huge expansion of the world market following the Second World War, the West left the Stalinist states far behind. Zheng offered the following explanation for this outcome.

He recognised that the post-war boom had demonstrated that he and his Trotskyist comrades had seriously underestimated the complexity and vitality of traditional capitalism and its potential for renewal. He attributed the boom to capitalism's ability to incorporate previously pre-capitalist formations into the world market under the new regime of neo-colonialism. This process would of course reach a limit as pre-capitalist formations were eliminated. Nevertheless, he was not afraid to draw the conclusion that Trotskyism's key doctrine – the permanent revolution – would be a much longer-term prospect than previously envisioned. The world socialist revolution would not be the result of a

---

1   See Appendix in this volume.

single upsurge but would inevitably pass through a series of high and low tides before finally succeeding.

In this series of waves, Zheng regarded the restoration of traditional capitalism in the former so-called 'socialist states', as an ebb tide, not a high tide. It was certainly not the second wave of socialist revolution he and his comrades had hoped for and expected. It was famously celebrated by Francis Fukuyama as 'the end of history' and the final victory of capitalism. Zheng naturally did not agree with Fukuyama, but he saw the collapse as a setback of the sort that socialists would repeatedly face in a protracted struggle for global proletarian revolution.

The October Revolution, Thermidor, and Stalinist Mode of Capitalism is the result of four decades of unremitting theoretical study of state capitalism that draws conclusions on the fate of that system as well as that of traditional capitalism. It also reflects Zheng's life-long belief in world socialist revolution and his conviction that a new revolutionary wave revolution will inevitably sweep the world.

Translation source: Zheng Chaolin, *Shishi yu huiyi* (History and recollections), vol. II, Hongkong: tiandi tushu youxian gongsi. pp. 399–420.

The October Revolution, Thermidor, and the Stalinist Mode of Capitalism

What Was the Nature of the October Revolution?
In less than a decade the twentieth century will come to an end and we should begin drawing up its balance sheet. For me it is an urgent task since I was born at the beginning of the century and am unlikely to see its end.[2]

The greatest event of the twentieth century was not either of its world wars, but the Russian Revolution of 1917. Revolution had been brewing since the turn of the century when capitalism entered its imperialist phase. Imperialism, the 'highest stage capitalism', created the conditions for socialist revolution – conditions that prevailed throughout the twentieth century and will persist into the twenty-first.

When the Russian Revolution began in February 1917 it polarised opinion among Russian Marxists. A majority, led by the father of Russian Marxism, Georgi Plekhanov, believed it was a democratic revolution that would pave the

---

2   That is to say, Zheng did not expect that he could live longer than 100 years.

way to capitalist development in Russia. Many 'Old Bolsheviks' agreed with Plekhanov. Only Lenin and Trotsky, who was not at the time a member of the Bolshevik Party, saw it as the prelude to a socialist revolution. Despite fiercely debating the nature of the revolution, all sides were committed to carrying it out. History proved Lenin and Trotsky right and Plekhanov wrong. Plekhanov based his argument on Russia's level of economic development. And indeed Russia, taken its own, was not ready for a socialist revolution. But he did not take into account that the world economy was ripe for socialist revolution and that, in the age of imperialism, the global economy determines the destiny of nation-states, not the other way around.

Shortly before the February Revolution, addressing a young workers' rally in Zurich to commemorate the twelfth anniversary of Bloody Sunday,[3] Lenin said:

> The peculiarity of the Russian revolution is that it was a *bourgeois-democratic* revolution in its social content, but a *proletarian* revolution in its methods of struggle ... It was a bourgeois-democratic revolution since its immediate aim, which it could achieve directly and with its own forces, was a democratic republic, the eight-hour day and confiscation of the immense estates of the nobility – all the measures the French bourgeois revolution in 1792–93 had almost completely achieved.[4]

Speaking of the 'the coming European revolution', Lenin continued

> Undoubtedly, this coming revolution can only be a proletarian revolution, and in an even more profound sense of the word: a proletarian, socialist revolution also in its content.[5]

Lenin did not mention the possibility of a proletarian revolution in Russia. But he believed a European revolution was inevitable. 'Europe', he said 'is pregnant with revolution'. Furthermore, conditions in Europe

---

3   On 22 January 1905 (9 January, old style), Russian soldiers of the Imperial Guard opened fire on unarmed workers marching towards the Winter Palace in St. Petersburg to petition the Tsar. In Lenin's 'Lecture on the 1905 Revolution' which was given in Zurich in 1917, he said that Bloody Sunday 'is rightly regarded as the beginning of the Russian Revolution'. See Lenin 1964b, pp. 236–53.

4   Lenin 1960–78 [1917c], pp. 238–9.

5   Lenin 1960–78 [1917c], p. 252.

precisely because of this predatory war, will lead to popular uprisings under the leadership of the proletariat against the power of finance capital, against the big banks, against the capitalists; and these upheavals cannot end otherwise than with the expropriation of the bourgeoisie, with the victory of socialism.[6]

A month after he gave this lecture in Switzerland, the February Revolution broke out. On 20 March, Lenin sent his first letter from Switzerland to revolutionary Russia *Letters from Afar, First Letter, the First Stage of the First Revolution*. He still saw the Russian revolution as a 'bourgeois revolution' and said working class should first achieve

> a democratic republic and complete victory of the peasantry over the landlords, instead of the Guchkov-Milyukov semi-monarchy, and then to *socialism*, which alone can give the war-weary people *peace, bread* and *freedom*.[7]

Although Lenin mentioned 'socialism', at this stage he still saw it as something to be achieved in the future. The priority for Bolsheviks was to complete the Russian bourgeois-democratic revolution.

But less than a month later, on April 17 (April 4, old style), Lenin returned to Russia, and published a new programme for the Russian Revolution, the *April Theses* (or to give it its full name *The Tasks of the Proletariat in the Present Revolution*). Lenin made ten key points.

1. Revolutionary defencism is permissible only on condition that 'the power pass to the proletariat and the poorest sections of the peasants aligned with the proletariat'.[8] This shows that Lenin had already abandoned his formula of 'the democratic dictatorship of the proletariat and the peasantry' in favour of 'the dictatorship of the proletariat.'
2. After the February revolution, power was handed to the bourgeoisie by the proletariat and the poor peasantry.
3. The Bolsheviks should oppose the bourgeois Provisional Government
4. The Provisional Government must be replaced by Soviet power.

---

6 Lenin 1960–78 [1917c], p. 253.
7 Lenin 1960–78 [1917], p. 308.
8 Lenin 1960–78 [1917d], p. 21.

5.   Rather than a parliamentary republic, the revolution must create a Paris Commune-type state. The standing army must be abolished. All officials must be elected, recallable, and paid no more than skilled workers.[9]

6.   Land reform must be carried out by local Soviets of agricultural labourers' and peasants' deputies.

7.   Banks must be merged into 'a single national bank' controlled by the Soviet of Workers' Deputies.

8.   The Bolsheviks' immediate task is not to 'introduce' socialism, but 'only to bring social production and the distribution of products at once under the control of the Soviets of Workers' Deputies'.[10] In other words, the immediate task was to carry out a 'socialist revolution', not to 'implement socialism.' 'Socialist revolution' and 'socialism' are two different concepts: Socialism is a social system and a way of organising production, while 'socialist revolution' is the prerequisite for socialism.

9.   Some internal party tasks (amendments to that party programme, changing the name of the party and so on) need to be carried out.

10. A new International is needed.

Lenin's April Theses marked a turning point in his understanding of the Russian Revolution. Previously, he maintained the Russian Revolution would remain bourgeois democratic in scope despite employing proletarian methods of struggle. Henceforth he conceived the revolution as proletarian in both 'methods of struggle' and 'social content'. The revolution would not only abolish feudalism but would also encroach on property rights of the capitalist class by imposing reforms such as the eight hour day.

The April Theses became the programme of the 1917 Revolution.

Trotsky had championed the Theory of Permanent Revolution since 1905. The central point of his theory was that although the tasks of the Russian Revolution were bourgeois-democratic, they could only be completed by a proletarian dictatorship. But if the proletariat seized power it would not restrict itself to democratic tasks but would inevitably implement at least some socialist measures (without waiting for the democratic tasks to be completed). The revolution would therefore infringe on capitalist as well as feudal property rights.

Trotsky recognised that Russia's backwardness and the fact that peasants were the majority of the population meant the revolutionary regime would be unstable and characterised by conflict between the working class and the

---

9   Lenin 1960–78 [1917d], p. 23.
10   Lenin 1960–78 [1917d], p. 24.

peasantry. This conflict could be mitigated within Russia but could only be resolved by international proletarian revolution. Therefore, the fate of the Russian Revolution was inseparable from that of the world revolution.

The ideas of Lenin and Trotsky converged in the 1917. They called for a proletarian socialist revolution not because they believed Russia was ready for socialism, but because they believed the world (in particular Europe) was. The Russian Revolution would trigger world revolution and the world revolution would save the Russian Revolution.

In the particular circumstances of this historical conjuncture, the masses responded to the call of their leaders and carried the revolution to victory. This demonstrates that, by the beginning of the twentieth century, the world capitalist system had matured to the extent that world revolution would break out.

The October Revolution Failed

However, history tells us that by the end of the twentieth century conditions were still not present for the *completion* of the world proletarian revolution.

The conditions required for the outbreak of revolution are not the same as those required for its success. History provides numerous precedents. In France, several mass revolutionary struggles failed before the 1789 Revolution finally overthrew the absolute monarchy. In Russia, the 1905 Revolution failed to overthrow the Tsarist regime. Both the outbreak of the revolution and its failure were dictated by objective circumstances. Before the Chinese revolution of 1911 previous attempts to overthrow the Imperial system also failed. Viewed as a whole, the bourgeois democratic revolution in the West consisted of a series of waves, now rising, now retreating. History has left us few examples of revolutions that succeed at the first attempt.

The October Revolution triumphed in Russia but failed on a global scale. Nevertheless, as a historical event it cannot be understood purely on the national level. Rather, given its historical context, the aims of its leaders, and the consciousness of the masses it was a failed proletarian socialist revolution, or more accurately, the first wave of the world socialist revolution.

That the October Revolution failed is a view that only a small minority dissent from today. Indeed, the recent transformations in Eastern Europe and the Soviet Union – a domino-style collapse with few precedents in history – is widely taken as evidence of the bankruptcy of socialism and Marxism as well as the failure of October. We disagree. The collapse in Eastern Europe and the Soviet Union demonstrates the bankruptcy of Stalinism but tells us nothing about the fate of socialism. We already regarded the October Revolution as a defeated revolution, moreover one that was defeated more than sixty years ago. To be precise, the defeat of the October Revolution, and of the first wave of world revolution, can be dated to the 1927 debacle of the Chinese Revolution. After 1927, the Soviet regime represented the October Revolution in name only. In essence it was Stalinist.

Amongst the various schools of political thought, only we Trotskyists have drawn this conclusion because we are the only current that has always insisted on the universality of the socialist revolution; that from the start rejected the idea of 'socialism in one country' and the Stalinist idea that socialism could be built in the Soviet Union or in any of the other so-called 'socialist countries'.

Why the October Revolution Failed
The October Revolution can be only understood as a component of the world revolution. It broke out in a weak link in the chain of global capitalism at a time when Lenin and Trotsky agreed world revolution was on the agenda.

Before the October Revolution, in September 1917,[11] in *State and Revolution*, Lenin wrote

> this revolution as a whole can only be understood as a link in a chain of socialist proletarian revolutions being caused by the imperialist war.[12]

Three months after October, Lenin optimistically told the Third All-Russia Congress of Soviets of Workers', Soldiers' and Peasants' Deputies

> today we see that the socialist revolution is maturing by the hour in all countries of the world ...
>
> Things have turned out differently from what Marx and Engels expected and we, the Russian working and exploited classes, have the honour of being the vanguard of the international socialist revolution; we can now see clearly how far the development of the revolution will go. The Russian began it – the German, the Frenchman and the Englishman will finish it, and socialism will be victorious ...[13]

Two months later, in a speech on war and peace at the Seventh Congress of the Russian Communist Party (Bolsheviks), his attitude was less optimistic. It was a disastrous moment when the Bolsheviks had just signed the discreditable Treaty of Brest-Litovsk with Germany. Speaking of world revolution, he said:

---

11   Actually in August 1917. Translator's note.
12   Lenin 1960–78 [1917e], p. 388.
13   Lenin 1960–78 [1918b], pp. 471–2.

This is the greatest difficulty of the Russian revolution, its greatest historical problem – the need to solve international problems, the need to evoke a world revolution, to effect the transition from our strictly national revolution to the world revolution.[14]

Regarded from the world-historical point of view, there would doubtlessly be no hope of the ultimate victory of our revolution if it were to remain alone, if there were no revolutionary movements in other countries. When the Bolshevik Party tackled the job alone, it did so in the firm conviction that the revolution was maturing in all countries and that in the end – but not at the very beginning – no matter what difficulties we experienced, no matter what defeats were in store for us, the world socialist revolution would come – because it is coming; would mature – because it is maturing and will reach full maturity. I repeat, our salvation from all these difficulties is an all Europe revolution ... [I]t is the absolute truth that without a German revolution we are doomed – perhaps not in Petrograd, not in Moscow, but in Vladivostok, in more remote places to which perhaps we shall have to retreat, and the distance to which is perhaps greater than the distance from Petrograd to Moscow. At all events, under all conceivable circumstances, if the German revolution does not come, we are doomed.[15]

There are many similar passages in Lenin's works. There is no need to quote them here. Lenin made this point extraordinarily clearly: unless it advances the cause of world revolution, the proletarian socialist revolution in Russia will collapse.

With respect to Trotsky I do not need to elaborate on his views either. From 1905, he maintained that Russian bourgeois democratic revolution could succeed only if the proletariat seized power and that after taking power, the proletariat would push the revolution beyond its bourgeois limits. At that point, the proletariat would collide with the peasantry and that conflict could only be resolved by world revolution. In other words, without world revolution, Russia's socialist revolution would end in defeat. There are many such passages in Trotsky's writings.[16]

Stalin maliciously distorted Trotsky's assertion that without global revolution, revolutionary Russia was doomed to fail. In Stalin's *October Revolution*

---

14 Lenin 1960–78 [1918c], p. 92.
15 Lenin 1960–78 [1918c], pp. 95, 98.
16 This summary of Trotsky's views is adapted from his 1929 preface to a reprint of *1905*.

& *Tactics of the Russian Communists*, [concerning the future of the Russian Revolution], he caricatured Trotsky's views:

> Well, then, since there is still no victory in the West, the only 'choice' that remains for the revolution in Russia is: either to rot away or to degenerate into a bourgeois state. It is no accident that Trotsky has been talking for two years now about the 'degeneration' of our Party. It is no accident that last year Trotsky prophesied the 'doom' of our country.[17]

I do not know if Trotsky would accept Stalin's interpretation of his views, but history has proved that the Soviet Union, the state established by the October Revolution, did indeed degenerate into to a bourgeois regime, which meant that this 'socialist country' ceased to exist.

How the October Revolution Failed

Lenin and Trotsky agreed on this point; without a world revolution Soviet Russia would cease to exist. They both expected revolutions to break out in the West. After the revolutions in Germany, Hungary and Bulgaria were defeated, they looked East to launch a new revolutionary wave. But the defeat of the Chinese Revolution in 1927 sealed the doom of the October Revolution.

Despite the dangers, Lenin and Trotsky refused to passively accept defeat. As revolutionaries they had a duty to struggle for survival and find a way out of the dead end. They recognised two main forces threatening the gains of October were the domestic bourgeoisie and landlord class on the one hand and the imperialist powers on the other. The domestic counterrevolutionaries had been routed during the civil war and the 'Red Terror' while class conflict on their home territory and inter-imperialist rivalries meant that foreign counterrevolutionary forces were unable to strangle Soviet Russia at birth. But as these enemies were defeated Russian revolutionaries did not notice that other hostile forces were taking shape within their ranks. They recognised negative tendencies within the party but did not regard them as seriously threatening the foundations of the October Revolution. At worst they might weaken the party's revolutionary resolve and make it easier for external enemies to overthrow the revolution. Lenin and Trotsky called these corrosive forces 'bureaucratism'. Shortly before his death, Lenin began to reflect seriously about the threat posed by the bureaucracy how to fight and overcome it. He proposed to Trotsky that they form an alliance to combat bureaucracy within the party. But

---

17   Stalin 1953, p. 394–5.

he died before acting on this proposal. Without his support, Trotsky could not achieve anything. The 'anti-bureaucracy movement' was replaced by another – the 'anti-Trotsky movement'.

At the time of Lenin's death, 'bureaucratism' was not yet an independent force, but during inner-party struggles it gradually revealed its true face. It turned out that this was not just a generic form of bureaucratic power. It did not represent a layer within the proletariat but a completely different social class – a fraction of the bourgeoisie. This was the social formation that Stalin represented. This layer usurped the state power established by the October Revolution. Among historical precedents the Thermidor at the end of the French Revolution could be taken as a good example for comparison. So after Stalin concentrated power in his hands people began to say that the Soviet Union had experienced its own version of Thermidor and referred to Stalin and his comrades as Thermidorians. In the sense of a great revolution retreating from high tide to ebb tide, the comparison is apt. But there is a key difference – Thermidor in the French Revolution was the result of a revolution overstepping its historical limits. After the Thermidor retreat, France remained a capitalist society. It did not regress to the *ancien regime*. But the Russian Thermidor did not leave Russia a socialist society. Neither was it a society in transit from capitalism to socialism (because it was no longer a proletarian dictatorship). It was a capitalist society or rather a capitalist society of a certain type. We need to pay close attention to the distinction between these two forms of Thermidor.

The Thermidor was accomplished in Russian simultaneously with the defeat of the 1925–27 Chinese Revolution. This was not a coincidence. When the waves of world revolution launched by the October Revolution receded in the West the degenerative forces gained ground in Russia. The more hindrances the revolution faced in the West, the stronger the bureaucratic bloc became. After revolution spread to the East, the bloc was able to impose its strategy on the direction of the revolution. It abandoned the strategy of Permanent Revolution that had led to the October victory and regressed to the discredited Menshevik line of forming an alliance with the bourgeoisie. As a result, the Chinese Revolution was defeated.

At the time of the 1925–7 Revolution in China, the global capitalist system had stabilised itself and the wave of world revolution sparked by the October was in retreat. Under these circumstances, even with correct leadership, achieving the victory of the revolution would have been extremely difficult. But if the revolutionary waves could have been sustained and the Thermidor was not accomplished in the Soviet Union, and on condition that the leadership did not make any mistakes, there might have been some hope of victory.

But once the revolutionary leadership was captured by the Thermidorians, the Chinese Revolution was doomed to defeat.

Was this just a coincidence? The last gasp of the Chinese Revolution was the failure of the Guangzhou Uprisings in December 1927, while the Soviet Thermidor was sealed at the Fifteenth Congress of the RCP (B) in December 1927 when Trotsky and Zinoviev were both expelled from the party.

Since then, the revolutionary high tide caused by the October has been in retreat, marking the end of the first wave of world revolution. But Marxist revolutionaries believe that a second wave will inevitably rise, and the capitalist system will be replaced by socialism through violent revolution. This is an iron law of social development.

Successive Waves of World Revolution

It should be noted that the leaders of the October Revolution entertained the possibility of defeat, but it did not occur to them that the revolution might have to pass through several high tides before its final victory. There is a line in the *Internationale* – 'This the final struggle'. The *Internationale* was composed in the aftermath of the defeat of the Paris Commune. Its author Eugène Pottier pinned his hopes on a future revolution that would avenge the Commune. This was understandable. Both leaders and masses at the time hoped that a new wave of revolutions would usher in the age of socialism. But we now know that the transition from capitalism to socialism will be a long process requiring several high tides before it is finally accomplished. Few revolutions have succeeded at the first attempt. It is hard to think of a single such case.

The October Revolution was defeated a long time ago. Following the debacle of the 1927 Guangzhou Uprising, the tide of world revolution receded, and the Soviet state degenerated into a special form of capitalism – a capitalist state under Stalinist control. The bankrupt regimes that people called 'socialist states' were all capitalist states of this type, and not at all socialist.

East and West Germany have already reunified and discarded the Stalinist mode of capitalism. Poland, Hungary, Czechoslovakia, Bulgaria and Romania have all embraced traditional capitalism. Albania and Yugoslavia are in the process of transition and the Soviet Union, while still resisting, must inevitably revert to old-style traditional capitalism.

As I write, newspapers are reporting an *Anti-Crisis Programme* launched by Mikhail Gorbachev. The programme asserts that the Soviet Union is facing three main threats – the disintegration of the union, the collapse of the national economy and armed forces, and the collapse of government and the legal system. The programme calls for a complete rewrite of the constitution. It also calls on the Soviet people to suspend strikes and end conflicts between the

Soviet Union's constituent republics and nations. In the entire programme, there is not a single mention of the word 'socialism'. On 22 April 1991, the 121st anniversary of Lenin's birth, the Supreme Soviet of the Soviet Union published a communique describing Lenin as a supporter of 'reforms'. We may deduce from all this that the Soviet Union will soon abandon even lip service to the legacy of October and follow the path of the East European 'socialist states'.

The era of world revolution triggered by October has passed. We find ourselves somewhere between two waves of world revolution. We do not know when the second wave will arrive. But we know it will come and we must prepare for it. The first step is to draw a balance sheet of the first wave of world revolution. And while we should not minimise its successes we must pay more attention to its failures.

A Bourgeoisie of a Special Type

Two years before the October Revolution, Lenin wrote *Imperialism, the Highest Stage of Capitalism*. This work analyses the general tendency of world development in the early twentieth century and concludes that a correct understanding of the First World War shows that world socialist revolution has been placed on the agenda. Marxist analyses should always begin by characterising the nature of the epoch. Lenin's work was not the only attempt to sum up the era. Others included Rudolf Hilferding's *Finance Capital*, Rosa Luxemburg's *Accumulation of Capital* and works on imperialism by Karl Kautsky and others.

Lenin's analysis was fundamentally sound. He correctly pointed out that the imperialist war was a predatory war with no progressive features in which there was nothing to choose between the two sides. He also said that capitalism had reached its final stage, which reflected the fact that laissez-faire capitalism as described in Marx's *Capital* had been replaced by monopoly capitalism. This meant that capitalists could no longer rely on market laws and free competition to survive. They were forced to establish monopolies, seize control of sources of raw materials and divide up the world market. The logical result was war between imperialist contenders. Once the world had been carved up there would be no space left for the development of capitalism, production would stagnate, and social development would regress. Scientific advances and inventions would not be deployed in production but left in the drawers of the monopolies. In other words, social conditions were ripe for socialist revolution.

When the Russian Revolution erupted, Lenin and Trotsky were quite correct to lead it in the direction of socialism. But as Lenin pointed out in *'Left-Wing' Communism: An Infantile Disorder*:

History as a whole, and the history of revolutions in particular, is always richer in content, more varied, more multiform, more lively and ingenious than is imagined by even the best parties, the most class-conscious vanguards of the most advanced classes.[18]

After analysing the phases of Europe's social development in the mid-nineteenth century, Marx and Engels concluded that the conditions for proletarian socialist revolution were already present. They therefore called for the 1848 European Revolution to be turned into a 'permanent revolution' that would establish a proletarian dictatorship. But the revolution failed. In later years Engels reflected on the events of 1848.

> History has proved us, and all who thought like us, wrong. It has made it clear that the state of economic development on the Continent at that time was not, by a long way, ripe for the elimination of capitalist production; it has proved this by the economic revolution[19]

The 'economic revolution' Engels was referring to was rapid development of the European economy after 1848. He concluded that 'The grave-diggers of the Revolution of 1848 had become the executors of its will'.[20]

In 1915, when Lenin completed *Imperialism, the Highest Stage of Capitalism* he too believed that the time was ripe for proletarian socialist revolution. Based on this understanding, he led a proletarian socialist revolution in Russia in 1917 that triggered revolutionary high tides in both West and East. His predictions were correct so far. But after a series of defeats in West and East, the revolutionary wave receded. This in turn triggered the Thermidor in the Soviet Union and it regressed to capitalism. These events demonstrated that history is indeed more complex than is understood the best leaders. Theories must be corrected in the light of experience. The failure of revolutions and the degeneration of the Soviet regime prove that while capitalist society was sufficiently developed to trigger a socialist revolution, it was not yet ripe for the success of the revolution. In other words, even the smartest brains had failed to grasp the complexities of the capitalist system. Just as Marx did not foresee the development from

---

18   Lenin 1960–78 [1920], p. 95.
19   Engels 1969, pp. 191–2.
20   Engels 1969, p. 193.

laissez-faire capitalism to monopoly capitalism, Lenin did not predict that monopoly capitalism would possess the vitality to find a way out from its impasse and significantly prolong the life of the capitalist system. Given these conditions, the failure of the October Revolution was inevitable.

As mentioned above, the grave diggers of the October Revolution were neither the native Russian bourgeoisie and landlord class nor foreign imperialists, but a counterrevolutionary force that emerged within the revolutionary camp – the Thermidorians who were created by the proletarian revolution.

Originally, the Thermidorians were the administrative staff of the party and government organs responsible for implementing the policies of the leadership. Some had been bureaucrats under the old regime; others were drawn from the Communist Party or activists from the masses. At first their numbers were small as the revolutionary regime, following the example of the Paris Commune, insisted that all officials must be elected, subject to recall and paid no more than skilled workers. But during the civil war these three principles became a dead letter. When the civil war ended, War Communism was replaced by the New Economic Policy. But the standing army, with its bourgeois experts and pay differentials was not disbanded. The proportion of elected officials declined and professional bureaucrats, now indispensable, had become increasingly arrogant. Although seriously ill, Lenin recognised the problem and took action to combat it. He created the Workers' and Peasants' Inspection to oppose bureaucratism. Towards the end of his life, he realised that Stalin had become the representative of the bureaucrats in the party's highest body – the Politburo. In his last testament, Lenin suggested that Stalin be removed from the post of General Secretary, but by then it was too late.

History showed that the internal force that subverted the revolution was not 'bureaucracy' or 'bureaucratism' in the abstract, but a small group of people who split from the 'revolutionary fortress' in opposition to the proletariat and used the authority and prestige of the October Revolution to usurp power. They developed into a class that dominated and exploited the working people of the Soviet Union.

They were a class of capitalists, but of a special type. They owned the means of production, although not individually but collectively. In the Soviet Union and the other 'socialist states', this class ruled over a specific form of state capitalism.

State Capitalism of a Special Type

When Lenin wrote *Imperialism, the Highest Stage of Capitalism*, he saw monopoly capitalism as the final stage of the capitalist development. But two years later he discerned that capitalism had again mutated – not into a completely new stage, but into a new phase of this 'final stage', from monopoly capitalism to state-monopoly capitalism. In August 1917, he wrote:

> The imperialist war has immensely accelerated and intensified the process of transformation of monopoly capitalism into state-monopoly capitalism. The monstrous oppression of the working people by the state, which is merging more and more with the all-powerful capitalist associations, is becoming increasingly monstrous.[21]

[At the time, all the imperialist countries were on the road to state-monopoly capitalism. The furthest advanced in this direction was Germany.]

One month later, in *The Impending Catastrophe and How to Combat It*, Lenin returned to the subject of state-monopoly capitalism:

> For if a huge capitalist undertaking becomes a monopoly, it means that it serves the whole nation. If it has become a state monopoly, it means that the state (i.e., the armed organisation of the population, the workers and peasants above all, provided there is revolutionary democracy) directs the whole undertaking. In whose interest? Either in the interest of the landowners and capitalists, in which case we have not a revolutionary-democratic, but a reactionary-bureaucratic state, an imperialist republic. Or in the interest of revolutionary democracy – and then it is a step towards socialism. For socialism is merely the next step forward from state-capitalist monopoly. Or, in other words, socialism is merely state-capitalist monopoly which is made to serve the interests of the whole people and has to that extent ceased to be capitalist monopoly.[22]

The State and Revolution and *The Impending Catastrophe and How to Combat It* were both completed before the October Revolution. So we can conclude that before taking power, Lenin had decided to implement a type of state-monopoly capitalism. Indeed, Lenin approached revolution and national construction based on a blueprint drafted in Marx's *Critique of the Gotha Programme*. In *State and Revolution*, he devoted a chapter to elaborating Marx's programme. He stated that there must be a transition period from capitalism to socialism (the first stage of communism), and the state in this transition period can only be the dictatorship of proletariat.[23] Both Marx and Lenin in the *Critique of the*

---

21   Lenin 1960–78 [1917e] p. 387.
22   Lenin 1960–78 [1917 f.], p. 362.
23   See Lenin 1960–78 [1917e], pp. 461–79.

Gotha Programme and *State and Revolution* defined the transition period in political terms, from the perspective of how he state will function. But after the October Revolution, Lenin began to redefine the transition period from an economic point of view. In his essay *'Left-Wing' Childishness and the Petty-bourgeois Mentality*, he wrote:

> [W]hat does the word 'transition' mean? Does it not mean, as applied to an economy, that the present system contains elements, particles, fragments of both capitalism and socialism? Everyone will admit that it does.[24]

The point Lenin makes here seems incontrovertible. Everyone, not just Lenin, would surely admit that during the transition period, the economic structure would contain elements of both capitalism and socialism.

Lenin differed from others in that he *advocated* 'state-monopoly capitalism' under the proletarian dictatorship during the period of transformation. Before October, he made this point clear in *The Impending Catastrophe and How to Combat It*:

> state-monopoly capitalism is a complete material preparation for socialism, the threshold of socialism, a rung on the ladder of history between which and the rung called socialism there are no intermediate rungs.[25]

After October, he returned to this idea in *'Left-Wing' Childishness and the Petty-bourgeois Mentality*:

> To make things even clearer, let us first of all take the most concrete example of state capitalism. Everybody knows what this example is. It is Germany. Here we have 'the last word' in modern large-scale capitalist engineering and planned organisation, subordinated to *Junker-bourgeois imperialism*. Cross out the words in italics, and in place of the militarist, Junker, bourgeois, imperialist state put also a state, but of a different social type, of a different class content – a Soviet state, that is, a proletarian state, and you will have the sum total of the conditions necessary for socialism ...

---

24   Lenin 1960–78 [1918d], p. 335.
25   Lenin 1960–78 [1917f.], p. 363.

At the same time socialism is inconceivable unless the proletariat is the ruler of the state. This also is ABC. And history (which nobody, except Menshevik blockheads of the first order, ever expected to bring about 'complete' socialism smoothly, gently, easily and simply) has taken such a peculiar course that it has given birth in 1918 to two unconnected halves of socialism existing side by side like two future chickens in the single shell of international imperialism. In 1918 Germany and Russia have become the most striking embodiment of the material realisation of the economic, the productive and the socio-economic conditions for socialism, on the one hand, and the political conditions, on the other.

A successful proletarian revolution in Germany would immediately and very easily smash any shell of imperialism (which unfortunately is made of the best steel, and hence cannot be broken by the efforts of any ... chicken) and would bring about the victory of world socialism for certain, without any difficulty, or with slight difficulty ...

While the revolution in Germany is still slow in 'coming forth', our task is to study the state capitalism of the Germans, to spare no effort in copying it ...[26]

We can quote many passages from Lenin that demonstrate that he had by then begun to contemplate possible courses of action if the proletarian revolution in Germany was delayed. In that event, even though the prospects for revolution were gloomy, Soviet Russia would need to be sustained by a programme of economic construction. But this would not amount to building 'socialism in one country', but a type of 'state capitalism', based on the German model. This 'state capitalism' would remain a type of capitalism. As Lenin wrote in *State and Revolution*:

> capitalism becomes **monopoly capitalism**. The latter must be emphasised because the erroneous bourgeois reformist assertion that monopoly capitalism or state-monopoly capitalism is no longer capitalism, but can now be called 'state socialism' and so on, is very common.[27]

It follows that in the absence of world revolution, even if state capitalism has been mastered and implemented in Soviet Russia, state-monopoly capitalism

---

26   Lenin 1960–78 [1918d], pp. 339–40.
27   Lenin 1960–78 [1917e], pp. 447–8.

is still a variant of capitalism, and certainly contains elements and components of capitalism during the transition period.

Lenin elaborated on what he said in 1918 on state capitalism in his pamphlet *The Tax in Kind* written in 1921 during the implementation of the New Economic Policy. From this we can see that Lenin's earlier discussions of the subject were not passing or ephemeral jottings but a key component of his theory of transition.

When Lenin discussed state capitalism in 1918, there was no Thermidorian social formation in the Soviet Union. By the time he returned to the subject in 1921, the Thermidorians had begun to reveal themselves but they were not in a dominant position. For the time being, state-monopoly capitalism only existed in the main imperialist countries. Lenin listed state-monopoly capitalism as only one of five economic sectors under the dictatorship of the proletariat, and not even the principal one. According to Lenin, the dominant economic sectors in the country back then were small commodity production and private capitalism. After Lenin's death, particularly after the Thermidor was completed and five-year plans were carried out, the Soviet economy grew rapidly while within it, the share of small commodity production and private capitalism shrank dramatically. But the Soviet republic existed in its name only. The standing army was re-constituted; officials were neither chosen nor recallable by universal suffrage but appointed by a superior authority; high salaries were paid not only to 'bourgeois experts', but also to specialists from all backgrounds. Temporary measures taken after the revolution became routine. There was no hope of reviving the three principles of the Paris Commune. In other words, the proletarian dictatorship had ceased to exist.

Under such circumstances, what does the implementation of state capitalism in Soviet Russia amount to? According to Lenin, under bourgeois rule, state capitalism is the last phase of the final stage of capitalist development. By contrast, state capitalism in countries under proletarian rule is a capitalist formation that continues to exist during the transition period. But what about state capitalism in countries where Thermidor has been accomplished?

State capitalism in these circumstances becomes a particular configuration and form of capitalism. The ruling class constitute a special class of capitalists. In a system of this type, property is not personally owned but collectively owned. The capitalist class, *as a whole*, possesses the means of production, land, mines, transportation, factories, shops, schools, hospitals, and so on. Everything that can be called 'property' is owned by this class. Neither private-monopoly capitalism nor laissez-faire capitalism can compete with state-monopoly capitalism as operated by this capitalist class. This system can in no way be described as a 'gateway' to socialism. Only a new proletarian revolution can lead such a state-monopoly society to socialism.

We need a special name for this sort of state capitalism to denote its particular features. For example, we might call it the 'Stalinist mode of capitalism' or 'Cadreism'. Above all, we need to describe the role this form of capitalism has played in its seventy-year history.

In countries where state monopoly capitalism is the outcome of normal capitalist development, it is theoretically possible that the process will continue until private monopolies as well as free competition are eliminated. However, this is unlikely because retaining some private monopolies and pockets of free competition is not without its advantages. In Soviet Russia state-monopoly capitalism was not created by normal capitalist development but was the result of the degeneration of the October Revolution. After the revolution, Russia entered a transition period from capitalism to socialism. A proletarian dictatorship was established, and the three principles of the Paris Commune were implemented. But because the revolutionary wave failed in both West and East, the conquests of the revolution were usurped by the Thermidorians who had formed within the Bolshevik Party. The Thermidor that followed the proletarian revolution was different from the one that occurred after the bourgeois revolution. It did not preserve the conquests of the proletarian revolution (by developing a mixed economy in the transition period) but promoted capitalism by adopting its most advanced form.

The Stalinist Mode of Capitalism Was an Efficient Method of Production for an Epoch

This special form of state-monopoly capitalism, or the Stalinist mode of capitalism, was an efficient mode of production when it was adopted and remained so for more than 60 years. During its early period, while the traditional mode of capitalism was struggling for survival due to cyclical crises, the 'five-year plans' transformed the old and backward Russian empire from an agricultural country into an industrial country. Dozens of modern cities with well-equipped modern factories were built on desolate plains. In the Second World War, on the strength of its industrial economy, the Soviet Union was able to resist the German aggressors and eventually turn the tables on them and win the war. In the post-war era, the Soviet Union stood alongside the traditional capitalist United States as one of two great world superpowers. If the Stalinist mode of capitalism had not been superior to the modes of production in its rivals, it would have been impossible for Russia to attain the achievements listed above.

But this mode of production was by no means socialist. What is socialism? People have long debated this question without reaching a consensus.

Even the leaders of 'socialist states' cannot agree on what they mean by social-ism. But Marx and Lenin both explicitly set out their concepts of socialism in their writings. Marx's *Critique of the Gotha Programme* and Lenin's *State and Revolution* are not opaque texts. What is more, they are compulsory texts for all cadres in 'socialist countries.' Concerning the question of 'socialism' ('the first stage of communism'), it has been made very clear in both books. Do today's 'socialist states' or even 'developed socialist states' correspond to the standards set out by Marx and Lenin? The question does not require an answer. In fact, their form of 'socialism' does not even meet the standards of the transition period (from capitalism to socialism) as described by Marx and Lenin. According to the passages from Lenin's *Impending Catastrophe and How to Combat It* cited above, a transitional regime [from capitalism to social-ism] must operate under the dictatorship of proletariat. State capitalism [as a method of production] can exist in both capitalist and transitional regimes, but since the ruling classes are not the same, neither are the natures of the systems. And we cannot arbitrarily define what is meant by 'proletarian dic-tatorship'. The dictatorship of proletariat [in a transitional regime] must con-form to the three principles of the Paris Commune and described by Marx. Some flexibility is permitted of course. Short term deviations from the three principles are allowed. But if the three principles are thoroughly abandoned, the proletarian dictatorship has been extinguished, and with it the 'transition period.'

After WWII, despite the fact that the Soviet Union was one of the world superpowers, beginning in the 1950s, the Stalinist mode of capitalism fell so far behind traditional forms of capitalism in terms of productivity that we finally saw the recent domino-style collapse in Eastern Europe and Russia. How can we explain this phenomenon?

Competition between Social Systems Is Decided by Their Modes of Production

This is a theorem of historical materialism. Capitalism triumphed over feudal-ism because of its superior productivity. Similarly, monopoly capitalism replaced laissez-faire because economies of scale and centralised manage-ment resulted in higher productivity. Subsequently state-monopoly capitalism superseded private monopolies.

However, the mode of production is ultimately determined by the level of productivity. The mode of production must keep in step with the development of the productive forces. By the beginning of twentieth century, the global mar-ket had completely been carved up, and firms could only increase their share of surplus value by restructuring and centralising production. Consequently, monopoly triumphed over laissez-faire. In contrast, in the nineteenth century, when Marx wrote *Capital*, monopolies did not necessarily enjoy an advantage.

So why did today's traditional capitalist mode of production prevail over the Stalinist form of capitalism? We need to trace this back to the end of WWII. Since the post-war recovery from the war, traditional capitalism unexpectedly thrived while Stalinist capitalism fell behind. Traditional capitalism increased production and reduced costs. Markets expanded and living standards improved. In the two decades from 1950 to 1970 science and technology progressed faster than in the previous two millennia. It is not that there was no progress at all in the 'socialist states', but they developed far slower than the traditional capitalist countries. Over decades it became clear that economic development under Stalinist capitalism had lagged far behind. The 'socialist' countries themselves, facing growing internal problems, recognised that the Stalinist mode of production was falling behind traditional capitalism. Consequently, they began experimenting with reforms to replace the Stalinist mode with the traditional mode of capitalism.

Why did the traditional mode of capitalism, previously regarded by socialists as having reached a dead end, unexpectedly revive? A variety of explanations have been offered.

One is that the increase in productivity was the result of the triumph of democracy over authoritarianism brought about by WWII. This engendered a boom of traditional capitalism.

But this is not a satisfactory explanation. We are not living in the early stages of capitalism when parliamentary democracy replaced feudal despotism, released the productive forces from their shackles and launched an era of prosperity. We are in the age of late capitalism. Some countries that earlier embraced parliamentary democracy have already abandoned it in favour of oligarchical dictatorship. Democracy and dictatorship, or a mixture of the two, can all serve as capitalist forms of government and are adopted according to the requirements of the situation. In general, we can say that democracy goes with laissez faire capitalism and dictatorship with monopoly capitalism. But in all cases, we should look to the economic structure to explain the form of government, not the other way around.

Another view is that the post-war boom can be explained by the unprecedented advance of science and technology referred to above.

But this also reverses cause and effect. Historically, the expansion of markets, especially following the voyages of discovery, fueled the development of commerce and demand for new commodities. This in turn stimulated invention and scientific development, not the other way round. To take another example, after the world market was carved up and new markets became hard to find, as

Lenin pointed out in *Imperialism, the Highest State of Capitalism*, capitalists began buying up patents with no intention of using them, simply to deny them to competitors.[28] Without new markets the recent huge advances in science and technology would not have happened.

We still need to explain why the global market suddenly expanded so dramatically.

I attempted to answer this question a few years ago in my article *On Reform*. There is no need to repeat my argument in full here. Based on Rosa Luxemburg's arguments in her *Accumulation of Capital*,[29] I drew my own, slightly different conclusions.

My main ideas are as follows:

Luxemburg examined Marx's treatment of 'extended reproduction' in the second volume of *Capital* and concluded that in a pure capitalist society a portion of goods must always remain unsold and accumulate in warehouses. If this situation were to persist, the entire system of capitalist production would fall into a state of paralysis. Since this has not happened it follows that we are not living in a pure capitalist society. Since its birth in the womb of pre-capitalist society, pure capitalism has always co-existed with pre-capitalist modes of production. When pre-capitalist formations disappeared in one country or even in an entire continent they never disappeared on a global scale and continued to provide a market for capitalism's 'surplus' commodities.

Luxemburg mistakenly assumed that in her epoch pre-capitalist formations were dying out. Therefore, she drew the same conclusion as Lenin – that capitalism had reached its final stage and could no longer move forward. However, post-WWII history showed that pre-capitalist forms continued to exist in former oriental colonies and retained great vitality. When the imperialist countries turned to neocolonialism, these pre-capitalist formations absorbed the commodities that could not find a market in a pure capitalist society. This was the secret of capitalism's post-war recovery and prosperity.

However, this age of prosperity cannot last forever. Pre-capitalist formations must ultimately disappear. The faster capitalism develops in the former colonies, the more rapidly pre-capitalist production will vanish. When this process reaches a certain degree, the unabsorbed portion of commodities will no longer find markets, and capitalism will grind to a halt.

In recent years, economic crises have begun to emerge in the advanced capitalist countries. They are indications that an era of capitalist paralysis has already begun.

---

28   See Lenin 1960–78 [1916], p. 276.

29   See Luxemburg 1951.

Prepare for Future Waves of World Revolution

We are living in an ebb tide of the world revolution. The first wave of the revolution triggered by the October Revolution has receded and the second wave has not yet arrived. We cannot predict when the next high tide will arrive, but it will surely come. This is not 'faith', but a scientific conclusion derived from studying the evolution of human society.

Human society has a long future ahead of it. In fact, we have not yet surpassed the pre-history of humanity. We still live in a society where a minority exploits the majority. Our task is to undermine this exploitative society and allow everyone to lead fulfilled lives as real human beings.

This is the ultimate goal of the revolution. But the most important task for revolutionaries during an ebb tide is to learn the lessons of the failure of previous revolutions. Just as the lessons drawn from the short-lived Paris Commune helped ensure the early success of the 1917 Revolution, the lessons of October must be absorbed to inform future revolutions that will surely occur in tens, and perhaps even hundreds.

This article merely expresses the hope that these lessons will be learned and presents a few opinions of my own regarding the last revolution. It is far from a comprehensive study and I hope other more qualified people will improve on my analysis. I only insist that they must meet certain criteria.

Firstly, and above all, they must believe that revolutions will inevitably break out in the future.

Secondly, they need to understand that the collapse of the so-called 'Eastern bloc' did not mark the bankruptcy of socialism, but the collapse of Stalinism. Stalinism was not the inheritor of the October Revolution, but its executioner.

What is more, they should realise that the democracy we have been discussing here is parliamentary democracy. This form of democracy is only progressive during an ebb tide of revolution. It remains an instrument of capitalist rule. True democracy, proletarian democracy, is inseparable from socialism. But there is no thing as 'non-democratic socialism'. If we ever achieve socialism, true democracy will be achieved at the same time.

Finally, a future, successful world revolution will inevitably occur in the most developed capitalist countries. When it arrives, the objective conditions for the victory of the subsequent world revolution will be far more favourable than those that gave rise to the October Revolution.

Completed on 15 May 1991

CHAPTER 12

On Cadreism (c. 1992)

Translated by Huang Ting

Translator's Introduction

Zheng Chaolin conceived the theory of *ganbuzhuyi* or *cadreism* during his long imprisonment, but the piece translated here was written in his old age after he was released. It was first published in Hong Kong in 1998 in the collection of his late works *Shishi yu Huiyi* (History and Memory).

In debates on the nature of nominally Marxist states, socialism is, naturally, a contested concept. What does it mean to say a state is socialist? Another contested concept is that of a workers' state. It is now almost universally accepted that the Soviet Union and its Eastern European clones, while nominally proletarian socialist states, strayed far from the ideals envisaged by early socialist, and especially Marxist, thinkers. Trotsky, grappling with the issue, called the Soviet Union a degenerated workers' state. After the Second World War, many of his followers called China and the new Eastern European states deformed workers' states. Others thought it absurd to call a state that the working class had played little or no part in creating, a workers' state of any sort. As for the Soviet Union itself, how far could a workers' state degenerate before it no longer merited the name?

Zheng was a lifelong observer of the 'socialist' experiments in both the Soviet Union and China. As an insider, so to speak, his observations are extremely valuable and are informed by his solid grasp of Marxist theory. When considering the nature of the Soviet regime he took as his starting point the traditional socialist view, shared by both Lenin and Trotsky, that socialism is fundamentally international and can only be established on a global scale or at least on the basis of cooperation among several advanced countries. It could certainly not be built in a single country. He concluded that Stalin's slogan 'Socialism in One Country' was the political expression of a formerly revolutionary cadre that had degenerated and congealed into a new ruling class that monopolised political and economic power and exploited the rest of the population. The Stalinist system was neither socialist nor a degenerated workers' state but a new type of class society he called 'cadreism'. He maintained that the degeneration of the workers' state into this new class society became inevitable because, contrary to Lenin's hopes, the Russian Revolution was not followed by the world revolution.

What Zheng calls 'cadreism' is not fundamentally different from what other scholars, and for that matter Zheng elsewhere, call state capitalism. State capitalism accurately describes the economic system, while 'cadreism' focuses on the social origins of the new ruling class. For Zheng they were different aspects of the same phenomenon: the degeneration of the cadres proceeded hand in hand with the development of the state capitalist system. In fact, Zheng himself calls cadreism 'a form of late capitalism'.

While Zheng offers us his observations and criticisms, he does not provide a solution to the problem facing socialists – that genuine common ownership of the means of production has never been realised since the emergence of the first class societies. While scarcity remains, it seems that those in charge of the production process will necessarily degenerate into a privileged class. Zheng maintained that only the combination of political conditions (a proletarian regime with genuine mass participation) and economic conditions (the latest technological achievements of capitalism) can provide the basis for socialism. The mere combination of a planned economy and the absence of private property is perfectly compatible with the existence of a ruling class that exploits the vast majority. Whatever the future prospects for the formation of a genuine socialist society, this article offers a critical and acutely observed appraisal of the 'fake' socialism of the Soviet experiment.

Translation source: Zheng Chaolin 1998, 'Ganbuzhuyi', *Shishi yu Huiyi* Volume III, Hongkong: tiandi tushu youxian gongsi, 318–24.

On Cadreism

Stalin, who in his spring 1924 pamphlet *Foundations of Leninism* solemnly declared that socialism cannot be built in one country, by the autumn of the same year had authored a resolution claiming the exact opposite – that socialism can be built in one country. What he wrote in the spring was a theoretical and academic thesis composed according to Marxist doctrine and Bolshevik tradition, as well as his own beliefs; what he wrote in the autumn went against his own principles, his tutor's instructions and the traditions of his party. He made this abrupt theoretical transition in order to meet the needs and interests of the new class (or new stratum) that was taking shape in the Soviet Union at the time.

At issue was a question of class struggle.

When the Bolshevik Party leaders Lenin and Trotsky launched the October Revolution, they viewed it as the prelude of a world proletarian socialist revolution. They believed that the world revolution would break out in the near future and, as a by-product, would save the Russian Revolution. They were equally sure that if the world revolution did not break out then the isolated Russian Revolution would be defeated.

They envisioned the defeat of the revolution would come in two possible forms: either the landlords and capitalists would defeat the proletariat and restore the *ancien regime*, or the proletarian regime would be overthrown by the armed intervention of the imperialists. They took pre-emptive measures to combat these two counterrevolutionary forces. It never occurred to them that the Russian Revolution might collapse due to the degeneration of revolutionary regime from the inside. But as Lenin wrote in *'Left-Wing' Communism: An Infantile Disorder*, history develops ways that are more complex, clever and cunning than the best minds of the most revolutionary leaders can conceive.

As early as 1927, ten years after taking power, the regime created by the October Revolution had already factually failed, but its revolutionary aura remained intact. It did not finally collapse until 1991 taking down what remained of its revolutionary reputation with it.

The initial success and eventual failure of the October Revolution contain lessons for us. Perhaps we can learn more from its failure than from its success. In any case, here we will concentrate on what we can learn from how it failed.

The masses and the revolutionary cadres succeeded in carrying out the October Revolution, prevented the restoration of landlord and capitalist classes and beat off the invasion of the imperialist forces. But the world revolution did not break out. True, there were revolutions in Germany, Hungary and Bulgaria but they were short-lived. According to its leaders' own assessment, the October Revolution was doomed to fail. But they won the civil war and the imperialist countries proved willing coexist with the revolutionary regime and eventually re-established trading and diplomatic relations. In these circumstances, revolutionary sentiment among the masses died down and the previously revolutionary cadres started to degenerate.

Lenin foresaw this before his death and took some measures to counter 'bureaucratisation' but he underestimated the phenomenon, seeing it as merely a matter of red tape and so on. But the degeneration of the cadres went far beyond this, so the measures Lenin proposed were inadequate.

The cadres degenerated gradually, but slowly and even imperceptibly they regressed far beyond what anything that could be called the bureaucratisation of a workers' state and developed into a new ruling class opposed to the proletariat. This class, which I call the 'cadre class', in terms of its role in social production, should be termed a stratum of the capitalist class, a capitalist stratum that necessarily arises in the era of late capitalism. When capitalism progresses from free competition to monopoly, small and medium corporations merge into large corporations, domestic corporations expand into a multinationals, individual and family ownership is replaced by joint-stock companies. The management of corporations becomes an advanced technical skill requiring sophisticated knowledge beyond the capability of the mere owners of capital who therefore are obliged to employ experts to do the job. Engels described this phenomena in his late writings, as did Lenin in *Imperialism, the Highest Stage of Capitalism*. Corporate managers, like workers, are employees of the capitalists. Capitalists consequently lose their managerial authority, are reduced to receiving dividends and annual bonuses and become as redundant in the society as unemployed workers. Of course the capitalists are not forced to rely on state handouts to survive.

This phenomenon reaches its logical conclusion when monopoly capitalism develops into state monopoly capitalism. Under state monopoly capitalism, corporate managers of all levels are employees of the state, while capitalists lead a parasitic life on the interest generated by their bank deposits.

Naturally, there will be managerial experts among the capitalists, and they also will be employed by the state to manage corporations. Experts, because they receive such high salaries, are also able save up enough to become capitalists. But in terms of the social division of labour, their roles are different. Employees, in the last analysis, are not the same as employers.

The October Revolution erased the capitalist class in the Soviet Union. Those with the ability to manage the state and the corporations became the ruling class of the Soviet Union. It wasn't their fault that the world revolution did not break out. Since it could coexist with the surrounding imperialist countries, what was the point of starting a world revolution? After Lenin died, Stalin appraised the situation at home and abroad and decided to represent the existing cadre class, abandon world revolution and head down the path of 'socialism in one country'.

We know that without a world revolution the Soviet Union was bound to perish. But Lenin and Trotsky only made allowance for and arranged defences against, domestic reaction and imperialist invasion. They never imagined that the revolution would perish at the hands of its own cadre. They saw evidence of degeneration but regarded it as mere 'bureaucratisation' and the measures they took were inadequate to the task of preventing the emergence of a new ruling class.

Where was this cadre class (under Stalin's leadership) leading the Soviet Union?

The cadres formed a group, guided by the theory of socialism in one country. They managed both the state and production. They were the rulers; the masses were the ruled. They made all decisions while the masses had no say. And they called this 'socialism'.

In fact, it was what Lenin, in 1918, called 'state capitalism'.

In 1918, in his pamphlet *Left-Wing Childishness and the Petty-Bourgeois Mentality* Lenin actually advocated that the Soviet Union adopt 'state capitalism'.

Lenin analysed the Russian economy of the period into five sectors

1. Patriarchal peasant farming;
2. Small commodity production;
3. Private capitalism;
4. State capitalism;
5. Socialism[1]

In his view, the sector that predominated was that of petty-bourgeois production. The main contradiction was not between state capitalism and socialism, but between the small-scale capitalist sector and state intervention of any sort, whether from the state capitalist or the socialist state sector.

In 1918, Lenin recommended that the Soviet Union adopt state capitalism, for two reasons: Firstly, it would be much more efficient than the existing Russian economy. Secondly it would not threaten the character of the Soviet state as a workers' and peasants' regime. He restated his position in September of 1921 when he wrote the pamphlet *The Tax in Kind*. In this pamphlet, he stated:

> It is Germany. Here we have 'the last word' in modern large-scale capitalist engineering and planned organisation, *subordinated to Junker-bourgeois imperialism*. Cross out the words in italics, and in place of the militarist, Junker, bourgeois, imperialist state put also a state, but of a different social type, of a different class content – a Soviet state, that is, a proletarian state, and you will have the sum total of the conditions necessary for socialism.[2]

Lenin's position is clear. A country may possess the economic conditions (the latest technological achievements of capitalism) but if it lacks the political conditions (a proletarian regime with mass participation in the planning process), it cannot establish socialism. It is the combination of these conditions that constitutes socialism.

The system of state capitalism built by the Stalinist cadre did not just exist in the Soviet Union. The system in Nazi Germany was similar. Under Hitler, the factories were managed by Nazi party members, not by capitalists. The differ-

---

1 Lenin 1960–78 [1918d] pp. 335–6.
2 Lenin 1960–78 [1921b], p. 334.

ence was that while there were no private capitalists in the Soviet Union, in Germany capitalists lost their management rights but held on to their property. The difference is not crucial. As Engels once said, under late capitalism capitalists would also 'lose their jobs' and become redundant coupon clippers.

The question was which class did the Soviet regime represent.

Lenin's words show that, to him, what was important was the class nature of the regime. Germany possessed all the necessary economic conditions for building socialism but because it represented the capitalist class, it could not become socialist. When Lenin wrote these words, the Soviet Union represented the proletariat. After Stalin took over the question was, did the Soviet regime still represent the proletariat?

This was a fiercely disputed question.

Stalin insisted that the system was socialist. In 1936, the Soviet Union published a new constitution, drafted by Bukharin and announced by Stalin, which said: Socialism has been established in the Soviet Union. There is almost no private property in the Soviet Union: industry and the land are both state owned, and farmers farm on land under collective ownership not private ownership. This was the system in the Soviet Union and it was later reproduced in the other socialist countries. It seemed to prove that socialism could be built in individual countries.

Lenin, Trotsky and Zinoviev believed that socialism could not be built in one country. But others, for example Kamenev, did not agree. They thought that even if the rule of bureaucrats replaced direct rule by the proletariat the state was still the product of the October Revolution, even though some cadres had degenerated into bureaucrats. Like a generally healthy person who has a malignant tumour, once the tumour of bureaucracy is removed, the state would recover.

During his last illness, Lenin worried about the bureaucratic degeneration of the state and allied himself with Trotsky to fight it. Unfortunately, he died soon afterwards and Trotsky, left without support, was defeated and deported by Stalin.

It should be noted that the Stalin faction at the outset consisted of degenerated bureaucrats but over time it developed into a new class ruling a new form of capitalism.

Trotsky was assassinated by Stalin four years after the Soviet Union announced the establishment of socialism. Even then, he should have been able to perceive the true nature of the system but right up to his death he maintained that the Soviet Union was a degenerated workers state.

Now that that state has perished, we can see clearly that it was neither 'socialist' nor a 'degenerated workers' state'.

We should be clear that the absence of private property does not equal socialism. The Soviet Union announced that all means of production including land were owned by the state. But the Soviet state was not owned by the proletariat but by the cadres. Consequently, all means of production including land were in fact owned by the cadres. Admittedly, property was collectively owned, but it was collectively owned by the cadre class. Workers, farmers and intellectuals outside the class of cadres were all ruled politically and exploited economically.

Some people think that a planned economy equals socialism. This is also quite wrong. Late capitalism has many features in common with a planned economy and old-style state capitalism also featured a planned economy. Take a look at what Lenin wrote in 1918. He said that state capitalist Germany not only had the latest technology of capitalism but production and distribution were also organised by state planners. In his later years even Marx said that the appearance of joint-stock companies was a step towards a planned economy.

After the demise of the Soviet Union, capitalists around the world shouted from the rooftops that socialism was bankrupt. From the above analysis we can see that it was not socialism that failed, but Stalin's cadreism.

Marx and Lenin both gave clear definitions of socialism. Marx's *Critique of the Gotha Programme* and Lenin's *State and Revolution* were both compulsory reading for cadres in the nominally socialist countries but it seems that not many who read them understood them.

Marx described the first stage of communism (i.e. socialism) in *Critique of the Gotha Programme* as the following:

> Within the co-operative society based on common ownership of the means of production, the producers do not exchange their products; just as little does the labour employed on the products appear here as the value of these products, as a material quality possessed by them, since now, in contrast to capitalist society, individual labour no longer exists in an indirect fashion but directly as a component part of the total labour.[3]

A socialist society (the first stage of communism) has not only abolished private property and established a planned economy, it has also developed to the point that products no longer appear in society as objects bearing value. Once products no longer have value, they are no longer commodities. Money – a special kind of commodity will cease to exist. Without commodities and cur-

---

3   Marx 1977 [1875], pp. 567–8.

rencies how could there be markets? So a so-called 'socialist market economy' is an absurdity like a circular square. It cannot exist in the real world.

Therefore, the idea that the Stalinist system was socialist is also absurd.

Some, while admitting that the Soviet Union was not socialist, still maintain that it was a 'degenerated workers' state'. But the manner in which the Soviet Union collapsed in 1991 exposed this illusion. Not a single worker took up arms to protect this 'workers' state' from oblivion.

So what on earth was the Stalinist system?

The Stalinist system was a special version of state capitalism. It was special because it featured nationalised property and central planning, and because it did not develop organically from capitalism but rather from the degeneration of cadres who were originally proletarian revolutionaries. Revolution eliminated the capitalist class and a revolutionary cadre took over the administration of the state and the economy. They adopted German-style 'state capitalism' as a tool to develop the productive forces and survive until the world revolution came to their rescue. But the world revolution never arrived, the masses became demoralised, and the cadre degenerated. The result was state capitalism without a capitalist class in the traditional sense of the word.

The cadres took on the role of the capitalist class.

So if we were to give it a more apt name, we should call what Stalin practiced *cadreism* and its ruling class a cadre class. But we must keep in mind that the cadres were also a stratum of the capitalist class, and that cadreism was a form of late capitalism.

CHAPTER 13

Letters across the Sea (1996–8)

Translation and explanatory notes by Gregor Benton

Translator's Introduction

Zheng was a prolific correspondent, and exchanged hundreds if not thousands of letters with Wang Fanxi, Lou Guohua, and other veterans. The correspondence was, where necessary, channelled through intermediaries in order to maintain secrecy. The exchange with which we conclude this book was his last. It shows many of Zheng's excellent qualities: his absolute concern for accuracy and truth, his non-sectarian approach to politics (Hu Qiuyuan was not a comrade), and his elephantine memory, as well as the reverence and esteem in which he was held by those around him. The translation was made from a source in my possession.

Zheng Chaolin and Hu Qiuyuan[1]

Since June 1996, Zheng Chaolin and Hu Qiuyuan, on either side of the Taiwan Strait, have been engaged in correspondence. At the age of 97, Zheng Chaolin has a clear memory and a quick mind, and continues to write articles. In recent years, however, he has suffered from cataracts, so his vision is poor. The characters he has in mind when writing are hard to identify. Some of Zheng Chaolin's letters to Hu Qiuyuan were first copied out, by me, and then the venerable Old Zheng appended his signature. I read Hu Qiuyuan's letters aloud to him. The contents of the two old men's letters are rich in historical value, so they

---

1   Hu Qiuyuan was among the Chinese students who returned to China sometime in the early to mid-1930s after studying in Japan. The majority of these returned students supported the Chinese Communist Party, but a few (notably Hu and Zheng Xuejia) showed some sympathy for Trotskyism and borrowed weapons from the Trotskyist armoury to attack the Chinese Stalinists. The leaders of the Communist Party were extremely hostile to Hu, Zheng, and the other members of their group, and attacked them in an effort to discredit Chen Duxiu and the real Trotskyists. Hu and his friends very quickly became associated with the Guomindang. Hu earned his living by writing for the Shenzhou Publishing Company.

have been compiled and released for publication, after obtaining the two men's consent.

Little Zhou,[2] March 1997

(1)   Origins

The three-volume collection of Chen Duxiu's *Selected Works*, edited by Ren Jianshu, a mainland scholar, contained a letter from Chen Duxiu addressed to H and S. According to a note, H is Hu Qiuyuan and S is Sun Hongyi. Ren Jianshu said the note was based on what Zheng Chaolin told him. Later, Shen Ji, Professor of History at Anhui University, pointed out that Sun Hongyi died in 1936, and Chen Duxiu cannot have written to someone who had already died. Zheng Chaolin believed that his own memory was correct. When, at the time [in the 1940s], He Zhiyu took Chen Duxiu's manuscript to Zheng Chaolin to discuss its possible publication, Zheng saw with his own eyes the letter to Hu Qiuyuan and Sun Hongyi (a copy, not in Chen's handwriting). During the editing of Chen Duxiu's *Last Articles and Letters*, Zheng and He Zhiyu decided to hide the names of the two addressees and to replace them with H and S. In order to clarify this matter, Zheng Chaolin asked people to see whether there was another person with the same name as Sun Hongyi, but none was found. The only way to solve this problem was to ask Hu Qiuyuan, who was still alive and in good health. The two men lived on either side of the Taiwan Strait. They didn't know each other's address and therefore could not communicate.

In recent years, the two sides of the Strait have become indirectly connected by mail. Mr Hu Qiuyuan has visited the Mainland twice. In 1995, Beijing published *Chinese Heart: Selected Writings of Hu Qiuyuan on Politics, Literature and Philosophy*. In his Preface, dated 4 April 1995, Mr Hu said that he lived in Xincun in Xindian, but failed to indicate a house number. Zheng Chaolin thought that Hu Qiuyuan must be well-known in Taiwan, and an incomplete address might suffice. So Zheng Chaolin sent a letter on 18 June 1996. After a long time without receiving a reply, he concluded that the letter had not arrived. Unexpectedly, five months later, a long letter arrived from Hu Qiuyuan, dated 14 November 1996. So the two old men started up a long correspondence and finally ended up solving the problem: S was not Sun Hongyi but Sun Jiyi. Apart from this question, they discussed many other little-known but valuable matters in their correspondence.

---

2   Little Zhou is Zhou Lüqiang, a Wenzhou Trotskyist now living in Shanghai.

(2)   Letter Dated 18 June 1996, Zheng Chaolin to Hu Qiuyuan

Mr Qiuyan:

Please forgive me for taking the liberty of writing to you. I saw from a new book published in Beijing last year under the title *Chinese Heart* that you are still alive and you live in Xindian in Taipei. I would like to ask your opinion regarding a certain controversy.

The problem is that we found a letter in in Mr Chen Duxiu's correspondence written to Mr Hu Qiuyuan and Mr Sun Hongyi on 19 November 1941. In 1948, He Zhiyu published this letter, replacing H with Hu Qiuyuan and S with Sun Hongyi. The rest was not changed. The letter was included in the *Selected Works of Chen Duxiu* published in Shanghai, still using the names Hu Qiuyuan and Sun Hongyi. However, in recent years people have begun raising questions and pointing out that Sun Hongyi died in 1936 so S cannot be Sun Hongyi. As a result, a controversy has arisen.

I personally read the manuscript of He Zhiyu's book. The original manuscript of this letter did indeed say 'Sun Hongyi'. I and He Zhiyu decided jointly to replace S with Sun Hongyi. I still think that was not wrong. In his letter, Chen Duxiu said of Sun Hongyi: I have not seen Mr Sun for more than twenty years, and I think fondly of my time in Beijing!

Counting back twenty years from 1941, that was indeed a year in which Chen Duxiu was teaching at Peking University. At that time, Sun Hongyi was a member of parliament in Beijing. It is quite possible that the two were introduced to each other by [Chen's fellow Communist leader] Li Dazhao. Li Dazhao was a native of Zhili Province, and he and Sun were from neighbouring counties.

Chen Duxiu's letter is available in *Chen Duxiu's Selected Works*, vol. 3, p. 567.

I am interested not in the contents of the letter but in whether the other recipient besides you was Sun Hongyi. In other words, I only ask whether you know Sun Hongyi? Do you know whether he was still alive during the War of Resistance and went to the rear to meet you? This is a small matter, but it has given rise to debate, and even small matters must be resolved. Today, only you can answer this question.

I hope you can enlighten me,
    Yours sincerely,
    Zheng Chaolin

(3)   Letter Dated 14 November 1996, Hu Qiuyuan to Zheng Chaolin[3]

Mr Chaolin:

On 18 June, I had the pleasure of reading your letter. Due to my revision of the old book *Outline of the History of Chinese Thought over the Past 130 Years*, together with several minor illnesses, my reply has been delayed. A heap of letters from friends awaits me. Today I will start answering them. It is my privilege to start by honouring yours, and by requesting your help in a certain matter.

I gradually became interested in historical materialism after 1923–24, and also gradually became convinced of socialism. Before the Shanghai Incident of 28 January 1932, the Japanese set fire to Sanyou Industrial Company in Shanghai. This is because the Japanese bandits feared Chinese national capitalism. I thought at the time that China must first develop national capitalism before implementing socialism. I first went to Europe in 1934, and in 1935, at the invitation of the Third International's Chinese delegation, I helped to edit *Jiuguo shibao* (National Salvation Times). After nearly a year of observation in Soviet Russia, I came to believe that China was incapable of Russian-style socialism, and I also give up Marxism. At the end of 1935, I wrote in *Salvation Times* that 'the Anti-Japanese resistance is everything, everything is subordinate to the anti-Japanese resistance'. First of all, I said that I had given up Marxism and socialism and firmly believed that China should develop national capitalism, but after recovering the Northeast, the large industries would be owned by the state, and China would have a new type of capitalism. After returning to China after the War of Resistance, I read writings by Sun Yat-sen that said that Chinese industry should be both publicly and privately owned. I was also aware that the German Social-Democratic Party advocated a 'mixed economy'. During the Anti-Japanese War, everyone was talking about socialism and believed that socialism equalled control of the economy, even Ma Yinchu was more or less of this opinion. After arriving in Chongqing, the government's control only made prices rise. An old friend of mine, Xue Nongshan (also known as Tieshan, originally a print-worker who later studied on his own account, became quite learned, wrote *A History of Chinese Peasant Wars*, and frequently wrote for *Dushu zazhi* [Readers' Magazine], joined the Trotskyists, and met Chen Duxiu early on), was chief editor of *Shishi xin bao* (News of the times) and asked me to write for it. I wrote 'The Theory of People's Livelihood is capitalism'. Wang Jingwei was angry when he read it, and instructed someone to bring a charge against me. At the

---

3   Note by Little Zhou: Mr Hu Qiuyuan originally wrote a total of 9 pages.

time, Mr Chen Duxiu wrote a letter on my behalf to the Guomindang Central Committee saying that the issues I had raised were worthy of study and that
power considerations should not be allowed to curtail academic freedom. I first
met Mr Chen in Hankou, when I lived close by him. I got on with him and we
enjoyed conversing together. He had already given up Trotskyism, but he was
still attached to democratic socialism.[4] After arriving in Chongqing, he gave a
speech at the Minsheng Company on 'The Meaning of the War of Resistance'
and advocated that China should first develop capitalism. That attracted a lot
of attention. Fortunately, Wang Jingwei capitulated to the enemy two months
later, so I was saved from prosecution. The Guomindang's *Yiwen zhoukan* (Arts
Weekly) held a discussion on socialism and capitalism (this was the third in a
series, obviously there was no conclusion).

At the time, Chen Duxiu lived in Jiangjin [in exile in Sichuan], but his article was not published, because the Soviet Russian Communists protested and
the Guomindang was unwilling to offend the Soviet Union. So he sent mimeographed copies of his article to close friends, and also published his private
letters. On one occasion he wrote to Xue Nongshan, and the letter mentioned
me, so Xue showed it to me. I don't remember what it said. However, while I
was revising my old work I came across an excerpt from a letter 'to H and S' in
An Outline History of Chinese Thought over the Past 130 Years (pp. 160–1). I then
thought that the H might refer to me, and the S to Xue Nongshan.[5]

Is that a permissible inference? Two or three years ago, I received a letter
from Anhui Documentary Centre from a gentleman asking the same question
as you. He also said that according to a close friend of Mr Chen, the person
who had served Mr Chen in his later years had said that H was indeed Hu Such-
and-Such. But who was S? The gentleman had written in the hope that I could
answer his question. At the time, I was suffering in hospital with bronchopneu-
monia. I didn't answer him. I don't know where his letter is, or even what his
name was.

My conclusion: Mr Chen's letter to H and S was 'maybe' to me and Xue Nongshan. If Mr Chen's relatives are sure that H is a reference to me, then S must be
Xue Nongshan. But I say 'maybe' because I can't say for sure.

Your present letter asks whether the other person besides me was Sun
Hongyi. I believe Sun Hongyi was twenty or thirty years older than me and we
had no background in common, so it's unlikely that a letter would be jointly
addressed to us. Moreover, according to your letter, Chen's letter began by say-

---

4   Hu's assertion about Chen and Trotskyism is debatable.
5   In certain transcriptions, Xue might be rendered with an initial 's'.

ing that he had not seen Mr Sun 'for more than 20 years ...', and his letter reminisced about old times and talked about current communist issues, with which Sun Hongyi was not concerned. I have an old colleague called Sun Jiyi[6] who had a literary reputation in Beijing in my early years. We met daily at the National Defence Commission, but Chen Duxiu's name never came up. So I stick by the above conclusion.

I said that I wanted to ask your help. I mentioned that two or three years ago, I received a letter from the Anhui Documentary Centre asking me who S was. I am embarrassed to say that I did not answer at the time due to illness, for which I apologise. I would like to ask you to write a letter on my behalf to the Anhui Documentary Centre or some other organ responsible for sorting out the affairs of leading Anhui public figures [of which Chen Duxiu was one] to ask whether anyone had earlier written a letter to Hu Such-and-Such asking who H and S were. If so, and if they are anxious to resolve this question, might I ask you to copy this letter to them? I would be most grateful!

Yours respectfully,
     With all best wishes,
     Hu Qiuyuan

(4)   Letter Dated 27 November 1996, Zheng Chaolin to Hu Qiuyuan[7]

Mr Qiuyuan:

I have received your reply. I took the liberty to write to you regarding a small matter. I received no reply for several months. I imagined that after receiving my letter you had decided not to answer. Who would have imagined that you would write a nine-page reply on such a small account. Thank you for your kindness!

---

6 Note by Little Zhou: The character *ji* in Sun Jiyi was not clear. A copy of the letter was sent to Professor Shen Ji of History at Anhui University. Shen Ji wrote to say: 'I checked biographical materials for the May Fourth period and found a Sun Jiyi. At the time, he was quite well known as a literary figure. After carefully examining Mr Hu's letter, it seems to me that Mr Hu wrote the character *ji* in its traditional form'.

7 Little Zhou's note: This letter and the ninth issue of *Chen Duxiu Research Trends* were sent at the same time but separately. Hu Qiuyuan only received the magazine and did not receive the letter. Later, Little Zhou sent him a copy of it. 'Sun X Yi' had been identified by Shen Ji as Sun Jiyi.

In the early 1930s, I was detained in Nanjing Central Military Prison, where I borrowed books and magazines from other political prisoners, so I knew that you were a writer. I read several of your articles in the magazine published by the Shenzhou Guoguang Society; I also read Vladimir Friche's *Sociology of Art*,[8] translated by you, especially your long preface to the book. It is a pity that I am now very old and almost blind. People have sent me your *Chinese Heart*, published in the mainland, but I am unable to read it. Someone read aloud to me your answer to my letter. I can't read it clearly myself. If I didn't have someone capable of making out my characters, I would be unable to send letters.

To return to the topic to hand: your reply has solved my problem.

First, in the letter written to you by Chen Duxiu (*Chen Duxiu's Selected Works*, vol. 3, p. 567) and published in Shanghai, it seems clear that the other recipient S cannot have been Sun Hongyi. In your reply, you say that you 'had no background in common' with Sun Hongyi – that is proof of the matter. Chen Duxiu cannot have written to two people who have 'no background in common'.

This error was mine alone. Whenever anyone asked me who H and S were, I would always say: H is Hu Qiuyuan, S is Sun Hongyi.

Second, S was definitely not Xue Nongshan, for Chen Duxiu said that 'I have had no contact with Mr S for more than twenty years', whereas at the time Xue Nongshan and Chen Duxiu were in the Guomindang rear,[9] and they met frequently.

Third, so who is S? Why did I originally say that he was Sun Hongyi? Because I saw a copy of this letter (not Chen Duxiu's original letter), and the recipients were Hu Qiuyuan and Sun Hongyi. Moreover, the letter said that Chen had not seen Mr Sun 'for more than 20 years', i.e., he had seen him at the time of the May Fourth Movement, when Chen and Sun were both in Beijing. So it was entirely possible that they had met at the time.

Luckily, there are a few words in your reply that suggest a good reason for my mistake. The Sun X Yi you mention in your letter (the character I have marked as X is unclear, at the start of the eighth line of the eighth page of the letter) had been misread by me as Sun Hongyi. When He Zhiyu sent you Chen Duxiu's articles (*My Fundamental Views*), he also sent them to Sun X Yi. Since you two knew each other, you would be able to write a letter (jointly or separately) to He Zhiyu expressing your opinion. He Zhiyu showed it to Chen Duxiu, and Chen Duxiu then wrote a letter to both of you.

---

8   Fo Licai (Vladimir Friche), *Yishu shehui xue* (Sociology of art), translated and with an introduction by Hu Qiuyuan, Shanghai: Shenzhou guoguang she, 1933.

9   The part of China unoccupied by the Japanese in 1937–45.

The question is, who was Sun X Yi? But that is a separate problem. That S is not Sun Hongyi has been established. We have also established why I mistook S for Sun Hongyi. In this way, the fundamental problem has been solved. Again, I thank you!

I know that Professor Shen Ji of the History Department at Anhui University has written to you asking this same question, and received no reply. I will write to him and enclose a copy of your letter. If anyone else asks this question, Shen Ji can enlighten them.

Yours sincerely,
    Zheng Chaolin

(5)   Letter Dated 19 December 1996, Hu Qiuyuan to Zheng Chaolin

Mr Chaolin:

After receiving your letter, I made two points:

(1)   The H in Mr Chen's letter is probably me. If so, then S must be Xue Nong-shan, not Sun Hongyi.

(2)   I asked you to send a copy of the letter to the institute in Anhui Province responsible for carrying out research on Mr Chen, for two or three years ago the said documentary centre wrote me a similar letter saying that H is definitely me and asking who S is. At the time, I failed to reply, either because of a minor illness or some small problem. I would now like to make amends by asking you to send a copy of the letter.

I then received from you *Chen Duxiu Research Trends*,[10] no. 9, and a letter dated 11 December. The characters in the letter are not very clear. The main point seems to have been to enquire whether I had received your reply and the magazine. I don't know whether the magazine refers to *Chen Duxiu Research Trends*. As for the letter, the one dated 11 December is just a few words long, and makes no mention of my previous letter.

There's another point I'd like to raise: seventy years ago, in Hankou, I came across a Mr Zheng Chaolin, who had studied in France. He had made some excellent translations of Marxist works, and later joined Chen Duxiu's group. When I first received your letter, I asked myself whether it was the same Zheng Chaolin. When I read it, the writing was spry and lively, and apparently written

---

10   A scholarly journal.

by someone younger than me, so I thought the name must simply be a coincidence. Today's letter bears the handwriting of someone over 90, which leads me to believe that it is indeed the same Mr Zheng Chaolin that I saw seventy years ago. If my speculation is correct, our affinity is indeed predestined.

Finally, I would like to take this opportunity to respectfully request the gentlemen and women of the Chen Duxiu Research Society, given that Mr Zheng's handwriting is hard to read, to answer the two points raised in my previous letter, and to let me know whether the Zheng Chaolin who wrote to me is indeed the Mr Zheng Chaolin I saw seventy years ago.

Happy New Year, and Happy New Year to the members of the Research Society!
Hu Qiuyuan

(6) Letter Dated 31 December 1996, from Zheng Chaolin to Hu Qiuyuan

Mr Qiuyuan:

I have received your letter of 19 December. I recall that when Wu Guozhen was Mayor of Shanghai, he checked the household register and found that there were 13 people (or was it 23?) in Shanghai called Wu Guozhen. I would dare to wager that there is no one other than me called Zheng Chaolin, in the past or in the present, in China or abroad. The Zheng Chaolin living out his later years in peace in Shanghai is the same Zheng Chaolin that experienced the defeat of the revolution in Wuhan seventy years ago. After today, starting with New Year's Day tomorrow, I can tell the people across the country that I am 97 years old.

So you and I once came across one another when we were young. I hope that we can still keep in touch in future. The question of who S was has already been solved (S was Sun Jiyi – when this letter was first published, I mistakenly remembered it as Sun Hongyi). But that doesn't mean that you and I have nothing more to talk about. Let's start by talking about your translation of the *Sociology of Art*. In the preface, you address Chen Duanben[11] as older sister. Obviously you know her. Can you tell me where she is? In the same preface, you talk about translation. Roughly speaking, you say that today translators in

---

11   Chen Duanben (1901–1990), an educator, was a friend of Hu Qiuyuan. Both attended the 1946 Republic of China Constituent Assembly. In 1956, Chen was appointed to the Wuhan Political Consultative Conference.

China can be divided into two groups. One group advocated literal translation, of which Lu Xun was the main example. Another advocated free translation, of which Lin Chaozhen was the main example. Lin Chaozhen is me. At the time, I was in Nanjing Central Military Prison. If anyone had known that Lin Chaozhen was me, you would definitely have been in trouble. However, in recent years I have come across historical materials that prove that you were not the only one to make this comparison. Qu Qiubai did too. See p. 998 of *Qiu Qiubai's Collected Essays*, published by Chongqing Publishing House in 1995 – I'll copy the page and send you it.

The magazine I mentioned is the 9th issue, which you have received. My reply to your long letter was sent at the same time as this magazine, but separately. It's hard to imagine that you received the magazine but not the letter. I will send you a replacement copy in a few days' time.

After receiving your long letter, I immediately sent a copy to Mr Shen Ji, Professor of History at Anhui University. He replied saying: 'The Anhui Documentary Centre Mr Hu Qiuyuan talks about does not exist, but the person he remembers sending a letter from Anhui was me, there is no one else'.

I hope you can read the characters written by an old man who is nearly one hundred years old.

I wish you health!
    Zheng Chaolin

Annex: Qu Qiubai on Zheng Chaolin

Stalin's *Lenin and Leninism* has been translated by Comrade Zheng Chaolin, and readers can refer to it. 'Transformative translation' (*gaiyi*) was originally advocated by the dramatist Hong Yu, and the original intention was to make writings accessible to Chinese readers. The 'literal translation' currently advocated by Zhou Zuoren[12] exerts a very baneful influence. Chinese grammar is completely different from foreign grammar. If a translation is literal, it becomes little more than an exercise book for elementary school students of foreign languages. As for Comrade Chaolin's translation, it is excellent (*Qu Qiubai lunwen ji*, p. 998).

---

12   The younger brother of the writer Lu Xun.

(7)   Letter Dated 18 January 1997, from Hu Qiuyuan to Zheng Chaolin (Note 1)[13]

Mr Chaolin:

On 31 December 1996 and 3 January 1997, I received from younger brother Little Zhou a letter dated 27 November 1996, for which my grateful thanks. One of the joys of receiving this second letter is that the handwriting in it is askew [and therefore by an old person], which proves that this Chaolin is the same Chaolin I once saw and whose translations I read. You said that there has only ever been one Chaolin in ancient and modern times. Today, he is a venerable old person of 97 years, how can one not rejoice? The second cause for joy is that you mention the preface to *The Sociology of Art*, which had long slipped from my mind, and while dipping into old writings, you found an article that mentions both Lu Xun and Lin Chaozhen.[14] That people who seventy years ago regarded their translations with great esteem are still alive, and in touch, is indeed cause for rejoicing! I mentioned in a previous letter that I had seen you once before. That was in the sixteenth year of the Republic [1927]. At the time, I was editing *Chinese Student* for the National Students' Union and I used to give publicity reports. On one occasion, you stood up and spoke. A friend sitting alongside me said that is Zheng Chaolin, and I seem to remember he said there was a problem with your legs.

I can say a few words about my relationship with Mr Duxiu. (a) In the early days of the Anti-Japanese War, *The Daily Times* (*Shidai ribao*) was run from the Derun building in Hankou, which happened to be quite close to where Mr Duxiu lived, and I used to call by to pay my respects and for a chat. (b) When my wife and mother first entered Sichuan, they were on the same boat as Mr Duxiu and Zheng Xuejia.[15] (c) When I first made my westward journey, I argued that China should implement capitalism. After reaching Sichuan, Mr Chen made a speech at the Minsheng Company in which he made the same proposal. After I arrived in Sichuan, in September or October 1938, I published this idea in *The Daily Times* edited by Xue Nongshan. When Wang Jingwei flew off the handle

---

13   Note by Little Zhou: The original letter contained the following three additional comments: (a) Little Zhou, please send a copy of this letter to Mr Shen, I greatly appreciate your kindness; (b) the character *ji* [presumably in the name Sun Jiyi] is correct; (c) Happy New Year to Little Zhou too – please read this letter aloud to the venerable Zheng.

14   A reworking of Zheng Chaolin's name.

15   Note by Little Zhou: I asked the venerable Zheng about his apparent lameness, and whether Hu had remembered rightly. Zheng said: "At the time I had athlete's foot, yes, so I was lame, so Hu remembered rightly. After so many decades, and he still remembers!"

and urged a charge to be brought against me,[16] Mr Chen wrote to the Guomindang Central Committee saying that my proposal was worth studying and shouldn't be suppressed. After that, Chen and Xue often mentioned my name in their correspondence, and Xue repeatedly showed up, which left a deep impression. (d) After Mr Duxiu's death, in Chongqing I wrote an obituary for Mr Chen Duxiu for the supplement published by *Saodang bao*. When Sun Fuyuan saw it, he persuaded me to change it to 'Obituary for Mr Chen Zhongfu'.[17]

I have already explained that H was me and S must have been Xue Nongshan. Now I come to think about it, Sun Jiyi was also a distinct possibility. Sun Jiyi was quite a famous writer in the early Republic of China, and must have been a little more than ten years older than I. Because at the time the pair of us were secretaries on the Supreme National Defence Council, we deeply sympathised with Mr Duxiu because of the vilification to which he was subjected.[18] He must have heard about it, whence the letter addressed to H and S. But all this happened half a century ago, and it's difficult to remember. I quoted the letter in *Outline of the History of Chinese Thought over the Past 130 Years*, because I was mentioned in it.

You are ten years older than I, and there are very few people left in your generation, and there aren't very many left in mine either. Over here, elder brother Yan Lingfeng is still hale, I don't know if you still remember him.

I wish you a Happy New Year, and please take care, I hope you live to reach one hundred years and more!

Hu Qiuyuan

(8)   Letter Dated 8 February 1997, from Zheng Chaolin to Hu Qiuyuan[19]

Mr Qiuyuan:

Several days ago, I received your reply of 18 January. I've been busy and only just got round to answering it.

---

16   Wang Jingwei, originally a Guomindang leftist, later became Japan's wartime puppet.
17   Chen Duxiu's courtesy name.
18   Wang Ming and other Chinese Stalinists vilified Chen, in part, and for complicated reasons, in an attempt to undermine Mao.
19   Note by Little Zhou: I sent this manuscript to Mr Hu Qiuyuan and asked him whether he agreed to its publication.

I'm an old man, nearly one hundred years old and almost blind, and I can only walk around indoors by holding on to tables and chairs, but I can still listen to people reading to me, I can still talk, and I can still write. I believe my job as a human being has not yet run its course, and that I should remain active as long as I am capable of it.

I not only remember two things you said in your translator's preface to *The Sociology of Art*, I also remember to this day that in one of your articles you expressed sympathy for Trotsky's misfortunes and sympathised with Chen Duxiu after his arrest and imprisonment. All that left a deep impression on me, and showed to me that you were made of different stuff than the 'left' literati of the day. A few years ago, I did some research on a certain question in historical materials relating to Lu Xun, and learned for the first time that you paid a price for sympathising with Trotsky and Chen Duxiu, i.e., you were attacked by other 'left' literati. Apparently Lu Xun signalled in a concealed way his outrage at the injustice done to you by those attacks,[20] by making use of a public opportunity to emphasise Chen Duxiu's contribution during the May Fourth Movement era.

From your recent letter to me, I gather that in the early years of the War of Resistance you publicly advocated that China should develop capitalism, which made Wang Jingwei furious, but fortunately Chen Duxiu approved of what you said – in the spirit of seeking truth from facts.[21] It seems to me that, at the time, it was not just the traitor Wang Jingwei and not just the Guomindang leaders who, while personally developing capitalism, opposed the promotion of capitalism by others.

Unfortunately, I no longer had the opportunity to read your writings after my release from prison.

The good impression I received in the Guomindang prison from reading your article made me think it would be a good thing to be able to communicate with you in old age.

I have already done as you asked, and sent Professor Shen Ji in Anhui University's History Department a copy of your recent reply. He wrote back to get your address, and I told him it. I imagine he too will write to you.

I wish you a Happy Spring Festival!
Zheng Chaolin

20   For Lu Xun's view of Chen Duxiu and the Trotskyists, see Gregor Benton, 'Chinese Trotsky-ism and the World of Letters'.

21   'Seek truth from the facts' was the slogan of the Chinese reformers starting in the late 1970s.

(9)   Letter Dated 29 March 1997, from Zhou Lüqiang to Hu Qiuyuan

Mr Qiuyuan:

Thank you for calling me Little Zhou and younger brother, it gives me a very warm, sweet and cordial feeling. More than fifty years ago, my friends called me Little Zhou, and now that I have passed the age of seventy, old friends still call me that. I am happy to bear that name. I refuse anyway to give in to old age, but in the eyes of the senior generation, the venerable Old Zheng and you yourself, I will always be Little Zhou.

I have already sent Mr Shen Ji a copy of your letter to Old Zheng. I have also copied several of your letters to two others, Mr Tang Baolin, editor-in-chief of *Chen Duxiu Research Trends*, and Mr Ren Jianshu, a Mainland scholar who studies Chen Duxiu.[22]

In dealing with your correspondence with Old Zheng, I was deeply touched by the rigorous pursuit of knowledge to which each of you is committed. You do not forget the letter from someone in Anhui a few years ago that you never answered, and you apologise again and again for your remissness. You are such an admirable person. The letters you send have great historical value, and it is important to publish them. Old Zheng agrees with my suggestion. So I have sorted out and copied the transcripts and will send them to you. Please review them. If you agree, they can be published on either side of the Strait [on the Mainland and in Taiwan]. In addition to the correspondence, the publication could be accompanied by recent photos and examples of your handwriting.

Old Zheng wrote a good hand in his early years, and right up to his eighties he continued to write clearly (see his handwritten inscription at the age of eighty), but in recent years he has suffered from cataracts and his vision has greatly deteriorated. However, he continues to churn out a ceaseless flow of articles and letters. We suggested that he dictate them into a tape-recorder which we would then sort out, but after one or two trials he gave up, probably because he was in the habit of thinking while writing, so he insisted on writing everything down on paper. His 'blind writing' is hard to read. In copying his letters, I originally planned to use traditional unsimplified characters,[23] but in writing them I became confused, and ended up with a mixture of simplified and unsimplified characters, which made proofreading even more complicated.

---

22   Tang and Ren are Mainland writers who specialise in researching Chen Duxiu and the Trotskyists.

23   Simplified characters were introduced by the Communists after 1949, whereas the Guomindang on Taiwan retain the traditional unsimplified script.

I attach a photo of Old Zheng. Please send us a recent photo of yourself. If in copying your letters I made any mistakes or if there is anything you would like to add or delete, please let me know. I won't send the manuscript to press without your consent.

I wish you all the best of health and a long life!
    Sincerely,
    Little Zhou

(10)   Letter Dated 21 April 1997, from Hu Qiuyuan to Zhou Lüqiang and for Chaolin

Mr Zhou, and please pass this letter on to Mr Chaolin:

I received the package of documents several days ago. I think you must have been waiting a long time for my reply. First of all, let me answer the points you raise.

    You say you want to publish our correspondence regarding H and S – I not only agree with the proposal, but I welcome it, for the letters have historical value. Regarding my tardy response to elder brother's letter, this was due to a minor illness that afflicted me after the Chinese New Year. As for a recent photo, I look old, less hale and healthy than Old Zheng. Little Zhou is also more than seventy, so I should stop calling him little and start calling him mister.

Respectfully yours, and wishing you a Happy New Year!
    Younger brother Hu Qiuyuan

(11)   Letter Dated 7 May 1997, from Zhou Lüqiang to Hu Qiuyuan

Mr Qiuyuan:

Your esteemed letter of 21 April arrived on 29 April. On the same afternoon, I went to read it aloud to Old Zheng. He was very happy. He took hold of your recent photo, brought it right up the tip of his nose, peered closely at it, and said: 'Hu Qiuyuan is in far better health than I'. Old Zheng told me to write a letter to thank you and wish you good health. If you visit the Main-land for the third time, he hopes you will pay him a visit to speak about old times.

In your masterpiece *Outline of the History of Chinese Thought over the Past 130 Years*, you make only a passing reference to Zhang Junli,[24] but you show a singular devotion to Chen Duxiu. You quote three letters and a long passage from an article, and you offer a detailed and penetrating analysis. It should be published together with the correspondence between you and Old Zheng. However, *Letters across the Sea* is already seven thousand characters long. This passage can only be submitted to Mainland journals. If it's too long, there's no way it can be used, so we have no choice other than to give up this treasured writing. However, if you have no word limit in Taiwan, you can use it. As for your obituary of Mr Chen Zhongfu, we do not have this material to hand. We intend to write to Mr Shen Ji to see if he can send it in time, in which case we will be honoured to incorporate it.

You began your letter by saying: 'I received the package of documents several days ago. I think you must have been waiting a long time for my reply'. This is true. We weren't worried about you being late, just that we thought you might not have received it. When I took it to the post office, I asked for it to be registered, and I was told that mail sent to Taiwan would not be registered. However, the letter you sent was indeed registered. Mail often goes astray, for reasons that cannot be clarified. Fortunately, things can now be copied, and you can keep a copy for the records, so if something goes missing, it can be sent again.

Old Zheng decided to arrange for *Letters across the Sea* to be published, but on the Mainland many factors must be taken into account, including personal relations and other things. It is difficult to say when it will appear. If it comes out first in Taiwan, please send a copy or a photocopy.

You are the older generation, please don't stand on ceremony, you can call me Little Zhou or even better, call me by my full name. If there is anything I can do for you, please feel free to let me know.

I wish you health and a long life,
    Little Zhou

When I read this letter to Old Zheng, he asked me to add two points. (1) Zheng has not received your reply to his letter of 8 February 1997, which we now know you did not receive. Fortunately, you did receive Little Zhou's copy of the manuscript. (2) You have already received the ninth issue of *Chen Duxiu*

---

24   Also known as Carsun Chang (1887–1969), a philosopher, public intellectual, and social-democratic politician.

Research Trends. It includes Zheng Chaolin's obituary of Chen Duxiu. I wonder if you noticed it? It was originally published under the name Yiyin[25] in the Trotskyist underground journal. Old Zheng no longer has copies of his early articles. The editor of *Trends* didn't know where the obituary had been found.

(12)   Letter Dated 29 May 1997, from Zhou Lüqiang to Hu Qiuyuan

Mr Qiuyuan:

The venerable Old Zheng has instructed me to send you the 11th issue of *Chen Duxiu Research Trends*. In it are three letters that passed between you and Old Zheng. They had already been sent to *Trends*. Regarding the subsequent letters, they have not yet seen them, so the editor asks in his introduction to the issue who S is, and adds: 'This might become a mystery for all times'. On 22 May, Mr Tang Baolin came to Shanghai to host the Fourth National Chen Duxiu Scholarly Seminar, which opened on the 25th. Old Zheng gave all the *Letters across the Sea* to Mr Tang Baolin. They will continue to publish them – the identity of S will no longer be a 'mystery for all times'. *Trends* is a publication of this scholarly association. It does not pay for manuscripts, but manuscripts can be submitted to other publications.

Mr Shen Ji has sent me a copy of your obituary of Mr Chen Zhongfu. A copy of it was sent to him by Mr Chen Wanxiong of the Hong Kong Commercial Press, it is from *Zhonghua zazhi* (China Magazine), vol. 3, no. 5 (16 May 1965), pp. 17–19. The text is clear, but the footnote on p. 19 is illegible. Shortly I will send you *Chen Duxiu Research Trends*.

Old Zheng says hello.

That's all for now, sincerely yours,
    Little Zhou

---

25   One of Zheng Chaolin's pen-names.

(13)   Letter Dated 31 May 1997, from Hu Qiuyuan to Zhou Lüqiang and Zheng Chaolin

Mr Chaolin:

I received your letter of 7 May several days ago. You noted that I 'show a singular devotion to Mr Chen'. There are two main reasons for that. First, at the time, the Westernisation faction (mainly the Peking University faction) was pessimistic about the war. Many people joined Wang Jingwei's 'low-profile club',[26] but Mr Chen was firmly convinced that the Resistance would triumph (so was Fu Sinian[27]). Second, in Chinese academic circles Mr Chen was treated very unfairly. He was denied freedom of speech. When Liang Qichao died, thousands of people attended his funeral. When Hu Shi died in Taiwan, hundreds did. When Mr Chen died in Jiangjin, fewer than a score gathered to bury him. Since *Letters across the Sea* is limited in length, there is no need to include my clumsy efforts. Now that *Zhonghua zazhi* has ceased publication, I have no outlet. What other publications would be interested in such a matter?

There is one other favour I would like to ask. Older brother asked me if I noticed Mr Zheng's obituary for Chen Duxiu in the ninth issue of *Trends*. To be honest, I am dim-sighted from old age and failed to notice it. I hope that you can send me a copy at your convenience.[28] I would be most grateful.

You say that you hope I can visit the Mainland for a third time. But during my second stay in Beijing, the Sino-Japanese Hospital told me that I should stop travelling long distances. Looking up into the cloudy sky, I utter unavailing cries of despair.

Wishing you and Old Zheng a long life.
    Younger brother Qiuyuan

---

26   A group associated with Wang Jingwei, Zhou Fohai and other pro-Japanese politicians in wartime China.

27   Fu Sinian (1896–1950) was an educator and linguist, and a leader alongside Chen Duxiu of the May Fourth Movement in 1919.

28   One must assume that Hu had lost or given away the issue containing the obituary.

(14)   Letter Dated 12 June 1997, from Zheng Chaolin to Hu Qiuyuan

Mr Qiuyuan:

Elder brother Little Zhou read your two letters aloud to me, and answered them on my behalf. Little Zhou has also compiled our correspondence and other documents into a booklet titled *Letters across the Sea*. Without him, I could have done nothing.

I remember that when I was being held in the Nanjing Central Military Prison in the 1930s, I often read articles by Hu Qiuyuan in publications of the Shenzhou Guoguang Society. In them were passages sympathising with Trotsky and Chen Duxiu, and you even brought up Lin Chaozhen's translations,[29] which is what caught my attention. At the time, I was unaware of the new writer's background. I am now taking the liberty of writing to you about the Sun Jiyi issue. I have learned from your reply that you and I saw each other in Wuhan. This unexpected discovery caused me to sigh with emotion, at something that happened exactly seventy years ago. At the time, I was only twenty-seven years old, and you were only eighteen.

Now, both you and I have grown old. Reading your letter, however, I am suddenly again full of vim and vigour, though I have eyes but am unable to read, legs but am unable to walk, it makes me so angry! You can judge my mood from a *ci* I wrote a few years ago:

Lin Jiang Xian

'I'm not the only one to have grown old' (borrowed from Fang Weng[30])

I sigh at the frustration of my lofty goals,
one hundred years along a rough and bumpy road.
Snow drifts among the mountains,
showers lash the little boat.
Straining to glimpse the glorious future,
a spring breeze, with the bright sun overhead.
Trudging across mountains and wading streams,
what is the old, declining man striving to achieve?

---

29   As we have seen, Lin Chaozhen was one of Zheng Chaolin's many pen-names.
30   Fang Weng was another name of the Southern Song poet Lu You (1125–1210).

Chasing the sun in the Abyss of Yu,[31]
Kua Fu will happily die of thirst.

It makes no sense for a person who has lost his labour power and relies on social support to prolong his life.

All best wishes,
    Zheng Chaolin

Mr Hu:

Old Zheng profoundly apologises for not having personally penned his previous two replies to you. This time, he insists on writing to you in person. I attach his original letter together with my copy of it. I also attach a copy of Old Zheng's 'Obituary for Comrade Duxiu'. I have sent your recent letter and your 'Obituary for Mr Chen Zhongfu' to *Chen Duxiu Research Trends*, for them to print.

I wish you an auspicious summer,
    Little Zhou

(15)   **Letter Dated 26 June 1997, from Hu Qiuyuan to Zhou Lüqiang and Chaolin**

Mr Chaolin:

I have received your two replies and the attached photos.

In the first letter, Mr Zheng included a copy of *Trends* (which I had not received before). Now I know that part of our *Letters across the Sea* has been published. I also received a copy of Mr Chen Duxiu's rebuttal of the court documents [allegedly] expressing 'deep self-repentance' and of the rainbow couplet.[32] At the trial in Suzhou,[33] the lawyer Zhang Shijian said [in a misguided attempt to defend him] that Chen now belonged to the Communist

---

31   The Abyss of Yu is the legendary place into which the sun sets. Kua Fu died racing the sun.
32   Chen Duxiu's couplet ran as follows: 'In behaviour, be fair and upright, open-minded and magnanimous, so that your conscience remains clear. In troubled times, continue to cherish broad-mindedness and lofty thoughts, with the energy of a rainbow'.
33   Note added by Little Zhou: Suzhou should be Jiangning.

Party opposition – he had the same goal as the Guomindang and should not be found guilty. Chen then told the judge that he still believed in communism and still opposed the Guomindang, so what lawyer Zhang had just said could not represent him. Replete with power and grandeur! I have long been acquainted with Mr Chen's calligraphy, and this couplet is handsomely written, many thanks.

The second letter, in Old Zheng's handwriting, is dated 12 June, and Mr Zhou has transcribed the characters. It is accompanied by the original obituary for Chen and the *ci* Lin Jiang Xian. Old Zheng says that we met seventy years ago and knew each other's names, and that we can now speak across the Strait, although even now it is not easy to do so. It is difficult [now], in 1997, and it wasn't easy in 1988 either.[34] Our predestined affinity has brought good fortune – how many of our generation lived to see the return of Hong Kong to China?

Old Zheng hopes that I can return to the Mainland and talk about old times. This is also my burning desire, but the doctor has forbidden me to undertake long journeys. Mr Shen Ji's letter mentioned that this October there will be a research symposium to discuss Mr Chen and Chinese culture, and hopes that I can write a paper. However, I've been working on an old paper for a year now, and I have not even got half-way through. Sometime soon, I will write to Mr Shen to apologise, and I hope Mr Zhou will convey my humble opinion.

Wishing Old Zheng and Mr Zhou a happy summer,
Hu Qiuyuan

Note by Little Zhou: In the second half of 1997, no further letters passed between Zheng Chaolin and Hu Qiuyuan. During the Spring Festival in 1998, Hu Qiuyuan sent two exquisitely crafted New Year cards to Zheng Chaolin and Zhou Lüqiang, signed by Hu Qiuyuan and Jing Youru. One card carried an inscription for Old Zheng: wishing Mr and Mrs Chaolin one thousand New Year happinesses. My card was similarly addressed, with the following sentence attached: 'The two letters and the publication have been received – because of chores and minor illnesses, I delayed in acknowledging them, thank you'. In the first month of 1998, Old Zheng fell ill and was hospitalised three times. On 20 July, he suffered a cerebral haemorrhage. He was in a coma for nearly a fort-

---

34 Perhaps a reference to the death of Jiang Jingguo and the start in Taiwan of the presidency of the Taiwan-born Lee Teng-hui, who dismantled many structures left over from the past.

night. He died on 1 August 1998, aged 98. After Old Zheng's death, I wrote to Mr Hu Qiuyuan to inform him of the sad news.

(16)   Hu Qiuyuan's Expression of Condolence on the Death of Chaolin

Teacher Chaolin's learning is known throughout China and abroad. He is an eminent and eloquent translator. In recent years, we have exchanged letters and established a close literary relationship. Hearing this news of his passing, I am saddened by the loss of a venerable Elder of the nation and pained at losing this my dear friend.

Hu Qiuyuan expresses his condolences

Tenth day of the eighth month of the fifteenth year of the Sexagenary Cycle (1998)

Attached:

Letter of 11 August 1998, from Hu Bukai to Zhou Lüqiang

Mr Zhou:

My father received your letter and was very saddened to hear of the death of the Elder Zheng. However, he recently had an operation on his eyes, so he is unable to write. He therefore specially asked me to write this letter of condolences. Please convey this message to Elder Zheng's family and friends, thank you.

Respectfully wishing you great peace!
    Hu Bukai

Annex 1: Chen Duxiu's Letter to H and S

This letter is the main subject of Zheng Chaolin's correspondence with Hu Qiuyuan – Zheng knows who H is, but who is S? In the letter, Chen informs his non-Trotskyist friends of his new view of Lenin and Trotsky, and appears to abandon Marxist theory for a pragmatic approach to political questions. See too his letter of 23 December 1941 to Zheng Xuejia, a former Trotskyist sympathiser who had later become associated with the Guomindang, in which Chen rejects Marxism as irrelevant not only to China but even to Russia and Western Europe.[35] On the whole, however, as Wang Fanxi notes elsewhere, Chen's final views are not irreconcilable with Marxism as Karl Kautsky and others understood it.

Dear Messrs H and S,

Three years have passed since I and Mr H parted, and it is more than twenty years since I last saw Mr S. Thinking back on my Beijing days [spent with Mr S], I cannot but feel nostalgic.[36]

I have seen your letters to Y[37] and your comments on my latest works, I thank you warmly for them. In formulating my opinions, I prefer to base myself on the historical and contemporary process of events rather than on vacuous isms, and I am even more loath to quote as a foundation for my thinking what others may have said in the past. This method of 'measuring by saints' words' is a weapon drawn from the armoury of religion, not of science.[38]

In 'My Basic Views', which I completed recently, I have also avoided bringing in any sort of ism. My seventh thesis [in that essay] proposes re-evaluating the Bolsheviks' theories and leaders (including both Lenin and Trotsky) not by some Marxist measure but on the basis of the lessons of more than two decades of Soviet history. If the Soviet Union had rational grounds for existence (no matter whether it succeeds or fails), no one could repudiate it, even if its existence were not in conformity with Marxism. To confine oneself to a definite 'circle' is to be 'sectarian'. The so-called 'orthodox' is the equivalent of what the Confucians of the Song dynasty called *daotong*.[39] None of these things were ever to my liking. That's why I came out against Confucianism when I found it to be wrong, and against the Third International when I found its policies to be wrong. And I'll take the same stance towards the Fourth, Fifth, and ... th Internationals. Shizhi[40] has called me 'an oppositionist for life', and it's true, though

---

35   For Chen's letter to Zheng Xuejia, see Ren Jianshu and Tang Baolin, *Chen Duxiu zhuan* ('A biography of Chen Duxiu'), 2vols, Shanghai: Shanghai renmin chuban she, 1989, vol. 2, p. 286.

36   H and S are Hu Qiuyuan and Sun Jiyi, as we have seen.

37   Y is He Zhiyu, who edited Chen Duxiu's last articles and letters.

38   A Buddhist term, meaning to take saints' words as the sole judgment and measure of truth or falsehood, right or wrong.

39   The legitimate legacy of Confucianism.

40   I.e., Hu Shi (Hu Shih) (1891–1962), a philosopher, writer, advocate of the vernacular literature, and one of modern China's most influential liberal scholars. Hu taught at Beijing

not by my design; facts forced me along this road. Figuratively speaking, if meat tastes good, no one cares about which butcher sold it. But if it tastes bad and one still likes it simply because it was sold by Lugaojian,[41] that would be an exercise of superstition. Superstition and prejudice cannot withstand the test of events or the passage of time; I'll have nothing to do with either of them. That's all for now. Even from this [short letter], I trust you can discern my attitude in searching for the truth.

If I write new articles, I'll certainly send them to you for comments. I've a lot more to say, but unfortunately my poor health prevents me from writing. Moreover, even if I do write, it's very hard to get things mimeographed.

Best wishes,
  Duxiu

19 January [1941]

Annex 2: Excerpts from Shen Ji's Letters to Zheng Chaolin

1.   *Letter Dated 11 December 1996*

Please be reassured that your letter of 28 November, together with a copy of Mr Hu Qiuyuan's letter and your letter to Mr Hu Qiuyuan, has been received. Mr Hu has a great sense of responsibility and provides evidence of what he knows. However, on page 8, he mentions an old colleague, Sun X Yi, in whose name the character represented here by 'X' is difficult to make out. I have searched through some reference books. In the years following the May Fourth Movement, there was a person named Sun Jiyi. Mr Hu seems to have written the non-simplified form of the X character as *ji*, is that right? If Mr Hu writes again, please let me know. Mr Hu Qiuyuan mentions an Anhui Documentary Centre, but there is no such unit. I was the recipient of the letter he remembers sending to Anhui, it could not have been anyone else.

University from 1917 to 1927; between 1918 and 1920, he helped edit Chen Duxiu's *Xin qingnian*. After May Fourth, 1919, Hu split from Chen Duxiu and was strongly criticised by the Communists. He was a supporter of the Guomindang, and pro-American.

41   Suzhou's best-known cooked pork shop, established several hundred years ago.

2.   *Letter Dated 26 December 1996*

I wish you a Happy New Year and good health! I received your letter of 15 December, you flatter me. You are my elder and my better. I have benefited immensely from your letters to me, especially from your upright character and your tact, which I greatly respect. I take as my personal model the rigour with which you pursue learning. You never echo the opinions of others, in which sense I am like you. But you acknowledge facts and are prepared to seek truth from them.

3.   *Letter Dated 24 February 1997*

Mr Hu Qiuyuan has already replied to my letter. He said he was 'rectifying past errors', so he had replied immediately.

As for Sun Jiyi, I have found out nothing about him. I checked in reference books and lists of pen-names used in modern times. I will return later to working on the question of who Sun Jiyi was. There's nothing to tell you at the moment.

Annex 3: Letter Dated 28 January 1997, from Hu Qiuyuan to Shen Ji

Mr Shen Ji:

I received your letter yesterday, and I reply today, in order to rectify past errors.

Earlier, I received your letter asking about H and S. At the time, I was ill, so I did not answer immediately. Even after recovering from my illness, I no longer knew where I'd put your letter, so I was unable to answer it. I kept thinking about it, it preyed on my mind. Recently Zheng Chaolin sent me a letter mentioning this matter. It occurred to me that he would know the people in Anhui working on this problem, so I asked him to check. Sure enough, he put me in touch with you. It must be fate. After repeated discussions by the three parties, it can be concluded that I am H and S is Sun Jiyi, the matter is now put beyond doubt. Our close affinity has led to the solving of this historical problem.

You will have seen that *Zhonghua* published an annotated version of my 'Obituary for Mr Chen Zhongfu', originally published in *Saodang bao* – I was very pleased. You ask me to write another article about Mr Chen. However, I am old and in declining health, and I am engaged in adding a chapter to *An Outline History of Chinese Thought over the Past 130 Years*, which will thus become *An Outline History of Chinese Thought over the Past 175 Years*. I have still not completed the draft, so it is difficult to respond your request. However, Mr Chen is mentioned five or six times in *An Outline History of Chinese Thought over the*

Past 130 Years. I published this book myself, and it is already sold out. It contains much criticism of a certain gentleman, so it is perhaps not convenient to send it to you. I will send you the new edition when it appears (it is more balanced).

Yours sincerely, wishing you a Happy New Year,
    Younger Brother Hu Qiuyuan

Annex 4: Shen Ji's Telegram of Condolence after Old Zheng's Death

I was shocked and greatly saddened to learn that Old Zheng has died suddenly. He was the same age as the century,[42] and suffered many setbacks in the course of his difficult life. He was independent in mind and action, treasured by others, constant in his thoughts and beliefs, and a model for us all. In the seventeen years that I have been his pupil and he my teacher, I saw that he had the refined air of a great master.

5 August 1998

---

42   I.e., born in 1901.

Appendices

Zheng Chaolin's Life and Death

Obituary of Zheng Chaolin by Wang Fanxi

Zheng Chaolin, a veteran of the Chinese Communist Party and of the Chinese Trotskyist movement, died on 1 August 1998, in Shanghai. He devoted his entire life to the cause of the liberation of the Chinese workers and peasants, and yet his achievement was far from restricted to the revolution.

Zheng was extremely versatile; his talents were numerous and many sided. He was at once a writer, a poet, a historian, a linguist, and a translator. His achievements were not only numerous but exemplary. In all respects he avoided a superficial approach and probed deeply into the essence of things, assiduously perfecting his skills and knowledge.

Naturally, he was first and foremost a faithful and unyielding revolutionary. His efforts and achievements in other fields took as their keynote his revolutionary thinking, and were imbued with his revolutionary spirit. Therefore I shall restrict myself in this obituary to writing a brief introduction to his life as a revolutionary.

Zheng Chaolin was born in Zhangping in Fujian Province in 1901, and as a boy received a traditional Chinese education. In 1919 he went to France as part of the Work-Study Programme (under which young Chinese students financed their studies by working part-time in French industry), and came under the influence of Western thought, particularly the Russian Revolution.

As a result, he gradually abandoned his attachment to the philosophy of Confucius and Mencius and even of Laozi and Zhuangzi and embraced the ideas propagated by Chen Duxiu and his co-thinkers, who advocated democracy and science. Shortly afterwards he embraced Marxism, and very soon progressed from thought to action.

In June 1922, when some young Chinese Marxists living in Europe held a meeting in Paris at which they set up the Youth Communist Party, Zheng Chaolin was among the eighteen delegates, who included Zhou Enlai, Zhao Shiyan, and Yin Kuan. In 1923, he was selected to go to Russia to study at Moscow's University for the Toilers of the East.

In July 1924, when the CCP urgently needed cadres as a result of the rapid development of the revolutionary situation in China, he was sent back to China together with Chen Yannian and others. He worked in the Propaganda Department of the Central Committee, edited party journals, drafted internal educational materials and external propaganda materials, and translated Bukharin's *ABC of Communism* while at the same time teaching at the party school, that is, Shanghai University.

From 1925 to 1927, when the Chinese Revolution grew apace, he participated in the famous May Thirtieth Movement and in the second and third Shanghai workers' risings. After Chiang Kai-shek's bloody coup of 12 April 1927, Zheng went with the Central Committee of the CCP to Wuhan, where he took part in the party's Fifth Congress. After the Congress, he was appointed head of Propaganda Department of the Hubei Provincial Committee.

After the final defeat of the revolution, he took part in the party's famous August 7th Conference, and soon afterward secretly moved back to Shanghai with the new Central Committee and took charge of the new party organ *Bolshevik*, as its chief editor.

In 1928, he went to Fujian to reorganise party affairs in the province. In 1929, he married comrade Liu Jingzhen. Not long afterwards, he was arrested for the first time by the Guomindang. Fortunately, his identity was not discovered, and after just forty days he was freed from prison as a result of the secret intervention of the party.

Between 1929 and 1930, he began to come into contact with Leon Trotsky's writings on the Chinese Revolution. Deeply impressed, he turned towards Trotskyism, together with Chen Duxiu and more than eighty veteran party members.

In May 1931, Zheng, Chen Duxiu and three other comrades represented the Proletariat group at the unification conference of the four Trotskyist groups. He was elected to the Central Committee of the new Trotskyist organisation and took charge of its Propaganda Department.

Not long afterwards, he was arrested by the Guomindang authorities and sentenced to fifteen years in prison, though he was freed after just seven years, when the Japanese War broke out.

After his release from prison, he rested and recuperated for a while in a village in Anhui Province together with his wife, and proofread and translated the remaining part of Trotsky's *The Revolution Betrayed* (one third of which had already been translated by two other Trotskyists in Nanjing Prison).

In 1940 he returned to Shanghai, where he joined the leadership of the Chinese Trotskyist organisation and the editorial board of its underground paper, *Struggle*. At the same time, he translated Volumes 2 and 3 of Trotsky's *History of the Russian Revolution*.

After the outbreak of a new World War in Western Europe in 1939, differences of opinions grew up in the Chinese Trotskyist leadership, principally in regard to what attitude to adopt to the Chinese resistance once the Anti-Japanese War in China became caught up in the wider war. A protracted dispute ensued, and spread from a political to an organisational split in 1942. Chaolin was a leading member of the group later known as the Internationalist Workers' Party of China (IWP).

On 7 December 1941 the Japanese army occupied Shanghai's foreign settlements and revolutionary activity directed against the Japanese became extremely difficult. From then until the Japanese defeat in August 1945, Chaolin put his main effort into writing. Apart from editing *Internationalist*, the underground Trotskyist journal, he wrote his memoirs and *Three Travellers*, a collection of political debates in the form of imaginary dialogues.

He also wrote *The ABC of Permanent Revolution* and *A Critical Biography of Chen Duxiu*. To earn a living, he translated some literary works, among them Ignazio Silone's *Fontamara* and a book by André Gide.

From August 1945 to May 1949, from the Japanese surrender and the civil war between the Guomindang and the CCP through to the Communist victory in China, he wrote numerous articles for *New Banner*, a publicly declared Trotskyist biweekly, which was banned by the Guomindang Government after twenty-one issues.

On the eve of the Communist occupation of Shanghai, the group to which he belonged reorganised as the IWP, which he helped lead. In the meantime, Chaolin systematically researched the social nature of the new China and wrote a pamphlet on the subject, *On State Capitalism*.

In the next two to three years, the IWP continued its activities under Communist rule and extended its influence. As a result, on 22 December 1952, its entire membership, together with all the other Chinese Trotskyists and even sympathisers, were netted up by the Maoist political police.

This development had naturally been foreseen. As a precaution, the other Trotskyist organisation, under Peng Shuzhi, had already transferred its leadership to Hong Kong. The group to which Zheng Chaolin belonged also decided to send someone [Wang Fanxi himself] to set up a liaison station in Hong Kong.

Chaolin himself, however, refused to go and insisted on staying behind in Shanghai, although he was fully aware of the great danger that he faced there. His St Peter-like spirit of self-sacrifice led him not to a martyr's grave but to a further twenty-seven years in prison, including physical and spiritual abuse.

In June 1979, as a result of changes in the leadership of the CCP and in response to calls by people both inside and outside China (in 1979 he was declared a Prisoner of Conscience by Amnesty International), Chaolin and eleven other Trotskyist survivors of Mao's prisons were restored to liberty. In all, Chaolin spent a total thirty-four years behind bars under first the Guomindang and then the CCP, thus equalling the record for political imprisonment set by the nineteenth-century French revolutionary Louis Auguste Blanqui.

In the nineteen years between his release in 1979 and his death in August 1998, Chaolin suffered from poor health as a result of his long years in prison, but he refused to live the sort of life that most retired people live, and put enormous effort into reflecting or writing about events in the world around him.

In those years, he achieved three main things, First, he helped various historians write true accounts of the Chinese Revolution and the CCP (including Chinese Trotskyism), to correct distortions made, consciously or unconsciously, by official historians, and in particular to refute past slanders and distortions directed by the CCP against Chen Duxiu. Second, he reflected independently and systematically on fundamental questions in the Chinese and the World Revolution, and put the process and outcome of those reflections into writing in his long essay 'On Cadreism'. Third, he repeatedly demanded of successive Congress of the CCP that they rehabilitate the Chinese Trotskyists, formally declare Trotskyists (in China and throughout the world) not to be counter-revolutionaries, and admit that the past suppression of the Chinese Trotskyists had been wrong.

He recorded his efforts in these three regards in writings of more than one million Chinese characters. Unfortunately, so far it has been possible to publish only a small part of them. Even though Chaolin enjoyed personal freedom after 1979 and was even named as a member of the Shanghai Municipal Political Consultative Committee, he continued to be labelled a 'counter-revolutionary' and to suffer discrimination.

In recent years, his memoirs were twice allowed to be published 'internally' (that is, for a restricted readership) and his translation of D. Merezhkovski's *Resurrection of the Gods* was republished, but none of his main works dealing with ideological and political questions, whether written in prison or after his release, has received permission to be published.

Because Chaolin all along resolutely maintained his opposition to Stalinism and Maoism, he has continued to be viewed as a 'counter-revolutionary'. Of his main writings, only his memoirs have appeared in English, in a volume titled *An Oppositionist for Life: Memoirs of the Chinese Revolutionary Zheng Chaolin*, published in the USA in 1996 by Humanities Press. His memoirs were also published in German in 1991 by isp Verlag Frankfurt, in a translation by Rudolf Segall under the title *Siebzig Jahre Rebell: Erinnerungen eines chinesischen Oppositionellen* ('Seventy years a rebel: Memoirs of a Chinese Oppositionist'). From these writings, foreign friends can get some idea of the life of this remarkable Chinese Marxist-Trotskyist.

Chaolin's wife Liu Jingzhen [alias Wu Jingru] died less than half a year after her and Chaolin's release from a labour camp in June 1979. Their son Frei, born in 1938, died in 1945. In his final years, Chaolin was cared for by his great niece.

Translated by Gregor Benton

A Self-Description at the Age of Ninety (Written 1 May 1990)
Zheng Chaolin

My name is Zheng Chaolin. I was born in 1901, so according to the old Chinese way of counting, this year I am ninety.

I was born in Zhangping, a small mountainous county in the south of Fujian province. My family was an old-established landlord family already in decline, but it still maintained the ancient trappings of culture and education. When I was a child, a 'foreign-style school' had already started up in my home town, but I still acquired my schooling at the old-style private academy, until finally, I was inserted into the graduation class of the foreign-style school, to get my certificate of primary education. I graduated under the old-style system of middle school, that is, after a course in traditional Chinese culture lasting only four years.

I graduated from middle school in the same year as the May Fourth Movement broke out. In our small county high up in the mountains, we heard only about the student movement to boycott Japanese goods and knew nothing about the 'new culture movement'.

In the spring of that year, while I was preparing to take my graduation exams, some Guomindang troops under Chen Jiongming invaded Fujian from Guangdong and occupied the southern corner of the province, including my home town. Chen Jiongming ordered each county under his control to select two students to go to France under the work-study scheme. Each student would get an annual subsidy of $300 from his local authority. That is how I ended up in France. Those who went from Fujian were work-study students like the rest of the Chinese in France; the only difference being that they received these local subsidies.

I experienced my 'New Culture Movement' on the boat from China to France. The first time I saw the radical journal *New Youth* and found out about the 'new culture movement' was on board the boat. Only then did I go through the struggle between the old culture in which I had received my schooling and the new culture that I learned about at sea.

In France, I got close to the progressive students on the work-study programme. I studied together with them, I struggled with them, and together with them, I organised the 'Communist Youth Party' and embarked on the road of revolution.

In 1923, the Communist Youth Party chose its first batch of members – twelve people in all, including me – to go to study at the Communist University for the Toilers of the East in Moscow. In the summer of 1924, the Moscow branch of the Chinese Communist Party chose its second batch of students to send back to China. I was among them.

As soon as I got back to Shanghai, I was allocated to work as secretary in the Party's newly founded Propaganda Department. My job was to write, translate, edit, and publish the Central Committee organ and its various publications, and at the same time to teach 'sociology' (that is, historical materialism) at Shanghai University. I participated in the May Thirtieth Movement and in Shanghai's second and third workers' insurrections.

In the spring of 1927, when the Central Committee moved to Wuhan, I, too, went to Wuhan and took part in the Fifth Congress there. After the Congress, I was allocated to the Hubei Provincial Committee to take charge of its Propaganda Department. I experienced the defeat of the revolution and attended the August 7 Conference. After that, I returned to do propaganda work in the Central Committee. In late September, the Central Committee moved back to Shanghai and so did I, to take charge of the Central Committee's Publishing Bureau and to edit the Party journal *Bolshevik*. In the summer of 1928, I was sent to Xiamen to sort out organisational work in the Fujian Provincial Committee. In late September I returned to Shanghai to continue editing Bolshevik.

At the end of 1928, I resigned from Bolshevik and from various other propaganda tasks because of differences of opinion with Li Lisan, then in charge of the Central Committee's propaganda work. After that, I had nothing to do save wait for the Central Committee to assign me new work.

This period marked the end of the first stage of my work in the Party.

During it, my main activity was literary propaganda, though I also did some oral propaganda, teaching, and organising. Everything I did was in line with the Central Committee's policy; that in its turn was based on the line set for China by the Communist International, which you were not allowed to doubt. So during this stage, I scarcely needed to do any thinking of my own about basic questions of line. After the August 7 Conference, I began to question the line of the Communist International and to consider wrong some of the Central Committee's policies, but whenever I made propaganda outside the Party, I stuck to its line.

Factions had already started fighting one another inside the Party. The main struggle was between the Chen Duxiu supporters around Wang Ruofei and the Central Committee faction of Comintern loyalists around Qu Qiubai; the General Labour Union faction, previously under Zhang Guotao and now under Luo Zhanglong, vacillated between these two groups. I personally inclined, for ideological and historical reasons, toward the Chen Duxiu group.

While editing *Bolshevik*, I went through the motions of propagating the policies of the Central Committee, but gradually, I exposed my own thinking. Because the revolution had been defeated, I could not but ponder certain fundamental questions of the Chinese Revolution, and in the course of this thinking, I gradually began to doubt the Comintern's position on the Chinese Revolution, both past and future. In the articles I wrote, I consciously or unconsciously betrayed my own ideas. The clearest instance of this was an unsigned editorial I wrote for the eleventh issue of Bolshevik, after the defeat of the Guangzhou insurrection, in which I clearly proposed that the Chinese Revolution had no choice but to institute a dictatorship of the proletariat, even though the Central Committee was proposing a democratic dictatorship of workers and peasants, in accordance with the Comintern line. The Central Committee then got Qu Qiubai to write another unsigned editorial for the fourteenth issue of *Bolshevik* correcting my previous editorial. But I had only just begun to develop my own ideas, which had not yet grown into a systematic vision of the Chinese and world revolutions.

After I had withdrawn from the Central Committee's Propaganda Department in early 1929, I continued my independent reflections.

It was then that I was first arrested. I had already married, and my wife Liu Jingzhen – from Kunming, a member of the Communist Party – worked together with me on Bolshevik and left the Central Propaganda Department together with me. We lived with other comrades in a Party building. When one of our number was arrested, the others, too, were implicated and seized. Through the intercession of the Central Committee, those of us who had got drawn into the incident were bailed out after spending forty-odd days at Longhua Garrison Headquarters.

Not long after that, we Chen Duxiu supporters set eyes for the first time on documents of the Soviet Trotskyist Opposition. We discussed them among ourselves and with Chen Duxiu; finally, we accepted Trotsky's proposals for the Chinese Revolution and for the world revolution. After that, we Chen Duxiu supporters and Chen Duxiu himself became Trotskyists and joined the international Trotskyist organisation.

This was a big event in my political life. It was of no less consequence than organising the Communist Youth Party in 1922.

On 1 May 1931, I was a delegate at the Chinese Trotskyists' Unification Congress, and was elected onto its Central Committee and put in charge of its Propaganda Department. Before three weeks had passed, our leadership was uncovered by the Guomindang, after we had been betrayed from within. The majority of the Central Committee members was arrested. I was among them, and was described as the ringleader. The death sentence was said to have been passed on me, but as a result of personnel changes in the Guomindang government, there was a new appointment to the Shanghai garrison and my death sentence was commuted to fifteen years.

The minority of Central Committee members who had escaped arrest, among them Chen Duxiu, restored the leadership and carried on the struggle, but in October 1932, they, too, were unearthed and arrested.

In jail, I continued to reflect independently on basic questions of the revolution and on other actual political questions.

Those of us arrested by the Guomindang during these two waves were not freed until late 1937, after the start of all-out war with Japan, the aerial bombing of Nanjing, and the Guomindang decision to move its capital east to Wuhan.

After my release, I decided that because communications with Shanghai were broken, I would go for a while to southern Anhui to escape the turmoil, recover my health, and await the opportunity to return to Shanghai. I never guessed that I would spend three years in Anhui, that my son would be born there, and that I and my wife would earn our living as schoolteachers. Not until 1940 did we leave Anhui through Zhejiang and sail to Shanghai via Ningbo.

Back in Shanghai, I joined the leadership of the Chinese Trotskyist organisation. At the same time, I translated into Chinese Trotsky's *History of the Russian Revolution* (vols. 2 and 3).

There was a controversy in the Trotskyist leadership about what attitude to adopt toward the war against Japan. There were three different points of view: that the war itself had a progressive meaning, and that we should support the Guomindang's resistance; that the war itself had a progressive meaning, and we should resist independently; and that the war was part of the Second World War and we should prepare to carry out proletarian socialist revolution during it, like Lenin in the First World War. I supported the third position. As a result of the dispute, the Chinese Trotskyists split.

During the dispute and the split, my group independently brought out a mimeographed journal that was at first nameless and was later officially published under the name *Guoji zhuyizhe* ('Internationalist'). After the Japanese surrender, we started to bring out *Xin qi* ('New Banner'), in lead type. I wrote numerous articles for the nameless publication, for Internationalist, and for

New Banner. Apart from that, I also wrote some books: *Buduan geming lun ABC* ('ABC of Permanent Revolution'), *San ren xing* ('Three Travellers'), and *Guojia ziben zhuyi lun* ('On State Capitalism').

These articles and books are products of my second stage, that is, they represent conclusions that I arrived at in the course of using my own brain and reflecting independently. Unfortunately, today I am no longer in a position to gather together my writings of that period. I myself value them above the writings of my first period, which were written according to a set line and cost me no great effort. Since *New Youth* (later period), *Guide Weekly*, *Bolshevik*, and other publications are still available, my articles must also have been preserved.

After 'Liberation', I had no wish to flee abroad. I had devoted my entire life to proletarian socialist revolution, in the world and in China. I was fully aware that the Stalinist system could not tolerate the existence of the likes of me in this world – we had already learned that from the Moscow trials of the 1930s. But I still wanted to stay in China. Sure enough, three and a half years after the 'liberation' of Shanghai, on 22 December 1952, 'like a thunderclap the net fell', and all the Chinese Trotskyists were arrested. Again, I was singled out as the ringleader. Someone like me, who never sought the limelight, arrested three times and twice named as ringleader!

This time, I (together with four others) was locked up for twenty seven years (from 22 December 1952, to 5 June 1979). We were never sentenced, and never even charged. Strange? People told us that there were not many prisoners like us, but there were a few.

Starting in 1964, I was allowed openly to express opinions in jail, to write books, and to criticise current policies and theories. For from then on, I was allowed to form a study group with other prisoners arrested in connection with the same case, Trotskyists who, like me, had not yet been sentenced (at first, there were three of us, then there were two). (In 1956, we were all brought together to study, but at that time, there were as many as a dozen in a study group and the sessions never lasted long, so it was impossible to speak out freely.) We studied so-called 'anti-revisionist documents', that is, the theoretical dispute between the Chinese and Soviet Communists. Afterwards, we each had to write a 'summary'. Although no one told us 'you may write whatever you like', I used the occasion to develop a comprehensive critique of the Stalinist system on the basis of the ideas that I had formed in the course of my isolated prison reflections. I decided to disregard any possible consequences. Finally, I wrote up my 'study summaries' into a book of eighty five thousand characters, which I called *Ganbu zhuyi lun* ('On Cadreism').

In 1965, each of us got a set of Mao's *Selected Works* (volumes 1 to 4) and was told to study 'Mao Zedong Thought'. Needless to say, after studying it, we were expected to write summaries. So I wrote another book, of one hundred and thirty five thousand characters, called *Yuzhong du Mao Zedong xuanji* ('Reading Mao Zedong's Selected Works in Jail'). Apart from this, after reading Stalin's Problems of Leninism, I wrote a further book of criticism, and at the same time, I wrote a great many articles on current affairs as reported in the press. During the Cultural Revolution, after the prison came under military administration, the army representative ordered all these political and non-political writings to be confiscated and destroyed.

But the ideas that I developed in jail were indestructible. In 1972, the serious offenders in our case (including those not yet sentenced), having spent twenty years in jail, were no longer kept behind bars but released into a régime of strict supervision; and in 1979, we were released from strict supervision and had our civil rights restored. At last we were as if restored to freedom. I myself was co-opted onto the Shanghai Municipal People's Consultative Committee.

But the Chinese Trotskyists arrested in December 1952 had still not been rehabilitated, and were still categorised as 'counter-revolutionaries'. In 1988, the Soviet Union completely reversed the verdicts on the three great wrongs perpetrated by the Moscow show trials of the 1930s: the 1936 trial of the 'Trotsky-Zinoviev anti-Soviet coalition', the 1937 Pyatkov-Radek trial, and the 1937 trial of Bukharin, Rykov, and others. In the same year, I wrote three letters to the Standing Committee of the Politburo of the Central Committee of the Chinese Communist Party demanding a reversal of the 1952 case against the Chinese Trotskyists, but like a stone dropping into the vast ocean, it disappeared without an echo.

In the eleven years between the restoration of my civil rights in 1979 and now, I have written no few articles and a number of books, and some of my letters are worth publishing and preserving. All in all, my output amounts to some eight hundred thousand characters. These are the works of my third period. Like my second period, they are the product of independent reflection, but the conclusions are not wholly the same as those of my second period. Only a small proportion of them has been published; the overwhelming majority has been copied or photocopied and circulated among a small number of readers.

During this third period, three books of mine have been published in China, but none of them was written in this period. One is my book of memoirs, written in the second half of 1944, during my second period. The manuscript, taken as evidence of my 'counter-revolutionary crimes', followed me into jail. After my civil rights were restored, it, too, became Party history material and was internally circulated, in an edition printed by the state publishers. The supplement, on Chen Duxiu and the Trotskyists, was newly written in 1980. The second book is *Yu Yin canji* ('Surviving Poems of Yu Yin'), which comprise the remnants of the poems I wrote in jail. The third is Merezhkovsky's *Resurrection of the Gods*, a novel that I translated and was published in the 1940s. As for what I have written in the last eleven years, I have no idea when it can be published.

It is a matter for rejoicing that now that I am celebrating my ninetieth birthday, important events are taking place in the world, and show who was right and who was wrong in the greatest debate of the century.

I mean the great debate about whether or not socialism can be built in a single country.

In early 1924, Lenin died. In the autumn of that year, the contours of the internal struggle in the Soviet Communist Party gradually became visible. It was not a debate about styles of work but a difference of opinion about what basic line to follow. Stalin proposed the theory that socialism can be built in a single country. This theory was incompatible with the Marxist tradition, and also with what Stalin himself wrote in early 1924, in the Foundations of Leninism. Thereupon, those old Bolsheviks like Zinoviev and Kamenev, who had previously sided with Stalin against Trotsky, gradually left Stalin and began to ally with Trotsky. The united opposition upheld the old view that socialism is only possible within the framework of world revolution, and opposed the Stalinists.

For sixty years now, Stalin and the Stalinists have used the reality of the Soviet Union, and later the reality of the 'socialist states' of Eastern Europe and elsewhere, to prove that socialism can indeed be built in one or a few relatively backward countries.

But what do the events of last year and this year in those countries show?

Seventy years ago, when I was around twenty, the socialist or social-democratic parties in various countries changed their names into communist parties (though, naturally, some did not change and continued to maintain their old positions). But this year and last year, we have seen the opposite happen: communist parties in various countries have changed their names into socialist or social-democratic parties (though, naturally, some have not changed and continue to maintain their old positions).

Seventy years ago, one process took place; now, seventy years later, the opposite process has taken place. What does this fact signify? Most say that it is an expression of the bankruptcy of socialism.

But that is wrong. It is merely an expression of the bankruptcy of Stalinism, of the doctrine of socialism in one country. We Trotskyists alone in the world have dared – and with justification – to reach this conclusion, for we alone over the last several decades have maintained that socialism cannot be built in one or a few countries. We have never conceded that the system realised in the Soviet Union or the other 'socialist states' is socialist.

Socialism cannot be built in a single country.

The greatest dispute in twentieth-century history, which has been going on now for almost seventy years, has finally been settled: Trotsky was right, Stalin was wrong.

It is good that I lived to the age of ninety to see the end of this dispute. Will I live long enough to see the outbreak of the second high tide of world revolution?

Translated by Gregor Benton

References

Benton, Gregor (ed.) 1997, *An Oppositionist For Life: Memoirs of the Chinese Revolutionary Zheng Chaolin*, translated by Gregor Benton, Atlantic Highlands, New Jersey: Humanities Press International.

Benton, Gregor 2015. *Prophets Unarmed: Chinese Trotskyists in Revolution, War, Jail, and the Return from Limbo*, Leiden/Boston: Brill

Chen Duxiu 1940, 'My Basic Views', in Gregor Benton, ed., *Chen Duxiu's Last Articles and Letters, 1937–1942*, London: Routledge, 1998, pp. 70–74. For the Chinese original see Zhuanji wenxue zazhi she, eds, *Shi'an zizhuan* ('Autobiography of Chen Duxiu'), Taibei: Zhuanji wenxue chubanshe, 1967, pp. 82–88.

Chen Duxiu 1980 [1938], 'Gei *Xinhua ribao* de xin' ('Letter to *New China Daily*'), reprinted in Zhang Yongtong and Liu Chuanxue (eds) 1980, pp. 112–33.

Daum, Walter, 1990 *The Life and Death of Stalinism: A Resurrection of Marxist Theory*, Seattle: Socialist Voice Press.

Deutscher, Isaac. 1949. *Stalin: A Political Biography*. Oxford: Oxford University Press.

Engels, Frederick 1989 [1871], Engels to Wilhelm Liebknecht, 13 April 1871, in *Marx and Engels Collected Works*, Volume 44, Moscow: Progress Publishers.

Engels, Frederick 1990 [1886], *Ludwig Feuerbach and the End of Classical German Philosophy*, in *Marx and Engels Collected Works*, Volume 26, Moscow: Progress Publishers.

Engels, Friedrich 2010 [1892] 'Socialism Utopian and Scientific', Marx-Engels Collected Works, Vol. 24, London: Lawrence and Wishart

Evans, Les, and Russell Block (eds) 1976, *Leon Trotsky on China*, New York: Monad Press.

Feigon, Lee 1983, *Chen Duxiu, Founder of the Chinese Communist Party*, Princeton: Princeton University Press.

Fo Licai (Vladimir Friche), *Yishu shehui xue* (Sociology of art), translated and with an introduction by Hu Qiuyuan, Shanghai: Shenzhou guoguang she, 1933.

Jiang Guangchi 1983, *Xuanji* ('Selected works'), Beijing: Renmin wenxue chuban she.

Lenin, V.I. 1960–78 [1899], 'Our Programme', *Collected Works*, Vol. 4, Moscow: Progress Publishers.

Lenin, V.I. 1960–78 [1905], 'Two Tactics of Social-Democracy in the Democratic Revolution', *Collected Works*, Vol. 9, Moscow: Progress Publishers.

Lenin, V.I. 1960–78 [1906], 'Preface to the Russian Translation of K. Kautsky's Pamphlet: The Driving Forces and Prospects of the Russian Revolution', *Collected Works*, Vol. 11, Moscow: Progress Publishers.

Lenin, V.I. 1960–78 [1907], 'Revolution and Counterrevolution', *Collected Works*, Vol. 13, Moscow: Progress Publishers.

Lenin, V.I. 1960–78 [1909], 'The Aim of the Proletarian Struggle in our Revolution'., *Collected Works*, Vol. 15, Moscow: Progress Publishers.

Lenin, V.I. 1960–78 [1912], 'Democracy and Narodism in China', Nevskaya Zvezda No. 17, 15 July 1912. *Collected Works*, vol. 18, Moscow: Progress Publishers: Moscow, 1975.

Lenin, V.I. 1974 [1914], *Karl Marx: A Brief Biographical Sketch With an Exposition of Marxism*, in *Lenin Collected Works*, Volume 21, Moscow: Progress Publishers.

Lenin, V.I. 1960–78 [1915], 'On the Slogan For a United States of Europe', *Collected Works*, Vol. 21, Moscow: Progress Publishers.

Lenin, V.I. 1960–78 [1915a], 'Several Theses', *Collected Works*, Vol. 21, Moscow: Progress Publishers.

Lenin, V.I. 1960–78 [1916], 'Imperialism, The Highest Stage of Capitalism', *Collected Works*, Vol. 22, Moscow: Progress Publishers.

Lenin, V.I. 1963 [1916], 'Imperialism, the Highest Stage of Capitalism', *Lenin's Selected Works* Volume 1, Moscow: Progress Publishers. 667–766.

Lenin, V.I. 1960–78 [1917], 'Letters from Afar', *Collected Works*, Vol. 23, Moscow: Progress Publishers.

Lenin, V.I. 1960–78 [1917a], 'Farewell Letter to the Swiss Workers', *Collected Works*, Vol. 23, Moscow: Progress Publishers.

Lenin, V.I. 1960–78 [1917b], 'Letters on Tactics', *Collected Works*, Vol. 24, Moscow: Progress Publishers.

Lenin, V.I. 1960–78 [1917c], 'Lecture on the 1905 Revolution', *Collected Works*, Vol. 23, Moscow: Progress Publishers.

Lenin, V.I. 1960–78 [1917d], 'The Tasks of the Proletariat in the Present Situation', *Collected Works*, Vol. 24, Moscow: Progress Publishers.

Lenin, V.I. 1960–78 [1917e], 'The State and Revolution', *Collected Works*, Vol. 25, Moscow: Progress Publishers.

Lenin, V.I. 1960–78 [1917 f.], 'The Impending Catastrophe and How to Combat It', *Collected Works*, Vol. 25, Moscow: Progress Publishers.

Lenin, V.I. 1960–78 [1918], 'The Proletarian Revolution and the Renegade Kautsky', *Collected Works*, Vol. 28, Moscow: Progress Publishers.

Lenin, V.I. 1960–78 [1918b], 'Report on the Activities of the Council of People's Commissars', *Collected Works*, Vol. 26, Moscow: Progress Publishers.

Lenin, V.I. 1960–78 [1918c], 'Political Report of the Central Committee', *Collected Works*, Vol. 27, Moscow: Progress Publishers.

Lenin, V.I. 1960–78 [1918d], 'Left Wing Childishness and the Petty-Bourgeois Mentality', *Collected Works*, Vol. 27, Moscow: Progress Publishers.

Lenin, V.I. 1960–78 [1919], 'The Deception of the People by the Slogans of Freedom and Equality', *Collected Works*, Vol. 29, Moscow: Progress Publishers.

Lenin, V.I. 1960–78 [1920], ''Left Wing' Communism: An Infantile Disorder', *Collected Works*, Vol. 31, Moscow: Progress Publishers.

Lenin, V.I. 1960–78 [1921], 'Fourth Anniversary of the October Revolution', *Collected Works*, Vol. 33, Moscow: Progress Publishers.

Lenin, V.I. 1960–78 [1921a], 'New Times and Old Mistakes in an Old Guise', *Collected Works*, Vol. 33, Moscow: Progress Publishers.

Lenin, V.I. 1960–78 [1921b], 'The Tax in Kind', Lenin's *Collected Works*, 1st English Edition, Volume 32, Moscow: Progress Publishers.

Lenin, V.I. 1960–78 [1923], 'On Cooperation', *Collected Works*, Vol. 33, Moscow: Progress Publishers.

Lenin, V.I. 1960–78 [1923a], 'Better Fewer But Better', *Collected Works*, Vol. 33, Moscow: Progress Publishers.

Luxemburg, Rosa 1951, *The Accumulation of Capital*, translated by Agnes Schwarzschild, London: Routledge and Kegan Paul.

Mao Tse-tung (Mao Zedong) 1975 [1928] 'The Struggle in the Chingkang Mountains' *Selected Works*, Vol. I, Beijing: Foreign Languages Press. Distributed by Pergamon Press, Oxford.

Mao Tse-tung (Mao Zedong) 1975 [1933] 'Pay Attention to Economic Work'. *Selected Works*, Vol. I, Beijing: Foreign Languages Press. Distributed by Pergamon Press, Oxford.

Mao Tse-tung (Mao Zedong) 1967 [1935], 'On Tactics Against Japanese Imperialism', *Selected Works*, Vol. I, Beijing: Foreign Languages Press.

Mao Tse-tung (Mao Zedong) 1975 [1937] 'Win the Masses in their Millions for the Anti-Japanese National United Front'. *Selected Works*, Vol. 1, Beijing: Foreign Languages Press. Distributed by Pergamon Press, Oxford.

Mao Tse-tung (Mao Zedong) 1975 [1938] 'Problems of War and Strategy' *Selected Works*, Vol. II, Beijing: Foreign Languages Press. Distributed by Pergamon Press, Oxford.

Mao Tse-tung (Mao Zedong) 'On New Democracy (January 15, 1940)'. In Mao's Road to Power: Revolutionary Writings 1912–1949, Vol. 7, edited by Stuart Schram and Nancy J. Rhodes, pp. 330–69. Armonk, NY: M.E. Sharpe, 2005.

Mao Tse-tung (Mao Zedong) 1967 [1942] 'Talks at the Yenan Forum on Literature and Art, May 1942' *Selected Works*, Vol. III, Beijing: Foreign Languages Press. Distributed by Pergamon Press, Oxford.

Mao Tse-tung (Mao Zedong) 1975 [1948] 'On the September Meeting' *Selected Works*, Vol. IV, Beijing: Foreign Languages Press. Distributed by Pergamon Press, Oxford.

Marx, Karl 1977 [1875], 'Critique of the Gotha Programme', *Karl Marx Selected Readings*, edited by David McLellan, Oxford: Oxford University Press.

Marx, Karl and Engels, Frederick 1969, *Marx and Engels Selected Works*, Volume 1, Moscow: Progress Publishers.

Marx, Karl 1975 [1844], *Economic and Philosophic Manuscripts of 1844*, in *Marx and Engels Collected Works*, Volume 3, Moscow: Progress Publishers.

Marx, Karl 1976 [1845], *Theses on Feuerbach*, in *Marx and Engels Collected Works*, Volume 5, Moscow: Progress Publishers.

Marx, Karl 1987 [1861–1863], *A Contribution to the Critique of Political Economy*, in *Marx and Engels Collected Works*, Volume 29, Moscow: Progress Publishers.

Marx, Karl 1997 [1885], *Capital, Volume II*, in *Marx and Engels Collected Works*, Volume 36, Moscow: Progress Publishers.

Marx, Karl and Frederick Engels 1976 [1848], *Manifesto of the Communist Party*, in *Marx and Engels Collected Works*, Volume 6, Moscow: Progress Publishers.

Marx, Karl and Frederick Engels 1988 [1872], Preface to the 1872 German Edition of the Manifesto of the Communist Party, in *Marx and Engels Collected Works*, Volume 23, Moscow: Progress Publishers.

Marx, Karl, and Frederick Engels 2010 [1848], 'Manifesto of the Communist Party', *Collected Works*, Vol. 6, London: Lawrence and Wishart.

Marx, Karl, and Frederick Engels 2010 [1848a], 'The Events of 1847', *Collected Works*, Vol. 6, London: Lawrence and Wishart.

Marx, Karl, and Frederick Engels 2010 [1850], 'Address of the Central Authority to the League, March 1850', *Collected Works*, Vol. 10, London: Lawrence and Wishart.

Marx, Karl, and Frederick Engels 2010 [1851–52], 'The Eighteenth Brumaire of Louis Bonaparte', *Collected Works*, Vol. 10, London: Lawrence and Wishart.

Marx, Karl, and Frederick Engels 2010 [1852], 'Revelations Concerning the Communist League Trial in Cologne', *Collected Works*, Vol. 11, London: Lawrence and Wishart.

Marx, Karl, and Frederick Engels 2010 [1859], 'Preface to a Contribution to the Critique of Political Economy', *Collected Works*, Vol. 29, London: Lawrence and Wishart.

Marx, Karl, and Frederick Engels 2010 [1867], 'Capital, Preface to the First German edition', *Collected Works*, Vol. 35, London: Lawrence and Wishart.

Marx, Karl, and Frederick Engels 2010 [1877], 'Letter to Otechestvenniye Zapiski', *Collected Works*, Vol. 24, London: Lawrence and Wishart.

Marx, Karl, and Frederick Engels 2010 [1878], 'Anti-Duhring', *Collected Works*, Vol. 25, London: Lawrence and Wishart.

Marx, Karl, and Frederick Engels 2010 [1882], 'Preface to the Second Russian Edition of the Manifesto of the Communist Party', *Collected Works*, Vol. 24, London: Lawrence and Wishart.

Miller, Joseph 2016, 'From Unity to Division. Chinese Trotskyism and World War II'.

Peng Shuzhi. 'Dui Shi Fan tongzhi "buduan geming lun? Haishi jieduan lun?" de dafu yu piping [Reply to and critique of Comrade Shi Fan's 'Permanent Revolution? Or Stage Theory?'] (6 January 1934)'. In Peng Shuzhi xuanji, 2:79–95. Kowloon: Shi yue chuban she, 1982.

Peng Shuzhi. 'Yu Shun Jun lun minzhu douzheng yu wuchan jieji duoqu zhengquan [Discussion with Shun Jun (Liu Bozhuang) on the struggle for democracy and the proletariat's seizure of power] (1933)'. In Peng Shuzhi xuanji, 2:32–68. Kowloon: Shi yue chuban she, 1982.

Ren Jianshu and Tang Baolin, *Chen Duxiu zhuan* ('A biography of Chen Duxiu'), 2 vols, Shanghai: Shanghai renmin chuban she, 1989, vol. 2, p. 286.

Schram, Stuart R. 'Mao Tse-tung and the Theory of the Permanent Revolution, 1958–69', *The China Quarterly*, no. 46 (1971): 221–44. www.jstor.org/stable/652262.

Sheng, Yueh 1971, *Sun Yat-sen University in Moscow and the Chinese Revolution: A Personal Account*, New York: Center for East Asian Studies, The University of Kansas.

Stalin, J.V. 1924, *Problems of Leninism*, First Edition.

Stalin, J.V. 1924a, *Problems of Leninism*, Second Edition.

Stalin, J.V. 1940, *Leninism*, London: Lawrence and Wishart.

Stalin, J.V. 1953 [1924], *Works Volume Six 1924*, Moscow: Foreign Languages Publishing House

Stalin, J.V. 1953 [1924], 'Foundations of Leninism', *Works* Volume 6, Moscow: Foreign Languages Publishing House. 71–196.

Sukhanov, N.N. 1922, *Zapiski o revoliutsii* (Notes on the Revolution), Berlin: Izd-vo Z.I. Grzhebina.

Trotsky Leon 2010 [1906, 1930], *The Permanent Revolution and Results and Prospects*, Seattle: Red Letter Press.

Trotsky Leon 1957 [1928], *The Third International After Lenin*, New York: Pioneer Publishers.

Trotsky Leon 2008 [1932], *History of the Russian Revolution*, Chicago, IL: Haymarket Books.

Trotsky Leon 1973 [1939–40], *Collected Writings 1939–1940*, New York: Pathfinder Press.

Wang Fan-hsi 1991, *Memoirs of a Chinese Revolutionary*, translated and with an introduction by Gregor Benton, second revised edition, New York: Columbia University Press

Zhang Yongtong and Liu Chuanxue, eds, 1980, *Houqi de Chen Duxiu jiqi wenzhang xuanbian* ('The later Chen Duxiu and a selection of his essays'), Sichuan: Renmin chuban she.

Zheng Chaolin 1998, *Shishi yu Huiyi* Volumes I–III, Hongkong: Tiandi tushu youxian gongsi.

Zheng, Chaolin 2015, 'A Self-Description at the Age of Ninety', in *Prophets Unarmed: Chinese Trotskyists in Revolution, War, Jail, and the Return from Limbo*, edited by Gregor Benton, Leiden/Boston: Brill, pp. 1108–15.

Index